CRITICAL INSIGHTS

Arthur Miller

CRITICAL
INSIGHTS

Arthur Miller

Editor
Brenda Murphy
University of Connecticut

Salem Press
Pasadena, California   Hackensack, New Jersey

Cover photo: AP/Wide World Photos

Published by Salem Press

© 2011 by EBSCO Publishing
Editor's text © 2011 by Brenda Murphy
"The *Paris Review* Perspective" © 2011 by Richard Beck for *The Paris Review*

∞ The paper used in these volumes conforms to the American National Standard for Permanence of Paper for Printed Library Materials, Z39.48-1992 (R1997).

Library of Congress Cataloging-in-Publication Data
Arthur Miller / editor, Brenda Murphy.
    p. cm. — (Critical insights)
Includes bibliographical references and index.
ISBN 978-1-58765-697-2 (alk. paper)
    1. Miller, Arthur, 1915-2005—Criticism and interpretation. I. Murphy, Brenda, 1950-
PS3525.I5156Z515 2010
812'.52—dc22
                                                              2010029183

PRINTED IN CANADA

Contents_____

About This Volume, Brenda Murphy   vii

Career, Life, and Influence_____

On Arthur Miller, Brenda Murphy   3
Biography of Arthur Miller, Paul Rosefeldt   8
The *Paris Review* Perspective, Richard Beck for *The Paris Review*   13

Critical Contexts_____

Best Intentions Far Awry: The Family Dynamic in Miller's
    All My Sons and *Death of a Salesman*, Pamela Loos   19
"It's All About the Language": Arthur Miller's Poetic Dialogue,
    Stephen A. Marino   33
The Freedom of Others: Arthur Miller's Social and Political Context,
    Katherine Egerton   54
The Critical Reception of Arthur Miller's Work, Jane K. Dominik   70

Critical Readings_____

Arthur Miller and the Art of the Possible, Steven R. Centola   97
Arthur Miller: Un-American, Christopher Bigsby   121
All My Sons and Paternal Authority, James A. Robinson   138
"There's No Place Like Home": Miller's "Poem," Frost's "Play,"
    George Monteiro   160
Asking "Queer Questions," Revealing Ugly Truths: Giles Corey's
    Subversive Eccentricity in *The Crucible*, J. Chris Westgate   173
Verse, Figurative Language, and Myth in *A View from the Bridge*,
    Stephen A. Marino   186
Uneasy Collaboration: Miller, Kazan, and *After the Fall*,
    Brenda Murphy   215
All About Talk: Arthur Miller's *The Price*, Gerald Weales   227
Both His Sons: Arthur Miller's *The Price* and Jewish
    Assimilation, James A. Robinson   241
The "Line to Measure From": Arthur Miller's *The American
    Clock* as a Lesson for the Ages, Susan C. W. Abbotson   265

Coming to Roost Again: Tragic Rhythm in Arthur Miller's
   Broken Glass, Terry Otten   286
Arthur Miller's Ironic Resurrection, Jeffrey D. Mason   297
The Fiction of Arthur Miller, Laurence Goldstein   330

Resources

Chronology of Arthur Miller's Life   357
Works by Arthur Miller   363
Bibliography   365

About the Editor   369
About *The Paris Review*   369
Contributors   371
Acknowledgments   374
Index   376

About This Volume

Brenda Murphy

This collection of essays offers a diverse selection of criticism on one of the most significant American playwrights of the twentieth century. The volume is divided into two parts. The first is composed of essays that were commissioned specifically for this volume. The second consists of reprinted essays that not only are interesting and revealing studies in themselves but also reflect the variety of work that Arthur Miller produced in his long and prolific career and the diversity of critical approaches that have been applied to it.

As background for the individual critical studies, the editor's introduction presents a general critical context for thinking about Miller's work, Richard Beck offers a perspective from *The Paris Review*, Paul Rosefeldt provides a concise biography of Miller, and Jane K. Dominik contributes a comprehensive account of Miller's plays in performance, focusing on the reception they received from their immediate critics in newspapers and magazines as well as later academic critics. Three additional newly commissioned essays suggest some of the ways in which Miller's work can be analyzed productively. Pamela Loos gives a lucid analysis of the operations of the family dynamic in the closely linked father-son plays *All My Sons* and *Death of a Salesman*. Stephen A. Marino demonstrates the extent to which Miller's language rewards close analysis by paying specific attention to *Death of a Salesman* in the context of a comprehensive discussion of Miller's poetic dialogue. Through an integration of biography and analysis of Miller's plays, Katherine Egerton shows how the playwright's political life informed his writing, as his life experiences led to the firmly held but evolving political beliefs reflected in the plays.

The section of reprinted essays begins with wide-reaching articles by two of Miller's most distinguished and prolific critics. Taking a broad view of Miller's career, Steven R. Centola examines what Miller has called "the art of the possible" in theater by analyzing the extraordinary suggestiveness with which the language of his theater reso-nates, whether the idiom be words or lighting, scene design, gesture, or action. Miller's major biographer, Christopher Bigsby, offers a sweep-ing analysis of the playwright's complex relationship, both artistic and political, with his country.

Following these two essays are articles that focus on individual plays. They are arranged in the chronological order in which the plays appeared. Beginning in the 1940s, with *All My Sons*, James A. Robin-son examines Miller's representation of the conflict between the mod-ernist and the liberal visions through the conflict between Joe and Chris Keller. Taking an intertextual approach, George Monteiro ana-lyzes the relationship between *Death of a Salesman* and Robert Frost's "The Death of the Hired Man" in the context of the biblical parable of the prodigal son. Focusing on the plays of the 1950s, through *The Cru-cible*'s Giles Corey, J. Chris Westgate presents a provocative argument for Miller's use of the character as a subversive voice expressing his critique of societies that "willingly or willfully marginalize anything aberrant as Other and then build their ideological identity upon that marginalization." Stephen A. Marino focuses on Miller's use of lan-guage to analyze the playwright's revision of *A View from the Bridge*, arguing that Miller remade the original myth-centered one-act play into a more psychologically and socially oriented two-act version. Brenda Murphy examines the complex collaboration between Miller and director Elia Kazan as *After the Fall* took shape during its premiere at New York's Lincoln Center.

The essays that follow are representative of the variety of criticism on Miller's still somewhat neglected later plays. Beginning with *The Price*, Gerald Weales analyzes Miller's use of, and questioning of, the "dramatic, social, and therapeutic uses of talk" in the play and argues that our understanding of it hinges on our willingness to admit that there may be efficacy in conversation. James A. Robinson examines Miller's representation of his father in *The Price* and his relationship to Judaism and the ethical questions it raised about his assimilation into

"American capitalistic culture." Susan C. W. Abbotson discusses *The American Clock*'s relationship to the Great Depression and its "lesson" about the necessity of combining community and individuality in future conceptions of society. Terry Otten analyzes the tragic rhythm in *Broken Glass*, which he traces to Miller's first discovery of tragedy in classical Greek drama and the plays of Henrik Ibsen. Jeffrey D. Mason contributes a trenchant analysis of the political satire in *Resurrection Blues* and its targets: "the power and cultural values of broadcast media, the deceitful rhetoric and compromise of military dictatorship, the wary and unbalanced relationship between the United States and Latin America, and the virtually palpable force of money in a global and corporate economy." Finally, Laurence Goldstein offers a review and reassessment of Miller's fiction, a heretofore neglected part of Miller's body of work that, Goldstein argues persuasively, will richly reward future readers and critics.

CAREER, LIFE, AND INFLUENCE

On Arthur Miller

Brenda Murphy

Arthur Miller's career in the theater spanned seven decades, from the 1930s, when he was writing prizewinning plays as an undergraduate at the University of Michigan, to the twenty-first century, when his last play, *Finishing the Picture*, was produced in 2004. It was a career that began in the spirit of the 1930s, with plays reflecting a leftist social consciousness, like the autobiographical *No Villain* (1936), later retitled *They Too Arise* and *The Grass Still Grows*, which was based partly on Miller's relationship with his father, a self-made wealthy coat manufacturer who lost his fortune during the Great Depression. Miller's leftist political stance was born in the economic and social conditions of the Depression and brought to greater sophistication during his years at Michigan. His politics stayed with him throughout his life, and a good deal of critical attention has been given to the enormous impact Miller had on the theater and the larger culture in a role that Eric Bentley has described as "the playwright as thinker." Miller created an Ibsenesque exposure of war profiteering in *All My Sons* (1947) and an attack on some of the basic values of American business culture in *Death of a Salesman* (1949), later revisiting this last issue through the lens of the Great Depression in *The American Clock* (1980). In *The Crucible* (1953), he exposed the excesses of McCarthyism by analogizing it with the Salem witch trials. With *After the Fall* (1964) and *Incident at Vichy* (1964), he became one of the first American writers to explore the significance of the Holocaust, and he continued this exploration in *Playing for Time* (1980) and *Broken Glass* (1994). During the 1960s, he became active in protesting the oppression of Eastern European writers under Soviet rule as the president of International PEN, dramatizing this oppression in *The Archbishop's Ceiling* (1977). In 2002, he was still at work, pointing out the excesses of American capitalism and the self-absorption of the mediatized twenty-first century in his dramatic satire *Resurrection Blues*.

Perhaps because he has so often been cast in the role of America's intellectual playwright, not as much attention has been paid to Miller's aesthetic innovations and their effect on the theater as to his ideas. Looking at the span of his career from 1936 to 2005, the degree of experimentation and innovation in his work is extraordinary. In his earliest years, his plays reflected the dramaturgy of the leftist Group Theatre and its star playwright, Clifford Odets, but Miller received a good education in world drama at Michigan, and the plays he worked on during the 1930s and early 1940s reflect a wide-ranging interest in both subject and dramatic form. One of his major projects from this period was a verse tragedy about Montezuma, which he eventually entitled *The Golden Years*. It was finally produced on the BBC as a radio play in 1987. Another was his first play to reach Broadway, *The Man Who Had All the Luck*, a dramatic parable that failed in the realistic format it was given by Joseph Fields in 1943 but was more successful in a 2002 production that recognized its true genre.

After his first Broadway failure, Miller resolved to write the best play that he could with the aim of becoming successful on Broadway, or, failing that, to stop writing plays and do something else. He worked on *All My Sons* for almost two years, writing in a form he had never tried before, the straightforward and carefully plotted Ibsenesque realism that he saw most serious playwrights of the time, such as Lillian Hellman and Robert Sherwood, using successfully to reach a Broadway audience.

Miller achieved the success he was hoping for; his first Broadway hit ran for 328 performances and established his reputation as a young playwright to be reckoned with. His next play, *Death of a Salesman*, was as innovative for the American, and indeed the world, theater audience to view as it was for Miller to write. Starting with the objective of dramatizing what he thought of as Willy Loman's way of thinking just as his mind is breaking down, Miller broke down the barriers between present and past, reality and "daydream," to dramatize the simultaneity of Willy's physical experience of what is happening to and around him in stage present with the reality running through his mind, which is perhaps even more real to him. To do this, Miller combined a colloquial realism with expressionism, a European theatrical idiom that had been devised to dramatize dreams or nightmares. The uniqueness of Miller's vision is found in the way in which the two styles of theater are intermixed to create the effect of simultaneity that allows audience members to believe that they are experiencing reality as Willy experiences it. It took the inventive collaboration of director Elia Kazan and scenic designer Jo Mielziner to achieve complete realization of Miller's aesthetic vision, but the result was a new form of theater that became known as "the American style" and was imitated throughout the world.

While other playwrights may have imitated the style of *Death of a Salesman*, Miller did not. His next two plays were as different from it, and each other, as they could be. *The Crucible* is in form and dramatic idiom a fairly straightforward realistic play, although some productions have shown that it can be pushed toward abstraction with interesting results. For Miller, the experiment was in the dialogue. He has said that he tried to create a new dialogic idiom for *The Crucible*. Reading the transcripts of the original Salem witch trials, he realized that he could not use the seventeenth-century vernacular as it was spoken, because it would be hard for the audience to listen to, and, since the speech did not come naturally to him, it would be difficult for him to create the kinds of rhythms he was looking for in the dialogue. Instead he used contemporary English laced with enough markers to suggest to the audience that this was the speech of an earlier time, such as formal grammar and some invented archaic constructions like "He have his goodness now." Like *Death of a Salesman*'s dialogue, much of *The Crucible*'s was originally composed in verse in order to give it the rhythm Miller was trying to achieve. In *A View from the Bridge* (1955), he retained some of the verse, contributing to the sense that the play he was writing was a classical tragedy. In that play, based on the ancient culture of Sicily, he introduces a character, Alfieri, who comments directly to the audience on the meaning of the action in the manner of the chorus in a Greek tragedy, elevating the story of Eddie Carbone, his wife, and his niece to one of primal tragic myth.

As the American theater became increasingly open to innovation and experiment during the 1960s and 1970s, Miller ranged more freely away from realism. In *After the Fall*, which takes place in the mind of Quentin at the same time that he addresses an unseen "Listener" in real time, Miller revisited expressionism, this time ranging all of the characters on an abstract mindscape of a set and having them come to life as Quentin thinks of them. *The Creation of the World and Other Business* (1972), which Miller adapted into the musical *Up from Paradise* (1974), is a comic parody of the biblical book of Genesis. *The American Clock*, which Miller called a "vaudeville," juxtaposes song and dance with a series of loosely connected scenes of the Depression that are drawn from Miller's own youth and from Studs Terkel's 1970 oral history *Hard Times*. Four one-act plays from the 1980s, *Elegy for a Lady* (1982), *Some Kind of Love Story* (1982), *Clara* (1987), and *I Can't Remember Anything* (1987), are among the most experimental of Miller's plays, eschewing realism for an almost postmodern conception of character and fragmented plotlines. *Mr. Peters' Connections* (1998) is a memory play in which, as the audience gradually realizes, the title character's memories come to life as they occur to him. *Resurrection Blues* might be described as "magical realism" if it were fiction. Not only does its plot about the televising of a crucifixion push the limits of what an audience will accept as a shared reality, it also mixes a recognizable reality with supernatural events. None of these experiments was particularly successful commercially, but each of them shows Miller pushing the boundaries of his art and creating something new and original for the theater.

Even when he stayed within the limits of the realistic theater, Miller pushed these limits with a sense of experiment. *The Price* (1968) and *A Memory of Two Mondays* (1955) both play on the genre of the memory play, although not as radically as *Mr. Peters' Connections*, *Salesman*, and *After the Fall*. Ostensibly a realistic play, with its suggestion that the characters are being overheard through surveillance equipment, of which some are aware and some are not, *The Archbishop's Ceiling* leads the audience to question the very definition of the reality to which even the most banal conversation refers. *The Ride Down Mt. Morgan* (1991) and *Broken Glass* (1994) both feature protagonists who lead audiences to question the reality of what has happened and is happening on stage and, perhaps, their own grasp of the real.

In short, Arthur Miller had a long career of exciting dramatic and theatrical innovation at the same time that he spoke out consistently for the values that most Americans affirm as decent or humane, for the individual's responsibility to both self and others, and for society's responsibility to each of its members. His achievement was unique. If he had written only *Death of a Salesman*, he would be considered one of the great American playwrights. Fortunately, he did far more than that.

Biography of Arthur Miller_____

Paul Rosefeldt

Arthur Miller, son of Jewish immigrants, was born on October 17, 1915, in New York City. His father, Isadore, was born in Austria and ran a prosperous garment business; his mother, Augusta Barnett Miller, was a schoolteacher. When his father's firm began to fail in 1928, the Millers moved to a suburban area of Brooklyn, an area that would be the model for the settings of *All My Sons* (1947) and *Death of a Salesman* (1949). From his mother, Miller inherited a strong sense of mysticism that would inform much of his later work. As a young boy, Miller resented his father's withdrawal, which was caused by his business failure. The figure of the failed father would later play a significant role in Miller's writing.

The young Miller came of age during the Great Depression of the 1930's. Seeing once-prosperous people on the streets begging for work affected him deeply. To him, the Depression signified the failure of a capitalist system of government and the tragedy of a generation of people who frequently blamed this failure on themselves. The events of the Depression and their impact on so many people's chances for success led Miller to probe individuals' relationships to their work and to consider critically the price they must pay for success or failure.

Like Biff Loman in *Death of a Salesman*, Miller was more athlete than scholar. His reading consisted largely of adventure stories and some of Charles Dickens's novels. Unable to get into college, he worked for his father, where he first became moved by the plight of salesmen. After rotating through a series of odd jobs, Miller worked in an automobile parts warehouse and saved enough money to enroll at the University of Michigan. He relates this experience in *A Memory of Two Mondays* (1955).

While working, Miller became an avid reader and was especially impressed by Fyodor Dostoevski's *The Brothers Karamazov* (1879-1880), a novel that features fraternal rivalry as well as the trial motif that Miller frequently returned to as a controlling theme in his own writing. At the university, he became interested in social causes and began to develop a strong liberal philosophy. He studied playwriting under Kenneth Rowe and won two successive Avery Hopwood Awards, one in 1936 for *Honors at Dawn* and another in 1937 for *No Villain*.

In 1938, he won the Theater Guild National Award for *They Too Arise*. Following the style of the 1930s, Miller's early plays focused on young idealists struggling to eliminate social injustice. After college, he worked for the Federal Theatre Project and wrote radio scripts. In 1944, he wrote a screenplay, *The Story of GI Joe*, which was later reworked and produced without a Miller credit.

That same year, he had his first Broadway production, *The Man Who Had All the Luck* (1944), but his drama of a man dismayed by his incredible success was unconvincing and not well received by critics or audiences. In 1947, Miller finally achieved success on Broadway with *All My Sons*, a better controlled and more topical work than *The Man Who Had All the Luck*, which had closed after four performances and had saddled Miller with a debt of more than fifty thousand dollars. In 1949, *Death of a Salesman* achieved unprecedented critical acclaim and established Miller as a significant American playwright.

Disturbed by such elements of the 1950's as the Cold War, the tactics of Senator Joseph McCarthy, and the betrayal by his onetime liberal friends who named names before the House Committee on Un-American Activities, Miller wrote *The Crucible* (1953), which connected the witch hunts of seventeenth century Salem, Massachusetts, to the search for communists in the 1950s. *The Crucible*, however, did not achieve immediate success. His next works were two one-act plays, *A Memory of Two Mondays* and *A View from the Bridge* (both 1955). An expanded version of *A View from the Bridge* (1956) tells the story of Eddie Carbone, a longshoreman who, driven by incestuous desires for his niece, informs on her boyfriend and the other illegal immigrants living with him. Miller here shows how those who persecute others often have their own hidden agendas, again drawing parallels with McCarthyism.

The mid-1950's were troubling times for Miller. After divorcing his first wife, Mary Grace Slattery, Miller married film star Marilyn Monroe in 1956 and became involved in her turbulent life and career. He was also cited for contempt of Congress for refusing to name names before the House Committee on Un-American Activities. Although he was acquitted on appeal, this ordeal exacted a financial and emotional toll on him. In 1961, his marriage to Monroe ended in divorce, and, in 1962, he married Ingeborg Morath, a professional photographer.

After a nine-year hiatus from the American stage, Miller wrote *After the Fall* (1964) and *Incident at Vichy* (1964). Miller returned to the form of family drama with *The Price* (1968), which depicts the rivalry of two brothers.

Continuing to experiment, Miller wrote *The Creation of the World and Other Business* (1972), a comedy based on the book of Genesis; *The Archbishop's Ceiling* (1977), a play about power and oppression in a European communist country; *The American Clock* (1980), a montage view of the Depression focusing on the trials of one family; and *Danger: Memory!* (1987), two short symbolic dramas exploring the mysteries hidden in past actions. Although these dramas failed to receive the critical acclaim of Miller's earlier works, the continual revivals of his dramas, both on stage and on television, and his burgeoning international reputation kept Miller in the forefront of American theater.

In the early twenty-first century, after an impressive career that spanned six decades, Arthur Miller became ill with cancer and heart disease. He moved to the Manhattan apartment of his sister, Joan Miller Copeland, where he received hospice care. In early February, 2005, at his request, he was moved by ambulance to his home in Roxbury, Connecticut, where he died a few days later, succumbing finally to heart failure. His final play, *Finishing the Picture*, was produced just months before his death and marked the end of a highly productive career.

From *Magill's Survey of American Literature*. Rev. ed. Pasadena, CA: Salem Press, 2007. Copyright © 2007 by Salem Press, Inc.

Bibliography

Bigsby, Christopher, ed. *Arthur Miller and Company*. London: Methuen, 1990. A series of impressions on Miller's works from noted writers and theater personalities. Presents a variety of insights into Miller and his work.

_____. *The Cambridge Companion to Arthur Miller*. New York: Cambridge University Press, 1997. Contains a detailed chronology, an essay on the tradition of social drama, and chapters on the early plays, the major plays, and Arthur Miller in each of the decades from the 1960s through the 1990s. Following chapters discuss Miller's involvement with cinema, his fiction, and his relationship with criticism and critics. Includes a bibliographic essay and an index.

Bloom, Harold, ed. *Arthur Miller*. New York: Chelsea House, 1987. Collection of essays on Miller's major drama from *All My Sons* to *The American Clock* includes a brief introduction discussing Miller's significance, important early essays (Raymond Williams and Tom F. Driver on the playwright's strengths and weaknesses), and later criticism by Neil Carson, C. W. E. Bigsby, and E. Miller Buddick. Supplemented with a chronology, a bibliography, and an index.

_____. *Arthur Miller's "Death of a Salesman."* New York: Chelsea House, 1988. Contains critical discussions published between 1963 and 1987, a chronology of Miller's life, a comprehensive bibliography, and an index. In spite of reservations about Miller's importance as a writer, Bloom explains in his introduction how the play "achieves true aesthetic dignity" and discusses the particular merits of the essays in this collection.

Brater, Enoch. *Arthur Miller: A Playwright's Life and Works*. New York: Thames & Hudson, 2005. Provides a basic introduction to Miller and some of his best-known plays. Includes seventy black-and-white photographs.

_____, ed. *Arthur Miller's America: Theater and Culture in a Time of Change*. Ann Arbor: University of Michigan Press, 2005. A collection of essays by Miller scholars.

Gottfried, Martin. *Arthur Miller: His Life and Work*. Cambridge, Mass.: Da Capo Press, 2003. The first full-length biography of Miller, this profile discusses the playwright's work in the context of his life.

Koon, Helene Wickham, ed. *Twentieth Century Interpretations of "Death of a Salesman."* Englewood Cliffs, N.J.: Prentice-Hall, 1983. These essays from the 1960s and 1970s emphasize the play's cultural significance, its status as a modern classic, and its style and point of view. The introduction provides biographical information and discussions of Miller's major themes, the play's relationship to classical tragedy, and Miller's manipulation of time. Includes a brief bibliography and chronology of events in Miller's life and times.

Koorey, Stefani. *Arthur Miller's Life and Literature*. Metuchen, N.J.: Scarecrow Press, 2000. A bibliographic guide to primary and secondary sources.

Martine, James J. *"The Crucible": Politics, Property, and Pretense*. New York: Twayne, 1993. Offers an in-depth analysis of *The Crucible* from a number of viewpoints, including the historical context of McCarthyism, the play's place in Miller's oeuvre, and how the play fits into the genre of tragedy.

Murphy, Brenda. *Miller: "Death of a Salesman."* New York: Cambridge University Press, 1995. Comprehensive treatment of Miller's play discusses its Broadway production, productions in English and in other languages, and media productions. Also provides a production chronology, a discography, a videography, an extensive bibliography, and an index.

Schlueter, June, and James K. Flanagan. *Arthur Miller*. New York: Frederick Ungar, 1987. Contains a comprehensive narrative chronology, a thorough first chapter on Miller's literature and life to 1985, chapter-length discussions of his major plays (including *The Archbishop's Ceiling*), and a concluding chapter on his later one-act plays. Includes extensive notes, a bibliography of Miller's work in all genres, a select secondary bibliography of books and articles, and an index.

 *the* PARIS REVIEW

The *Paris Review* Perspective_____

Richard Beck for *The Paris Review*

In 1951, Arthur Miller traveled to Hollywood. He was trying to sell a screenplay. Two years earlier, *Death of a Salesman* had made Miller famous, and now he wanted to cash in his cultural capital. Miller found himself both repelled and attracted by the atmosphere of sex and power that surrounded him in Los Angeles. The guest list for a party thrown in his honor contained the following subsection:

> *Buffet for Arthur Miller*
> 1. Mona Knox
> 2. Ruth Lewis
> 3. Cheryl Clark
> 4. Diane Cassidy
> 5. Kazan Girl

"Kazan" was Elia Kazan, one of Miller's closest collaborators and friends. Kazan's "Girl" was Marilyn Monroe.

Miller and Monroe did not begin their affair at that particular party—"flying homeward . . . I knew my innocence was technical merely," Miller wrote in his memoir, *Timebends*—but by 1956 Miller was divorced and married again. That year, he received a subpoena from the House Un-American Activities Committee. The timing was no coincidence; after nearly a decade of headlines, blacklists, and hearings, the committee's power was waning. "Pinko Playwright Weds Sex Goddess," one newspaper read: the red scare was back on the front page.

The hearing itself was a transparent sham. The questioning about Miller's 1953 play *The Crucible*, an allegorical denunciation of Senator Joseph McCarthy's culture of fear, lasted for all of thirty seconds, and committee chairman Francis E. Walter privately told Miller that in exchange for a photograph with Monroe, the hearing would be called off entirely. Even a circus can have its serious moments, though, and when asked to name names, Miller refused. In the last half century, this act has continued to resonate with all the symbolic force of his best plays. Held in contempt, Miller was threatened with a year of prison time before the case was thrown out of court on appeal. He emerged from the hearings transformed: the newly minted conscience of American liberalism. It did not go unnoticed that with his serious bearing and 6'1" stature, Miller looked a little like Abraham Lincoln.

Language is Miller's weak spot. Although not a realist himself, Miller came out of the social realism movement that swept through the American theater in the first half of the twentieth century, and some of his less fortunate lines seem determined to make upper-class audiences appreciate the homespun rhythms of working-class or immigrant speech (his grandparents had originally lived in Poland). "Gotta break your neck to see a star in this yard," says Willy Loman, gazing up past the tenement buildings, in *Death of a Salesman*. Even after he stepped into the national spotlight, Miller maintained that he spent a few weeks every year working in a factory in order to keep in touch with the working classes. This, as his biographer Christopher Bigsby writes, is "stretching things a little."

Where Miller shines is structure. Speaking to Bigsby in 1999 for his second interview with *The Paris Review*, Miller said that "a play arrives at an almost palpable architectural form," and this is an important key to his work. Even read on the page, it is possible to sense the power and grace of Miller's dramatic constructions. On stage, their momentum has no equal in American drama. As Miller said to *The Paris Review* in 1966, "Everything is inevitable, down to the last comma."

Miller's foundation is domesticity. There is no personal or collective sin that he does not channel through the textures of family life. In *All My Sons*, Chris Keller's plans for marriage unravel as he discovers that his father, who manufactured faulty airplane parts during World War II, is responsible for the deaths of twenty-one pilots. John Proctor's past infidelities in *The Crucible* open his wife Elizabeth to accusations of witchcraft. It is Miller's signature that these wrongs have already been committed by the time the curtain rises on the play's first act. His moral interest lies in what we do with our guilt.

This technique is at the core of Greek tragedy as well (Oedipus is twice guilty by the time he takes the stage in *Oedipus Rex*), but Miller was not simply borrowing a clever dramatic device. Writing at a time when Freudian psychoanalysis, with all its denial and repression, was thick in the air, Miller worked toward a notion of history in which the past could suddenly and destructively intrude on the present. If that sounds like a commonplace today, it is in part because Miller made it so. "I came back" is Willy Loman's opening line. In a sense, he is ventriloquizing his fractured past. He is driven to suicide by the things that come back to him.

This way of thinking about history took on a special—sometimes painful—political resonance in the 1950s. "I would not deny I might have signed it," Miller said when asked about a petition before the HUAC. With that evasive, uneasy wording, he might have been speaking for the whole American left. Miller was part of a political generation that had seen Marxism and its national embodiment—the Soviet Union—as a beacon of hope, only to watch in horror as their old beliefs produced not peace and equality but Stalin's pogroms. "I used to think that if people had the right idea they could make things move accordingly," Miller said in 1999. "Now it's a day-to-day fight to stop dreadful things from happening."

Today, Miller the public figure is remembered as a fairly uncomplicated moral hero, but that misunderstands both his life and his writing. It is worth remembering that Miller, a second-generation immigrant who became one of the country's most celebrated artists, may have critiqued the American dream, but he also lived it like few others can. In the final scene of *The Crucible*, choosing between life and death, John Proctor says, "I think it is honest, I think so; I am no saint." The line lives in the architecture of Miller's greatest plays.

Bibliography

Bigsby, Christopher. *Arthur Miller: 1915-1962*. Cambridge, MA: Harvard UP, 2009.

Miller, Arthur. "The Art of Theater No. 2." Interview with Olga Carlisle and Rose Styron. *The Paris Review* 38 (Summer 1966).

_____. "The Art of Theater No. 2, Part 2." Interview with Christopher Bigsby. *The Paris Review* 152 (Fall 1999).

_____. *Collected Plays 1944-1961*. Ed. Tony Kushner. New York: Library of America, 2006.

_____. *The Portable Arthur Miller*. Ed. Christopher Bigsby. New York: Penguin, 2003.

_____. *Timebends: A Life*. New York: Grove Press, 1987.

Pells, Richard H. *The Liberal Mind in a Conservative Age*. New York: Harper & Row, 1985.

Saunders, Frances Stonor. *The Cultural Cold War: The CIA and the World of Arts and Letters*. New York: New Press, 2001.

Whitfield, Stephen J. *The Culture of the Cold War*. Baltimore: Johns Hopkins UP, 1991.

CRITICAL CONTEXTS

Best Intentions Far Awry:
The Family Dynamic in Miller's *All My Sons* and *Death of a Salesman*_____

Pamela Loos

"Miller's tragedies are about men who are not 'at one' with society," according to William B. Dillingham, "because they have sinned against it or have refused to assume their rightful place in it" (339-40). Indeed, the fathers of *All My Sons* and *Death of a Salesman* are both out of sync with society: Willy Loman fails to understand himself and esteems a career path that goes against who he truly is, and Joe Keller fails to recognize that, besides being responsible for his family, he must also be a moral person within the larger world. In both plays, the fathers' conflicts ripple across their families and cause their deaths. Willy Loman's inability to reconcile himself with society causes both his own and his son Biff's wrenching unhappiness; Joe Keller's own conflict with society causes the death of his son Larry as well as of scores of other men's sons. Ultimately, the fathers' conflicts push them both to suicide, allowing no opportunity for them to be restored to society and leaving their families in despair.

As important as the fathers are in these plays, however, neither of the fathers is his play's key focus. Rather, the two plays emphasize the entire family dynamic as the fathers near the end of their working lives and look to their sons to take up their work and become successful businessmen. Wives and sons go to great lengths to protect their families, lies that have been perpetuated for years are exposed, family members fail to understand themselves and one another, and fathers and sons have conflicting views about what is important in life. At the end of each play, a son comes to some realizations about himself and his father, tries to explain them to his father, and becomes a catalyst in his father's destruction.

When *Death of a Salesman* opens, Willy is in his early sixties, about the same age as Joe Keller, and, like Joe, he has two grown sons, though both of his are still alive. Also like Joe, he insists that his son become a successful businessman. His conflict with society is primarily twofold. First, he is torn about his own self. As Miller explains, "In the deeper, psychological sense, he is Everyman who finds he must create another personality in order to make his way in the world, and therefore has sold himself" (Fuller 243). Trying to make a living as a salesman, Willy finds that he must develop a personality that is at odds with his true self—he must split himself in two between his job and who he actually is. This split has serious consequences, as it causes Willy to misunderstand himself and his family by defining success solely on business terms and, as we will see later, forcing this definition upon his sons. Gerald Weales points out that audiences have mixed reactions to Willy and his struggle: "Is Willy, for instance, a born loser, or is he a game little fighter who, having been sold a bill of goods about the American Dream, keeps slugging it out against unequal odds?" (xvi).

The second part of Willy's conflict follows from this split as he insists on a vision for his older son, Biff, that is thoroughly at odds with who Biff is. Miller says, "Biff wants not to be an integer, a simple little factor, in this gigantic business and industrial operation that the United States is. . . . He is a precursor of the hippy movement in a way" ("Interview" 507). Willy, though, wants Biff to be a successful businessman, and this faulty vision creates a key conflict in the play. Willy's vision goes against Biff's nature and so pits him against his natural place in society. It creates a conflict between father and son, a conflict within Biff himself, extreme disruption in the family, and havoc in the world at large for those with whom Biff comes in contact.

As the play opens, we find that Willy has been plagued for years by Biff's inability to hold a job (let alone become the successful businessman Willy would like him to be), and Biff, too, has been unhappily drifting and getting into trouble. Trying to figure out what went wrong, Willy replays earlier years, years he sees as greatly successful during which he filled his sons' heads with advice about how to become successful. As a salesman, Willy believes that success does not come just from being liked but from being well liked, and he instills this belief in his sons. While many would agree that likability may be an ingredient for success in the world at large, for Willy, this trait takes on enormous proportions at the expense of other key characteristics or skills, and it is, arguably, one of the reasons he is forced to split himself in two. After all, a salesman has to sell himself in order to sell his products. But this insistence is problematic for Willy as well as for his boys. When applied to the boys' lives, it means that being well liked becomes more important than studying hard. It means that Willy does not really believe a teacher will fail Biff, since, after all, Biff is so well liked. It means that Biff's stealing and cheating are okay as long as he remains well liked. It means it is fine to make fun of the neighbors, since this only reinforces the idea that they are *not* well liked. In short, the sons are filled with seriously flawed advice, and it is at least partially as a result of this advice, in addition to his disillusionment about Willy's unfaithfulness to his wife, that Biff runs into trouble and has a problematic adulthood.

Despite all of his problems, however, Willy still sees Biff as the son of promise. Happy, on the other hand, as A. Howard Fuller sees it, is "the victim of the neglect of the father, whose chief concern is always directed toward Biff. Happy suffers, accordingly, a general moral decline" (242). Willy seldom speaks to Happy, even though Happy is intent on making his father proud of him, and it may be this neglect and Happy's resultant determination to make his father proud of him that causes him to misunderstand his father and his brother. For instance, Happy is shocked when his mother, Linda, tells him and his brother that his father wants to die, and he wants Biff to stay and find a job near home, not recognizing how this would be completely against Biff's nature and would only intensify his psychic turmoil. Like Biff, Happy suffers disillusionment over his life. Happy tells Biff, "I don't know what the hell I'm workin' for. Sometimes I sit in my apartment—all alone. . . . My own apartment, a car, and plenty of women. And still, goddammit, I'm lonely" (23). But unlike his brother, he does not let his life and faults bother him too much. He takes bribes and sleeps with executives' wives and girlfriends. He even denies that Willy is his father while trying to pick up a woman in a restaurant.

Linda's relationships with her husband and sons further complicate the family dynamic. In the play's opening description, Miller writes of Linda that "she more than loves him [Willy], she admires him, as though his mercurial nature, his temper, his massive dreams and little cruelties, served her only as sharp reminders of the turbulent longings within him, longings which she shares but lacks the temperament to utter and follow to their end" (12). Like Kate in *All My Sons*, Linda is her husband's protector: Kate goes so far as to help cover up her husband's immoral acts, and it seems that Linda, if in Kate's situation, would likely do the same. As Willy's protector, Linda believes she is helping him, but in fact she is not helping him in the way he most needs, for Willy does not need protection but rather a clear, honest view of himself and the world. Further, she is concerned with Willy's welfare not only at her own expense but also at the expense of her sons. When the sons were young, she played no role in their upbringing other than supporting Willy's parenting, allowing him to instill in them an unrealistic view of the world and themselves. Now that they are grown, she is unable to show Willy who Biff really is.

While Linda has the utmost patience with Willy, she seems to have little patience for her sons, and when she speaks to them, it is nearly always about Willy. She hopes against hope that by telling her sons that Willy is thinking of killing himself they can prevent Willy from doing it, since she has no understanding of how to prevent it on her own. Again, as his protector, she has taken no time to look beyond Willy's illusions and so is unable to help him understand himself and prevent his suicide. Her lack of involvement with her sons adds to the tragic situation as well and keeps her from helping Willy understand Biff, one of the key problems in the play.

As the play's action rises, Biff, like Chris Keller in *All My Sons*, is so torn by events that he says he will do just what he does not want to do. For Biff, this means moving home and making money for his parents, even though he hates the city where they live. At Bill Oliver's office, however, Biff comes to some realizations and changes his mind about what he must do. When Oliver keeps him waiting for hours and does not remember who Biff is, Biff is snapped into reality. He realizes how his family perpetuates lies, how even he, for example, found himself believing he had been a salesman for Oliver when he had in fact never been more than a shipping clerk. At the same time, Biff realizes he has spent too much time trying to force himself to be something he truly has no inclination to be. He later tries to explain to Willy: "I stopped in the middle of that building and I saw—the sky. I saw the things that I love in this world. . . . What am I doing in an office, making a contemptuous, begging fool of myself, when all I want is out there, waiting for me the minute I say I know who I am! Why can't I say that, Willy?" (132).

Biff realizes he has been falling for lies and, as a result, has been at war with his own true self. Like Chris Keller, Biff becomes the truth teller to his whole family. Wanting to avoid upsetting the family dynamic and exposing their fathers as liars, both of these sons refuse to acknowledge the truth until circumstances force them to.

For Biff, even after his striking realizations in Oliver's office and his recognition that Willy, too, must know the truth, the truth telling still does not come easily. The first barrier to the truth arises when Happy tells Biff to lie to Willy about what happened with Oliver and even fabricates a lie that he insists Biff should use. Second, Biff struggles to tell Willy the truth because of Willy's own insistence that there must be some good news. Telling Willy the news about Oliver would be tough enough, given Willy's desire to see Biff become a successful businessman, but Miller heightens the difficulty by having Willy admit that he has just lost his own job.

Miller drives Biff's truth telling further in the family's kitchen near the play's end. Willy gives Biff the final push when he insists that Biff has been operating out of spite for years. Biff's love for his father and his need for his father's acceptance are so great that he tells almost all of the truth: that he has been in jail, that he never got anywhere in life because his father filled him up with hot air when he was a boy, that he and his father are both "a dime a dozen" (132), and that he knows about the hose Willy put down in the cellar to kill himself. Biff knows that the truth will be overwhelming to Willy, but he sees that revealing it is the only way to put the negative past behind him and his family and keep them from repeating it.

Unlike in *All My Sons*, however, where all secrets seem to come out, at no point in the play does Biff tell his mother and Happy one secret, the one event after which he let go of his dreams—that, as a young man, he found Willy with a mistress. That Biff does not reveal this secret bolsters his argument that he is no longer acting out of spite, for if he were, it is likely that he would rail against Willy for being unfaithful.

Biff again cuts through the family's illusions right before the curtain falls on Willy's funeral. He says that Willy was never really meant to be a salesman, since, despite all of Willy's high-flying accounts of his success on the road, selling was not what truly satisfied Willy. Biff reminds everyone of how Willy enjoyed working on his house as well as how skillful he was in doing it. His rightful place, according to Biff, was making a ceiling of his own, not cajoling customers and convincing a boss of his salesmanship. His place was as a craftsman, literally maintaining a home that could be a valued place of peace for his family—no traveling, no arm-twisting, no tricks required. And it is this final truth telling that enables Biff to understand himself. Linda and Happy, meanwhile, remain static—Linda still does not understand why Willy killed himself, and Happy continues to spout grandiose plans.

Like Willy, Joe Keller in *All My Sons* has worked hard for his family his whole life, most especially for his son Chris. Chris, though, is expected not just to earn money from the business, but also to take it over after his father retires. Like Willy, Joe has a vision for his son and is shocked and angry when this vision does not match what his son actually wants.

The essential conflict in this play, however, is not that regarding Chris's career. Over the course of the play, it is revealed that Joe is responsible for allowing faulty airplane parts to be shipped from his factory, causing the deaths of twenty-one pilots during World War II. When the truth comes out, he defends himself by arguing that scrapping the parts would have cost his business a great deal of money, and he invokes his responsibility to his family to justify his actions. As Dillingham describes it, "Keller's extreme allegiance to a lesser good, the family, destroys his social consciousness; he becomes merely a shell, a man without conscience" (342). The conflict is thus between the morally limited Joe and his idealistic son as they confront the truth about Joe's actions.

As Robert W. Corrigan points out, however, while Arthur Miller's "judgments are absolute, they are also exceedingly complex. There is no doubt that he finally stands four-square on the side of the community, but until the moment when justice must be served, his sympathies are for the most part directed toward those ordinary little men who never discovered who they really were" (29). Whereas Willy's conflict stems from the split between who he really is and who his job forces him to be, Joe's stems from the discordance between his morality within his family and his morality within the larger world. Unlike Willy, Joe has a strong understanding of himself, but he fails to recognize that he is responsible not just to his family but also to society. Willy is in some ways morally lacking, too—he allows his boys to cheat and steal, for example, and is unfaithful to his wife—but Joe's immorality has graver consequences than Willy's. Joe causes the deaths of twenty-one pilots, allows his business partner to take the blame and be sent to jail, causes his son, Larry, to commit suicide, and is ultimately the cause of his own suicide.

As the play opens, Joe Keller is described as near sixty, a "heavy man of stolid mind and build, a business man these many years, but with the imprint of the machine-shop worker and boss still upon him" (6). He appears to be a magnet in the neighborhood—neighbors come and go from his yard, and a young boy comes to play games with Joe. He is easily content with simple things, like reading the newspaper on the porch, and enjoys spending time with his family. He is a traditionalist and romantic, repeatedly teasing Chris and Ann about their relationship and supporting Chris's desire to marry Ann even though he knows it will deeply disturb his wife, Kate.

Like Willy, Joe wants to be well liked, though he is much more skilled than Willy in getting people to like him and using them to his advantage. He has been able to convince people that his partner, Steve, was responsible for shipping the faulty airplane parts, not him. We also see his bravado when he turns home from prison and decides to walk down the whole street to show his neighbors that he has been found innocent. After he returns home, Joe holds card parties to ensure he is back in the neighbors' good graces. Rather late in the play, however, one neighbor reveals that no one in the neighborhood truly believes Joe is innocent. Perhaps Joe himself realizes this, too, but he knows that giving parties and inviting people to his home ingratiates him with them. His skill is also seen later in the play, when George arrives with word from his father about the faulty parts. Joe dismisses Steve's argument and tries to win over George by offering to get George a job and new life in the neighborhood and to give his father a new start as well. Joe thinks that if George believes Joe has their best interests at heart, perhaps George will not try to reopen the case, perhaps he will believe Joe always had his and his father's best interests at heart and so never would have claimed that Steve was guilty if it had not been true.

Even though Joe can understand and manipulate people, he can still be surprised by them, especially his son Chris. He is surprised that Chris wants to marry Ann and that he would be willing to give up the family business to do so. Further, he is shocked at Chris's wrenching anguish when he finally realizes that Joe knowingly shipped the faulty airplane parts. Whereas Willy's lack of understanding of Biff wears on Willy, his son, and the rest of the Loman family for many years, Joe's lack of understanding of Chris only truly surfaces during the course of the play. Rather than the deep-seated disappointment and frustration Willy shows for Biff, Joe is intensely shocked as he suddenly realizes that he does not understand Chris.

Toward the first surprise, that Chris wants to marry Ann, Joe is unenthusiastic, and it is only after Chris probes him that Joe admits he wishes Chris would not go through with the marriage because Kate will be against it. Joe would rather keep the status quo than disturb his wife's psyche, however out of kilter it may be and however harmful it might be to his own son and others.

Much more upsetting to Joe, though, is Chris's statement that, if he must, he will leave the family business to marry Ann. Joe, who built the business to pass on to his son, is shocked. In Joe's mind, it is imperative that Chris continue the business—his own life's work has meaning only if Chris continues the business. His language is intense: "What the hell is *this*?" and "Are you crazy?" (17). He cannot understand how Chris could think of leaving, even if Chris does find the job uninspiring. To him, a man's satisfaction comes from continuing what his father not only started but also improved and handed down. He is shocked that his son feels differently and that he could so cavalierly think of walking away: "But don't think like that. Because what the hell did I work for? That's only for you, Chris, the whole shootin'-match is for you!" (17).

This last point is repeated near the end of the play when Chris confronts Joe about shipping out the faulty parts. Joe justifies his actions by saying, "Chris, I did it for you" (70). As Joe sees that this explanation has no effect on Chris, he offers other excuses—that he did not expect the parts to get used after all and that plenty of other people engaged in shady business practices during the war. The irony and the tragedy is that, while Joe does have expertise in understanding people and sometimes in winning them over, he does not understand his own son, whom he loves so much, and so does not see that such explanations will not justify him before his son. Ann, Kate, and even neighbors see Chris for who he is, but his father does not.

Chris is "thirty-two; like his father, solidly built, a listener. A man capable of immense affection and loyalty" (11). He is educated. Like Biff Loman, Chris has given in to his father's wishes for him, even though doing so has put Chris at odds with his own self. He has not been torn apart by making compromises to try to please his father like Biff, but Chris is definitely tired of compromise and ready to change. "I've been a good son too long, a good sucker. I'm through with it," he says (17). Unlike Biff, Chris has no deep need for his father to understand him, and he no longer appears intimidated by what his father wants. He stands firm when Joe says Chris should rethink marrying Ann and when Joe becomes upset when he says he could leave the plant.

Chris is greatly respected and admired by Ann and George. Their belief in Chris is so thorough that at first they readily believe Chris over their own father about the shipment of the faulty airplane parts. Chris's mother and his neighbors also see him as an idealist, but they do not consider this a positive quality. Sue Bayliss, for instance, asks Ann to keep Chris away from her husband, Jim, because Chris makes Jim unhappy about the compromises he has made. Sue tells Ann, "Chris makes people want to be better than it's possible to be" (44), a line similar to one said later by Joe. Chris's idealism is also seen when he explains to Ann how he felt after returning from the war. People should have been changed by such a profound event, should have realized their responsibility to each other, he says. Instead, "there was no meaning in it here; the whole thing to them was a kind of a—bus accident. . . . nobody was changed at all" (36).

We see Chris's disillusionment come to fruition near the end of the play. Whereas Joe sees cheating as part of life, Chris goes through most of the play avoiding thinking about how many people cheat and compromise in life, and he is overwhelmed by disgust when he does, especially as he is pressed to do after finding out about his father's immorality. He rails: "This is the land of the great big dogs, you don't love a man here, you eat him! That's the principle; the only one we live by—it just happened to kill a few people this time, that's all. The world's that way, how can I take it out on him? What sense does that make? This is a zoo, a zoo!" (81).

Chris is disgusted with himself as well for being a coward for too long, for blocking out the evidence about his father's guilt. And he comes to the realization that his father does not live up to his expectations: "*I* know you're no worse than most men but I thought you were better. I never saw you as a man. I saw you as my father" (82). Chris is destroyed by finding out about his father's guilt. Like Biff, his first reaction is to leave and find a job in another city. Doing so, however, would be a compromise, just what he is sick of doing, and one of the worst sort, involving morality and his father: "I could jail him! I could jail him, if I were human any more. But I'm like everybody else now. I'm practical now. You made me practical . . . and I spit on myself" (80). Also like Biff, Chris realizes he cannot just run away. Chris cannot be as inhuman as he sees everybody else being; he cannot just let his father's crime go. Still, he cannot tell his father what to do—he needs Joe to know that he needs to go to jail and to be willing to do it.

Up until the very end of the play Joe's allegiance to his family blinds him to his responsibility to be moral outside his family. Though Joe is devastated after Chris blasts him about his lack of morality, Joe is not concerned about his lack but about his relationship with Chris. Joe remains adamant in his belief that his responsibility to his family supersedes all of his other responsibilities, even when Kate points out that this vision excuses his immoral act. Only after Joe hears Larry's suicide letter does he accept what he has been told. Joe gravely admits, "Sure, he was my son. But I think to him they were all my sons. And I guess they were, I guess they were" (83). He realizes he has a moral responsibility in the world at large. While Willy never hears the truth about his true place in the world, Joe finally does.

Unlike Linda Loman at the end of *Death of a Salesman*, Kate does not realize that her husband is suicidal. Miller describes Kate as "in her early fifties, a woman of uncontrolled inspirations, and an overwhelming capacity for love" (18), and Samuel A. Yorks describes her as "easily the strongest individual in the play. She is shown as superior in force of character to all the others, especially in times of emotional crisis" (22). Like Linda Loman, Kate can be anxious and superstitious, and she cares deeply for her husband. She protects him too, like Linda does Willy, but Kate extends her protection further, becoming an accomplice to Joe's cover-up. As an accomplice, however, she gains a certain control over her husband, making her a powerful figure in the family.

She is able to persevere in her belief that Larry is still alive, for if he were dead, she reasons, it would mean that Joe killed him. Thus Joe is made complicit in her illusion. Because of her belief, she is able to insist that Ann and Chris cannot get married and, when Joe confronts her about the marriage, slap him in the face. Throughout the play she directly connects Joe to the faulty parts and to Larry's death, although she does not reveal this until late in the play. Her revelation is what finally causes Chris to insist that his father tell the truth. In some ways, then, Kate, not George, causes the confrontation between Chris and Joe. Miller himself later wrote about the ambiguity surrounding Kate and suggested that a part of her wants vengeance on her husband (*Timebends* 135-36).

Unlike Willy Loman, who missed Biff's message about who he and his son are, by the end of *All My Sons* Joe Keller finally understands that he has made a mistake and that both of his sons wanted him to be moral in the world at large. As Chris does, Biff spells out all the answers for his father. Thus Joe seems to have the potential to reconcile himself with his family and society, whereas Willy, in the end, does not even seem to see his problems, never mind being able to face them.

The resolution to *All My Sons* seems simpler than that of the later *Death of a Salesman*. In *All My Sons*, Joe's deliverance hinges on his recognition that his actions were immoral and his readiness to suffer the consequences of them. He seems to meet at least the first point, if not the second. In *Death of a Salesman*, however, Willy's deliverance hinges on whether he will understand and accept himself and Biff. This seems a taller order. Perhaps it could be said that the outcome of Miller's later tragedy acknowledges the unlikelihood of two characters simultaneously coming to major realizations, as well as how a single, initial blind spot can often multiply into many more. It seems quite natural that Willy's blind spot about his true self has also kept him from seeing Biff's true self, for instance. If *All My Sons* had been written later in Miller's career, perhaps Joe's blind spot, his illusions about his moral responsibilities, would manifest itself further in the Keller family dynamic rather than just in Joe's business decisions. Perhaps the play's resolution would be more complex, too.

Regardless of their resolutions, both plays exemplify Miller's view that tragedy ought to focus on the "heart and spirit of the average man" ("Tragedy" 7). We identify not only with the plays' fathers but also with their sons and wives. In both plays, the importance of family is not only a major topic of discussion among the characters but is also illustrated dramatically as the characters alternately act to avoid upsetting their families, even though doing so is highly detrimental to them in the long run, and to save them by revealing the truth. In both plays, the family members' interactions make us realize the danger of ignoring reality and upholding lies, even in the interest of not hurting those we love. Still, despite his characters' familial and personal flaws, in tragedies, Miller writes, "and in them alone, lies the belief—optimistic, if you will, in the perfectability of man" ("Tragedy" 7). Characters such as Biff and Chris model this idea, as both believe humanity can be better and bring enlightenment to their families.

Works Cited

Corrigan, Robert W. "Robert W. Corrigan on the Achievement of Arthur Miller." *Arthur Miller*. Ed. Harold Bloom. Philadelphia: Chelsea House, 2000.

Dillingham, William B. "Arthur Miller and the Loss of Conscience." *Arthur Miller: Death of a Salesman—Text and Criticism*. Ed. Gerald Weales. New York: Viking Press, 1977.

Fuller, A. Howard. "A Salesman Is Everybody." *Arthur Miller: Death of a Salesman—Text and Criticism*. Ed. Gerald Weales. New York: Viking Press, 1977.

Miller, Arthur. *All My Sons*. 1947. New York: Penguin Press, 1975.

_____. "Arthur Miller: An Interview." *The Theater Essays of Arthur Miller*. Ed. Robert A. Martin and Steven R. Centola. New York: Da Capo Press, 1996.

_____. *Arthur Miller: Death of a Salesman—Text and Criticism*. Ed. Gerald Weales. New York: Viking Press, 1977.

_____. *Timebends: A Life*. New York: Grove Press, 1987.

_____. "Tragedy and the Common Man." *The Theater Essays of Arthur Miller*. Ed. Robert A. Martin and Steven R. Centola. New York: Da Capo Press, 1996.

Weales, Gerald. "Introduction." *Arthur Miller: Death of a Salesman—Text and Criticism*. Ed. Gerald Weales. New York: Viking Press, 1977.

Yorks, Samuel A. "Samuel A. Yorks on Joe Keller and His Sons." *Arthur Miller*. Ed. Harold Bloom. Philadelphia: Chelsea House, 2000.

"It's All About the Language":
Arthur Miller's Poetic Dialogue_____

Stephen A. Marino

In a 2003 interview with his biographer, Christopher Bigsby, about the inherent structure of his plays, Arthur Miller explained, "It's all about the language" (Bigsby, "Miller"). Miller's declaration about the centrality of language in the creation of drama came at the end of his almost seventy-year career. He had completed his final play, *Finishing the Picture*, and a little more than a year later, he became ill and subsequently died in February 2005. Thus Miller's statement can be seen as a final avowal about how language operates in dramatic dialogue, a concern that had obsessed him since the start of his career when he wrote his first play, *No Villain*, at the University of Michigan in 1935.

Despite Miller's proclamation, not enough critical attention has been paid to the sophisticated use of language that pervades his dialogue. Throughout his career, Miller often was subject to reviews in which critics mostly excoriated him for what they judged as a failed use of language in his plays. For example, in the *Nation* review of the original production of *Death of a Salesman* in 1949, Joseph Wood Krutch criticized the play for "its failure to go beyond literal meaning and its undistinguished dialogue. Unlike Tennessee Williams, Miller does not have a unique sensibility, new insight, fresh imagination or a gift for language" (283-84). In 1964, Richard Gilman judged that *After the Fall* lacks structural focus and contains vague rhetoric. He concluded that Miller's "verbal inadequacy [has] never been more flagrantly exhibited" (6). John Simon's *New York* review of the 1994 Broadway production of *Broken Glass* opined that "Miller's ultimate failure is his language: Tone-deafness in a playwright is only a shade less bad than in a composer." In a June 2009 review of Christopher Bigsby's authorized biography of Miller, Terry Teachout judged that Miller "too often made the mistake of using florid, pseudo-poetic language" (72).

These reviews illustrate how, as a language stylist, Arthur Miller was underappreciated, too often overshadowed by his contemporary Tennessee Williams, whose major strength as a dramatist for many critics lies in the "lyricism" of his plays. As Arthur K. Oberg pointed out, "In the established image, Miller's art is masculine and craggy; Williams', poetic and delicate" (303). Because Miller has so often been pigeonholed as a "social" dramatist, most of the criticism of his work focuses on the cultural relevance of his plays and ignores detailed discussions of his language—especially of its poetic elements. Most critics are content to regard his dialogue as "colloquial," judging that Miller best used what Leonard Moss described as "the common man's language" (52) to reflect the social concerns of his characters. The assumption is often made that the manufacturers, salesmen, Puritan farmers, dockworkers, housewives, policemen, doctors, lawyers, executives, and bankers who compose the bulk of Miller's characters speak a realistic prose dialogue—a style that is implicitly antithetical to poetic language.

This prevailing opinion of Miller as a dramatist who merely uses the common man's language has been reinforced largely by a lack of in-depth critical analyses of how figurative language works in his canon. In his November 1998 review of the Chicago run of the fiftieth anniversary production of *Death of a Salesman*, Ben Brantley noted that, "as recent Miller scholarship has suggested again and again, the play's images and rhythms have the patterns of poetry" (E3). In reality, though, relatively few critics have thoroughly examined this aspect not only of *Salesman* but also of Miller's entire dramatic canon.[1] Thomas M. Tammaro judges "that critical attention to Miller's drama has been lured from textual analysis to such non-textual concerns as biography and Miller as a social dramatist" (10).[2] Moreover, classroom discussions of Miller's masterpieces *Death of a Salesman* and *The Crucible* (1953) mostly focus on these biographical and social concerns in addition to characterization and thematic issues but rarely discuss language and dialogue. Five years after his passing, it is time to recognize that

Arthur Miller created a unique dramatic idiom that undoubtedly marks him as significant language stylist within twentieth- and twenty-first-century American and world drama. More readers and critics should see his dialogue not exclusively as prose but also as poetry, what Gordon W. Couchman has called Miller's "rare gift for the poetic in the colloquial" (206).

Although Miller seems to work mostly in a form of colloquial prose, there are many moments in his plays when the dialogue clearly elevates to poetry. Miller often takes what appear to be the colloquialisms, clichés, and idioms of the common man's language and reveals them as poetic language, especially by shifting words from their denotative to connotative meanings. Moreover, he significantly employs the figurative devices of metaphor, symbol, and imagery to give poetic significance to prose dialect. In addition, in many texts Miller embeds series of metaphors—many are extended—that possess particular connotations within the societies of the individual plays. Most important, these figurative devices significantly support the tragic conflicts and social themes that are the focus of every Miller play. By deftly mixing these figurative devices of symbolism, imagery, and metaphor with colloquial prose dialogue, Miller combines prose and poetry to create a unique dramatic idiom. Most critics, readers, and audiences seem to overlook this aspect of Miller's work: the poetry is in the prose and the prose is in the poetry.

Indeed, poetic elements pervade most of Miller's plays. For example, in *All My Sons*, religious allusions, symbols, and images place the themes of sacrifice and redemption in a Christian context. In *Death of a Salesman*, the extended metaphors of sports and trees convey Willy Loman's struggle to achieve the American Dream. In *The Crucible*, the poetic language illustrates the conflicts that polarize the Salem community as a series of opposing images—heat and cold, white and black, light and dark, soft and hard—signify the Salemites' dualistic view of the world. In *A View from the Bridge*, metaphors of purity and innocence give mythic importance to Eddie Carbone's sexual, psychological, and moral struggles. *After the Fall* uses extended metaphors of childhood and religion to support Quentin's psychological quest for redemption. *The Ride Down Mt. Morgan* connects metaphors of transportation and travel to Lyman Felt's literal and figurative fall, and *Broken Glass* uses images of mirrors and glass to relate the world of the European Jew at the beginning of the Holocaust to Sylvia and Phillip Gellburg's shattered sexual world.

That most critics continue to fail to recognize Miller's sophisticated use of poetic elements is striking, for it is this very facility for which many other playwrights are praised, and the history of drama is intimately intertwined with the history of poetry. For most of Western dramatic history, plays were written in verse: the ancient Greek playwrights of the fifth century B.C.E. composed their tragedies in a verse frequently accompanied by music; the rhyming couplets of the *Everyman* dramatist were the de rigueur medieval form; and English Renaissance plays were poetic masterpieces. Shakespeare's supremacy as a dramatist lies in his adaptation of the early modern English language into a dramatic dialogue that combines prose and poetry. For example, Hamlet's "quintessence of dust" speech is lyrical prose. In the twentieth century, critics praised the verse plays of T. S. Eliot, Maxwell Anderson, Christopher Isherwood, and W. H. Auden.

Even more baffling about this critical neglect is that Miller readily acknowledged his attraction to poetry and dramatic verse. His views on language, particularly poetic language, are evident in the prodigious number of essays he produced throughout his career. Criticism has mostly ignored this large body of nonfiction writing in which Miller frequently expounds on the nature of language and dialogue, the tension between realistic prose and poetic language in twentieth-century drama, and the complex evolution of poetic language throughout his plays.[3] For example, in his 1993 essay "About Theatre Language" he writes:

It was inevitable that I had to confront the problem of dramatic language. . . . I gradually came to wonder if the essential pressure toward poetic dramatic language—if not of stylization itself—came from the inclusion of society as a major element in the play's story or vision. Manifestly, prose realism was the language of the individual and private life, poetry the language of man in crowds, in society. Put another way, prose is the language of family relations; it is the inclusion of the larger world beyond that naturally opens a play to the poetic.

. . . How to find a style that would at one and the same time deeply engage an American audience, which insisted on a recognizable reality of characters, locales, and themes, while opening the stage to considerations of public morality and the mythic social fates—in short, the invisible? (82)

* * *

Miller's attraction to poetic dramatic dialogue can be traced back to his development as a playwright, particularly his time as a student at the University of Michigan in the mid-1930s and the early years of his great successes in the 1940s and 1950s, when his views on dramatic form, structure, aesthetics, and language were evolving. Miller knew little about the theater when he arrived in Ann Arbor from his home in Brooklyn, but during these formative college years, he became aware of German expressionism, and he read August Strindberg and Henrik Ibsen, whom he often acknowledged as major influences on him. Christopher Bigsby has pointed out that Miller always remembered the effect that reading Greek and Elizabethan playwrights at college had on him (*Critical Study* 419). However, Miller was markedly affected by the social-protest work of Clifford Odets. In his autobiography, *Timebends* (1987), Miller describes how Odets's 1930s plays *Waiting for Lefty* (1935), *Awake and Sing* (1935), and *Golden Boy* (1937) had "sprung forth a new phenomenon, a leftist challenge to the system, the poet suddenly leaping onto the stage and disposing of middle-class gentility, screaming and yelling and cursing like somebody off the

Manhattan streets" (229). Most important for Miller, Odets brought to American drama a concern for language: "For the very first time in America, language itself had marked a playwright as unique" (229). To Miller, Odets was "The only poet, I thought, not only in the social protest theater, but in all of New York" (212).

After Miller won his first Avery Hopwood Award at Michigan, he was sent to Professor Kenneth Rowe, whose chief contribution to Miller's development was cultivating his interest in the dynamics of play construction. Odets and Rowe clearly were considerably strong influences on Miller as he developed his concern with language and his form broke out of what he termed the "dusty naturalistic habit" (*Timebends* 228) of Broadway, but other influences would also compel him to write dramatic verse. The work of Thornton Wilder, particularly *Our Town* (1938), spoke to him, and in *Timebends* Miller acknowledges that *Our Town* was the nearest of the 1930s plays in "reaching for lyricism" (229). Tennessee Williams is another playwright whom Miller frequently credited with influencing his art and the craft of his language. He credited the newness of *The Glass Menagerie* (1944) to the play's "poetic lift" (*Timebends* 244) and was particularly struck by *A Streetcar Named Desire* (1947), proclaiming that Williams had given him license to speak in dramatic language "at full throat" (*Timebends* 182).

Moreover, Miller practiced what he had learned and espoused. In fact, he reported that when he was first beginning his career he was "up to [his] neck" in writing many of his full-length and radio plays in verse ("Interview" 98). When he graduated from Michigan and started his work with the Federal Theatre Project in 1938, he wrote *The Golden Years*, a verse play about Montezuma. In a letter to Professor Rowe, he reported that he found writing verse much easier than writing prose: "I made the discovery that in verse you are forced to be brief and to the point. Verse squeezes out fat and you're left with the real meaning of the language" (Bigsby, *Arthur Miller* 155). Also, he explained that much of *Death of a Salesman* and all of *The Crucible* were originally written in verse; the one-act version of *A View from the Bridge* (1955) was written in an intriguing mixture of verse and prose, and Miller regretted his failure to do the same in *The American Clock* (1980) (Bigsby, *Critical Introduction* 136).

However, Miller found an American theater hostile to the poetic form. Miller himself pointed out that the United States had no tradition of dramatic verse ("Interview" 98) as compared to Europe. In the 1930s, Maxwell Anderson was one of the few American playwrights incorporating blank verse into his plays, and the English theater witnessed some interest in poetic drama in the 1940s and 1950s, most notably with Christopher Fry and T. S. Eliot. In reality, dramatic verse had been in sharp decline since the late nineteenth century, when the realistic prose dialogue used by Henrik Ibsen in Norway was adopted by George Bernard Shaw in England and then later employed by Eugene O'Neill in the United States. Miller also judged that American actors had difficulty speaking the verse line ("Interview" 98). Further, Miller came of age at a time when American audiences were demanding realism, the musical comedy was gaining in dominance, and commercial Broadway producers were disinterested in verse drama.

Christopher Bigsby has pointed out that Miller was "in his own mind, an essentially poetic, deeply metaphoric writer who had found himself in a theater resistant to such, particularly on Broadway, which he continued to think of as his natural home, despite its many deficiencies" (*Critical Study* 358). Struggling with how to accept this reality, Miller accommodated his natural inclination to verse by developing a dramatic idiom that reconciled his poetic urge with the realism demanded by the aesthetics of the American stage. Thus he infused poetic language into his prose dialogue.

* * *

Let's examine how some of these poetic devices—symbolism, imagery, and metaphor—operate in Miller's masterpiece, *Death of a*

Salesman. From the outset of the play, Miller makes trees and sports into metaphors signifying Willy Loman's struggle to achieve the American Dream within the competitive American business world. Trees symbolize Willy's dreams, sports the competition for economic success.[4] Miller sustains these metaphors throughout the entire text with images of boxing, burning, wood, nature, and fighting to make them into crucial unifying structures. In addition, Miller's predilection for juxtaposing the literal and figurative meanings of words is particularly evident in *Salesman* as the abstract concepts of competition and dreaming are vivified by concrete objects and actions such as boxing, fists, lumber, and ashes.

Trees are an excellent illustration of how Miller uses literal and figurative meanings. Two references in act 1, scene 1, immediately establish their importance in the play. When Willy unexpectedly arrives home, he explains that he was unable to drive to Portland for his sales call because he kept becoming absorbed in the countryside scenery, where "the trees are so thick, and the sun is warm" (14). Although these trees merely seem to distract Willy from driving, he also indicates their connection to dreaming. He tells Linda: "I absolutely forgot I was driving. If I'd've gone the other way over the white line I might've killed somebody. So I went on again—and five minutes later I'm dreamin' again" (14). Willy's inability to concentrate on driving indicates an emotional conflict larger than mere daydreaming. The play reveals how Willy often exists in dreams rather than reality— dreams of being well liked, of success for his son Biff, of his "imaginings." All of these dreams intimately connect to Willy's confrontation with his failure to achieve the tangible aspects of the American Dream. He is a traveling salesman, and his inability to drive symbolizes his inability to sell, which guarantees that he will fail in the competition to be a "hot-shot salesman." The action of the play depicts the last day of Willy's life and how Willy is increasingly escaping the reality of his failure in reveries of the past, to the point where he often cannot differentiate between reality and illusion.

The repetition of the mention of trees in Willy's second speech in scene 1 cements the importance of trees in the play as a metaphor for these dreams. He complains to Linda about the apartment houses surrounding the Loman home: "They should've had a law against apartment houses. Remember those two beautiful elm trees out there? When Biff and I hung the swing between them?" (17). However, these trees are not the trees of the real time of the play; rather, they exist in Willy's past and, more important, in the "imaginings" of his mind, the place where the more important dramatic action of the play takes place.

Miller's working title for *Death of a Salesman* was "The Inside of His Head," and certainly Willy's longing for the trees of the past illustrates how dreaming works in his mind. Throughout the entire play, trees—and all the other images connected to them—are complicated symbols of an idyllic past for which Willy longs in his dreams, a world where Biff and Hap are young, where Willy can believe himself a hotshot salesman, where Brooklyn seems an unspoiled wilderness. The irony is that, in reality, the past was not as idyllic as Willy recalls, and the play gradually unfolds the reality of Willy's failures. The metaphor of trees also supports Willy's unresolved struggle with his son Biff. Willy's memory of Biff and himself hanging a hammock between the elms is ironic as the two beautiful trees' absence in the present symbolizes Willy's failed dreams for Biff.

Throughout the play, Miller significantly expands upon the figurative meaning of trees. For example, in act 1, scene 4, Willy responds to Hap's claims that he will retire Willy for life by remarking:

You'll retire me for life on seventy goddam dollars a week? And your women and your car and your apartment, and you'll retire me for life! Christ's sake I couldn't get past Yonkers today! Where are you guys, where are you? The woods are burning! I can't drive a car! (41)

Willy's warning that "the woods are burning" extends the tree metaphor by introducing an important sense of destruction to the trees of

Willy's idyllic world of the past. Since the trees are so identified with Willy's dreams, the image implies that his dreams are burning too—his dreams for himself as a successful salesman and his dreams for Biff and Hap. The images of burning and destruction are crucial in the play, especially when Linda reveals Willy's suicide attempts—his own form of destruction, which he enacts at play's end. We realize that since Willy is so associated with his dreams, he will die when they burn. In fact, Willy repeats this same exact line in act 2 when he arrives at Frank's Chop House and announces his firing to Hap and Biff. He says: "I'm not interested in stories about the past or any crap of that kind because the woods are burning, boys, you understand? There's a big blaze going on all around. I was fired today" (107). This line not only repeats Willy's warning cry from act 1 but also foreshadows Biff's climactic plea to Willy to "take that phony dream and burn it" (133). The burning metaphor—now ironic—also appears in Willy's imagining in the Boston hotel room. As Willy continues to ignore Biff's knock on the door, the woman says, "Maybe the hotel's on fire." Willy replies, "It's a mistake, there's no fire" (116). Of course, nothing is threatened by a literal fire—only by the figurative blaze inside Willy's head.

Once aware of how tree images operate in the play, a reader (or keen theatergoer) can note the cacophony of other references that sustain the metaphor in other scenes. For example, Willy wants Biff to help trim the tree branch that threatens to fall on the Loman house; Biff and Hap steal lumber; Willy plaintively remembers his father carving flutes; Willy tells Ben that Biff can "fell trees"; Willy mocks Biff for wanting to be a carpenter and similarly mocks Charley and his son Bernard because they "can't hammer a nail"; Ben buys timberland in Alaska; Biff burns his sneakers in the furnace; Willy speculates about his need for a "little lumber" (72) to build a guest house for the boys when they get married; Willy is proud of weathering a twenty-five-year mortgage with "all the cement, the lumber" (74) he has put into the house; Willy explains to Ben that "I am building something with this firm," something "you can't feel . . . with your hand like timber" (86). Finally, there are "the leaves of day appearing over everything" in the graveyard in "Requiem" (136).

Miller similarly uses boxing in literal and figurative ways throughout the play. In act 1, scene 2, Biff suggests to Hap that they buy a ranch to "use our muscles. Men built like we are should be working out in the open" (24). Hap responds to Biff with the first sports reference in the text: "That's what I dream about, Biff. Sometimes I want to just rip my clothes off in the middle of the store and outbox that goddam merchandise manager. I mean I can outbox, outrun, and outlift anybody in that store" (24). As an athlete, Biff, it seems, should introduce the sports metaphor, but, ironically, the sport with which he is identified—football—is not used in any extensive metaphoric way in the play.[5] Instead, boxing becomes the extended sports metaphor of the text, and it is not introduced by Biff but rather by Hap, who reinforces it throughout the play to show how Willy has prepared him and Biff only for physical competition, not business or economic competition. Thus Hap expresses his frustration at being a second-rate worker by stressing his physical superiority over his managers. Unable to win in economic competition, he longs to beat his coworkers in a physical match, and it is this contrast between economic and physical competition that intensifies the dramatic interplay between the literal and the figurative language of the play.

In fact, the very competitiveness of the American economic system in which Willy and Hap work, and that Biff hates, is consistently put on physical terms in the play. A failure in the competitive workplace, Hap uses the metaphor of physical competition—boxing man to man—yet the play details how Hap was considered less physically impressive than Biff when the two were boys. As an adult, Hap competes in the only physical competition he can win—sex. He even uses the imagery of rivalry when talking about his sexual conquests of the store managers' girlfriends: "Maybe I just have an overdeveloped sense of competition or something" (25). Perhaps knowing that they cannot win, the Lomans resort to a significant amount of cheating in competition:

Willy condones Biff's theft of a football, Biff cheats on his exams, Hap takes bribes, and Willy cheats on Linda. All of this cheating signifies the Lomans' moral failings as well.

The boxing metaphor also illustrates the contrast between Biff and Hap. Boxing as a sports metaphor is quite different from the expected football metaphor: a boxer relies completely on personal physical strength while fighting a single opponent, whereas in football, a team sport, the players rely on group effort and group tactics. Thus the difference between Biff and Hap—Hap as evoker of the boxing metaphor and Biff as a player of a team sport—is emphasized throughout the text. Moreover, the action of the play relies on the clash of dreams between Biff and Willy. Biff is Willy's favorite son, and Willy's own dreams and disappointments are tied to him. Yet Hap, the second-rate son, the second-rate physical specimen, the second-rate worker, is the son who is most like Willy in profession, braggadocio, and sexual swagger. Ultimately, at the play's end, in "Requiem," the boxing metaphor ironically points out Hap's significance as the actual competitor for Willy's dream, for he decides to stay in the city because Willy "fought it out here and this is where I'm gonna win it for him" (139).

Biff's boxing contrasts sharply with Hap's. For example, Biff ironically performs a literal boxing competition with Ben, which juxtaposes with the figurative competition of the play. The boxing reinforces the emphasis that has been placed on Biff as the most physically prepared "specimen" of the boys. Yet Biff is defeated by Ben; in reality he is ill prepared to fight a boxing match because it is a man-to-man competition, unlike football, the team sport at which he excelled. He is especially ill prepared for Uncle Ben's kind of boxing match because it is not a fair match conducted on a level playing field. As Ben says: "Never fight fair with a stranger, boy. You'll never get out of the jungle that way" (49). Thus the literal act of boxing possesses figurative significance. Willy has not conditioned Biff (or, by extension, Hap) for any fight—fair or unfair—in the larger figurative "jungle" of the play: the workplace of the American economic system.

Willy, too, uses a significant amount of boxing imagery, much of it quite violent. In the first imagining in act 1, Biff asks Willy about his recent sales trip, "Did you knock them dead, Pop?" and Willy responds, "Knocked 'em cold in Providence, slaughtered 'em in Boston" (33); when he relates to Linda how another salesman at F. H. Stewarts insulted him, Willy claims he "cracked him right across the face" (37), the same physical threat that he will later make against Charley in act 2 on the day of the Ebbets Field game. Willy wants to box Charley, challenging him, "Put up your hands. Goddam you, put up your hands" (68). Willy also says, "I'm gonna knock Howard for a loop" (74). Willy uses these violent physical terms against men he perceives as challengers and competitors.

As with the tree metaphor, this one is sustained throughout the scenes with a plethora of boxing references: a punching bag is inscribed with Gene Tunney's name; Hap challenges Bernard to box; Willy explains to Linda that the boys gathered in the cellar obey Biff because, "Well, that's the training, the training"; Biff feebly attempts to box with Uncle Ben; Bernard remarks to Willy that Biff "never trained himself for anything" (92); Charley cheers on his son with a "Knock 'em dead, Bernard" (95) as Bernard leaves to argue a case in front of the Supreme Court; Willy, expressing to Bernard his frustration that Biff has done nothing with his life, says, "Why did he lay down?" (93). This last boxing reference, associated with taking a dive, is a remarkably imagistic way of describing how Biff initially cut down his life out of spite after discovering Willy's infidelity.

* * *

Miller also uses images, symbols, and metaphors as central or unifying devices by employing repetition and recurrence—one of the central tenets of so-called cluster criticism, which was pioneered in the 1930s and 1940s.[6] In short, cluster criticism argues that the deliberate repetition of words, images, symbols, and metaphors contributes to the unity of the work just as significantly as do plot, character, and theme. These clusters of words can operate both literally and figuratively in a text—as I. A. Richards notes in *The Philosophy of Rhetoric*—and, therefore, contribute significantly to the overall aesthetic and thematic impact. For example, in *Arthur Miller, Dramatist*, Edward Murray traces word repetition in *The Crucible*, examining how Miller, "in a very subtle manner, uses key words to knit together the texture of action and theme." He notes, for example, the recurrent use of the word "soft" in the text (64). My own previous work on *The Crucible* has examined how the tenfold repetition of the word "weight" supports one of the play's crucial themes: how an individual's struggle for truth often conflicts with society.

Let's examine an intriguing example of word repetition from *Death of a Salesman*.[7] The words "paint" and "painting" appear five significant times in the play. The first is a literal use: at the end of act 1, Willy tells Biff during their argument, "If you get tired of hanging around tomorrow, paint the ceiling I put up in the living room" (45). This line echoes Willy's previous mockery of Charley for not knowing how to put up a ceiling: "A man who can't handle tools is not a man" (30). In both instances, Willy is asserting his superiority on the basis of his physical prowess, a point that is consistently emphasized in the play.

The second time "paint" appears is in act 2, when Biff and Hap abandon Willy in Frank's Chop House to leave with Letta and Miss Forsythe. Hap says to Letta: "No, that's not my father. He's just a guy. Come on, we'll catch Biff, and honey we're going to paint this town!" (91). Of course in this line Miller uses the cliché "Paint the town red" for its well-known meaning of having a wild night of partying and dissolution—although it is notable that Miller uses a truncated form of the phrase. Nevertheless, here the cliché takes on new significance in the context of the play. Willy defines masculinity by painting a ceiling, but Hap defines it by painting the town with sexual debauchery and revelry, lording his physical superiority and his sexual conquests over other men.

The third, fourth, and fifth repetitions occur in act 2 during the imagining in the hotel room when Biff discovers Willy with the woman. When the woman comes out of the bathroom, Willy says: "Ah—you better go back to your room. They must be finished painting by now. They're painting her room so I let her take a shower here" (119). When she leaves, Willy attempts to convince Biff that "she lives down the hall—they're painting. You don't imagine—" (120). Here, painting is simultaneously literal and metaphorical because of its previous usage in the play—but with a high degree of irony. Willy's feeble explanation that Miss Francis's room is literally being painted is a cover-up for the reality that Willy himself has painted the town in Boston. Biff discovers that Willy's manhood is defined by sexual infidelity—ultimately defining him as a "phony little fake."

* * *

Another relatively unexplored aspect of Miller's language is the names of his characters. Miller chooses his characters' names for their metaphorical associations in most of his dramatic canon. Justin Kaplan and Anne Bernays's 1997 text *The Language of Names* revived some interest in this technique, which is known as literary onomastics and is considered a somewhat minor part of contemporary literary criticism. Kaplan and Bernays examine the connotative value of names that function in texts as "symbolic, metaphoric, or allegorical discourse" (175). Although some scholars have discussed the use of this technique in individual Miller plays, most readers familiar with the body of Miller's work notice how consistently he chooses the names of his characters to create symbols, irony, and points of contrast.

For example, readers and critics who are familiar only with *Death of a Salesman* among Miller's works have long noted that Willy's last name literally marks him as a "low man," although Miller himself chuckled at the overemphasis placed on this pun. He actually derived the name from a movie he had seen, *The Testament of Dr. Mabuse*, in which a completely mad character at the end of the film screams, "Lohman, Lohman, get me Lohman" (*Timebends* 177-79). To Miller, the man's cry signified the hysteria he wanted to create in his salesman, Willy Loman. Many critics also have noted the significance of the name of Dave "Singleman," the eighty-year-old salesman who stands alone as Willy's ideal.

Despite Miller's consistent downplaying in interviews of the significance of his characters' names, an examination of his technique reveals how extensively he connects his characters' names to the larger social issues at the core of every play. For example, the last name of *All My Sons'* Joe Keller, who manufactures faulty airplane parts and is indirectly responsible for the deaths of twenty-one pilots, resembles "killer." In previous work on the play, I have noted the comparison of the Kellers to the Holy Family, and how, therefore, the names of Joe and his son, Chris, take on religious significance. Susan C. W. Abbotson has noted how the first name of *The Ride Down Mt. Morgan's* Lyman Felt suggests the lying he has lived out. She also has analyzed the similarities between Loman and Lyman, and has argued that Lyman is a kind of alter ego to Willy some forty years later. Frank Ardolino has also examined how Miller employs Egyptian mythology in naming and depicting Hap ("Mythological").

An intriguing feature of Miller's use of names is his repetition of the same name, or form of the same name, in his plays. It is striking how in *Salesman* Miller uses the name "Frank," or variations of it, five times for five different characters, a highly unusual occurrence.[8] In act 1, during Willy's first imagining, when Linda complains to Biff that there is a cellar full of boys in the Loman house who do not know what to do with themselves, Frank is one of the boys whom Biff gets to clean up the furnace room. Not long after, at the end of the imagining, Frank is the name of the mechanic who fixes the carburetor of Willy's Chevrolet. In act 2, in the moving scene in which Howard effectively fires Willy and Willy is left alone in the office, Willy cries out three times for "Frank," apparently Howard's father and the original owner of the company, who, Willy claims, asked Willy to "name" Howard. Willy also meets the boys in Frank's Chop House and, in the crucial discovery scene in the Boston hotel room, Willy introduces the woman to Biff as Miss Francis, "Frank" often being a nickname for Francis.

There are significant figurative uses of "Frank" too, for, although the word means "honest" or "candid," all of the Franks in *Salesman* are clearly associated with work that is not completely honest. Biff uses the boy Frank and his companions to clean the furnace room and hang up the wash—chores that he should be doing himself. Willy somewhat questions the repair job that the mechanic Frank does on "that goddam Chevrolet." Despite Willy's idolizing of his boss, Frank Wagner, Linda indicates that Frank, perhaps, promised Willy a partnership as a member of the firm, a promise that kept Willy from joining Ben in Alaska and that was never made good on by either Frank or his son, Howard. Miss Francis promises to put Willy through to the buyers in exchange for stockings and her sexual favors, but it is uncertain whether she holds up her end of the deal, since Willy certainly has never been a "hot-shot" salesman. And, of course, Frank's Chop House is the place where Stanley tells Hap that the boss, presumably Frank, is going crazy over the "leak in the cash register." Thus Miller clearly uses the name Frank with a high degree of irony, an important aspect of his use of figurative language in his canon. Of course, all this business dishonesty emphasizes how *Salesman* challenges the integrity of the American work ethic.

Miller's careful selection of names shows that he perhaps considered the names of his characters as part of each play's network of figurative language. As Kaplan and Bernays note, "Names of characters . . . convey what their creators may already know and feel about them and how they want their readers to respond" (174). Thus, in his choice of names, Arthur Miller may very well be manipulating his audience before the curtain rises, as they sit and read the cast of characters in their playbills.

Finally, being aware of Miller's use of poetic language is crucial for however we encounter his plays—as readers who analyze drama as text or as audience members in tune with the sound of the dialogue. It is, indeed, "all about the language"—the language we read in the text and the language we hear on the stage.

Notes

1. Although some critics have examined Miller's colloquial prose, only a few have conducted studies of how poetic devices work in his dialogue. Leonard Moss, in his book-length study *Arthur Miller*, analyzes Miller's language in a chapter on *Death of a Salesman*, a section of which is titled "Verbal and Symbolic Technique." In an article titled "*Death of a Salesman* and Arthur Miller's Search for Style," Arthur K. Oberg considers Miller's struggle with establishing a dramatic idiom. Oberg judges that Miller ultimately "arrives at something that approaches an American idiom to the extent that it exposes a colloquialism characterized by unusual image, spurious lyricism, and close-ended cliché" (305). He concludes that "the play's text, although far from 'bad poetry,' tellingly moves toward the status of poetry without ever getting there" (310-11). My 2002 work *A Language Study of Arthur Miller's Plays: The Poetic in the Colloquial* traces Miller's consistent use of figurative language from *All My Sons* to *Broken Glass*.

In other studies discussing individual plays, some critics have noted poetic nuances in Miller's language. In "Setting, Language, and the Force of Evil in *The Crucible*," Penelope Curtis maintains that the language of the play is marked by what she calls "half-metaphor" (69), which Miller employs to suggest the play's themes. In an article published in *Notes on Contemporary Literature*, John D. Engle explains the metaphor of law used by the lawyer Quentin in *After the Fall*. Lawrence Rosinger, in a brief *Explicator* article, traces the metaphors of royalty that appear in *Death of a Salesman*.

2. Thomas M. Tammaro also points out that the diminished prestige of language studies since the height of New Criticism may account for the lack of a sustained examination of imagery and symbolism in Miller's work. Moreover, Tammaro notes that Miller's plays were not subjected to New Critical theory even when language studies were prominent (10). In his new authorized biography *Arthur Miller: 1915-1962*, Christopher Bigsby clearly recognizes Miller's attempts to write verse drama, but this work is largely a critical biography and cultural study, not a close textual analysis.

3. Most notable among these works are the following: "The Family in Modern Drama," which first appeared in *The Atlantic Monthly* in 1956; "On Social Plays," which appeared as the original introduction to the one-act edition of *A View from the Bridge* and *A Memory of Two Mondays*; the introduction to his 1957 *Collected Plays*; "The American Writer: The American Theater," first published in the *Michigan Quarterly Review* in 1982; "On Screenwriting and Language: Introduction to *Everybody Wins*," first published in 1990; his 1993 essay "About Theatre Language," which first appeared as an afterword to the published edition of *The Last Yankee*; and his March 1999 *Harper's* article "On Broadway: Notes on the Past and Future of American Theater."

4. For a more detailed discussion of these metaphors, see *"Death of a Salesman*: Unlocking the Rhetoric of Poetic Power" in my 2002 volume *A Language Study of Arthur Miller's Plays*. Also, in "Figuring Our Past and Present in Wood: Wood Imagery in Arthur Miller's *Death of a Salesman* and *The Crucible*," Will Smith traces what he describes as a "wood trope" in the plays.

5. When Biff discovers Willy with the woman in the hotel room in act 2, she refers to herself as a football (119-20) to indicate her humiliating treatment by Willy and, perhaps, all men.

6. Frederick Charles Kolbe, Caroline F. E. Spurgeon, and Kenneth Burke pioneered much of this criticism. For example, Spurgeon did groundbreaking work in discovering the clothes imagery and the image of the babe in *Macbeth*. Kenneth Burke, in *The Philosophy of Literary Form*, examines Clifford Odets's *Golden Boy* as a play that uses language clusters, particularly the images of the "prizefight" and the "violin," that operate both literally and symbolically in the text (33-35).

7. In his work *Arthur Miller*, Leonard Moss details the frequent repetitions of words in the text, such as "man," "boy," and "kid." He notes that forms of the verb "make" occur forty-five times in thirty-three different usages, ranging from Standard English to slang expressions, among them "make mountains out of molehills," "makin a hit," "makin my future," "make me laugh," and "make a train." He also notes the nine-time repetition of "make money" (48). Moss connects these expressions to Miller's thematic intention: illustrating how the American work ethic dominates Willy's life.

8. In "'I'm Not a Dime a Dozen! I Am Willy Loman!': The Significance of Names and Numbers in *Death of a Salesman*," Frank Ardolino takes a mainly psychological approach to the language of the play. He maintains that "Miller's system of onomastic and numerical images and echoes forms a complex network which delineates Willy's insanity and its effects on his family and job" (174). Ardolino explains that the name imagery reveals Biff's and Willy's failures. He sees the repetition of "Frank" as part of Miller's use of geographical, personal, and business names that often begin with *B*, *F*, *P*, or *S*. Thus the names beginning with *F* "convey a conflict between benevolence and protection on the one hand and dismissal and degradation on the other" (177). Benevolent Franks are Willy's boss, the boy Frank who cleans up, and the repairman Frank. Degrading Franks are Miss Francis and Frank's Chop House, which contains the literal and psychological toilet where Willy has his climactic imagining of the hotel room in Boston.

Works Cited

Abbotson, Susan C. W. "From Loman to Lyman: The Salesman Forty Years On." *"The Salesman Has a Birthday": Essays Celebrating the Fiftieth Anniversary of Arthur Miller's "Death of a Salesman."* Ed. Stephen A. Marino. Lanham, MD: University Press of America, 2000.

Ardolino, Frank. "'I'm Not a Dime a Dozen! I Am Willy Loman!': The Significance of Names and Numbers in *Death of a Salesman.*" *Journal of Evolutionary Psychology* (August 2002): 174-84.

_____. "The Mythological Significance of Happy in *Death of a Salesman.*" *The Arthur Miller Journal* 4.1 (Spring 2009): 29-33.

Bigsby, Christopher. *Arthur Miller: A Critical Study.* New York: Cambridge UP, 2005.

_____. *Arthur Miller: 1915-1962.* London: Weidenfeld & Nicolson, 2008.

_____. *A Critical Introduction to Twentieth-Century American Drama, Volume Two: Tennessee Williams, Arthur Miller, Edward Albee.* New York: Cambridge UP, 1984.

_____. "Miller and Middle America." Keynote address, Eighth International Arthur Miller Society Conference, Nicolet College, Rhinelander, WI, 3 Oct. 2003.

Brantley, Ben. "A Dark New Production Illuminates *Salesman.*" *New York Times* 3 Nov. 1998: E1.

Burke, Kenneth. *The Philosophy of Literary Form.* 2d ed. Baton Rouge: Louisiana State UP, 1967.

Couchman, Gordon W. "Arthur Miller's Tragedy of Babbit." *Educational Theatre Journal* 7 (1955): 206-11.

Curtis, Penelope. "Setting, Language, and the Force of Evil in *The Crucible.*" *Twentieth Century Interpretations of "The Crucible."* Ed. John H. Ferres. Englewood Cliffs, NJ: Prentice-Hall, 1972.

Engle, John D. "The Metaphor of Law in *After the Fall.*" *Notes on Contemporary Literature* 9 (1979): 11-12.

Gilman, Richard. "Getting It Off His Chest, But Is It Art?" *Chicago Sun Book Week* 8 Mar. 1964: 6, 13.

Kaplan, Justin, and Anne Bernays. *The Language of Names.* New York: Simon & Schuster, 1997.

Krutch, Joseph Wood. "Drama." *Nation* 163 (1949): 283-84.

Marino, Stephen. "Arthur Miller's 'Weight of Truth' in *The Crucible.*" *Modern Drama* 38 (1995): 488-95.

_____. *A Language Study of Arthur Miller's Plays: The Poetic in the Colloquial.* New York: Edwin Mellen Press, 2002.

_____. "Religious Language in Arthur Miller's *All My Sons.*" *Journal of Imagism* 3 (1998): 9-28.

Miller, Arthur. "About Theatre Language." *The Last Yankee.* New York: Penguin, 1993.

_____. "The American Writer: The American Theater." *The Theatre Essays of Arthur Miller.* Ed. Robert A. Martin and Steven R. Centola. New York: Da Capo Press, 1996.

_____. "Arthur Miller: An Interview." Interview with Olga Carlisle and Rose Styron. 1966. *Conversations with Arthur Miller.* Ed. Matthew C. Roudané. Jackson: UP of Mississippi, 1987. 85-111.

_____. *"Death of a Salesman": Text and Criticism.* Ed. Gerald Weales. New York: Penguin Books, 1967.

_____. "The Family in Modern Drama." *The Theatre Essays of Arthur Miller.* Ed. Robert A. Martin. New York: Viking Press, 1978.

_____. "Introduction to the *Collected Plays.*" *The Theatre Essays of Arthur Miller.* Ed. Robert A. Martin. New York: Viking Press, 1978.

_____. "On Broadway: Notes on the Past and Future of American Theater." *Harper's* Mar. 1999: 37-47.

_____. "On Screenwriting and Language: Introduction to *Everybody Wins.*" *The Theatre Essays of Arthur Miller.* Ed. Robert A. Martin and Steven R. Centola. New York: Da Capo Press, 1996.

_____. "On Social Plays." *The Theatre Essays of Arthur Miller.* Ed. Robert A. Martin. New York: Viking Press, 1978.

_____. *Timebends: A Life.* New York: Grove Press, 1987.

Moss, Leonard. *Arthur Miller.* New Haven, CT: College and University Press, 1967.

_____. "Arthur Miller and the Common Man's Language." *Modern Drama* 7 (1964): 52-59.

Murray, Edward. *Arthur Miller, Dramatist.* New York: Frederick Ungar, 1967.

Oberg, Arthur K. "*Death of a Salesman* and Arthur Miller's Search for Style." *Criticism* 9 (1967): 303-11.

Otten, Terry. *The Temptation of Innocence in the Dramas of Arthur Miller.* Columbia: U of Missouri P, 2002.

Richards, I. A. *Richards on Rhetoric: I. A. Richards—Selected Essays, 1929-1974.* Ed. Ann E. Berthoff. New York: Oxford UP, 1991.

Rosinger, Lawrence. "Miller's *Death of a Salesman.*" *Explicator* 45.2 (Winter 1987): 55-56.

Simon, John. "Whose Paralysis Is It, Anyway?" *New York* 9 May 1994.

Smith, Will. "Figuring Our Past and Present in Wood: Wood Imagery in Arthur Miller's *Death of a Salesman* and *The Crucible.*" *Miller and Middle America: Essays on Arthur Miller and the American Experience.* Ed. Paula T. Langteau. Lanham, MD: University Press of America, 2007.

Spurgeon, Caroline F. E. *Leading Motives in the Imagery of Shakespeare's Tragedies.* 1930. New York: Haskell House, 1970.

Tammaro, Thomas M. "Introduction." *Arthur Miller and Tennessee Williams: Research Opportunities and Dissertation Abstracts.* Ed. Tetsumaro Hayashi. Jefferson, NC: McFarland, 1983.

Teachout, Terry. "Concurring with Arthur Miller." *Commentary* 127.6 (June 2009): 71-73.

The Freedom of Others:
Arthur Miller's Social and Political Context_____

Katherine Egerton

Arthur Miller saw his efforts in the theater as political work. He used drama to teach, to hector, to cajole, and to reassure audiences all over the world that ideas matter, that politics should never be business as usual, and that the plight of the individual must not be forgotten amid the machinations of the powerful. Jeffrey D. Mason, in his book *Stone Tower: The Political Theater of Arthur Miller*, argues that "Miller's individual was not simply a man alone or apart, but specifically one who dissents from the majority view, an independent thinker who follows his convictions and goes his own way" (40). Because of the length of Miller's career, his political and cultural influences span the twentieth century, from the Great Depression through the early days of the new millennium. Along the way, his writing was shaped by the politics of World War II, McCarthyism and the Cold War, the social and political upheavals of the 1960s, and capitalism's uneasy and uncertain triumph from the days of Ronald Reagan onward. His ideals did not always fit the taste of the times, at least in the United States, which accounted for Miller's marginalization at home as well as his increasing popularity abroad.

Both sides of Miller's family came from the small Polish town of Radomizl. They were part of the huge exodus of Jews from Eastern Europe in the late nineteenth century, seeking a much-hoped-for prosperity and freedom from anti-Semitic persecution. The journey for Miller's father, Isidore, was particularly fraught. At the age of six, Isidore was left behind by his family when they traveled to the United States. In his biography of Arthur Miller, Christopher Bigsby speculates that the child was thought to be retarded (6). Eventually, a ticket was sent, and Isidore Miller traveled—alone, by train and then in steerage for the transatlantic journey—to rejoin his family in New York. Because of the chaos of immigration and his parents' lingering fears about his

Critical Insights

mental fitness, Isidore Miller received little schooling and, despite the fact that he had a head for figures, never learned how to read. Miller's mother, Augusta, was born soon after her parents arrived in New York as immigrants. Both Isidore and Augusta grew up on Broome Street on the lower East Side of Manhattan, where they were surrounded by and worked in the garment trade, which would remain the Miller family business.

Despite his inauspicious beginning, Isidore Miller thrived in the tenement world, no matter how stifling the sweatshop atmosphere. He sewed coats for his parents and soon was hiring other boys to do piecework (Bigsby 13). As a teenager, he went on the road to sell the family wares, traveling to the Midwest with sample cases. As it was for both Isidore and Augusta, the main goal of these young immigrants was to become American, to refashion life in new ways, embracing the new and forgetting their parents' shtetl culture. Both Isidore and Augusta grew up paying less and less attention to Jewish observances, and they passed down this lack of religiosity to their own children. On reflection, Arthur Miller understood the price required by this fast track to assimilation. "The original impulse of the immigrant," he explained, "was to become an American, not, as is the fashion now, to emphasize the ethnicity of everybody, to show how different people are. There is something to be said for both, because my parents' generation was deformed by having, in effect, to conceal themselves" (Bigsby 24). Augusta Miller, however, loved to read, and she also enjoyed music and the theater and other forms of cultured entertainment that her husband could not share. Miller's own family, and the world in which they lived, formed his first and most lasting subject. Miller never exhausted this first, best source of material, from his first play written when he was a student at the University of Michigan through *Death of a Salesman*, with its iconic image of a salesman with his sample cases; *The American Clock*, which dramatized his own family; and the late work *Broken Glass*, about a Jewish man's struggle to assimilate without becoming lost.

Isidore Miller did not merely succeed at making and selling coats, he excelled. At the height of his business in the early years of the twentieth century, his company was one of the largest manufacturers of women's coats in the United States. By the time Arthur Miller was born in 1915, his parents were not just comfortable but wealthy. They lived in a handsome apartment in Harlem, close to Central Park, and Miller's childhood was marked by both plenty and safety from the dangers and uncertainties his parents had known. This affluence, however, proved to be temporary, in part because of Isidore Miller's participation in the popular sport of stock market speculation. When the bubbles burst, they burst hard, and the money that had paid for the fine life in Harlem quickly disappeared. Of all the events that would have impacts on Miller's life and art, none can compare with the Great Depression. Even before the stock market crash of 1929, the Millers had decamped to still-rural Brooklyn, to a neighborhood of modest means and making do. In his 1980 play *The American Clock*, Miller fictionalized his family's Depression-era life, and his younger sister, Joan Copeland, played the role of their mother in the Broadway premiere. Like many of his later plays, however, *The American Clock* proved more popular on the English stage than it did in the United States.

With the national economic crisis, the Millers' hard-won success vanished rapidly, and young Arthur's life was utterly changed. These events affected him all the more because of his age. Miller later described the acute sensitivity of adolescence as "your most sensitive moment of consciousness," "when you walk into a moment of history" (Bigsby 40). Family tensions also flared, both between Miller's parents, whose marriage had never been easy, and among the members of the extended clan, now reliant on each other for support. In Brooklyn, Miller shared a bedroom with his maternal grandfather, while Isidore's father, still relatively affluent, refused to bail out his relatives.

Through the Great Depression, some aspects of normalcy remained. Miller attended high school in Brooklyn, where, like *Death of a Salesman*'s young Biff Loman, he put in more effort on the sports fields than in the classroom. Playing football, he suffered the knee injury that would later disqualify him from military service in World War II. While he worked many odd jobs, he enjoyed the relative freedom of Brooklyn's open spaces, which allowed him occasionally to escape his parents' financial preoccupations. He also made some contacts that were to shape the rest of his life. From one, a friend of his brother Kermit, he learned that the University of Michigan awarded cash prizes to student writers. With another, he first encountered the ideas of Karl Marx, and the conversations they had showed him another way to view his family's upheaval as well as the larger social changes taking place all around them. The primacy of political ideas, and the need to communicate them to others, would always remain a priority in Miller's work.

Despite his indifferent academic performance, especially compared to Kermit's, Miller finished high school determined to go to college and become a writer. An early stab at taking night classes at City College was short-lived, and Miller's poor school record meant that scholarships were out of reach. In order to make it to the University of Michigan, he needed to save money and to convince the university to overlook his academic deficiencies. It took Miller nearly two years to earn the funds he needed by working in a large auto parts warehouse that, like many New York businesses at the time, normally refused to hire Jews. He depicts similar circumstances in his late play *Broken Glass*, set in Brooklyn in 1938, in which Miller makes Phillip Gellburg the only Jew employed by his firm.

Although Miller's family might have found his plans misplaced, they made real sacrifices to support them. His older brother Kermit, more likely to succeed in college, instead turned his attention back to their father's struggling business, and despite their father's protests that Arthur, too, belonged there, Miller managed to save most of his earnings rather than contribute them to the strained family budget (Bigsby 69). This fraternal dynamic reappears in *The Price*, in which two brothers revisit their life choices, which are obviously informed by the Millers' life choices, years after their father has died.

The anti-Semitism that Miller encountered at work and in the wider adult world of New York became another theme that would shape much of his work, particularly early in his career, although not everyone Miller encountered even realized he was Jewish. Miller remained interested in the peculiar strengths, both pro and con, of ethnic identity, in how it can create both community and division. His 1945 novel, *Focus*, explores this idea through a man who, while not a Jew, is taken to be one after he starts wearing glasses. Even this level of crass stereotyping, Miller's novel argues, can be transformative—not for the accusers but for the accused.

After nearly two years of working in the warehouse, Miller again appealed to the University of Michigan to admit him, which it did after having rejected him twice. It helped that the university had no mathematics requirement and thus forgave his inability to pass algebra in high school. Once in Ann Arbor, Miller quickly found a place at the student newspaper, the *Michigan Daily*, where he both reported and served as night editor. Having made it to Michigan, he also had to prove that he had the academic ability to stay there, and he had a lot of ground to make up. He was also counting on the money that winning the Avery Hopwood Award would provide, and so had to work on his literary writing at the same time.

The university's proximity to the American automobile industry gave Miller a new view of radical labor politics. In 1937, the *Michigan Daily* sent him to the city of Flint to cover a labor strike at a General Motors factory. The striking workers were attempting to unionize the factory's unskilled laborers, many of whom were black southerners brought to Michigan by companies looking for what managers hoped would be a more docile workforce. The United Auto Workers (UAW) finally gained negotiating powers with General Motors and a stronger foothold in the industry. At the Ford Motor Company, racial tensions were further fanned by Henry Ford's well-known and virulent anti-Semitism. President Franklin D. Roosevelt's New Deal had authorized collective bargaining, and the governor of Michigan was also sympathetic to the unionization efforts, but despite this support, corporate management fought the strikers both with violence and with subterfuge, infiltrating the unions with paid spies. As Christopher Bigsby observes, "Miller would feature company spies in his second Hopwood play, while the issue of informing and betrayal was to remain central to his work. This is where he experienced it for the first time" (119). Like Clifford Odets, the author of *Waiting for Lefty*, a 1935 play about taxi drivers planning to strike, Miller found drama a particularly apt vehicle to spread the word about labor solidarity.

Fueled by this experience, Miller wrote his first play, *No Villain*, in six days. The play, drawn from portraits of the strikers he had observed in Flint, won the Avery Hopwood Award for Drama in 1936, and the accompanying $250 prize allowed him to continue his education. Miller would repeatedly revise and expand this first play, later winning $1,250 for a version called *The Grass Still Grows* in 1939. Even in this earliest play, Miller focused on some of his most persistent ideas and on his lifelong drive to connect what Robert A. Martin has called his "public and private conflicts" (98). In his essay "Arthur Miller: Public Issues, Private Tensions," Martin discusses Miller's focus on "a major dramatic question that reflected both the public issue and the private tension between family members that result in a betrayal of either a legal or social aspect of the American Dream" (98). This tension would inform nearly every play Miller ever wrote, befitting the dramatic need to have closely related characters on stage provide a bridge to the audience's own world.

Like many young people of his generation, Miller was also radicalized by the Spanish Civil War and the bombing of Guernica in April, 1937. Looking back on this time in 1973, he explained that "to most supporters of the Spanish loyalists, their struggle was far more profound than any politics could embrace; the Spanish civil war was a battle of angels as well as the lowly poor against the murderous rich" ("Miracles" 130). Miller came close to joining the fight directly. While still a junior at Michigan, he drove to New York with his friend Ralph

Neaphus, who was heading to Spain to join the republican Abraham Lincoln Brigade. Held back, however, by his still-unfinished work in Michigan, his mother's certain disapproval, and a deepening relationship with Mary Slattery, another young Michigan radical who was also working her way through school and who would become his first wife in 1940, Miller remained behind. Neaphus never came home (Bigsby 125-26).

Returning to Brooklyn after graduating, Miller continued to hone his craft, writing both plays and fiction. For a few short months, he joined the Federal Theatre Project (FTP) until Congress disbanded it in 1939, in part because of the left-leaning politics of many FTP artists. Even after the FTP's demise, Miller worked briefly for the government's Works Projects Administration, collecting oral histories in the South for the Library of Congress. Miller was writing, but his work that now found an audience happened not in the theater but on the radio. He wrote many short radio plays, often on patriotic themes, for NBC's *Cavalcade of America* series and others, honing his skills with dialogue and storytelling. He also adapted other literary works for radio, including, improbably, Jane Austen's *Pride and Prejudice*.

Even though he was making a living writing for the radio, Miller felt disconnected both from the war and from the lives of working people. Because so much of his earlier writing was based on the lives of workers, he felt the need to remain immersed in that world. This led him to sign on as a shipfitter at the Brooklyn Navy Yard. Bigsby notes the irony of the fact that Miller would soon be suspected for his political affiliations at the same time he was laboring in the shipyard (222). Miller was also drawn to help the war effort because Kermit, his older brother, had enlisted and was fighting in France. Arthur, again feeling that his older brother was shouldering a burden that should have fallen to him, redoubled his efforts. Brooklyn's waterfront was also a rich source of stories, which Miller would later revisit in *A View from the Bridge*.

Miller's first chance to succeed on Broadway was an abject failure.

In 1944, *The Man Who Had All the Luck* closed after only a few performances, despite the fact that the play won a National Award from the Theatre Guild. While continuing to write prose fiction and radio drama, he looked to the Norwegian playwright Henrik Ibsen as he revised a play he had begun in 1943, in the midst of World War II (Bigsby 269). Miller saw in Ibsen's social dramas techniques that were both moral and practical. The resulting play, *All My Sons*, relies on the dramatic structure and insistent moral voice found in Ibsen's work. Based on a real incident, the play tells the story of a manufacturer whose shady wartime business practices caused the deaths of twenty-one pilots. After the war, his family learns just how personal those losses were. *All My Sons* was a hit in 1947, although it nearly missed its historical moment because in the postwar period audiences were beginning to look back on manufacturers like Joe Keller as heroes.

All My Sons catapulted Miller into a brand-new income bracket. After years of scraping by on his and Mary's earnings, Miller found himself with enough money to buy two homes. Shortly after that success, and because he was studying New York's Italian community for a play about the waterfront, he traveled to Italy, where he met some Holocaust survivors but came away from the meeting without fully understanding their experiences. Connecting with their story would take Miller more than a decade, beginning with *Incident at Vichy* and *After the Fall*, both of which premiered in 1964, and *Playing for Time*, an adaptation of Fania Fénelon's *The Musicians of Auschwitz*, which was televised nationally in 1980. Images from the Holocaust would resonate in other Miller plays throughout his career, including *Broken Glass*.

Miller's next play, and the one for which he is most remembered, focused not on the aftermath of the war in Europe but on what he would soon call "the Tragedy of the Common Man." Just as he was moving away from elements of theatrical realism in *All My Sons*, Miller invoked a family story, that of his Uncle Manny, always selling on the road. He also drew on a vignette written while he was still in high school, in which a young narrator named Arthur meets a salesman who, drowning in failure, commits suicide (Bigsby 325). Through his story, Miller tried to change people's expectations about tragedy and about drama itself. Complemented by Elia Kazan's direction and Jo Mielziner's set, *Death of a Salesman* was an artistic triumph. However, like *All My Sons*, it was seen by some as insufficiently patriotic because it questioned the values of American capitalism. Ironically, *Death of a Salesman*, the story of a family haunted by poverty, would make Miller rich, securing his income for life and finally separating him from the working class.

Salesman's success, beyond ensuring his family's economic future, solidified Miller's sense of obligation to speak out for his own beliefs and for the rights of other artists. This would remain a priority for the rest of his life. A particularly high-profile opportunity arose with the 1949 Cultural and Scientific Conference for World Peace, held at New York's Waldorf-Astoria Hotel. This came at a moment when American views of the Soviet Union were shifting rapidly, and many who still admired the Soviet Union, either because they were sympathetic to Marxist ideology or because they were grateful to the Soviets for fighting alongside the United States during World War II, were coming under siege. Miller knew that his participation in the Waldorf Conference, alongside fellow playwright Clifford Odets and composers Dmitri Shostakovich and Aaron Copland, would be provocative to those now hunting for communists, and he was right. Later, in his 1985 autobiography, *Timebends*, Miller reflected that "for me, . . . the conference was an effort to continue a good tradition that was presently menaced" (234). Miller saw this growing anti-Soviet bias as an issue of integrity: "I thought one must speak out against it or forfeit something of honor and the right to complain in the future" (234). Bigsby explains in *Arthur Miller: 1915-1962* that the Waldorf Conference "was seen as disastrous for the communists. . . . Far from breeding peace and harmony, [it] had, in fact, played its part in prompting a cultural cold war which would affect a generation of writers and intellectuals" (363). For Miller, this cultural cold war would soon become much more personal.

Miller's eventual encounter with Senator Joseph McCarthy[1] and the House Un-American Activities Committee (HUAC) would affect both his work and his public reputation for the rest of his life. The history of congressional interest in leftists in the arts dates back to the late 1930s, when the investigatory HUAC called Hallie Flanagan, the head of the Federal Theatre Project, to account for the political affiliations of the FTP's members. After World War II, HUAC became a standing congressional committee looking into political subversion and suspected communist propaganda. The committee's interest in writers, particularly those involved with the film industry, intensified when HUAC became concerned that Hollywood studios were producing films that could be considered pro-Soviet. Starting in 1947, writers and filmmakers who refused to testify before HUAC about their knowledge of communists in the industry were being blacklisted and thus became unable to work. In 1952, Elia Kazan was subpoenaed to name fellow communists involved with the Group Theatre in the 1930s. He visited Miller ahead of his appearance to tell his friend and colleague that he planned to cooperate with the committee. Miller later wrote that he "felt sympathy going toward [Kazan] and at the same time I was afraid of him. Had I been of his generation, he would have had to sacrifice me as well. And finally that was all I could think of. I could not get past it" (*Timebends* 333). Miller's disgust at Kazan's capitulation led him to recast the story of the Salem witch trials as a modern political parable. *The Crucible* opened in New York in 1953, winning that year's Tony Award for best new play.

By exploring the witch panic in Salem, Miller found a way to confront—and combine—his two greatest sources of stress. One, in public, was the growing power of those who were trying to rid American culture of the influence of anyone who persisted in seeing the Soviet Union as a past and potentially future source of good in the world. The other, in private, was the final unraveling of his troubled marriage, triggered by a Hollywood encounter with the most desirable woman in America. Miller had first met Marilyn Monroe at a party in

1951, before she became America's ultimate sex symbol. Just after his marriage to Monroe in 1956, which created huge interest in the media, Miller himself was subpoenaed to testify before HUAC. Ten years later, in an interview with Olga Carlisle and Rose Styron, Miller speculated that the committee would not "have bothered me if I hadn't married Marilyn. And in fact I was told on good authority that the then Chairman, Francis Walter, said that if Marilyn would take a photograph with him, shaking his hand, he would call off the whole thing" ("Interview" 109-10). Miller refused to cooperate with the committee and was cited for contempt of Congress. His conviction was later overturned on appeal.

His marriage to Marilyn Monroe catapulted Miller to a level of fame that overshadowed both his Broadway success and his refusal to name names for HUAC. Under the glare of intense journalistic scrutiny, he tried to shape Monroe's career in a more dramatic vein through a screenplay derived from *The Misfits*, a novella he had written during the six-week Nevada sojourn required for a quick divorce from his first wife. By the time production began on the John Huston film, the new marriage was the one on the rocks. In his final play, *Finishing the Picture*, Miller would return to this time, dramatizing a film cast and crew idled by a drug-addled star who is paralyzed by the weight of great expectations. Miller and Monroe divorced in 1961, and *The Misfits* was the last film she would make.

Some of the most famous images from *The Misfits* came not from the film but from photographs taken on the set by Henri Cartier-Bresson and Inge Morath, who were documenting the production for Magnum Photo. Magnum's exclusive access to the film's set introduced Morath to Miller just as his second marriage evaporated in the desert heat. Morath, soon to be Miller's third wife, created a bridge between Miller's disparate worlds. On the one hand, as an Austrian and a refugee from World War II, she would turn his attention again to Europe and to the continent's postwar chaos. As a photographer for Magnum, she complemented his art with her own skill and fiercely sharp insight into the human condition. In 1964, Miller and Morath visited the site of the Mauthausen concentration camp in Austria (Bigsby 665). Only after this trip did Miller begin to deal directly with the Holocaust in plays including *After the Fall*, *Playing for Time*, and *Broken Glass*.

This shift of Miller's political focus led to a new avenue for his activism. In 1965, Miller became the president of International PEN, a writers' organization founded in 1921 to fight censorship around the world. Speaking in 2001, Miller observed that writers, particularly when they succeed, have "an opportunity . . . to affect the freedom of other people" ("Panel"). Miller's work with PEN defined his public profile, particularly in the United States, at a time when many assumed his best work was behind him. He used his status as a literary lion—and, thanks to Monroe, as a celebrity—to advocate for writers around the world, most notably convincing Nigerian general Yakubu Gowon to release playwright Wole Soyinka from prison in 1967. Miller's experiences meeting writers living under state censorship, including the Czechoslovakian playwright Václav Havel, led to his 1977 play *The Archbishop's Ceiling*. The title refers to the play's setting, once an elaborate palace but now the home of a writer who has become a government agent. The others who assemble there, including a famous dissident and an American writer who wrongly thinks he can help his friends more than they can help themselves, confront the constant possibility that they are being overheard by the authoritarian regime of a country that very much resembles Czechoslovakia. The only possible victory for Sigmund, the play's dissident writer, is to stay put, where "he is loved, he creates our memories. Therefore, it is only a question of time when he will create the departure of these tanks and they will go home" (84). From the 1960s onward, Miller devoted time and energy to helping writers thrive and publish in their own countries, to say what they believed needed to be said. As a result, he found his own works banned in the Soviet Union.

During 1968, one of the century's most tumultuous years, Miller kept his expansive view focused on political upheaval at home, the war abroad, and his own family on stage. *The Price*, which opened on Broadway in 1968, explored the strained relationship between two brothers whose lives have taken different trajectories. One of them has, like Miller's own brother, Kermit, stayed close to home so that the other might pursue fame and professional success. Both are haunted by their dead father's life as they meet to sell off his possessions, debating the nature of filial responsibility and what makes for success. In the same year, Miller served as a delegate to the Democratic National Convention in Chicago. Because Lyndon Johnson had already declared that he would not run for another term as U.S. president, the delegates on the convention floor clashed over the future of the party, while protesters against the Vietnam War clashed with National Guardsmen in the city streets outside the hall.

In the latter part of his career, Miller found that the most appreciative audiences for his work were often the ones farthest from home. In the years following the production of *After the Fall* in 1964, Miller became disenchanted with the tastes and priorities of the American theater, particularly in its most commercial forms. His 1972 comedy *The Creation of the World and Other Business* was not a success. Foreign interest in his work intensified as Americans seemed less interested in Miller's social vision, and he met with warmer receptions abroad. In England, the National Theatre and director David Thacker provided Miller with a home away from home, and his plays were also highly sought after in Israel and many other countries. Befitting a dramatist who, throughout his career, sought opportunities to make the theater a strong social force, Miller welcomed the invitation to direct *Death of a Salesman* at the People's Art Theater in Beijing in 1983. While his memoir of this experience, *"Salesman" in Beijing*, records his self-image as a teacher who could bring universal values to China, Belinda Kong, in her essay "Traveling Man, Traveling Culture: *Death of a Salesman* and Post-Mao Chinese Theatre," explains how Miller, once again, was playing a political role he himself did not fully understand. Kong describes how, from the "Chinese perspective," Miller's production was "but one act in a lived national drama, staged between artist-intellectuals and party leaders, begun long before Miller's arrival" (38). As in the early days of the Cold War, Miller's necessarily limited knowledge of a distant political situation enabled others to direct his voice to different ends.

Miller's later plays, smaller in scope than his earlier successes, continued to comment on a country that had become less interested in hearing what he had to say. In the 1980s, Miller turned his attention to the one-act play, an intimate form lending itself to introspection and theatrical minimalism. When he returned to larger projects, he continued to pursue the themes of individual rights and responsibilities. In *The Ride Down Mt. Morgan*, a wealthy bigamist living in the go-go eighties fails to understand that he cannot have everything he wants. *The Last Yankee* explores the legacy of the American Dream from the perspective of a Connecticut carpenter and his chronically depressed wife. Sometimes Miller returned to stories long untold, as in *Broken Glass*, which tells about one Jewish woman's reaction to Kristallnacht in 1938. Even though these newer plays did not find large audiences in New York, many of Miller's major early works have in recent years been revived on Broadway to great acclaim. His penultimate play, the savage comic satire *Resurrection Blues*, never played in New York, but after several productions in American regional theaters, it was produced at London's Old Vic Theatre under the direction of filmmaker Robert Altman. In a Swiftian style that Miller had practiced in many a newspaper op-ed, the play flirts with the idea that there are no depths to which American television will not sink in pursuit of advertising dollars, including making plans to broadcast a mysterious South American freedom fighter's crucifixion.

While Miller's career rose from powerful and specific historical moments, the plays themselves transcend their times. Writing in *Timebends*, Miller reflected that the meaning of *The Crucible* "is somewhat different in different places and moments. I can almost tell what the political situation in a country is when the play is suddenly a hit there—it is either a warning of tyranny on the way or a reminder of tyranny just past" (348). When Miller himself returned to *The Crucible* to prepare the screenplay for director Nicholas Hytner's 1996 film version, the spectacle in Washington no longer seemed an essential part of the play even to him. The larger stories, themes, and characters connected with new audiences in new generations. Thanks to his first drama teacher at the University of Michigan, Dr. Kenneth Rowe, Miller always admired the power of the classical Greek theater to transmit a culture's core beliefs. By the time of his death in 2005, Miller had lived to see his own work, at once grounded in history, carry his ideals far beyond their original contexts. "Theatre," Miller wrote in 1993, "like politics, is always the art of the possible" ("About Theatre Language" 78), and Miller pursued this art as vigorously at the end of his life as he did at his fame's greatest height.

Note

1. While the U.S. senator from Wisconsin worked closely with HUAC, because he was not a member of the House of Representatives, he did not serve on the committee.

Works Cited

Bigsby, Christopher. *Arthur Miller: 1915-1962*. Cambridge, MA: Harvard UP, 2009.

Kong, Belinda. "Traveling Man, Traveling Culture: *Death of a Salesman* and Post-Mao Chinese Theatre." *Arthur Miller's Global Theater*. Ed. Enoch Brater. Michigan: U of Michigan P, 2007. 35-56.

Martin, Robert A. "Arthur Miller: Public Issues, Private Tensions." *Studies in the Literary Imagination* 21.2 (1988): 97-106.

Mason, Jeffrey D. *Stone Tower: The Political Theater of Arthur Miller*. Ann Arbor: U of Michigan, 2008.

Miller, Arthur. "About Theatre Language." *The Last Yankee*. New York: Penguin, 1993. 75-98.

_____. *"The Archbishop's Ceiling" and "The American Clock": Two Plays*. New York: Grove Press, 1989.

_____. "Arthur Miller: An Interview." Interview with Olga Carlisle and

Rose Styron. 1966. *Conversations with Arthur Miller*. Ed. Matthew C. Roudané. Jackson: UP of Mississippi, 1987. 85-111.

_____. "Miracles." *Echoes Down the Corridor: Collected Essays, 1944-2000*. Ed. Steven R. Centola. New York: Viking Press, 2000. 126-38.

_____. *"Salesman" in Beijing*. New York: Viking Press, 1984.

_____. *Timebends: A Life*. New York: Penguin, 1987.

"A Panel of Writers Talks About the Writers' Organization PEN." *Charlie Rose*. Guests Arthur Miller, Nora Ephron, Frances Fitzgerald, and John Guare. PBS. 23 Apr. 2001. http://www.charlierose.com/view/interview/3152

The Critical Reception of Arthur Miller's Work_____
Jane K. Dominik

Arthur Miller's reputation and stature as one of the three greatest American playwrights of the twentieth century has rested primarily on only two plays he wrote within a four-year period: *Death of a Salesman* and *The Crucible*, which premiered in 1949 and 1953, respectively. However, while accumulating approximately sixty years of productions around the world as well as critical attention and acclaim, the two plays have overshadowed much of Miller's other dramatic work. His writing career spanned sixty-eight years and encompassed many other plays, with, on average, four to six written every decade. Some of his plays have received critical recognition; those that have not fared well critically nonetheless reflect Miller's persistent themes and formal experimentation. If he had not written another play after *Death of a Salesman*, Miller's significance as a playwright still would have endured. In a 1998 poll of eight hundred theater professionals asked by the Royal National Theatre (Lahr, "Making" 49) to nominate significant twentieth-century plays, of the 188 writers nominated, Miller ranked as the most frequently nominated playwright, and *Salesman* was named the second most significant of the 377 plays nominated ("NT2000"). However, as Miller stated in an interview, not writing "would be like cutting my heart out" (Bigsby, *Companion* 182).

The works of the other two members of the American playwriting triumvirate, Eugene O'Neill and Tennessee Williams, reside primarily in the psychological worlds of their characters, varied though those worlds are. Miller's drama, in contrast, weds the psychological with the social, and therein lies one of the largest critical challenges for his plays and their productions. In his plays, Miller persistently asserts what many American critics and audiences have viewed as political challenges, and, as Jesus is quoted as saying in the New Testament, "No man can be a prophet in his own country." The thought and courage—some might say the artistic audacity—that led Miller to shine a light on war profiteering a mere two years after the end of World War II, to criticize the American Dream and capitalism during a period of economic growth, and to compare the actions of the House Un-American Activities Committee with the Salem witch trials, as well as his willingness to write from his personal life, including reflections of his original family, his father's loss of wealth during the Great Depression, and his marriages, opened the door for personal scrutiny, at times distracting critics and audiences from focusing on the plays themselves. That Miller's intent was to distill the essence of these issues, events, and people to their universal elements has not always been recognized or appreciated. The lens Miller holds up through his plays has often been distorted by audiences and critics alike, and this, combined with reports and rumors about the playwright's political leanings, has detracted, to a certain degree, from his critical success. However, as critics, including Christopher Bigsby in this volume, have pointed out, the universality of Miller's work has been borne out in productions around the world, and Miller's stature as a playwright has been greater abroad than in the United States.

Beyond plot and theme, Miller's experiments with dramatic form require a flexibility and design onstage that critics and the public have not always accepted or embraced. On one hand, when Miller strayed from realism or naturalism, critics pounced on his departure, criticizing his efforts because they did not fit with his previous work; on the other hand, when Miller revisited themes and characters, he was criticized as repetitious and it was suggested that his playwriting days were effectively behind him. While he credited the Greek playwrights and the nineteenth-century Norwegian playwright Henrik Ibsen as foundations for his work, Miller also sought forms that would allow expression of his themes, stream of consciousness, and "timebending." Though some critics, even after his death, have persisted in labeling him a realist or naturalist, Miller's plays elude any clear categorization, instead embracing elements of realism, naturalism, expressionism, impressionism, surrealism, minimalism, and abstract symbolism. Other critics have recognized Miller's explorations of dramatic form, which were encouraged and enhanced by the European designers and American film directors with whom he collaborated. For his part, Miller recognized the narrow expectations of American theatrical audiences and attempted, through both his plays and his essays, to enlarge the parameters of form and content on the stage to make them capable of embracing his thematic preoccupations: guilt, responsibility, illusions, dreams, family, betrayal, the "birds coming home to roost" (Bigsby, *Company* 49), and success and failure in capitalistic America.

Miller never saved the reviews of his plays and often lambasted critics for their myopic preference for so-called realism and their predilection for treating theater primarily as entertainment. Over the course of his career, however, he received a number of prestigious awards: Miller garnered a Pulitzer Prize, seven Antoinette Perry Awards for Excellence in Theatre (Tony Awards), two New York Drama Critics' Circle Awards, an Off-Broadway Theater Award, a Laurence Olivier Award, an Academy Award, an Emmy Award, the John F. Kennedy Lifetime Achievement Award, and the Dorothy and Lillian Gish Prize. In 2002, Spain awarded him the Premio Príncipe de Asturias de las Letras, calling him the "undisputed master of modern drama."

In 1934, having saved money by working at various jobs, including one in an automobile parts warehouse, Miller appealed the rejection of his initial application to attend the University of Michigan because he heard the university gave prizes for writing, specifically the prestigious Avery Hopwood Award in playwriting (Bigsby, *Company* 23, 25). His later belief that playwrights are born, not made (or trained), ostensibly arose from his own success. Having reportedly seen only one or two plays and having to ask a friend who lived down the hall during his first college Easter vacation how long an act was (Miller, *Timebends* 211), Miller wrote his first play, *No Villain*, which won the coveted award in 1936. His second play, *Honors at Dawn*, won the next year, and *The Great Disobedience* earned second place the following year. He rewrote *No Villain*, titling it *They Too Arise*, in 1937, and with it won the Theater Guild Bureau of New Plays Award; he revised the work yet again under the title *The Grass Still Grows* in 1939 (Bigsby, *Companion* xiv). The *No Villain* versions set the stage for one of Miller's perpetual themes: a father and his two sons unwittingly find themselves in conflict over socialist and capitalist points of view, and the sociopolitical issues threaten to destroy the family. He thus achieved an early integration of the social and personal themes that would mark his later plays. *Honors at Dawn* focused more on the conflicts between two brothers, one of whom represented socialism and the other capitalism. *The Great Disobedience*, which addressed the need for prison reform, also set the stage for later plays that dealt with specific social problems. Structurally, these student plays reflect the impact of Miller's original influences, namely, the ancient Greek playwrights and Ibsen.

In 1939, Miller began to write radio plays to earn money, the best known of which are *The Pussycat and the Expert Plumber Who Was a Man*, *William Ireland's Confession*, *The Four Freedoms*, *Grandpa and the Statue*, *The Story of Gus*, *The Guardsman*, and *Three Men on a Horse* (Bigsby, *File* 59-60). Miller followed the four plays he wrote in the 1930s with six more in the 1940s. With the undergraduate awards under his belt, he next wrote two plays under the Federal Theatre Project: the first, coauthored with Norman Rosten in 1939, was titled *Listen My Children*; and the second, *The Golden Years*, was written in 1940. The project ended, however, and the latter play had to wait until 1987 for its radio broadcast on the BBC in England and until 1990 for its first theatrical production. *The Golden Years* was Miller's first use of historical metaphor to address current political threats; in the play, Hernán Cortés's conquest and destruction of the Aztecs were intended to shed light on the West's initial disbelief and inaction as Adolf Hitler gained power in Europe. Miller's next play, *The Half-Bridge*, written from 1941 to 1943 (Bigsby, *Companion* 43) and set on a ship during World War II, remains, like his undergraduate plays, unpublished and unproduced.

During this time, Miller also began his foray into nonfiction and fiction writing. A collection of reportage on World War II soldiers was published as *Situation Normal* in 1944, and he completed his only published novel, *Focus*, which addresses anti-Semitism and fascism, in 1945. The novel had sold ninety thousand copies by the time *Salesman* premiered in 1949 (Miller, "Brooklyn" 12). However, neither the novel nor its eventual film adaptation in 2001 attracted much critical acclaim. After being criticized at times for supposedly avoiding writing from a Jewish sensibility, Miller wrote *Broken Glass* (1994), his only other work that deals overtly with a Jewish theme.

More significant in terms of his playwriting is that in 1945 Miller completed the first of his ten one-act plays, *That They May Win*, which centered on the financial difficulties of a returning World War II veteran and his wife. Finally, in 1944, Miller gathered material for a screenplay, *The Story of G.I. Joe*, but withdrew from the project before filming began (Miller, *Timebends* 288).

Miller's foray into Broadway theater came on November 23, 1944, with *The Man Who Had All the Luck*. Featuring two brothers—as four of Miller's student plays did and six of his later ones would—*Luck* centers on the guilt of one brother over his undeserved luck as the other fails to become a professional baseball player despite his rigorous training under their father. A father's differing treatment of his supportive and prodigal sons would be a theme Miller would return to in later plays. Using the play's title for their own pithy evaluations, critics were less impressed with the play itself than they were with the promise shown by the new, twenty-nine-year-old playwright. The play closed after only four performances but won the Theatre Guild National Award. Critics pointed out what was to become Miller's challenge: "to focus his plot and his characters so that a clear dramatic image will be created," as critic George Freedley wrote in the *New York Daily Telegraph*. Failing to appreciate Miller's desire and attempt to bring something new to the American stage, and reflecting the staid state of American theater in the 1940s, critics articulated what would remain their primary complaints about Miller's writing: it was too complex, with too many ideas and story lines, and too philosophical and political. As would later critics, some found his work melodramatic and did not like that the play so directly asserted ethics and principles.

Miller's response was one of both disappointment and determination. He felt that the play had failed in part because of its lengthy scenic changes and determined "never again [to have] anybody move scenery in any play of his" (Miller, "Brooklyn" 11). He also decided that if he did not succeed with his next playwriting effort, he would abandon the craft (Miller, *Plays* 16); in hindsight, however, it is doubtful that he would have done so. Fortunately, both for the man who believed one was born to be a playwright and for the American theater, Miller's next attempt did succeed on Broadway three years later.

Opening on January 29, 1947, and running for 328 performances, *All My Sons* was much more unified than the plays that preceded it, but it retained a strong political element. In the play, two sons are destroyed by their father's selfish decision to ship faulty airplane parts in order to keep his business flourishing, a decision responsible for the deaths of twenty-one pilots during World War II. Miller avoided any changes of scenery, utilizing a single setting; the various characters congregate in the Kellers' backyard as the familial tragedy unfolds. Once again intersecting the public with the private, examining morals and political challenges, Miller took a risk by offering this play, which exposed the profiteering and immorality of business that occurred alongside the military's courage and heroism, only two years after the war had unified the country.

Brooks Atkinson, in a review for *The New York Times*, remarked that Miller had distinguished himself as "a genuine new talent" with the "honest, forceful drama" ("Play"). He praised the play's "pithy yet unselfconscious dialogue" and vivid characters, calling the work "a piece of expert dramatic construction. Mr. Miller has woven his characters into a tangle of plot that springs naturally out of the circumstances of life today." Not all critics were so positive in their responses, however. Richard Watts, Jr., writing for the *New York Post*, qualified his praise, saying that while the play has "force and passion," the story is "uneven," even "clumsy." He also found the "symbolism and social crusading" unwieldy and overwrought. Ward Morehouse, in a review for *The Sun*, asserted that the play had too many plot threads (Bigsby, *File* 17-19).

Although with this new play Miller had certainly simplified the issues raised and the structure of the work in comparison with his earlier plays, it still proved too complex for some. Morehouse and other critics asked him to explain his play, which he did in a piece written for *The New York Times* (Miller, *Timebends* 134). Critics have also criticized as implausible the scene in the play in which Ann reveals Larry's letter, but Miller compared this device to the coincidence inherent to the Greek drama *Oedipus* (134). Miller later wrote that with *All My Sons*, he "had exhausted [his] interest in Greco-Ibsen form" (144).

Miller credited Brooks Atkinson for the success of *All My Sons* and for Miller's subsequent recognition as a playwright intent on making theater socially relevant as well as entertaining (*Timebends* 138). The play earned Miller the New York Drama Critics' Circle Award and remains one of his strongest and best-known works. It was soon produced in Europe, and even as late as 1977, a production in Israel broke all previous box-office records there. Ironically, even as he earned money from the production of his first Broadway success, Miller returned to his working-class roots, deciding to accept a minimum-wage factory job; his experience, however, was short-lived, though his desire to stay in touch with people from whom he could create characters and his sense of the moral remained (Miller, *Timebends* 138-39).

The success of *All My Sons* established Miller as a new playwright and gave him permission, once again, to attempt a new dramatic structure that included multiple settings, time shifts, and complex philosophical and political ideas on the stage. Miller set about writing his next play, *Death of a Salesman*, the play on which his reputation as a major playwright rests most prominently. Reportedly, since the work's premiere, there has never been a night without a performance of *Salesman* somewhere in the world. More critical books and articles have been written about *Salesman* than about any other of Miller's plays. The first act was written in twenty-four hours, the second in the following six weeks. However, it was an idea that had been germinating for years; at the age of seventeen, Miller had written a two-page short story, "In Memoriam," about a downtrodden salesman (Lahr, "Birth" 110).

The play premiered on February 10, 1949, and, despite the producers' fear that a title with "death" in it would mean certain death for the production, it ran for 742 performances. Neither the title nor the play's complexity prevented audiences from buying tickets or critics from raving about Miller's new drama. The producers also feared that the audience might not follow the story or the play's frequent time shifts; however, Jo Mielziner's set design, which allowed most locations to be on the stage simultaneously, with only set pieces quickly rolled on and off for the remainder, and his lighting design, which included techniques to denote the time changes, enabled audiences to follow the stream-of-conscious, fluid play and prevented the long scenery changes Miller had come to loathe. Alex North's music, which utilized leitmotifs, and minor costume changes also helped audiences to recognize the story's time changes.

The instant success of *Salesman* changed Miller's life immediately. He wrote later in his 1987 autobiography *Timebends* that as the reviews were coming in, on the drive home from the theater on opening night he and his wife could already feel the difference between them (193). Critics were nearly unanimous in their praise of *Salesman*; Howard Barnes recognized that Miller had "grown enormously in artistic stature since *All My Sons*," and Watts stated his belief that Miller's promise as a budding playwright had been fulfilled. All aspects of the production were applauded. Kappo Phelan acknowledged that the work was both experimental and classical, praising the writing and the "extraordinary performances." Boyd Martin, writing for the Louisville,

Kentucky, *Courier-Journal*, stated that "as a production, it is unique and almost stylized . . .[the] setting imaginative and elastic, . . . direction vital and fluid, . . . [and] cast superb," going on to say that the play was poetic and both an artistic and popular hit; he concluded that "as a playwright [Miller could] be looked to with keen anticipation in the future." Brooks Atkinson of *The New York Times* considered *Salesman* "one of the finest dramas in the whole of the American theater," commenting on the masterly direction and Lee J. Cobb's heroic performance as Willy Loman (*"Death"*). He continued, "Miller has accomplished some remarkable things," adding that the play and staging were "daring and experimental." Howard Barnes, writing for *The New York Herald Tribune*, concurred, calling *Salesman* "a great play of our day," with "majesty, sweep and shattering dramatic impact," "consummately performed."

Cue magazine named *Salesman* the best play of 1948-49 season with "a production of [the] highest caliber." The play won the New York Drama Critics' Circle Award and the Tony Award (over Tennessee Williams's *A Streetcar Named Desire*) and earned Miller his one Pulitzer Prize. Later, its television adaptations in 1966, 1985, and 2000 would receive Emmy nominations. The original production had audience members weeping and, perhaps, even affected certain social conditions. After one performance, for example, Miller learned that, after seeing the play, "Bernard Gimbel, head of the department store chain, . . . gave an order that no one in his stores was to be fired for being overage" (*Timebends* 191).

John Chapman of the *Daily News* predicted that "everybody . . . [would] have much more to say about" *Salesman* in the coming years, and they have (*"Death"*). The play has been produced worldwide over the past sixty years—Miller directed it himself in China and Sweden—proving its versatility across cultures and countries as well as its universality. Even in China, as Miller wrote in his book *"Salesman" in Beijing* in 1984, where footballs, punching bags, and large refrigerators were foreign to actors and audience members alike, audiences understood well the pressure of fathers on sons and the expectations and failures that exist in a strict social system.

The fiftieth-anniversary production, imported from the Goodman Theatre in Chicago to Broadway, utilized revolves and cubes that swung in and out of the darkness in a set designed by Mark Wendland. (Revolves had first been used to stage the play by designer Fran Thompson at the Royal National Theatre in London in 1996.) Chicago critics thought the Goodman production, which extended its sold-out run, to be a landmark, and Ben Brantley called it "rare and splendid [with an] interpretation that rejuvenate[d] a classic." Chris Jones of *Variety* recognized the production's "post-modern concept"; Brantley found the sets "miraculously fluid"; and Richard Christiansen of the *Chicago Tribune* commented on "Robert Falls's beautiful, innovative staging, . . . Michael Philippi's poetic lighting, and Richard Woodbury's dynamic . . . score," calling the production "a new standard of excellence for an ageless drama." Brantley asserted that Brian Dennehy and Elizabeth Franz gave the "performances of their careers" in a "reimagined" production. Roma Torre wrote, "People will be talking about [Dennehy's performance] for decades." The production won a Tony Award for best revival of a play, and Dennehy and Franz, as well as director Robert Falls, earned Tony Awards; two other members of the cast, Kevin Anderson and Howard Witt, were also nominated for Tonys. In addition, Miller received the Antoinette Perry Special Lifetime Achievement Award. By its fiftieth anniversary, *Salesman* had sold about eleven million copies, making it the most successful modern play ever published (Lahr, "Making" 42).

Having firmly launched his career as a playwright in the 1940s, Miller wrote four plays during the 1950s: an adaptation of Ibsen's *An Enemy of the People*, *The Crucible*, and two one-acts, *A Memory of Two Mondays* and *A View from the Bridge*, the latter of which he developed into a successful two-act play in 1956 for a London production directed by Peter Wood.

Miller was approached by Fredric March and Robert Lewis in 1950 to adapt Ibsen's *An Enemy of the People* (*En folkefiende*, first published in 1882) to overcome its previous stilted translations and make it more contemporary. The play opened on December 28, 1950, but ran for only thirty-six performances. In the era of McCarthyism, when Americans' fear of the spread of communism was fanned, critics lambasted Miller for adding an ironic line about America, which was, in fact, in Ibsen's original script (Bigsby, *Company* 80). A screenplay titled *The Hook* followed in 1951, but when Miller refused to change the characters to make them more politically palatable, the script was pulled; later, director Elia Kazan would collaborate with Miller on the making of the 1954 film *On the Waterfront* (Bigsby, *Company* 126).

Still, Miller refused to shy away from controversial issues, running instead into the lion's mouth with the writing of *The Crucible*. Indeed, as he wrote the play, he did not know that he would be called before the House Un-American Activities Committee (HUAC) in 1956. Utilizing the Salem witch hunts and trials as a metaphor for the growing dangers of McCarthyism, Miller's new play premiered January 22, 1953. Although its initial run was only 197 performances, *The Crucible* has since been the most frequently produced of Miller's plays, both in the United States and abroad; along with *Salesman*, it is one of Miller's two most studied and most popular plays. Miller blamed the initial reaction to the play in part on its staging, which the director, Jed Harris, had seen as a Dutch genre painting (*Timebends* 344). While critics recognized the power in, and implications of, Miller's drama, most agreed that there was little effective emotion in the production.

Walter Kerr of the *New York Herald Tribune* considered the play a "step backward" in Miller's dramaturgy, while others concurred with Kerr's view of the play's traditional form and style and failed to accept the parallels Miller drew between the two historical periods in his effort to make universal assertions (Bigsby, *File* 30-35). However, the production won both the Tony Award and the Donaldson Award, and the play's London production, mounted soon after, fared much better, perhaps because of Britain's social and critical distance on the work's subject matter. Despite its somewhat inauspicious beginnings, *The Crucible* has gone on to become the playwright's most popular work, and Miller's script for the 1996 film adaptation of the play earned him an Academy Award.

Miller wrote only two other plays in the 1950s, both of which were initially one-acts. *A Memory of Two Mondays*, a slice of life set in an automobile parts warehouse, and *A View from the Bridge*, a memory play about the protective jealousy of a longshoreman for his niece, which results in a tragic murder-suicide, premiered together on September 29, 1955, and ran for 149 performances. As Miller himself pointed out, one-act plays are a hard sell on Broadway; by the time audiences drive into New York and pay for dinner and parking, they want to sit for more than half an hour. Nevertheless, Miller wrote ten one-act plays that have been produced, two of which he later developed into full-length plays. For the two-act version of *A View from the Bridge*, which Miller called his "Greek drama," he developed the two female leading roles, emphasized the neighborhood and its people, changed some of the one-act version's poetic meter to prose, and intensified the triangular relationships (Otten 78). For the two-act's production directed by Peter Brook in London, the set design "soared to the roof," providing a fuller sense of Eddie's environment (Miller, *View* viii).

After his critical success in the 1940s and early 1950s, Miller was absent from the theater until 1964. During the meantime, he wrote hundreds of pages for other plays but did not complete them. He also wrote the screenplay for the film *The Misfits*, in which his wife, Marilyn Monroe, was to star. Miller returned to the theater with *After the Fall*, produced by the Repertory Theatre of Lincoln Center. Producer Robert Whitehead brought together Miller and director Elia Kazan, from whom Miller had been estranged since Kazan had named names before HUAC to save his directing career. The dynamics between the two must have been interesting both artistically and personally, given that one of the play's characters, who is based on Kazan, names names, an action that results in another character's suicide.

After the Fall opened at the American National Theater and Academy's Washington Square Theatre, the temporary home for the new, twenty-six-actor theater company, on January 23, 1964, and ran for fifty-nine performances. Even before the play opened, protests began based on rumors that much of the work was based on Miller's marriage to Marilyn Monroe, an affront to those fans still mourning her death two years earlier. Ironically, however, throngs clamored for tickets, perhaps in part fueled by interest in the movie star. That Barbara Loden, the actress portraying Maggie, wore a blonde wig did little to separate Monroe from the character of Maggie. Although Miller insisted he was surprised at the public's reaction, the play, along with Miller's lengthy account and attempt to make sense of his failed marriage in *Timebends*, left him disinterested in discussing his second marriage further, despite incessant questions in interviews, at conferences, and at other appearances throughout the remainder of his life. Surprisingly, Miller's final play, *Finishing the Picture*, which premiered at the Goodman Theatre in Chicago on September 21, 2004, less than five months before his death, was first drafted in 1977-78 and centers on an emotionally fragile actress's inability to complete the filming of a movie (Bigsby, *Study* 437).

As the Lincoln Center Repertory began, Elia Kazan stated, "We want the playwrights to think of our theater as a place where they can state their convictions clearly and without restriction, without a bow to any convention or stricture." Miller reported that *After the Fall* consisted of a "new form, continuous stream of meaning . . . the way a mind would go in quest of a meaning" ("Ad-Libs" 69). Distilled from more than 5,000 pages, however, the play is 180 pages long and runs three and one-half hours (Norton). It includes several plotlines and themes, including the Great Depression, the Holocaust, marriage and divorce, and an actress's drug- and alcohol-fueled demise. The critical and popular failures of *After the Fall* stemmed, in large part, from the play's unfinished nature.

Critics were divided in their recognition and appreciation of Miller's efforts. Walter Kerr of the *New York Herald Tribune* found it to be a "thoroughly bad play: structurally inchoate, verbally-vague, psychologically imperceptive . . .[its] exhaustive self-revelation disingenuous, self-serving, and insensitive" and its staging "chopped up," with mixed metaphors and abstract stage and realistic props. Yet, as John Chapman asserted, the play got "the Repertory Theatre of Lincoln Center off to an impressive start" ("*After*"). A writer for the Associated Press called it "a strange, stirring, and sensation-tinged experience; a beautiful, remarkable play." Martin Gottfried wrote that "no single play in memory has produced so powerful an effect," comparing it with *Tea and Sympathy*, *Picnic*, and *Cat on a Hot Tin Roof* ("*After*").

Others noted the significance of the play not only in Miller's oeuvre but also in American drama. Norman Nadel wrote in the *New York World-Telegram and Sun* that the play advanced drama as the works of August Strindberg and Eugene O'Neill had before it. Howard Taubman of *The New York Times* wrote that the play "may mark a turning point in the American drama" and that it was Miller's most mature drama; he called Kazan's direction "unfaltering in its perception and orchestration" and Loden's performance "stunning." In Taubman's view, the company gave "every indication of becoming a true ensemble." Commenting favorably on the staging, acting, music, and costumes, Caldwell Thomas of the *Harvard Crimson* stated, "Together they have enabled the American theatre to take a giant step." Sheridan Morley noted years later that, while *After the Fall* is not Miller's greatest play, it marked a turning point in his life. Harold Clurman asserted that had Miller "not written this play, he might never have been able to write another. We may now look to a future of ever more creative effort." *After the Fall* was the first play to be published in the *Saturday Evening Post*, which also printed photographs from the original production ("*Saturday*").

Twenty-six years later, the play received a significantly better critical reception in a revival staged by Michael Blakemore in London; the production starred a black actress, Josette Simon, as Maggie, and her performance was hailed as "smashing" (Allen), "magnificent" (Shaw), and "riveting" (Paton). Critics said that Simon provided "an exquisite portrayal" (Cairney) that "wholly eclipses the memory of Monroe" (Wardle).

Miller provided a second play for the new repertory company with *Incident at Vichy*, which was based on World War II interrogations. It opened December 3, 1964, and ran for ninety-nine performances. Miller's only other play of the 1960s, *The Price*, his first commercial play since the two-act version of *A View from the Bridge*, proved to be a popular and critical hit. The play rose from the same drafts dating back to 1950 that *After the Fall* had, although the two plays are quintessentially different, both in content and in form. *The Price* is, arguably, one of Miller's five best works, even though it is not as widely known as others such as *Death of a Salesman*, *All My Sons*, and *A View from the Bridge*. It reprises earlier preoccupations of Miller's, including the Great Depression and supportive and prodigal sons, who here meet for the first time in twenty-eight years, sixteen years after their father's death, to decide what to do with ten rooms of furniture he left behind.

The Price opened February 7, 1968, ran for 429 performances, and was nominated for the Tony Award for best play. Late in rehearsals, Miller had taken over the direction of the production from Ulu Grosbard (Greenfeld). Critics considered the play one of Miller's best: Tony Lawrence asserted that it was "every bit as good as *Salesman*," and Clive Barnes called it one of Miller's two or three best plays and "one of the most engrossing and entertaining plays that Miller [had] ever written—superbly, flamboyantly theatrical." Mike Stein stated that the play was "destined to become a classic." In Miller's *New York Times* obituary in 2005, *The Price* was listed as his last critical and commercial hit (Berger).

Miller wrote four plays in the 1970s, two of them one-acts: *Fame* and *The Reason Why*. These two plays, which were performed in New York's Theatre Workshop in 1970, have not garnered much attention. *Fame* was later filmed in 1978 for television; *The Reason Why* was filmed in 1969. Miller's next play, *The Creation of the World and Other Business*, was based on the story of Adam and Eve, Cain and Abel. Opening November 30, 1972, it ran for only twenty performances. Miller later adapted it for the musical stage under the title *Up from Paradise*, which was performed at the University of Michigan, opening April 23, 1974. *The Archbishop's Ceiling*, which is based on Miller's experience at a dinner party in Czechoslovakia in 1970 when he was president of International PEN (Bigsby, *Companion* 5), an organization that describes itself as an "association of writers working to advance literature, defend free expression, and foster international literary fellowship," returns to his themes of paranoia and government infiltration. The play opened April 30, 1977.

Miller continued his playwriting despite many critics' insistence that his greatest works were behind him. The most notable of the plays he produced during this next period was that based on Studs Terkel's 1970 book of interviews about the Great Depression, *Hard Times*. Miller selected stories and characters from Terkel's book to create *The American Clock*, placing memories of his own family center stage and returning thus to themes of sons and fathers, economic disaster, and the impacts on the individual of ineffectual social systems. First presented at the Spoleto Festival, *The American Clock* opened in New York on May 24, 1980; it lasted only twelve performances. Once more, Miller had taken over the direction of his play, this time from Dan Sullivan, as Miller believed that Sullivan did not understand the concept of the play. Labeled "a vaudeville," *The American Clock* features an enormous cast and a large number of locations, requiring more scenic fluidity than any other of Miller's plays.

Subsequent productions have continued to tackle this difficult play, with varying success. Peter Wood's production at the Royal National Theatre in London in 1986 was reviewed by Clive Hirschhorn as follows: "Peter Wood's lively direction does its best to balance the private and public aspects of a rather lopsided play, and he is aided in this difficult task by a large . . . [and] terrific [cast]" ("Striking"). The production was able to include many more songs of the period than the New York production had. In 1997, James Houghton's production of *Clock* at his Signature Theatre Company in New York met with critical favor.

Miller next adapted a book by Fania Fénelon about an orchestra made up of women in a Nazi concentration camp who play music to stay alive. *Playing for Time* was first written for television in 1980 and earned four Emmy Awards the following year, including one for Miller's script. Miller then adapted the work for the stage, and it opened on September 5, 1985. It remains a powerful, if lesser-known, play.

Miller followed this work with two sets of one-acts. In November 1982, under the title *Two-Way Mirror*, two one-acts, *Some Kind of Love Story* and *Elegy for a Lady*, opened. The two differ significantly in form and content: the first is based on an actual case of a falsely accused man, and the second is an abstract study of love, true devotion, and mutual understanding. In January 1987, under the title *Danger: Memory!*, another pair of one-acts, *I Can't Remember Anything* and *Clara*, opened. The two are again of contrasting themes and forms. The first is a slice-of-life play about two elderly neighbors who attempt to come to terms with their aging and seeming purposelessness. *Clara* focuses on the denial and guilt of a father who knowingly allowed his daughter to date a former convict, only to find her murdered.

Miller continued to write plays in the 1990s, producing four that also varied in form and subject matter, reflecting his thematic and formal tendencies as well as his interest in continuing to experiment with form. A screenplay, *Everybody Wins*, was written in 1990, and Miller's most unusual play of the decade, the satirical, surreal *The Ride Down Mt. Morgan*, followed a year after. Tired of the standard American theater, Miller chose to have *Mt. Morgan*'s world premiere directed by Michael Blakemore in London ("Miller's Tale"). In both this production and the Williamstown one, which was directed by David Esbjornson and found its way to Broadway, the disparate themes center on a bigamist who is discovered by his two wives after he crashes his car on a mountain. The play requires constantly shifting locales as well as differentiation between the imagination of the bigamist, Lyman Felt, and the reality he must face. Critics respected the complexity of the play but were unsure what to make of it. The latter production earned a Tony Award nomination.

Two years later, Miller wrote *The Last Yankee*, first as a one-act and then as a full-length play; as in *After the Fall*, the two acts do not appear to mesh formally. Act 1 finds two men in the waiting room of a mental hospital ready to visit their wives; act 2 introduces the wives and offers a disturbing portrayal of the complexities of marriage.

Continuing with this theme, but returning to a more traditional structure, Miller wrote *Broken Glass* in 1994. This play is about the Holocaust and its effects as well as the blind innocence of those outside Nazi Germany. As with many of Miller's earlier plays, to avoid the necessity of distracting and time-consuming scenery changes, the set was a modern metaphoric environment, complete with an onstage cellist; furniture for the various locales was readily rolled on and off the set.

Once again, critics varied in their responses. Writing of the production at the Royal National Theatre in London, Clive Hirschhorn stated that *Broken Glass* was Miller's best play since *The Price* ("*Broken*"). Others also lauded the work, calling it "deeply compassionate" (Peter), "a heart-breaking piece of writing" (Darvell), a "compelling, full-blooded drama" (Stone), and "demanding and refreshing," "one of [Miller's] strongest plays for many years . . . a gripping and . . . powerfully affecting drama" (Spencer). Critics called Miller "as vital a writer as . . . ever" (Hagerty) and praised the "superb production," "inspired, masterly direction," and "completely brilliant performance by Henry Goodman" (White) as well as the "virtuous performance" of Margot Leicester (Shaw). One called it a "wise and profound play" that had received "the brilliant production it deserves" (Shaw). Others disagreed, calling the play "dramatically underpowered and burdened with an overly dramatic ending" (Johns), its writing "factitious" (Wolf), and Miller an "overrated playwright" (Macauley) writing about "too many issues." *Broken Glass* won the Tony Award in New York and the Olivier Award in London. When director David Thacker took the production to Israel, it met with acute resonances among its audiences (Neill).

Miller's final play of the twentieth century, *Mr. Peters' Connections*, was produced in 1998 at the Signature Theatre Company; its British premiere followed at the Almeida Theatre in London. The play sounds like a swan song as a man reflects on the various people and relationships in his life. Both productions were well received by the critics, reflecting, perhaps, that they had finally changed their expectations of Miller and American drama.

As the new century broke, Miller, now in his eighties, managed to write three plays in the last four years of his life. *Untitled* was written in 2001 for the poet-playwright and president of the newly formed Czech Republic, Václav Havel. *Resurrection Blues*, written in 2002, concerns wealth, corruption, drugs, and a plan to televise a crucifixion. Miller's final play, *Finishing the Picture*, was completed in 2004. He also wrote a piece for a London newspaper that he then published in 2001 as a book titled *On Politics and the Art of Acting*, which once again commented on the state of the American government and the country's political leaders.

In addition to his stage plays, radio plays, and films, Miller wrote three collections of short stories—*I Don't Need You Any More* (1967), *Homely Girl, a Life, and Other Stories* (1992), and *Presence* (2007)—three books with his wife, Ingeborg Morath, as photographer; three collections of essays; and a children's book, *Jane's Blanket* (1963). Miller's autobiography, *Timebends* (1987), as well as collections of essays by the playwright—*The Theatre Essays of Arthur Miller*, edited by Robert A. Martin and Steven R. Centola (1978/1996); *Echoes Down the Corridor*, edited by Centola (2000); and *The Crucible in History, and Other Essays* (2000)—offer very useful perspectives from the writer himself.

Controversy about Miller's plays continues, but many critics recognize Miller's singular effect on the development of American drama in the twentieth century. Numerous books of criticism provide varying perspectives on Miller's work over the past sixty years, and we are now, in effect, in the second and third generation of critics. Collections of critical essays by single authors include books by Harold Bloom, Neil Carson, Alice Griffin, Ronald Hayman, Sheila Huftel, Leonard Moss, Edward Murray, Benjamin Nelson, Terry Otten, and June Schlueter and James K. Flanagan. Collections of critical essays by multiple authors include volumes edited by Christopher Bigsby, Enoch Brater, Steven Centola, Robert W. Corrigan, Robert Martin, and James J. Martine. Collections of essays on *Death of a Salesman* include those edited by Harold Bloom, Brenda Murphy, Stephen A. Marino, and Gerald Weales. Collections of essays on *The Crucible* include those edited by John H. Ferres, James Martine, and Gerald Weales; in addition, Bernard F. Dukore has published a volume that addresses both *Salesman* and *The Crucible*. Also quite useful are Bigsby's *Arthur Miller: A Critical Study*, published in 2005, and his *File on Miller*, published in 1987. Two books of interviews are *Conversations with Arthur Miller* (1987), edited by Matthew Roudané, and Bigsby's *Arthur Miller and Company* (1990).

Only three biographies of Miller exist to date: Martin Gottfried's *Arthur Miller: His Life and Work* (2003), Enoch Brater's *Arthur Miller: A Playwright's Life and Work* (2005), and the first volume of Christopher Bigsby's *Arthur Miller: 1915-1962* (2008), which analyzes Miller's life to 1962 (the next volume is slated for publication in the near future). Finally, interested students may find more information about Miller and his works by accessing the Web sites of the Arthur Miller Society (http://www.ibiblio.org/miller) and *The Arthur Miller Journal* (http://www.stfranciscollege.edu/academics/publications/miller).

Those who have doubted the universality and endurance of Miller's drama are quickly having their opinions changed as new productions and the publication of new editions and criticism continue the analysis and discussion of his work. Still, perceptions of Miller and his work remain divergent across national boundaries. Miller once noted that plays other than *Death of a Salesman* are often hailed outside the United States as his finest work, and British scholar Christopher Bigsby pointed out in 1990 that in Britain the playwright is "treated as a living writer who continues to write plays that address our culture. In America, he's still thought of as a realist who wrote great plays many years ago" (quoted in Goldfarb). Yet, both within and outside the United States, Miller's insistence on voicing his political views has meant that his plays have often been banned.

While *All My Sons*, *Death of a Salesman*, *The Crucible*, *A View from the Bridge*, *The Price*, and *Broken Glass* are still considered Miller's best plays, *After the Fall*, *The Archbishop's Ceiling*, *The American Clock*, *The Ride Down Mt. Morgan*, and *Mr. Peters' Connections* deserve further critical attention devoted to exploring their production possibilities and analyzing more accurately Miller's dramaturgy, developing themes, and place in American drama. It will also be of interest to see which, if any, further works Miller's estate chooses to publish and what light these might shed on Miller's concerns, his writing process, and the development of his art.

Works Cited

Allen, Carol. *"After the Fall." London Talkback Radio*. Undated transcript, Royal National Theatre Archives, London.

Atkinson, Brooks. *"Death of a Salesman*: Arthur Miller's Tragedy of an Ordinary Man." *The New York Times* 20 Feb. 1949.

_____. "The Play in Review: *All My Sons*." *The New York Times* 30 Jan. 1947.

Barnes, Clive. Rev. of *The Price*, by Arthur Miller. *The New York Times* 7 Feb. 1968.

Barnes, Howard. "A Great Play Is Born." *New York Herald Tribune* 11 Feb. 1949.

Berger, Marilyn. "Arthur Miller, Legendary American Playwright, Is Dead." *The New York Times* 11 Feb. 2005.

Bigsby, Christopher. *Arthur Miller*. London: Weidenfeld & Nicolson, 2008.

_____. *File on Miller*. London: Methuen, 1987.

_____, ed. *Arthur Miller: A Critical Study*. New York: Cambridge UP, 2005.

_____, ed. *Arthur Miller and Company*. London: Methuen Drama, 1990.

_____, ed. *The Cambridge Companion to Arthur Miller*. New York: Cambridge UP, 1997.

Brantley, Ben. "A Dark New Production Illuminates *Salesman*." *The New York Times* 3 Nov. 1998.

Brater, Enoch. *Arthur Miller: A Playwright's Life and Work*. London: Thames & Hudson, 2005.

Cairney, Jennifer. "Stage and Screen Reviews: *After the Fall*." *London Weekly Diary*. Undated clipping, Royal National Theatre Archives, London.

Chapman, John. "*After the Fall* Overpowering." *Daily News* 24 Jan. 1964.

_____. "*Death of a Salesman*: A Fine Play, Beautifully Produced and Acted." *New York Daily News* 11 Feb. 1949.

Christiansen, Richard. "Brilliant Revival Proves a Golden Anniversary for *Salesman*." *Chicago Tribune* 29 Sept. 1998.

Clurman, Harold. "Arthur Miller: Theme and Variations." *Playbill* Mar. 1964.

Cue 18 Apr. 1949: 16. Untitled clipping, Harry Ransom Humanities Research Center, University of Texas, Austin.

Darvell, Michael. "Pick of the Week: *Broken Glass*." *What's On* 10 Aug. 1994.

Freedley, George. "Arthur Miller Tries but Fails in *The Man Who Had All the Luck*." *New York Daily Telegraph* 25 Nov. 1944.

Goldfarb, Michael. "Arthur Miller and Reverence Abroad." *Newsday* 29 July 1990.

Gottfried, Martin. "*After the Fall*—A Second Look." Undated clipping, Harry Ransom Humanities Research Center, University of Texas, Austin.

_____. *Arthur Miller: His Life and Work*. New York: Da Capo Press, 2003.

Greenfeld, Josh. "Writing Plays Is Senseless, Arthur Miller Says, 'But I Love It.'" *The New York Times* 13 Feb. 1972.

Hagerty, Bill. "Miller Shatters Glass Houses." *Today* 5 Aug. 1994.

Hirschhorn, Clive. "*Broken Glass*." *Sunday Express* 17 Aug. 1994.

_____. "A Striking Success." *Sunday Express* 17 Aug. 1986.

Johns, Ian. "Short Take." *London Theatre News*. Undated clipping, Royal National Theatre Archives, London.

Jones, Chris. "*Death of a Salesman*." *Variety* 5 Oct. 1998.

Kazan, Elia. "Theater: New Stages, New Plays, New Actors." *The New York Times Magazine* 23 Sept. 1962.

Kerr, Walter. "*The Fall*: The Eye Is 'I.'" *New York Herald Tribune* 16 Feb. 1964.

Lahr, John. "Birth of a Salesman." *The New Yorker* 25 Dec. 1995: 110-11.

_____. "Making Willy Loman." *The New Yorker* 25 Jan. 1999: 42-49.

Lawrence, Tony. "*The Price*: Huntington Hartford." *The Hollywood Reporter*. Undated clipping, Harry Ransom Humanities Research Center, University of Texas, Austin.

Macauley, Alastair. "Miller's *Broken Glass*." 9 Mar. 1995.

Martin, Boyd. "Playwright Arthur Miller Looks for Weaknesses of Human Nature." [Louisville, Kentucky] *Courier-Journal* 24 Apr. 1949.

Miller, Arthur. "Arthur Miller Ad-Libs on Elia Kazan" (1964). *Conversations with Arthur Miller.* Ed. Matthew C. Roudané. Jackson: UP of Mississippi, 1987. 68-77.

_____. "Brooklyn Boy Makes Good." Interview by Robert Sylvester (1949). *Conversations with Arthur Miller.* Ed. Matthew C. Roudané. Jackson: UP of Mississippi, 1987. 9-18.

_____. *Conversations with Arthur Miller.* Ed. Matthew C. Roudané. Jackson: UP of Mississippi, 1987.

_____. *Plays One.* London: Methuen, 1958.

_____. *"Salesman" in Beijing.* New York: Viking, 1984.

_____. *Timebends: A Life.* New York: Grove Press, 1987.

_____. *A View from the Bridge.* New York: Viking Press, 1960.

"Miller's Tale." *London Evening Standard* 10 Feb. 1992.

Morehouse, Ward. *"The Man Who Had All the Luck* Is Folksy, Philosophical, and Tiresome." *The [New York] Sun* 24 Nov. 1944.

Morley, Sheridan. "Miller's Tale: Life After Marilyn." *Sunday Mirror* 17 June 1990.

Nadel, Norman. "Miller Play One of Inward Vision." *New York World-Telegram and Sun* 24 Jan. 1964.

Neill, Heather. "It's All Grist to His Miller." *London Times* 4 Feb. 1995.

Norton, Elliot. "Arthur Miller's *Fall* to Break with Custom." *Theatre Arts* Jan. 1964.

"NT2000 One Hundred Plays of the Century." Accessed 2 Sept. 2009. http://spot.colorado.edu/~colemab/NT2000/NT2000.html

Otten, Terry. *The Temptation of Innocence in the Dramas of Arthur Miller.* Columbia: U of Missouri P, 2002.

Paton, Maureen. "Haunting Tale of a Tragic Star." *Daily Express* 21 June 1990.

Peter, John. "A Raw Slice of Humanitiy." *Sunday Times* 14 Aug. 1994: sec. 10, 20-21.

Phelan, Kappo. *"Death of a Salesman." The Commonweal* 4 Mar. 1949.

"Saturday Evening Post to Print Miller's Play." *The New York Times* 11 Jan. 1964: 15.

Shaw, Roy. "Theatre." *The Tablet* 27 Aug. 1994.

Spencer, Charles. *"Broken Glass* Reveals a Life Shattered by Images of War." *Daily Telegraph* 5 Aug. 1994.

Stein, Mike. Rev. of *The Price,* by Arthur Miller. WNEW, Radio TV Time Recordings. Undated transcript, Harry Ransom Humanities Research Center, University of Texas, Austin.

Stone, Bill. "Miller Offers a Prayer for Oppressed Minorities." Undated clipping, Royal National Theatre Archives, London.

Taubman, Howard. "Arthur Miller's Play Opens Repertory." *The New York Times* 24 Jan. 1964.

Thomas, Caldwell. "Arthur Miller's Comeback." *Harvard Crimson* 27 Jan. 1964.

Torre, Roma. Rev. of *Death of a Salesman,* by Arthur Miller. NY1-TV. 11 Feb. 1999.

Wardle, Irving. "When Miller Made Maggie from Marilyn." *The Independent on Sunday* 24 June 1990.

Watts, Richard, Jr. "*Death of a Salesman* a Powerful Drama." *New York Post* 11 Feb. 1949.

White, Grelle. "A Question of Impotence." *Watford Observer* 19 Aug. 1994.

Wolf, Matt. Rev. of *Broken Glass*, by Arthur Miller. *Variety* 15 Aug. 1994.

CRITICAL
READINGS

Arthur Miller and the Art of the Possible___

Steven R. Centola

While commenting on the difference between playwriting and screen-writing in his Preface to *Everybody Wins*, Arthur Miller used the following illustration to illuminate his point about the subtextual dimension of the theater:

> If a telephone is photographed, isolated on a table, and the camera is left running, it becomes more and more what it is—a telephone in all its details. . . . Things go differently on a stage. Set a phone on a table under a light and raise the curtain, and in complete silence, after a few minutes, some thing will accrete around it. Questions and anticipations will begin to emanate from it, we will begin to imagine meanings in its isolation—in a word, the phone becomes an incipient metaphor. Possibly because we cannot see its detail as sharply as on film or because it is surrounded by much greater space, it begins to animate, to take on suggestive possibilities, very nearly a kind of self-consciousness. Something of the same is true of words as opposed to images. The word is not and can't be any more than suggestive of an idea or sensation; it is nothing in itself. ("On Screenwriting and Language" vi)

Indeed, in itself a word is nothing. If we believe the structuralists, a word is a symbol, a signifer or sign, a marker of meaning that points to something, some referent or vast reservoir of negotiable meanings beyond itself. The diacritical nature of language inevitably means that even small differences in sound and sense will produce tremendous variance in the determination and reception of meaning. Even more significantly, and perhaps more problematically, if we take a post-structuralist approach to language, a word points to an endless chain of linked signifiers, and given the arbitrary nature of the signifier and the system of which it is a part, this endless linked series of associations inevitably multiplies the potential meanings of every word and every sequence of words forming sentences in written texts. The nuance that every word takes on and generates in the reader's mind is affected by the nuances all these words have in combination with each other, and all of this is then complicated by unanticipated associations which generate a host of linked associations and impressions, which collectively form unexpected meanings as they stimulate the reader's imagination and even tap into the unconscious. Perhaps for this reason, then, Miller, almost sounding a little like a deconstructive theorist, characterizes the word as nothing, but for Miller in its very nothingness lie the richness, density, and infinite possibilities of the word. After all, Miller tells us, "a description in words tends to inflate, expand, and inflame the imagination, so that in the end the thing or person described is amplified into a larger-than-life figment" ("On Screenwriting and Language" v). And that is the crucial part of the equation for the playwright: how to generate, shape, and string together words; how to invent and hone theater language in such a way that what is created constructs metaphorically an impression of reality that is powerful and suggestive enough to stimulate an imaginative response within the audience. As Miller recognizes, the possibilities inherent within the whole dramatic event are limitless, for the fundamental indeterminacy of meaning—an indeterminacy that Roland Barthes says inevitably results from the plural nature of the play text as a discourse that can be experienced only in the art of production—poses no nihilistic threat in Miller's world. Such indeterminacy instead opens up the possibility for rich speculative and imaginative discovery and generates endless opportunities for creative and diverse interpretations—possibly, even, a reinscription of oppositions, both with his own work and in the life and condition of humanity he depicts in his art. Miller's comments on the limitless and constantly mutating accretions accumulating around the words spoken and objects presented on the stage not only call attention to the subtextual dimension of the theater, but also show why this very important feature of dramatic art makes the theater what Miller described in 1999 as "the art of the possible" (*Echoes* 312).

Although in his commentary on the difference between the cinema and the theater Miller does not give enough credit to good film directors who can skillfully use the camera's eye to capture, isolate, and present certain aspects of individual objects or scenes on the screen in such a way that endows these scenic images with tremendous symbolic significance, he does make an important point about the special nature of theatrical presentation that causes words and objects on the stage to gather accretions around them and take on a subtextual dimension that knows no bounds. Whether it is the word or the scenic image, lighting or sound, gesture or action, the language of the theater resonates with extraordinary suggestiveness at almost any moment in a good play. And that suggestiveness resonates with a stream of endless associations and impressions that change not only from performance to performance but also for every new audience. Christopher Bigsby effectively describes the magical transformation that occurs during a theatrical performance:

> Theatre is a form of alchemy and if the end-product is not always gold at least certain transformations have been effected. Fredric March, Lee J. Cobb, Dustin Hoffman, and Warren Mitchell have all played the part of Willy Loman in *Death of a Salesman*. They spoke the same lines to the same characters but they spoke them differently to different audiences, in different sets, in front of different people, in different theatres, at different times on different continents. . . . Whenever any of us open our mouths we speak the past. The words we use have passed through other mouths. They've been shaped, over time, by pleasures not our own. They're like our own, but they're not our own. They've shed and accumulated meanings. Perhaps that's the reason we're drawn to the theatre. It enacts our own central dilemma as actors inhabit someone else's words and struggle to make them their own, just as we try to imprint ourselves on the given. ("British View" 19-20)

As Bigsby points out, the theater is a place of transformation. The theater is a place where nature is transmuted into art, where reality meets and fuses with illusion, where text and subtext, character and action, word and gesture become one, where opposites are held in balanced suspension, and that, of course, is why the theater is the realm of the possible.

The theater, unlike everything else—the cinema, the novel, and the poem—is a living spectacle. That is why Clive Bloom says that the

> visceral, three-dimensionality of the theatrical space, at once muscular presence and fragile voice, is the sinful nature of raw knowledge. Unlike film and television, even and especially unlike commercial radio, the theatre offers an authenticity which is shocking and peculiarly distressing . . . a type of primary authenticity which unravels or questions the inauthenticity of popular consumer culture and the values of the American system." (Introduction to *American Drama* 2-3)

"The sinful nature of raw knowledge," the peculiar "authenticity" of the theatrical event, as Bloom puts it, derives mainly from the fact that it is a live performance and therefore its success depends on the performance, and oftentimes the interpretation, of the performer who responds to cues within the script and directorial decisions, and helps to turn word into speech and action, which transmutes art into life and makes a text a living presence on the stage for a live audience. The theater is not limited to or constrained by the script. That is certainly the play's beginning, but that is most definitely not its end. Undeniably, because it is a collaborative art form, the play, even more so than the novel, the cinema, or the poem, transcends the author's intentions and understanding and essentially takes on a life of its own in each performance. The world of the play can never be entirely circumscribed by the playwright's intentions any more than an author writing in any other genre of literature can completely know or predict the implication, association, or interpretation of every single word for each individual reading, and reacting to, a particular work. To borrow a phrase from John Barth, who used it in a different context, focusing more on

the art of narrative composition than on the act of reading or responding to literary works, we can accurately characterize the genre of
drama as "a literature of replenishment" (*The Friday Book* 206). Text
and subtext, word and gesture, speech and action—all of these are
fused into a remarkably coherent orchestration of sound and silence,
light and darkness, time and space, past and present, reality and illusion. Opposites maintain a steady equilibrium in a carefully balanced
and beautifully suspended presentation that momentarily, almost mag-
ically, transports us not only to an imagined world inhabited by invented
people, but that also mysteriously invades our deepest consciousness
and somehow suspends our individual ego while facilitating a group
consciousness that affects us not only in the theater but also long after
we experience the magic of the theatrical event. "What the performance of a play gives an audience," says Robert A. Martin, "is less a
set of ideas, propositions, or abstractions about life and how to live it
than what Arthur Miller has called a 'felt experience,' the imaginative
sharing and participation in the lives and action of imaginary characters" ("The Nature of Tragedy" 97). "The performance is mythic; our
sensibilities are enlivened by imaginary characters and we become engaged in their conflicts . . . [and by vicariously living through the characters' conflicts in the theater] we also see how their lives illuminate,
by association, our own lives as individuals and as members of a larger
society" (98). For all of these reasons, Arthur Miller is right in calling
theater "the art of the possible" (*Echoes* 312).

What about Miller's own theater—a theater that has addressed the
problems of war-profiteering crimes, anti-Semitism, the Holocaust,
the Salem Witch Trials of 1692, the Great Depression, the inherent
flaws in the American Dream of material success, mental illness, memory loss, infidelity, bigamy, incestuous desire, corruption in the American criminal justice system, censorship and the invasion of privacy in
totalitarian countries, and other problems threatening to diminish the
value of human life in the modern age? His theater emphasizes the
tragic conditions of human existence, a theater that oftentimes depicts

frustration, anguish, and failure as the prevailing condition of people trapped by circumstances and the crush of overwhelming forces in their society or within their own psyche. Can we justifiably call Miller's theater the art of the possible too? I believe that we can, and my purpose in this essay is to attempt to explain why I believe that his humanist values and postmodernist perspective provide audiences worldwide with a vision of humanity that is uplifting and life-affirming. His plays offer hope and solace for a world desperately seeking to find a glimmer of hope in a world of darkness. In spite of his tragic vision and brutally honest confrontation with the dark forces of human depravity, Miller's plays show the possibility for redemption, transcendence, even triumph in the face of seemingly overpowering odds and adversity most inimical to human enterprise and achievement. Miller's theater is not escapist in nature, but neither is it fatalistic, pessimistic, or nihilistic. It is a drama of hope not despair, transcendence not reduction, and, above all else, the limitless potentialities and possibilities of the human spirit.

When I interviewed Arthur Miller in August 2001, he spoke of one of his more recent creations: *Mr. Peters' Connections*, which was produced at the Signature Theater in 1998. The play is set in a dilapidated nightclub, which Mr. Peters has entered to meet his wife. On one level, it seems as if they may be interested in purchasing and renovating the establishment for future use, but during the course of his conversations with other characters, it becomes clear that Mr. Peters seems uncertain of why he's even in this particular setting. On another level, though, it is easy to view the set as completely symbolic, representing the interior consciousness of Mr. Harry Peters, an elderly man on the verge of death, trapped somewhere between life and death, between consciousness and unconscious reverie. As the play progresses and Mr. Peters engages in spirited, but sometimes puzzling and even depressing, conversations with both real and imagined characters, some alive and in the present and some dead and resurrected from memories and images of the past, it becomes evident to the audience that Mr. Peters is primarily concerned with finding some thread to his life experience that ties everything together into a neat package, an orderly and meaningful whole that has purpose, design, definition, and clarity. His obsessive interest in finding the unseen inherent order is blatantly shown through his repetitive questioning of both himself and the others about the "subject" he searches for in their conversation. Early in the play, Mr. Peters, on the verge of understanding his dilemma but never completely coming to full conscious awareness of his insight, says: "I just cannot find the subject! Like I'll be strolling down the street, and suddenly I'm weeping, everything welling up.—What is the subject? Know what I mean? Simply cannot grasp the subject" (8). Clarifying the significance of this repeated insistence by Mr. Peters on finding and understanding "the subject," Miller, in his Preface to the play, tells us that Mr. Peters is searching for "the secret, the pulsing center of energy, what he calls the subject—that will make his life cohere" (viii). By the play's end, Mr. Peters is no more certain of what the subject is than he was at its beginning, and this lack of resolution—this failure to reach a definitive position about the subject—was not received well by Miller's critics, and is perhaps even primarily responsible for the play being greeted with what Robert Brustein has characterized as "the worst reviews of Miller's career" ("Still Searching for Theater" 29-30).

Undoubtedly, one of the negative reviews Brustein refers to is his own. Writing for the *New Republic* in 1998, Brustein describes *Mr. Peters' Connections* as "windy, tiresome, self-conscious, and full of moony maundering." Associating what he views as the play's structural flaws with the playwright's inability to articulate his vision coherently, Brustein assumes that Miller unintentionally creates a formless play that lacks resolution. Brustein writes:

> Miller is so eager to get things off his chest that he hasn't bothered to provide his new play with a plot, a form, or even much effort at characterization. . . . *Mr. Peters' Connections* is like a long confession to a friend which has yet to be proofed or edited. . . . He [Mr. Peters] is looking for some con-

tinuity with his history in "the hope of finding a subject." It is like watching Arthur Miller at his typewriter wrestling with the same elusive goal. ("Still Searching for Theater" 29-30)

Brustein is not alone in identifying Harry Peters' struggle for certitude with Miller's own personal frustrations, both as a writer seeking to find the perfect form for his vision and as an alienated artist who has sadly witnessed the terrible transformation of the world surrounding him. Writing for the *Village Voice*, Michael Feingold argues that Harry Peters is nothing more than a mouthpiece for Arthur Miller. Feingold writes: "Like his hero, the 82-year-old Miller barely seems to be connecting to the outside world these days. His connections are to his memories, to his puzzlement over the countless ways life has changed in this half-century, and to whatever method he uses now to get words on paper" ("The Old Miller Stream" 147). Making the same assumption, Nina Raine and Frances Stonor Saunders, reviewing the play for the *New Statesman* during its production in London during the fall 2000 season, also identify the playwright with his character: "thoughts of a dry brain in an off-Broadway season. As Mr. Peters (or, rather, Miller) repeatedly exclaims: 'There is no subject any more'" ("Miller's Tale" 30). This brief sampling of the critical response to the New York and London productions of *Mr. Peters' Connections* reveals two trends in the reviewers' response to the play: one, the tendency to identify the author with his character and, two, the conclusion that Miller, and his play, present the audience with a grim, maybe even pessimistic, view of the human condition, a view in their minds undoubtedly invited by the play's unsettling approach to its central thematic interest, which echoes jarringly in the phrase "There is no subject any more." While many have taken *Mr. Peters' Connections* to be a radical departure from Miller's other works and have read the play as a depressing conclusion to a long and distinguished career, the play's thematic center can actually be seen as perfectly consonant with the playwright's vision throughout his career and, in fact, offers its audiences a vision of hope and human possibility, not despair.

In our discussion in August 2001 Miller confirmed that there is a subject in *Mr. Peters' Connections*; the playwright identifies it for us in his play. Humanity, as Miller put it in our conversation, the human mind, is the subject. Miller does not find it disturbing or depressing that there is no inherent order or purpose to life and human existence. The greatness of humanity lies in its ability to forge meaning out of chaos. The human mind, Miller believes, shapes, defines, clarifies, orders, and gives purpose and meaning to life and human existence. In its unmediated state, life is chaos. Entropy is more than just a theory; it is the fundamental condition of the expanding universe, within which we struggle to resist the forces of chaos and destruction and to elevate and ennoble the human condition. The human mind alone brings light into a world of darkness, and because of its power of transcendence and capacity for reason and logical discourse, the human mind is worthy of celebration. "What is the subject?" asks Mr. Peters. Miller answers: we are—and his play implicitly provides this answer by showing us Mr. Peters' thoughtful attempt to wrest some meaning out of his life's experiences. In essence, his quest parallels that of Oedipus and other great tragic figures who seek to understand the conditions of life and their own unique role in shaping their personal destiny. Mr. Peters is no tragic figure, but his efforts are noble and commendable and comment positively on the potential of humanity for honest self-exploration. *Mr. Peters' Connections*, like so much of Miller's work, is ultimately a tribute to the art of the possible.

Earlier in his career, Miller wrote plays that more forcefully explored this subject in the tragic mode and seemed, even more so than *Mr. Peters' Connections*, to have little to do with human possibility. In *All My Sons* and *Death of a Salesman*, for example, we are presented with characters who clearly seem to be and even controlled by environmental forces that severely diminish their capacity for free choice. However, nothing is that simple in Miller's world. There always remains a strong interplay between freedom and fate, a paradoxical balance between deterministic forces at play in the lives of individuals and the exercise and expression of one's own free will that invariably triggers some catastrophic event.

All My Sons tells the story of a successful Mid-Western manufacturer of airplane parts who knowingly allows defective engines to be shipped to the United States Army during the Second World War. As a result of his war-profiteering crimes, twenty-one American pilots die when the cracked cylinder heads cause their planes to malfunction and crash. Exonerated by the courts for his role in the catastrophe, Joe Keller, the play's central character, triumphantly returns to his community and futilely attempts to return to a life of normalcy, pretending the crime never occurred. The semblance of family harmony is maintained until his son, Chris, himself under pressure as his fiancée's brother forces him to acknowledge his own acquiescence, questions Joe about his role in the sordid business transaction. Chris, who fought bravely in combat during the war and had seen many of his troops perish under his command, has a different outlook from his father on the question of an individual's social responsibility. After several powerful scenes of intense debate over the individual's relation to society, Chris finally discloses his father's guilt and challenges him to accept responsibility for his actions. Until his son forces him to acknowledge his wrongdoing, Joe Keller steadfastly maintains his innocence and justifies his anti-social behavior by proclaiming his right to do anything necessary to keep the business from collapsing and ensure his family's survival. Ultimately, as a suicide letter discloses that his older brother preferred death over the ignominy that issued from his father's war crime, Chris convinces his father that he has an obligation to others in society as well. Tortured by his guilt and unable to deal with the shame in his son's eyes, Keller tries to escape from his intolerable situation by putting a bullet in his head. The play ends with Chris facing with horror his own complicity in his father's death. With Joe Keller's suicide, the play forcefully repudiates anti-social behavior that derives from the myth of privatism in American society.

So why should we see this play as exemplifying what Miller calls "the art of the possible"? Where is the hope and possibility in a man's suicide following his realization of the enormity of his anti-social behavior? In an interview with Henry Brandon in 1960, Miller made a statement that seems to point toward an understanding of the process of indirection that enables his drama to leave us with hope, while presenting his audiences with portraits and chronicles of despair. Miller said: "a playwright provides answers by the questions he chooses to ask, by the exact conflicts in which he places his people" (quoted in *Theater Essays* 227). In *All My Sons*, as in the rest of his drama, Miller conveys a sense of possibility for humanity by showing his audience the opportunity for choice; for the selection of a different course of action in his characters' lives. Like Willy Loman in *Death of a Salesman*, Eddie Carbone in *A View from the Bridge*, and Maggie in *After the Fall*, Joe Keller chooses to see himself as a victim of others, and of circumstances imposed on businessmen like himself during the Second World War. He adopts a counterfeit innocence and embraces the illusion that he is a victim of society, of the competitive business world, of the culture that makes it imperative for a man in American society to feel driven by the need to prosper, provide for the family, and succeed in attaining the forever elusive, unquestionably mythic American Dream. Keller denies his personal culpability so that he can preserve his false image of himself and maintain the illusion that he has regained his rightful place in society. He blinds himself from the impulses that make him a danger to himself and others in his society. Keller cannot face what Miller calls "the murder in him, the sly and everlasting complicity with the forces of destruction" (quoted in *Theater Essays* 256). Keller chooses his behavior; it isn't chosen for him or forced on him. His betrayal of trust and refusal to accept responsibility for others sets in motion the chain of events that lead to his self-destruction. Through showing us what happens when a man nullifies the value of the social contract through the performance and justification of indefensible anti-social acts, Miller emphasizes the importance of socially responsible behavior and makes clear why crimes against society must be censured. The sense of possibility in *All My Sons* derives from one simple fact: Joe Keller chose his fate and could have chosen differently. Among other things, *All My Sons* shows that the impulse to betray others and deny responsibility for the welfare of society, when left ungoverned, can run rampant and wreak havoc on the individual, his family, and his society—even, perhaps, civilization as a whole. The Kellers, and many of those around them, choose to blame everyone else for their dilemma, but the play actually shows its audiences that they are the authors of their destiny and failure to accept the tremendous burden of their freedom and responsibility is itself the cause of their personal tragedy.

In an essay published in 1964, Richard Loughlin offers an interesting perspective on the way *All My Sons* leaves its audiences with a sense of hope for the future. Discussing the play as a tragedy in Aristotelian terms, Loughlin argues that

> The spectacle of the crimes and sufferings of another stimulates our sympathy; it reminds us of the perils and uncertainties of the human condition and of the golden thread of strength of character that ties us all together. Such meditation on life's challenges and values may prompt us to rededicate our lives to those ideas of the good, the true, and the beautiful that any work of art enshrines. What ideals are apparent or implied in *All My Sons*? Honesty, brotherhood, patriotism, and true love, to mention the most obvious ones. ("Tradition and Tragedy in 'All My Sons'" 27)

More recently, Hersh Zeifman discussed the play's extraordinary fusion of form and vision as deriving from the playwright's "rage for order, for an anodyne to [our] 'helplessness before the chaos of existence'" ("All My Sons After the Fall: Arthur Miller and the Rage for Order" 107). In its "relentless Ibsenite . . . linearity, chronology, causality . . . the quest for order is dramatized in the play . . . not only formally but thematically: the conflict between Chris Keller and his father is precisely the struggle between order and chaos"(108). In their "life-

and-death struggle of ethics and values," the Kellers present audiences with an important lesson about "relatedness" and the necessity for "a connection with the larger family of humanity" (108). The conflict they experience speaks directly to every member of the audience, for as Robert A. Martin points out,

> Miller's great achievement as a playwright allows us to see and understand particular characters or groups of characters as possessing universal, human traits, even as we also see how their lives illuminate, by association, our own lives as individuals and as members of our larger society. In recognizing these larger concerns, we recognize as well that Miller's plays are not exclusively about individuals, but more precisely, are about humanity and human societies with all their contradictions and complications. ("The Nature of Tragedy" 98)

Nowhere is this aspect of Miller's drama more evident than in his masterpiece, *Death of a Salesman*, for in its searing portrait of a family in conflict, Miller achieves a near-perfect synthesis of the social, moral, psychological, personal, and metaphysical levels of experience, and shows how the death of a single individual touches everyone in his family and audiences that witness his tragic collapse.

Much like *All My Sons*, *Death of a Salesman* presents us with an individual, and a family, that have lost their ability to separate fact from fiction, truth from lies, reality from illusion. The Lomans are so deeply entrenched in the life-lie they have embraced that they find it nearly impossible to communicate with each other without resorting to the clichéd rhetoric they have imbibed from the prevailing success myths in their capitalistic society. *Death of a Salesman* is possibly Arthur Miller's greatest play. It has been called the quintessentially American play, and perhaps it has generated more critical and scholarly discussion over the efficacy of the popular concept of the American Dream than any other work of literature dealing with American society. Studies of this play invariably discuss Willy Loman's self-delusion and moral confusion in relation to Miller's indictment of the competitive, capitalistic society that is responsible for dehumanizing the individual and transforming the once promising agrarian American dream into an urban nightmare. But whether it is approached as a tragedy of the common man, a social drama indicting capitalism and American business ethics, a sociological consideration of work alienation and its impact on identity, a cultural critique of the American family and stereotypical gender roles in American society, a modern morality play about today's Everyman, or a complex psychological study of guilt, repression, and psychosis, *Death of a Salesman* is a compelling drama that makes for an intensely moving and hauntingly memorable theatrical experience. Despite its overwhelming sense of tragic inevitability, the play gains most of its power from Miller's ability to turn the self-destructive journey of Willy Loman into a tribute to the worth and nobility of the human spirit. Even in the very process of showing the devastating consequences that result when the individual succumbs to the lure of denial and self-delusion, *Death of a Salesman* somehow manages to affirm the value of human life and the potential for every individual to strive to achieve the impossible dream of human perfectibility.

Miller's masterpiece tells the story of the irrepressible sixty-three-year-old traveling salesman, Willy Loman, who strives to retrieve his lost dignity and his family's love on the last day of his life. This icon of the American theater represents every person, both in American society and throughout the world, who has ever felt displaced from his rightful position in his society and longed to attain a sense of peace and belonging in a world that suddenly seems foreign and even hostile to his pretensions. Using a highly suggestive multiple set to emphasize the subjective nature of the play, Miller collapses past and present and takes us inside the mind of Willy Loman to show us how an individual nurtured on success-formula platitudes and get-rich-quick schemes buys fully into the notion of the American Dream without ever really evaluating or understanding how false and incomplete are the values he embraces in his venal American society. Desperate to make sense of his life and to avoid seeing himself as a failure, both as salesman and father, Willy Loman tries to escape the burden of responsibility for the choices he has made and, instead, seeks facile solutions to complex personal and economic problems. Willy's painful struggle "to evaluate himself justly" ("Tragedy," *Theater Essays* 4) is what grips audiences around the world, for everyone, not just people who are culturally or ideologically predisposed to embrace the American Dream, can understand the anguish that derives from "being torn away from our chosen image of what and who we are in this world" ("Tragedy," *Theater Essays* 5).

During this last day in his life, Willy drifts back and forth between the past and the present, groping for answers to his problematic relationship with his son Biff, and futilely trying to ease his conscience about past indiscretions and missed opportunities that he fears have cost him the love, respect, and honor that society has trained him to expect as customary entitlements for male heads of household in the American family. As he sets up and then destroys opportunities for disclosures that would reveal his role in creating the destiny he seeks to avoid, Willy repeatedly attempts to deny his role in any wrongdoing in the past that would demand his acknowledgment and acceptance of responsibility for his own, and his sons', failures. He tries to preserve an inflated image of himself as both salesman and father and convince others that the identity he has manufactured is real. As a result of submerging himself so thoroughly in his life-lie, Willy experiences a complete disengagement from reality and virtually drives himself mad. His psychological disorientation is strongly evoked in the play's setting, lighting, music, and dramatic structure, particularly in director Robert Falls' postmodernist set design for the play in 1999, which vividly conveys and externalizes the fragmentation rending Willy apart and driving him inevitably to his tragic suicide.

Again, one has to wonder how a play that depicts the unmitigated frustration and failure of delusional and desperate characters can succeed in conveying any sense of hope and possibility for its audiences.

According to Zygmunt Adamczewski, Willy's tragic suicide "gives poignancy to existence in protest" as an individual who senses "the loss of his self," the fact that "he is not what he is" (*Tragic Protest* 190, 191). In other words, Willy's tragic protest comments on the paradoxical condition that defines human existence: the constant struggle within the individual between self and society, right and wrong, love and hate, joy and sorrow, consciousness and unconsciousness, work and play, success and failure, past and present, life and death. Life is flux, and human life is frequently characterized by internal conflict. If the value of a human life may ultimately be determined by the extent to which an individual struggles against contradictory and entropic impulses in an effort to give existence purpose and meaning, then it is easy to see why *Death of a Salesman* is so popular and successful and moves audiences around the world with its searing presentation of the Loman tragedy. Willy Loman's battle is everyone's battle, for despite his particular failings and annoying eccentricities, Willy's futile attempt to resist reduction and atomization, and his constant flight from his alienated condition, reflect a universal need for personal triumph over the forces that deny individuality and threaten to diminish our humanity. Life is change: conflict, tension, a war of wills and desires, an everlasting struggle to bring order to chaos and impose meaning on a fundamentally absurd world. It is the entropic condition that Willy Loman resists, and because of Willy's fierce determination to fight an impossible battle against the inherent conditions of human existence, Miller tells us that "There is a nobility . . . in Willy's struggle" (*Beijing* 27). Willy, explains Miller, "is trying to lift up a belief in immense redeeming human possibilities" (*Beijing* 29). That is the attraction and glory of Willy Loman: his limitless hope in the face of hopelessness and refusal to accept defeat even when thoroughly defeated. Willy's persistent struggle to resist the force of entropy in his life is ultimately what defines the tragic spirit of Miller's vision in *Death of a Salesman*.

Miller's play gives us an unblinking look at the terrifying darkness that lies coiled within existence. Attendant to this dark vision is the discovery that the light enkindled by human kindness and love can give human life a brilliance and luster that will never be extinguished. Willy dies, but death does not defeat Willy Loman; as the Requiem demonstrates, Willy will continue to live on in the memories and lives of others. Through his remarkable fusion of opposites that express both the form and the vision of the play, Miller reveals the condition of tension that is life and human existence. Because of its perfect integration of form, character, and action, *Death of a Salesman* is a modern masterpiece that celebrates, as Chris Bigsby eloquently states, "the miracle of human life, in all its bewilderments, its betrayals, its denials, but, finally, and most significantly, its transcendent worth" ("Poet" 723).

"*The Crucible*," writes Miller, "is, internally, *Salesman*'s blood brother. It is examining the questions I was absorbed with before—the conflict between a man's raw deeds and his conception of himself, the question of whether conscience is in fact an organic part of the human being, and what happens when it is handed over not merely to the state or the mores of the time but to one's friend or wife" ("Brewed in *The Crucible*," *Theater Essays* 172-173). The powerful manner in which *The Crucible* explores these questions explains why it is also regarded as a masterpiece of the modern stage. *The Crucible* is Arthur Miller's most frequently produced play and speaks to people all over the world of the need to resist tyranny and oppression. Miller's play transcends cultural and geographical boundaries with its inspired depiction of one man's heroic struggle to preserve his honor when threatened by a corrupt state authority. With its intense dramatic action and its absorbing look at the debilitating effects of guilt, fear, repression, personal betrayal, mass hysteria, and public confession, *The Crucible* shows how an individual can rise above the conditions surrounding him and transform guilt into responsibility and thereby defeat the deterministic forces, both within and outside him, that threaten to destroy his identity as well as his humanity.

The Crucible dramatizes one of the darkest episodes in American history: the Salem Witch Trials of 1692. Making just a few alterations to the historical record in the interest of intensifying the play's dramatic action and clarifying and revealing the characters' hidden motivation, Miller shows what happens when girls in the repressive Puritan community of Salem Village in 1692 make unfounded accusations of witchcraft against their neighbors. Hundreds are arrested and convicted of witchcraft and nineteen innocent people are hanged. Among those incarcerated is John Proctor, a citizen of the community, a successful farmer and landowner who has committed adultery with Abigail Williams, one of the principal accusers and witnesses for the state. Proctor's guilt over his infidelity and conviction that he is a sinner, and therefore not like the falsely accused, temporarily causes him to sign a phony confession of witchcraft in an effort to save his life and protect his family. But when he realizes that his confession must be made public and therefore will be used to damage the credibility of his friends and neighbors and justify their persecution, Proctor fiercely denounces the court and tears up his confession. In a powerful dramatic scene, Proctor insists that his name not be used to damage the reputation of others, and even though his inspiring act of courage and nobility leads directly to his execution, it simultaneously becomes the basis for his own personal redemption.

Ironically, because of Proctor's defiant act of heroism and decision to die a noble death rather than live ignobly, it is easier to see how *The Crucible* demonstrates the possibility for human transcendence than is at first evident in both *All My Sons* and *Death of a Salesman*. Yet the conditions for such individualistic behavior are certainly far less favorable in the Puritan community of 1692 that Miller dramatizes in *The Crucible* than in the American society of the 1940s he depicts in *All My Sons* and *Death of a Salesman*. Because Salem Village was a theocracy, every facet of an individual's life in that community could arguably be seen as demonstrating the inevitable intersection of the societal and personal dimensions of a person's experience. In essence, everything a person said or did in Salem Village in 1692 could have been construed as having a direct bearing on society and, therefore, would unquestionably receive the close scrutiny of the larger community. Yet, in spite of the strong limitations and constraints placed on an individual's personal liberties and freedoms in that society, John Proctor is able to rise above the deterministic conditions surrounding him and find the courage and strength needed to denounce the court's inane proceedings. Through the crucible of his personal suffering, Proctor embraces values that are life-affirming, and with his acceptance of his personal responsibility for the welfare of others, Proctor defeats death and wins a victory for humankind.

Perhaps the situation that was most inimical to the potentialities of the human spirit in the twentieth century was the Holocaust. Yet, even in this most disturbing spectacle of human depravity and unspeakable atrocity, Miller finds hope for the triumph of the human spirit. As Edward Isser rightly asserts, "Arthur Miller is perhaps the foremost spokesman for a universalist and humanistic interpretation of the Holocaust" ("Arthur Miller and the Holocaust" 155). This horrible testament to human depravity and the capacity for evil and despicable acts of human aggression looms large in three plays, a novel, a screenplay, and even an autobiography by Miller.

Miller first tackles this subject in his novel *Focus* (1945), which establishes strong parallels between the Nazi movement in Europe and the Anti-Semitism promoted in America by the Christian Front and other hate groups who persecuted Jews during the Second World War. Only after experiencing the unjust persecution that results from being mistakenly identified as a Jew does the novel's central character find the courage to stand up to the fascists persecuting Jews in his neighborhood, and counter their barbaric behavior with socially responsible action. In *After the Fall*, Miller creates even greater discomfort for his audiences by asking them to find within themselves the locus of evil that gives rise to such movements as nazism and the terrible hate crimes associated with the Holocaust. To concretize this direct association between private and public acts of aggression, the silhouette of a concentration camp tower is illuminated periodically in *After the Fall*, as the play's central character, Quentin, struggles to understand why his own personal acts of betrayal and cruelty are linked in his mind with the horrors that occurred at Auschwitz and other concentration camps. Quentin ultimately accepts his culpability in the horrors he detests because he realizes that no one is innocent after the fall. In *Incident at Vichy*, detainees awaiting interrogation by their Nazi captors are fearful that, if discovered to be Jews, they will be sent in locked boxcars to concentration camps in Poland for extermination. Each prisoner adopts what ultimately amounts to an ineffective strategy for explaining his captivity and dealing with the absurd impending interrogation. One by one, they are treated inhumanely by their captors, checked for circumcision, and then sent to certain death in the camps. Only one prisoner, the psychiatrist Leduc, is able to elude this horrible destiny as a result of the heroic and noble sacrifice of an Austrian Prince, who hands over his pass to freedom and courageously proves that it is possible to resist tyranny and oppression by transforming guilt into responsibility.

The advent of the Holocaust is the subject of *Broken Glass*. The play's central character, Sylvia Gellburg, suffers severe hysterical paralysis as she learns that old Jews and young children are being abused and ridiculed in Germany during *Kristallnacht*. Her anxiety over their condition and unconscious association of the Nazis' cruelty with her husband's abusive treatment of her and condescension toward Jews triggers the emotional disorder that leaves her physically incapacitated until her husband's unexpected death. Perhaps, though, Miller's most disturbing and direct treatment of the Holocaust occurs in his television screenplay adaptation of Fania Fénelon's memoirs: *Playing for Time*. This brutally frank depiction of the anguish and heroism of a woman captive in a concentration camp during the Second World War celebrates the courage and nobility of spirit exhibited by an individual who refuses to relinquish her dignity and act in a way that degrades the human species. In spite of the unspeakable horrors and ordeals she faces and the severe constraints imposed on her by her captors, her environment, and her impossible situation, Fania Fénelon, says Miller, shows that "it was possible to exercise free will even in a concentration camp" (quoted in Atlas 32).

Among other things, says Miller, his Holocaust drama teaches us an important lesson about ourselves:

> that we should see the bestiality in our own hearts, so that we should know how we are brothers not only to these victims but to the Nazis, so that the ultimate tenor of our lives should be faced—namely our own sadism, our own fear of standing firm on humane principles against the obscene power of mass organization. ("The Shadow of the Gods," *Theater Essays* 187)

The lessons do not end there. In his Holocaust drama, as in all of his other plays, the twin pillars on which his characters' personal morality rests are freedom and responsibility. As a character struggles not only to survive but also to do so with honor and integrity, Fania Fénelon demonstrates that it is imperative that the individual accept the possibility for free, and responsible, choices and behavior. In *Playing for Time*, Fania Fénelon counters the evil darkness of the Nazis with her commitment to a morality that fosters and promotes compassion, understanding, tolerance, honesty, and self-discipline. She selects and upholds values that ennoble the human species and affirm the value and importance of every individual life. In the most abhorrent conditions that are most inimical to the exercise of free will, a concentration camp prisoner finds it possible to prove that human beings are capable of the most courageous moral action even when faced with the threat of imminent death.

By writing so powerfully about the Holocaust, Miller may be suggesting that though art cannot guarantee the survival of humanity, it can help to justify and validate the worth of human existence. Miller clearly creates art for life's sake. He once said that the Great Depression made him "impatient with anything, including art, which pretends that it can exist for its own sake and still be of prophetic importance" ("The Shadows of the Gods," *Theater Essays* 179). For Miller, literature, and particularly the theater, must "speak to the present condition of man's life and thus would implicitly have to stand against injustice as the destroyer of life" (*Timebends* 596). Nowhere is this commitment made more evident than in his harrowing screenplay of humanity's darkest hour and greatest triumph. In the midst of a hellish landscape of human suffering and depravity, one woman faced the ultimate challenge to her dignity and proved that nothing, not even the threat of a horrible death, could force the individual to act ignobly or relinquish her sense of personal responsibility. Fania Fénelon' s triumph is ultimately a triumph of the human spirit—one that Miller presents dramatically to confirm the possibility of giving meaning and dignity to human existence.

Regardless of the conditions and limitations on the individual in Miller's plays, his characters have the ability to choose the course of action that determines their values and behavior. The moral truth that speaks so loudly in Miller's plays derives from a single premise: we are free to create our destinies. His characters have the ability to face and accept what is real and thereby to discover the truth about their lives and identities. Although characters like Joe Keller, Willy Loman, Eddie Carbone, and Lyman Felt do not exercise their freedom to choose honestly and responsibly, that fact does not mitigate the possibility for such expression of their free will to occur.

Bigsby has long maintained that for Arthur Miller the theater has always been "a realm of possibility" (*American Drama* 248). By creating plays that show the human will as inexhaustible and irrepressible, Miller expresses a vision of humanity that shows that transcendence is coexistent with consciousness, and this special attribute of human existence both curses and blesses humanity because it invariably sets us off on a lifelong journey to attain the impossible dream—a more-than-American dream for perfection. Struggle endows our lives with meaning; the theater of Arthur Miller offers the following message to his audience: as long as we continue to wrestle with our givens, resist the forces of chaos and entropy, and struggle to impose order on the natural world and our mental landscape, we will have an opportunity, a possibility, for a meaningful life. No easy task, admits the playwright, but entirely within the realm of the possible.

Works Cited

Adamczewski, Zygmunt. *The Tragic Protest*. The Hague: Martinus Nijhoff, 1963.

Atlas, James. "The Creative Journey of Arthur Miller Leads Back to Broadway and TV." *New York Times* 28 September 1980, Sec. 2:1+.

Barth, John. "The Literature of Replenishment: Postmodernist Fiction." *The Friday Book*. Baltimore: Johns Hopkins UP, 1984. 193-206.

Bigsby, Christopher. "A British View of an American Playwright." *The Achievement of Arthur Miller: New Essays*. Ed. Steven R. Centola. Dallas: Contemporary Research P, 1995. 15-29.

_____. "Arthur Miller: Poet." *Michigan Quarterly Review* 37 (Fall 1998): 713-25.

_____. "Arthur Miller: The Moral Imperative." *Modern American Drama, 1945-1990*. Cambridge: Cambridge UP, 1992. 72-125.

Bloom, Clive, ed. Introduction. *American Drama*. New York: St. Martin's P, 1995. 6-20.

Brustein, Robert. "Still Searching for Theater." *New Republic* 3 August 1998: 29-30.

Feingold, Michael. "The Old Miller Stream." *Village Voice* 26 May 1998: 147.

Isser, Edward R. "Arthur Miller and the Holocaust." *Essays in Theatre* 10.2 (May 1992): 155-64.

Loughlin, Richard L. "Tradition and Tragedy in *All My Sons*." *English Record* 14 (February 1964): 23-27.

Martin, Robert A. "The Nature of Tragedy." *South Atlantic Review* 61 (1996): 97-106.

Miller, Arthur. "Brewed in *The Crucible*." *The Theater Essays of Arthur Miller*. Edited by Robert A. Martin and Steven R. Centola. New York: Da Capo P, 1996. 172-74.

_____. *Echoes Down the Corridor*. New York: Viking, 2000.

_____. "Foreword to *After the Fall*." *The Theater Essays of Arthur Miller*. 255-57.

_____. Interview with Steve Centola. Roxbury, Connecticut, 9 August 2001.

_____. *Mr. Peters' Connections*. New York. Penguin, 1999.

_____. *Salesman in Beijing*. New York: Viking, 1984.

_____. "On Screenwriting and Language." *Everybody Wins*. New York: Grove Press, 1990. v-xiv.

_____. "The Shadows of the Gods." *The Theater Essays of Arthur Miller*. 174-94.

_____. "The State of the Theater." Interview with Henry Brandon. *The Theater Essays of Arthur Miller*. 223-36.

_____. *Timebends: A Life*. New York: Grove P, 1987.

_____. "Tragedy and the Common Man." *The Theater Essays of Arthur Miller*. 3-7.

Raine, Nina, and Frances Stonor Saunders. "Miller's Tale." *New Statesman* 14 August 2000: 30-32.

Zeifman, Hersh. "All My Sons After the Fall: Arthur Miller and the Rage for Order." *The Theatrical Gamut: Notes for a Post-Beckettian Stage*. Ed. Enoch Brater. Ann Arbor: U of Michigan P, 1995. 107-20.

Arthur Miller:
Un-American[1]

Christopher Bigsby

When Arthur Miller died, fifty-six years to the day after the Broadway opening of *Death of a Salesman*, he prompted the kind of respect we have come to expect from certain sections of the American media. According to the *New York Times*, "Even in his finest work, he sometimes succumbed to overstatement. . . . Themes, motifs, moral conclusions often glare from his plays like neon signs in a diner window." The on-line *Wall Street Journal* headed its assessment of America's leading playwright: "The Great Pretender: Arthur Miller Wasn't Well Liked— and for good reason." It went on to ask, "How much attention would now be paid to Miller if he hadn't married Monroe?" For its part, the *New Criterion* marked Miller's passing with an article headed, "Arthur Miller: Communist Stooge," and accused him of being the "source of radical chic clichés."

These were not typical but they did offer a reminder of the fact that he had often worked in a hostile critical environment. At the memorial held in New York's Majestic Theatre, Edward Albee felt obliged to confront the *New Criterion*'s hostility, being, in turn, dismissed by the magazine as a representative of "the left-liberal glitterati of yesteryear." But, then, Miller did engage, for much of his life, in a debate with America and its values, challenging its myths, confronting it with disquieting realities. In a country which Willy Loman described as "the greatest country in the world" (a phrase which drops with ease from the lips of successive Presidents), Miller could tell you the number of children who went to bed hungry every night and, on a visit to Turkey with Harold Pinter, upbraided the American ambassador for his country's collusion with torturers. No wonder the right-wing *New Criterion* recognised a natural enemy. There is a novel by Walter Abish called *How German Is It?* I want to ask of Arthur Miller, how American was he?

Every day, American children stand up in their classrooms, place their hands on the hearts and intone the Pledge of Allegiance, I suspect never asking themselves why they do so or even realising that similar ceremonies are not carried out in other countries. Incidentally, in the 1930s they held their hands out in what looked so like a Nazi salute that it was decided that your home is where your heart is. They affirm their allegiance to the flag of the United States (that phrase, "of the United States" was added, incidentally, when it was discovered that while affirming a unified country individuals were actually thinking of the flag of Italy, Germany, or even, heaven forbid, the United Kingdom).

During World War II, Miller wrote a radio play (*In the Beginning Was the Word*) in which the Bill of Rights is suspended and a man is assaulted for failing to salute the flag. Things have not changed much. Not so long ago, Congress was asked to pass a bill making it an offence to desecrate the flag, quite as if it were a fragment of the true cross. So, children pledge allegiance to the flag of the United States and the country for which it stands, one nation, under God, indivisible (or, as a young Miller thought, in a dirigible), with liberty and justice for all. Why else would they do so, however, if virtually every phrase of that pledge were not contestable. One nation? Indivisible? Under God? With liberty and justice for all? This is not the place for me to point out the divisions within the United States. Red and blue election maps are a ready reminder, as are the divisions of race which mean that only one television show appears on both the top ten watched by black Americans and the top ten watched by white Americans (the bad news being that it is *CSI*). A recent book, by Samuel Huntington, which deals, with a curious sense of alarm, with the rise in the percentage of Hispanics, is called *Who Are We*—228 years after the Declaration of Independence, while a review was headed "José can you see?" the joke turning on the fact that José is, indeed, now the most popular name in both California and Florida. Nor do I need to underline the threat to liberty represented by the Patriot Act and Guantánamo Bay, with their suspension of due process, nor the lack of access to justice by whole sections of American society.

But where would that pledge of allegiance place Arthur Miller who, as a Jew, grew up to find himself excluded from many universities, jobs and hotels in this country, an atheist who is told that it is unthinkable that a President of the United States should not be in daily dialogue with God and that religion should invade schools as it already has Congress and the White House? And who can forget the sight of Richard Nixon on his knees beside Henry Kissinger?—one guilty of a felony, the other, arguably, of war crimes. What price liberty and justice for all for a man hauled before a Committee (whose Senate equivalent included both Richard Nixon and Robert Kennedy) which declared him un-American, which told him that betrayal was the sign of a real American and withdrew from him that sign of a citizen, a passport? And this, incidentally, was the time when that phrase "Under God" was intruded into a pledge of allegiance which celebrated a country which in its founding documents established the separation of church and state. Why was it introduced then? Because during the Cold War there was a battle going on with godless communism, just as today militant Christianity is invoked as Islam is perceived as the primary threat. But how American was Arthur Miller or, perhaps more usefully, what have American attitudes been towards a man who in 1999 was voted by British playwrights, directors, actors, critics and reviewers, the leading playwright of the 20th century but who saw play after play close within days in New York over a period of some thirty years and was not merely dismissed but abused?

The truth is that he ran into trouble early on. When he left university, he already had an FBI file for his opposition to the Fascists in Spain. He wrote to the President of the United States and received a reply helpfully informing him that his letter had been forwarded to the Bureau. The first play he submitted for Broadway production was rejected by producers as "too Jewish," though those producers were themselves Jewish. Why, then, reject a fellow Jew's play? Because there was fierce anti-Semitism, especially in New York, and because Jews were anxious for it not to be felt that they were trying to get America entangled in a European war. This was a country, remember, in which one of the most popular radio programmes was that featuring the Christian priest Father Coughlin who borrowed his rhetoric from Joseph Goebbels, and in which President Roosevelt was known to many as President Rosenfeld. In his 2005 novel, *The Plot Against America*, Philip Roth recalled that time in a fabricated past which sees the Jews driven out of New York as Charles Lindbergh becomes President of the United States. But, lest this might seem absurd, the fact is that the proposal that he should become president was actually made and the relevant dialogue in the book is authentic. It was Alfred Kazin who recalled that "three months after Pearl Harbor, Charles Lindbergh, at an America First rally had threatened the 'Jewish race'" insisting that "instead of agitating for war, the Jewish groups in this country should be opposing it in every possible way, for they will be the first to feel its consequences."

Miller's 1945 novel, *Focus*, was an attack on American anti-Semitism, which might be thought an odd book to publish as a war against fascism came to its end but he wrote it, he explained, when "a sensible person could wonder if such a right of Jews to exist had any reality at all. . . . Roosevelt, friend of Jews, had denied landing privileges to the *St. Louis*, the ship carrying a couple of hundred Jews allowed to leave by the Germans." In 1938, 67% of Americans voted to exclude Jews entirely in the knowledge that a high proportion of those fleeing persecution were Jewish. The following year, 83% opposed easing immigration quotas. In August, 1941, four months before Pearl Harbour, the *Telegraph Register* published an editorial which predicted that, "If this country goes to war, we predict that opposition to the Jews will gain uncontrollable momentum." On a trip south for the Library of Congress in 1941, Miller himself was threatened by a man with a shotgun who thought that the federal insignia on the side of his vehicle was a sure sign that he was Jewish. But it was not only the South. New Jersey, Miller recalled, was Ku Klux Klan territory.

From Italy, meanwhile, came radio broadcasts; in one, in March

1942, Ezra Pound declared: "Had you the sense to eliminate Roosevelt and the Jews at the last election, you would not now be at war. . . . The 60 kikes who started this war might be sent to St. Helena as a measure of world prophylaxis and some super-kikes or non-Jewish kikes along with them." As Miller was to say of Pound, "He knew all America's weaknesses and he played them as expertly as Goebbels ever did." Later, Pound was awarded the Bollingen Prize, and lest it might be thought that Pound was entirely at odds with Americans back home, in 1940, a *Fortune* magazine poll asked Americans if they had heard any criticism of Jews in the previous month. 46% said they had. By 1946, a year after the war and the publication of *Focus*, the figure had reached 64%. In 1944, the army magazine, *Yank*, decided not to run a story about Nazi atrocities against the Jews because of latent anti-Semitism in the Army. The reporter, it was decided, should "get something with a less Semitic slant."

In 1945 *PM* magazine reported the contents of a US Armed Forces correspondence course which observed that "the Jew is an offensive fellow unwelcome in this country. . . . The Gentile fears, and with reason, the competition of the Jew in business and despises him as a matter of course." The Jew, in other words, was un-American, and Miller was a Jew. As late as 1962, on the occasion of an NBC adaptation of *Focus*, an entry in Miller's FBI file described it as "strictly Communist propaganda" aimed at fostering "race hatred between Jews and Gentiles."

In 2003 some of the tape recordings made by Richard Nixon in the White House came into the public domain. The tapes reveal Billy Graham, unofficial pastor to a succession of presidents, as remarking that, "the Bible says here are Satanic Jews and that's where our problem arises," while Nixon, President of the United States of America, can be heard saying, "the Jews are an irreligious, atheistic, immoral bunch of bastards." Which situates Arthur Miller, Jew, not merely as un-American, but as an immoral bastard.

Not that Miller was failing to play into the hands of those who would later accuse him of anti-Americanism. In 1947, the year of his first great success, *All My Sons*, the Communist *Daily Worker* saluted him for his play *You're Next*, which attacked the House Un-American Activities Committee. It was sponsored by Stage for Action, a Communist group, and performed four hundred times that year. In September, he attended an open rally sponsored by the Jewish chapter of the Congress of American Women at which he made a presentation to the Head of the League of Polish Women. The Congress was placed on the Attorney General's List and classified as a Communist organisation. In November he published a piece in *Jewish Life* which the California Committee on Un-American Activities designated as a Communist publication. He also attended a dinner of the American Russia Institute which his FBI file noted fell within the purview of Executive Order 9835 and which had been classified as Communist. He did all this in the year he finally broke through into the Broadway theatre with *All My Sons*.

It was in 1947 that President Truman had approved the introduction of a loyalty investigation for anyone entering civilian employment in any department or agency of the Executive branch of the Federal Government. Within two years of the end of the war, a new war was under way, a cold war. The Soviet Union, a wartime ally, was now the enemy, the Soviet Union which for Miller, as for many others, had, during the 1930s, been a working model of Marxist principles and which had then been such a force during the war that it might have been lost without it. In a recent American poll half of respondents did not know that the Soviet Union had been on the same side as the Americans. Meanwhile, many of those who had been on the left in the 1930s moved across to the right. These were to be the neo-cons of that period, more fiercely antagonistic to their former allies than those previously on the right. Often they moved right by way of Trotskyism. These would become the new super-patriots, a few going on to take part in covert actions designed to undermine the left, at home and abroad, by subverting American cultural life. A number of these would regard Miller as the enemy and their reviews of his work would often carry a special venom. *Partisan Review* became a focus for some of these, a magazine that failed to review *All My Sons, The Crucible* and *A View from the Bridge* while publishing a spiteful review of *Death of a Salesman*.

Not that responses to *All My Sons* had been unanimously positive. The *New York Herald Tribune* review of that and another play was headed, "Two More Duds," while *The Daily Mirror*'s review was headlined, "All My Sons Not Very Convincing." The *Daily News* offered a variation: "A Lot Goes On But Little Happens in Backyard Drama." *The Nation* review was a little more disturbing. Its reviewer noted that it "seems rather unnecessarily to express explicitly his warm respect for all the leftist pieties."

Meanwhile, the US army banned *All My Sons* from production at its bases in Europe following an article in the *New York Journal American* which warned of the army's purchase of a "Pro-Red Play." The same article revealed that Miller was a "member of several Red Fascist organizations and a contributor to the *New Masses*, official Communist Magazine." *Counter Attack*, an anti-Communist newsletter, insisted that the play "would help Stalin in his efforts to convince the Germans that the U.S. is controlled by heartless plutocrats." Miller, it helpfully explained, was a "COMMUNIST PLAYWRIGHT." The National Commander of the Catholic Veterans sent a telegram to the Secretary of War demanding to know who was responsible for the approval of the play. And in case you are thinking that the army is not usually known for its theatrical commitment, in a ruined post-war Europe productions had to be licensed and performances on army bases were frequently the only ones available. Why was it banned? Because it was thought that a play which suggested that there were corrupt capitalists in the United States could be seen as un-American; that it might, in particular, push Europeans into the hands of the communists, and this was a time when bribery, private and public, was being used by the US government, to stop the Italians from voting for the communists.

Miller thus found that a play that was popular at home was banned abroad by the American authorities, a ban supported by *The New Leader* magazine which agreed that the play would inflame European feeling against the United States. "The 'calumniators' of this country," it asserted, "have enough ammunition . . . without our wrapping it in 'prize' packages for foreign convenience in propaganda and gloating." At the same time, a copy of the screenplay for *All My Sons* fell into the hands of an FBI source in Hollywood who denounced it as "the product of a thorough-going Collectivist philosophy," suggesting that all industrialists are "criminal monsters." The agent then proceeded to identify a cast member of the film as a member of the Los Angeles Communist Party. When I showed Miller this document he said, "I think it will give you a pretty good sense of where things were leading up to *The Crucible*." Incidentally, it was not only the FBI which was positioning Miller as an Un-American. Jack Warner, head of Warner Brothers, in a secret session of HUAC, denounced it and identified Elia Kazan as "one of the mob."

Miller followed the success of *All My Sons* with the dramatically more original *Death of a Salesman*, seemingly about a salesman destroyed by his too complete embrace of the American dream, at least as he interprets it. But salesmen were the storm-birds of capitalism, generating the demand which justified supply and was America not launched on one of the greatest booms in its history? Meanwhile, here was a playwright suggesting that cars and refrigerators were always breaking down and that employers had no loyalty to loyal staff, even if they were apparently psychotic. Accordingly, that organisation renowned for its sophisticated critical capacity, those most loyal of loyal Americans and hence those most ready to ex-communicate those whose patriotism was regarded as suspect, and deny them First Amendment rights, the American Legion, organised picketing of the road version of the play, effectively urging Americans not to attend the work of an ostensibly American playwright, but, then, the definition of the word 'American' was already narrowing.

The film version, which Miller intensely disliked, besides provoking the studio quickly to shoot and distribute a film to show alongside *Salesman* stressing the importance and delights of being a salesman, would prompt another FBI memo which noted that its producer had taught at the Los Angeles Communist training school and that Miller had a long record of supporting Communist fronts; not, as it happened, untrue.

Not all reviewers were positive about the stage production of *Salesman*. The *Hudson Review* found it trite, devoid of merit. *The Nation* thought it unpoetic and unmemorable. Eric Bentley thought it displayed bad poetry while any virtues it might have must have come from Kazan, and Miller sued him for saying so. Mary McCarthy suggested that it was "enfeebled" by its author's desire for universality, a code word then for Marxist beliefs. Willy Loman, she suggested, was no more than a "suffering statistic."

Partisan Review's Eleanor Clark, a Trotskyite married to one of Trotsky's secretaries, who had served in the OSS during the war, dismissed it as boring, stuffed full of gloom, the product of a second-rate mind. It was, she explained, "of course the capitalist system that has done Willy in; the scene in which he is brutally fired after some forty years with the firm comes straight from the party literature of the 'thirties, and the idea emerges lucidly enough through all the confused motivations of the play that it is our particular form of money economy that has bred the absurdly false values of both father and sons." The play, she concludes, displays an "intellectual muddle and a lack of candor regardless of Mr. Miller's conscious intent [that] are the main earmark of contemporary fellow traveling." Later, Robert Brustein, consistently hostile to Miller, attacked it as a "social realist melodrama" about a man who is a victim of "a ruthless, venal and corrupt system." Miller, he insisted, like O'Casey, confronted audiences "less with works of art than political acts."

It is true that Miller was less than wise in 1949 when he attended the Waldorf Conference on World Peace, a patent communist front event. His Marxism of the 1930s and his awareness of the gallantry of Soviet forces in the Second World War meant that he was not willing to perform the sudden conversion which presented the Soviet Union as the new enemy, which in fact it was, while former Nazis were welcomed in providing that they had skills of the kind America needed. Among their number was Wernher von Braun, whose rockets, built by slave labour, had killed thousands in England. He now began the work that would one day lead the American flag to be planted on the moon and Neil Armstrong to fluff the only line he was required to deliver.

At that same conference, however, were gathered together those former communists who would now be among Miller's leading critics, and members of the recently born CIA, with brown paper bags of cash to pay for a spoiling campaign by those members of the New York intellectuals who now had a new cause. Some of these became part of that illegal CIA operation, finally exposed in 1967, to infiltrate student and women's organisations, unions and the arts, using the latter, through a series of dummy foundations, to fight a cultural battle with the Soviet Union, even sponsoring a production of *Porgy and Bess*, aware as they were that race was a key area of vulnerability.

Miller's attendance at the Waldorf Conference was helpfully heralded by *Life* magazine, which published photographs of the subversives who would be attending, including Arthur Miller. Afterwards, the New York *Journal American* drew the cultural implications of Miller's attendance to the attention of the American public, suggesting that the man who had suggested that an American industrialist would knowingly sell defective combat equipment to the armed forces had now "lifted the ideological curtain around his identity a bit higher when 'Death of a Salesman' reached Broadway. Here was another picture of doom and gloom in an American family. . . . Suddenly the data on Mr. Miller began to add up to a recognizable pattern. . . . in its negative delineation of American life . . . the play strikes a shrewd blow against the values that have given our way of life its passion and validity."

William Barrett, in *Commentary*, consistently hostile to Miller, spoke of those who attended as Stalin's emissaries while Robert Warshow described Miller as "a danger to culture." *Life*'s after-conference report helpfully identified those involved as willing or unwilling, conscious or unconscious agents of a foreign power. This, then, was Arthur Miller, not merely un-American but anti-American. Eleanor Clark's review of *Death of a Salesman*, incidentally, appeared four months after the play's opening and after the Waldorf Conference.

Not having the sense he was born with, however, Miller now chose to adapt an Ibsen play at the request of two actors—Fredric and Florence March—threatened with blacklisting. Miller had several friends who he had worked with in radio who were already losing their jobs at this time while his own sister, the actress Joan Copeland, herself lost work once her connection to Miller became more widely known.

The play was *An Enemy of the People* and he could hardly have chosen a more appropriate title because that was what he was presented as being when, three years after *The Crucible*, he was summoned before the paradoxically titled House Committee on Un-American Activities and asked to name names, names in which the Committee of course had no interest, neither Miller nor his erstwhile radio and theatre friends ever constituting a threat to the Republic. What, after all, could Sid Caesar, for example, have leaked to the Russians? A Jewish joke. Or Jerome Robbins? A subversive dance step or two.

Response to *The Crucible* was direct and unequivocal. E. G. Marshall, who played the Reverend Hale, was blacklisted, as was Beatrice Straight, who played Elizabeth Proctor, though she cleared herself by paying five hundred dollars. Madeleine Sherwood, who played Abigail, was listed in *Red Channels* as a communist, though largely because she had suggested that actress Lee Grant had attacked HUAC and was blacklisted for ten years. A number of reviews were once again ideologically freighted. The *New York Post* reviewer saw it as a "loaded allegory," while insisting that the real threat lay not at home but in despotic communism. The same point was made by *The New Leader*, which saw the real analogy as the Soviet Union. In the *New Re-*

public Eric Bentley insisted that "It is true that people today are being persecuted on chimerical grounds. It is untrue in that communism is not, to put it mildly, merely a chimera." In his book *What is Theatre?*, he elaborated, "The analogy between 'red-baiting' and witch hunting" could "only seem complete . . . to communists." It was a play, he suggested, "for people who think that pleading the Fifth Amendment is not only a white badge of purity but also a red badge of courage." In *Commentary*, in an article subsequently reprinted and distributed by the CIA supported American Committee for Cultural Freedom as part of its anti-Communist drive, Robert Warshow insisted that the real parallel with Salem was eastern Europe, especially Czechoslovakia. The Salem trials, he insisted, anyway "were not political and had nothing to do with civil rights, unless it is a violation of civil rights to hang a murderer." Which murderer, you might ask? The play, he insisted, offered "a revealing glimpse of the way the Communists and their fellow-travelers have come to regard themselves."

When he was invited to travel to Belgium for the French-language premiere of the play, Miller was denied renewal of his passport. That signal evidence of one's nationality was thus taken away from him before he was officially declared to be un-American when he was later indicted for Contempt of Congress following his HUAC hearing in 1956.

The Crucible did win some awards, but not the Pulitzer (which that year went to William Inge's *Picnic*). In fact, Miller only won one Pulitzer. He did not even win when no other play was deemed worthy. No Pulitzer was awarded in 1947, the year of *All My Sons*, or in 1964, the year of *After the Fall*, or 1968, the year of one of his most successful plays, *The Price*. And this is my larger point.

It was not, as we have seen, only a matter of know-nothing politicians, or self-serving megalomaniac drunks like McCarthy who saw Arthur Miller as being outside the circle of the permissible. Nor was it only the former Trostskyites and those who wrote for *New Leader*, *Commentary* and *Partisan Review*, though they sustained their vendetta a surprisingly long time. In 1997, for example, *Commentary* responded to the new film version of *The Crucible* by saying, "It is hard to believe that audiences were ever moved by this play [which is] so smothered in its unrevealed purpose that it can barely breathe," while, in 2003, it described him as "a strange artefact of an American Left whose formulaic slogans were once a fixture on the cultural scene." The fact is that the echo of these reviews continued to reverberate in subsequent decades with attacks by Susan Sontag, Richard Gilman, Philip Rahv, Walter Kerr, John Simon and others, and in 1984, the American Gerald Bordman would sum up his achievement in the *Oxford Companion to American Theatre* in a devastatingly reductive sentence: "Miller was a firmly committed leftist, whose political philosophising sometimes got the better of his dramaturgy." Note the tense—*was*. Note the year—1984. In 2003, plainly oblivious to this entry, OUP wrote to Miller soliciting an endorsement for a new edition of the book. I pointed out his own entry. He declined to offer an endorsement.

In 1987, *The New Republic* even published a coruscating review of Miller's autobiography, a book otherwise hailed as a classic. The cover promised an article on "the pretensions of an American playwright" while the article itself dismissed *Salesman* as a minor work and *After the Fall* as "a disastrous confessional orgy." "Are we seriously to believe," it asked, "that our country's bands of revolutionary Marxists, who have destroyed whole societies and murdered huge populations, have been merely the maladjusted products of Oedipal problems with Dad? Or that this explains the Marxist political motivations of guilt-ridden, middle-class intellectuals like Miller?" *Commentary*, meanwhile, noted that he had been a Marxist and that Stalin had murdered millions. It denounced all of his work from the 1970s onwards and said that as a playwright he was "drained."

Those who studied *Death of a Salesman* and *The Crucible* in high school and university must have thought that it was impossible for an American writer to be more celebrated. In fact, seldom has an American writer been more vilified or more peremptorily dismissed. In *Par-*

tisan Review Susan Sontag had found *After the Fall* "wretched." Stanley Kauffmann, in *The New Republic* suggested that *Salesman* had always been "a flabby, occasionally false work." In 1972 he said that "Going to Arthur Miller's new play is like going to the funeral of a man you wished you could have liked more. The occasion seals your opinion because there is no hope of change." Struggling to account for Miller's success abroad, he suggested that it was because his language "improves with translation," not, perhaps, an entirely convincing explanation for his success in Britain. Walter Kerr accused him of "wrapping himself in the cloak of seer, prophet, founding father and dormitory prefect." Martin Gottfried, who would go on to write a biography, saw him as "a slackening artist." It may well be, he suggested, "sadly, that the playwright has had his day."

William Dean Howells once remarked that anyone can make an enemy; the problem is to keep him. This was a skill that Miller had evidently acquired with respect to Robert Brustein, who over several decades conducted a sustained critique which amounted to a vendetta. Miller, he insisted, dealt in "domestic realism—plays in which people discuss their problems over hot meals." *After the Fall* was "scandalous," *Incident at Vichy* was "an old dray horse about to be melted down for glue." *The Price*, he suggested, was "impervious to modern moods." For Richard Gilman *A View from the Bridge* was "dismal," *After the Fall* was "not even the simulacrum of a drama," *Incident at Vichy* was "a windy, dated sermon." Delmore Schwartz wrote a review for *Commentary* which referred to the "retarded conscience of Arthur Miller," a piece which became so abusive that even *Commentary* refused to run it, while Leslie Fiedler, another former Trotskyite, described him as "an over-rated playwright, whose dramas were as devious as his public life." A Philip Rahv review of *After the Fall* was headed, "The Myth of Profundity," and described the play as "pretentious and defensive . . . more pitiable than ingratiating." In *Incident at Vichy* he was misinterpreting life and history and attempting to replace analysis of historical forces with moralistic gestures.

Miller himself insisted that a number of his plays, and those of others, had simply been "chewed up and spat out," in America. "Americans," he suggested, "obey criticism as if it were a public duty." He had, he acknowledged, been "invisible in my own country." In a review of *Timebends* a British critic suggested that he had been born in the wrong country. You might think so from the number of performances his plays had in America. *After the Fall* ran for 59 performances, *Incident at Vichy* for 99. *Fame* and *The Reason Why* ran for 3, *The Creation of the World and Other Business* for 20, *Up From Paradise* 5. *The Archbishop's Ceiling* ran for less than four weeks, *The American Clock* for 12 performances. *Broken Glass* had an eight-week run, *Mr. Peters' Connections*, some three weeks, *Resurrection Blues* just over four and *Finishing the Picture* just over six.

And there was something else un-American about him. Americans are dedicated to the pursuit of happiness. You have to be British, or still better German, to realise how strange this is as a national objective. It is not, as Gatsby discovered, that you are dedicated to being happy. Far from it. Americans are dedicated to pursuing happiness, which logically means that happiness itself is a deferred project. What Americans are not is dedicated to a tragic view of life, still less believers in the absurd. When Beckett's *Waiting for Godot* was first staged in America it was not seen as a bleak examination of the paradoxical search for order and meaning in a universe which lacks both. It was advertised as "the laugh sensation of two continents," and starred Bert Lahr and Tom Ewell. One of the reasons Eugene O'Neill despaired of American audiences was that in his view they lacked a tragic sense of life. Fearing that his last plays would prove too depressing for Americans, he left his last plays to be performed in Sweden on the principle, no doubt, that it was impossible to depress Swedes any more than they were already.

There is, it seems to me, too, something un-American about Miller. His models were the playwrights of ancient Greece and Ibsen. Like them, he insisted on the crucial significance of the past but did so in a country which leans into the future. History, Henry Ford memorably remarked, is bunk. This, incidentally, is the same Henry Ford who banned Jews from his plants and published the rabidly anti-Semitic and fraudulent Protocols of the Elders of Zion. For Miller, the past is vital. We contain it. The link between past actions and present consequences constitutes the moral spine of our existence. From time to time Americans are interested in guilt. Why else would psychoanalysts have so many yachts? Miller, though, is interested in responsibility. History, for Miller, is not a juggernaut crushing the bones of those who can do no more than submit to its logic. His is not a theatre of victims, apparently will-less, awaiting compensation for living. Beyond that, there is a natural politics to Miller's work, a social critique of a kind entirely familiar from European theatre. The op-ed pieces he regularly sent off to the *New York Times* are of a piece with his plays.

But, then, his plays have always brought us news, often news from the past, but always bearing on the present. When *Broken Glass*, set in 1938 at the time of Kristallnacht when the destruction of the Jews began, was in rehearsal, ethnic cleansing was in process in Bosnia. And, incidentally, when the play opened in the United States, it did so in New Haven and then moved to New York where it did not do particularly well. It was nominated for, but did not receive, a Tony. In England it opened at the National Theatre and won the Laurence Olivier Award as best play of the year. More plays by Arthur Miller have been staged by the National Theatre than by any other playwright with the single exception of Shakespeare. And that is another clue to his success in Britain. His plays have been produced at the National Theatre, the Royal Shakespeare Company, the Bristol Old Vic, the Young Vic, the West Yorkshire Playhouse—all subsidised theatres. And we have no *New York Times* that can decide whether a play lives or dies, comes into New York or not.

Is Arthur Miller an American playwright? Perhaps not, as judged by those obituaries. I am afraid that we in England rather suspect he is ours. Certainly he has always been granted considerably more respect in Britain than he has here. On his death *The Independent*, a national newspaper in the UK, cleared its front page of news and dedicated it entirely to Miller. But in truth, I have to admit, he is really a playwright for the world. There is no moment when one of his plays is not being performed somewhere. It is true that his reputation in his own country had been recovering, largely, though, I think because of revivals of two of his plays from the 1940s and 50s—*Death of a Salesman* with Brian Dennehy and *The Crucible*, with Liam Neeson, though it is true that *Resurrection Blues* would not be produced in England until 2006, so perhaps the pendulum has swung. Besides, when he died, all manner of people suddenly realised what they should have known all along, that losing Arthur Miller was like losing Chekhov or Ibsen, or Strindberg. And where was he born, where did he grow up, where was he shaped as a man and a writer? Well, even I have to admit that he was made in America. How American was he? As American as a person of that background could be, son of a Polish immigrant, husband to an Austrian woman, who modelled his plays on the ancient Greeks and Ibsen, who wrote plays set in ancient Mexico, late 20th century Czechoslovakia, and Colombia, if you acknowledge that he went out into the world where he fought to release imprisoned writers, if you accept that he was and is a writer for all seasons and all places.

From *The Arthur Miller Journal* 1, no. 1 (2006): 3-17. Copyright © by St. Francis College. Reprinted with permission of *The Arthur Miller Journal*.

Note

1. The following is the text of Christopher Bigsby's keynote address delivered March 4, 2005, at the conference "Writing, Teaching, Performing America" sponsored by the American Theatre and Drama Society at the University of Kansas, Lawrence.

All My Sons and Paternal Authority_____

James A. Robinson

In a 1958 essay, "The Shadows of the Gods," Arthur Miller located the struggle between father and son "at the heart of all human development" because their conflict symbolizes larger issues of power and its renewal. The son's "struggle for mastery—for the freedom of manhood," the playwright asserted, "is the struggle not only to overthrow authority but to reconstitute it anew" (*Theatre Essays*, 185, 193). *All My Sons* (1946) and *Death of a Salesman* (1948), as well as the earlier, unproduced "They Too Arise" (1938), all concentrate in different ways on the battle between a father and two sons to reconstitute authority. This issue lies at the heart of *All My Sons* in particular, where the father-son relationship is linked to the play's central themes: the inseparability of past and present, and the connectedness of man to man. The past abuse of power by the father, Joe Keller, has not only killed innocent American fighter pilots, but brought about the death of his younger son Larry; the present discovery of that abuse outrages the surviving son Chris, whose accusations help precipitate his father's suicide. The play appears to repudiate the father's authority and reconstitute it in Chris, the idealistic proponent of brotherhood and social responsibility.

The repudiation and reconstitution, however, are riddled with ambivalence, as signaled both by the abruptness of the ending and by fundamental flaws in Chris's moral character. That ambivalence points to Miller's anxiety about the usurpation of authority, a disquietude produced partially by his own relationship with his father, but mostly by the conflict among Jewish, modernist and liberal elements within his own vision. The Jewish traditionalist yearns for the unimpeded passage of authority from generation to generation, seeing it as sanction for other human connections. The modernist suspects discontinuity and fragmentation are the ultimate reality, while the liberal strives to assert the value of brotherhood in the face of this chaos. The relationship between Joe and Chris Keller in *All My Sons* provides an intriguing early arena for this unresolved tension—one whose implications obviously go well beyond the vision of Arthur Miller.

The conflict between these impulses issues from Miller's identity as a contemporary Jewish American; and before turning to the text of the play, it may be helpful to explore its cultural sources at some length. Miller himself, it should be noted, has generally discouraged this approach, stressing instead the universality of the father-son conflict. In a 1966 interview, the playwright typically claimed that the father-son relationship was "a very primitive thing in my plays. That is, the father was really a figure who incorporated both power and some kind of moral law which he had either broken or fallen prey to. He figures as an immense shadow.... The reason that I was able to write about the relationship, I think now, was because it had a mythical quality to me" (Roudané, 89-90).[1] A Jungian would argue that that "mythical quality" is universal, especially for men. But if so, Miller's upbringing in a patriarchal Jewish culture undeniably served to reinforce for him the mythic authority of male ancestors, and their connection to the moral law.

As the sacred text of a patriarchal religion, the Torah is rich in stories about fathers and sons (Abraham and Isaac, Isaac and Jacob, Jacob and Joseph, Solomon and David, David and Absalom—to name but a few). Moreover, modern Jewish literature often focuses on this relationship, with Miller's contemporaries Karl Shapiro, Delmore Schwartz, Bernard Malamud and Saul Bellow exhibiting a particular interest in the subject.[2] Since *All My Sons* is not an overtly ethnic play, however, little attention has been paid to how Miller's religious background may have determined his choice and treatment of this common Jewish subject.[3] Miller's recent volume of memoirs, *Timebends*, serves to correct this oversight. For in it, he recalls Orthodox services he attended as a child in which the gathering of male ancestors and descendants bodied forth a continuity of authority that had a powerful impact on his young, impressionable mind, preparing the way for the metaphoric use of fathers and sons in later plays.

In *The Jewish Family: Authority and Tradition in Modern Perspective*, the Jewish sociologist Norman Linzer notes that in Jewish tradition, parents symbolically represent God, tradition and history to their children. "As each reinforces the other," he asserts, "the child is exposed to a massive authority system that encompasses the entire Jewish past and is realized in the present" (71). It is precisely this "massive authority system," as embodied in male ancestors, that Miller describes in his account of childhood experiences in the 144th Street synagogue in Harlem. *Timebends* recollects Miller's awed feelings of "power and reassurance" as his great-grandfather

> would keep turning my face toward the prayer book and pointing at the letters, which themselves were magical, as I would later learn, and apart from their meaning were lines of an art first inscribed by men who had seen the light of God, letters that led to the center of the earth and outward to the high heavens. Though I knew nothing of all that, it was frightening at times and totally, movingly male.
>
> From where I sat, on my great-grandfather's lap, it was all a kind of waking dream; the standing up and then the sitting down and the rising and falling of voices passionately flinging an incomprehensible language into the air while with an occasional glance I watched my mother up in the balcony with her eyes on me and [Miller's brother] Kermit, on my great-grandfather and grandfather and father all in a row. (36-37)

This "totally, movingly male" experience with his elders was grounded in the relationship of Jehovah, a transcendent paternal authority, to man: "the transaction called believing," he learned from these occasions, "comes down to the confrontation with overwhelming power and then the relief of knowing that one has been spared its worst" (37). That power is transmitted through the sacred books of the Torah as handed down by generations of holy men "who had seen the light of God," books read in Orthodox services where Miller's keenest memories are of his male forebears lined up "all in a row," with himself and his brother at the end of the line of transmission. This striking image has several implications for nearly all Miller's subsequent drama. It identifies the realm of power as an exclusively male domain. It invests enormous authority in male ancestors, linking them through a long, unbroken chain to an ultimate (male) authority. It indicates that meaning resides not simply in the ancestors, but in the connection to their living descendants: a major reason for Miller's obsessive interest in the relationship between past and present. It implies that brotherhood depends for its validation on this unbroken succession from a divine source. Finally (and most important), awareness of this succession produces "reassurance," a sense of belonging to both history and community.

Given the significance (and repetition) of this experience in Miller's early childhood, it is no wonder that Miller invests Joe Keller in *All My Sons*, Willy Loman in *Death of a Salesman*, and even the deceased father in the later *The Price* (1968) with such formidable—indeed, "mythical"—power over two sons. They all stand for the authority of God over man, collective over individual, past over present. Nor is it surprising that the transmission of authority from father to son via inheritances (emotional and/or economic) becomes a central concern in these plays. In *Sons*, this takes the secular form of a business legacy which Joe Keller wishes his son Chris to assume. This symbol of continuity is deeply corrupted by Joe's behavior, as we shall see. Yet the idea of continuity still appeals strongly to the traditionalist in Miller, as the play's obsession with the connection between past and present demonstrates.

But if Orthodox Jewish religion provided the young Miller with the father-son relationship as a mythic signifier of continuity and meaning, his experiences as a modern American Jew challenged that signification. American history can be read as a series of ruptures with authority—the Puritans, the Revolution, the Civil War. Miller himself remarks in *Timebends* that American writers see themselves as "self-conceived and self-made, . . . as though they were fatherless men abandoned by a past that they in turn reject" (115). This is particularly true for children of immigrants—like Miller—children whose desire for integration with the mainstream culture encourages them to repudiate Old World customs and strictures, thus to symbolically rebel against authority.[4] The pressure to assimilate thus became an incentive toward discontinuity, a break from the connection to ancestors, from the past—and from the transcendent source of meaning that Miller's Judaism had promoted.

As Irving Malin has observed, "The archetypal Jew embraces the rule of the father; the archetypal American rebels against the father. Two mythic patterns clash: in this clash [Jewish] writers find tense, symbolic meaning," resulting in the depiction of "imperfect father-son relationships in which rebellion supplants acceptance; violence replaces tenderness; and fragmentation defeats wholeness" (pp. 35, 33). The description perfectly fits *All My Sons* (as well as *Death of a Salesman*), which describes the violent rebellion of two sons against their father. But Miller is torn in his sympathies. Beneath the overt condemnation of the father's duplicity and destructiveness, the playwright longs for the continuity of authority—and the deep connection between past and present—represented by Joe's relationship with Chris; and the problem of the play's ending indicates his confusion over that connection's loss.

This longing for continuity was intensified, I would suggest, by the effect on Miller of the Holocaust—the epitome of catastrophic discontinuity, the full dimensions of which were revealed the year before Miller began work on *All My Sons* in 1946. Twenty years later, two years after *After the Fall* (1964) had employed the concentration camp as setting and symbol, Miller interpreted the camp as "the final expression of human separateness, and its ultimate consequence. It is organised abandonment": a radical symbol, in other words, of discontinuity and fragmentation, and thus "the logical conclusion of contemporary life" (*Theatre Essays*, 289). But fifteen years earlier—much closer in time of composition to *Sons*—Miller had also dealt with the Holocaust as an agent of discontinuity, and connected it more explicitly to a Jew's relationship with his ancestors. In the short story "Monte Sant'Angelo," Miller describes the alienation experienced by Bernstein, an American Jew visiting Italy, who has "no relatives that I know of in Europe. And if I had they'd have all been wiped out by now" (*I Don't Need You Any More*, p. 56). Moreover, he takes "no pride" in the experience of his earlier European ancestors, symbolized for him by his father's vague memories of "a common barrel of water, a town idiot, a baron nearby." Rather, he feels only "a broken part of himself" that makes him wonder "if this was what a child felt on discovering that the parents who brought him up were not his own, and that he entered his house not from warmth but from the street, from a public and disordered place" (61). Bernstein has been thrice displaced: by the European Jew's historical marginalization, by immigration, and by the Holocaust, which has wiped out all traces of family in his ancestral homeland. Significantly for *All My Sons*, the sense of alienation bred by radical discontinuity, by the breaking of the chain of ancestral transmission, is figured by an analogy involving a child's discovery about the duplicity of his parents.

Ultimately, Bernstein has a mysterious encounter with an Italian Jew who has been so thoroughly assimilated into the surrounding Catholic culture that he has lost all consciousness of his Jewishness. The stranger's retention of traces of his ethnic heritage, however, moves the American toward a sense of connection, by means of this "proof as mute as stones that a past lived. A past for me, Bernstein thought" (69). The action of *All My Sons*, with the Holocaust fresh in Miller's memory, moves in the opposite direction, from a dramatization of the deep connection between father and son based on a shared personal history toward the modern sense of discontinuity and dispossession experienced by Bernstein early in the story. For Chris Keller, father and brother are likewise links to a deeply felt past that has, over the course of three years, been wiped out. He thereby encounters, in the void at play's end, a displaced version of the sense of discontinuity experienced by many American Jews following the war: a discontinuity that is also at the center of modernism. His desire to affirm his brotherhood with other American victims of the war assumes great poignancy when placed in the context of Miller's awareness of the slaughter of 6 million European Jews—inhabitants of the continent from which his own ancestors had emigrated earlier in the century, and thus symbolic fathers and brothers to him (as *After the Fall* makes clear). And that context explains, from a different angle, the centrality for Miller of the father-son relationship. It not only symbolizes for him the connection of past to present, a connection needed to fully understand and embrace one's cultural identity; its collapse also demonstrates the power of modern historical forces that shatter this identity, and threaten both continuity with the past and human brotherhood. While the traditional Jew in Miller longs to affirm this connection, the modern Jew cannot deny its weakness and vulnerability.

As so often in Miller, the Depression also played a profound role in his attitude toward the father-son relationship, complicating for him its traditional signification of authority and continuity. His recollected childhood impression of his father Isidore was one of awe: this successful immigrant clothing manufacturer maintained a self-assured "baronial attitude" that caused his young son to view him as an agent of "undefinable authority" and "moral force" (*Timebends*, 24). And this relationship affected his political attitudes. Before 1932, *Timebends* reveals, "life's structure was so fixed that it was not only Grandpa Barnett, a Republican, who was full of indignation at this Roosevelt even presuming to contest President Hoover's right to another term—I felt the same way. The truth, I suppose, was that we were really royalists to whom authority had an aura that was not quite of this world" (111). But the boy's reactionary attitude was overthrown by two events. One was gradual: his father's steady loss of income, causing a decline in both their standard of living and the father's morale. As *Timebends* reports,

[By the fall of 1932] There was an aching absence in the house of any ruling idea or leadership, my father by now having fallen into the habit of endlessly napping in his time at home. . . . Never complaining or even talking about his business problems, my father simply went more deeply silent, and his naps grew longer, and his mouth seemed to dry up. I could not avoid awareness of my mother's anger at this waning of his powers; . . . I must have adopted my mother's early attitudes toward his failure, her impatience at the beginning of the calamity and her alarm as it got worse, and finally a certain sneering contempt for him that filtered through her voice. (109, 112: my ellipses)

Torn between love for his father's "warm and gentle nature," despair over "his illiterate mind," and anger and contempt for his failure, the 17-year-old Miller was vulnerable to his mother's criticisms of the father, which "divided us against ourselves" (113). No one remained more divided than the young Miller, who observed the collapse of his primary domestic symbol of authority—contributing to the apparent confusion about the father's authority that is evident in the plot of *All My Sons*.

The other cause of Miller's new suspicion toward authority also planted the seed of his political liberalism. The teenaged Miller heard a college student outside a local drugstore one day, preaching on class differences in America and predicting a world-wide socialist revolution that would overthrow the capitalist system. As Miller remembers,

This day's overturning of all I knew of the world revolutionized not only my ideas but also my most important relationship at the time, the one with my father. For deep down in the comradely world of the Marxist promise is parricide. For those who are psychically ready for the age-old adventure, the sublimation of violence that Marxism offers is nearly euphoric in its effects; while extolling the rational, it blows away the restraints in the Oedipal furies, clothing their violence with a humane ideal. . . . I had never raised my voice against my father, nor did he against me, then or ever. As I knew perfectly well, it was not he who angered me, only his failure to cope with his fortune's collapse. Thus I had two fathers, the real and the metaphoric, and the latter I resented because he did not know how to win out over the general collapse. . . . [But] if Marxism was, on the metaphorical plane, a rationale for parricide, I think that to me it was at the same time a way of forgiving my father, for it showed him as a kind of digit in a nearly cosmic catastrophe that was beyond his powers to avoid. (*Timebends*, 111-114: my ellipses)

Ambivalence riddles the passage. Respect for his father co-exists with both contempt and an Oedipal desire to murder him; he loved the "real" father, resented the "metaphoric" one; Marxism offered him a rationale for both parricide and forgiveness. Obviously, the economic dislocations wrought by the Depression transformed Miller, opening him up to the arguments of a Marxist ideology that viewed as reactionary the reassuring sense of continuity which his traditional view of the father-son relationship offered. Inevitably, this made its mark on *All My Sons*. In it, an idealistic son—indeed, two such sons, one dead, one alive—destroy a father who represents the capitalist business ethic. But, as I will argue below, the final scene undercuts this apparent affirmation of the son's new authority through the doubt it casts on his behavior. The liberal critique of the father's behavior is sincerely felt, and consistent with the play's assault on other sources of authority in American capitalist society. But the traditionalist—and the loyal son—in Miller remain uncomfortable with the void left by the father's death, and the ruptured relationship that provoked it.

At stake for Miller is an issue that goes to the heart of *All My Sons*, and much of his drama. If the father-son connection so central to the faith of his own fathers can be sustained, it offers a transcendently sanctioned model of relatedness that sanctions human brotherhood as well. Raymond Williams once remarked about Miller's early tragedies, "in both father and son there are the roots of guilt, and yet, ultimately they stand together as men—the father both a model and rejected ideal; the son both an idea and a relative failure. But the model, the rejection, the idea and the failure are all terms of growth, and the balance that can be struck is a very deep understanding of relatedness and brotherhood" (Weales, 319). The father-son relationship obsesses Miller as traditionalist, because its loss threatens his sense of connection with all other men. His anxiety about that loss—the anxiety of the Jewish modernist, who perceives discontinuity and fragmentation in the wake of the Holocaust—also subverts the explicit, liberal affirmations of brotherhood by Chris Keller in *All My Sons*. Its troubling, abrupt ending fails to resolve the problems the play has posed; and we are left with a survivor incapable of asserting the authority required to restore the symbolic connection with other men he has broken.

* * *

Perhaps his experiences in childhood and youth exerted their subconscious pressure as Miller wrote *The Man Who Had All the Luck* in the early 1940's. That play's subplot concerned a father's desire to make his son into a perfect baseball player, and Miller recalled in his introduction to the 1957 *Collected Plays* that "in writing of the father-son relationship and of the son's search for his relatedness there was a fullness of feeling I had never known before; a crescendo was struck with a force I could almost touch. The crux of *All My Sons* was formed . . ." (*Theatre Essays*, 126). The relationship of Joe and Chris Keller is inseparable from the latter's search for relatedness in *All My Sons*. The son's quest for a transcendent sense of connection—for brotherhood— is generated by a desire to give meaning to his wartime experience; but this conflicts with the major source of authority in his life, a relationship with his father that the idealistic son ultimately sacrifices to that desire for meaning. In seeking to substitute the authority of brotherhood for that of the father-son relationship, he tragically exposes himself—as well as Miller—to the modern sense of discontinuity that potentially explodes meaning altogether.

The force exerted by the father-son relationship is only the dominant one in a field of forces, for a summary of the plot reveals Miller's modernist subversion of various forms of authority operating in bourgeois American life. Frank Lubey, a minor character, represents the most easily satirized one, astrology. Lubey is a neighbor of Joe Keller, a Midwest manufacturer of aircraft engines whose younger son, Larry, was a World War II pilot reported missing in action nearly three years before the play begins. Joe's wife Kate refuses to accept her son's death; Lubey flatters her delusion by maintaining that Larry couldn't have died on the day he was reported missing because it was a favorable day in his horoscope. By play's end, the son's death—by suicide—is revealed in a letter produced by Ann, his former fiancée, who has arrived to become engaged to the surviving son, Chris. Larry's letter thus explodes the easy target, astrology; but it also exposes Kate's more conventional faith in a God who "does not let a son be killed by his father" (*Plays*, I, 114), since the letter reveals that Joe's conviction for supplying aircraft defective engines (resulting in the death of 21 American pilots) prompted Larry's suicide. In this overtly secular play, divine authority is apparently dismissed by revealing the self-delusion of the only two characters who profess belief in it. But, as we shall see, Kate's assertion and subsequent loss of faith in the sanctity of the father-son relationship has deeper implications, since it represents the battle being fought within the playwright's own imagination.[5]

The revelation of the son's death leads to that of the father, who has resisted admission of his guilt partly because of his adherence to another, strictly secular source of authority. the business ethic. Despite his previous exoneration on appeal after shifting the blame to his business partner—Ann's father Steve—Joe now perceives his responsibility for the deaths and shoots himself. He has been forced to this recognition by the idealistic Chris, who has read Larry's letter to Joe to make him quit hiding behind his rationalizations of his crime as everyday business. Earlier, Joe had claimed after admitting the crime to Chris, "I'm in business, a man is in business; a hundred and twenty [engines] cracked, you're out of business; . . . You lay forty years into a business and they knock you out in five minutes, what could I do, let them take forty years, let them take my life away?" (115). Later, he claims a broader sanction for his deed in its typicality: "Did they ship a gun or a truck outa Detroit before they got their price? Is that clean? It's dollars and cents, nickels and dimes; war and peace, it's nickels and dimes, what's clean? Half the Goddam country is gotta go if I go!" (125). Keller's morally specious defenses of manslaughter are unacceptable to both sons, and (presumably) to Miller's audience. A problem play, *All My Sons* indicts war profiteering and the capitalist ethos that justifies it. Miller's embodiment of that callous capitalist code in a father whom two sons help destroy recalls Miller's interpretation of Marxism in *Timebends*, cited above: "deep down in the comradely world of the Marxist promise is parricide." On the socioeconomic level, Miller thus asserts the necessity for disputing and ultimately overthrowing the paternal authority of a man corrupted by a capitalistic system that privileges the profit motive over human life. As he remarked in the 1957 "Introduction"—in rhetoric with unmistakable Marxist echoes—the play attacks "the concept of a man's becoming a function of production or distribution to the point where his personality becomes divorced from the actions it propels" (131). The ending thus reasserts Joe's connection to the consequences of his crimes by breaking his connection to his sons.[6]

Despite his negative associations with capitalism, however, Joe Keller's authoritative presence compels respect, especially in his surviving son. Their relationship points to the strong patriarchal model of Miller's Jewish tradition, inspiring the admiration in a son required to maintain that tradition. The Joe/Chris relationship is the most intense in the play. Described by the stage directions as a man "capable of immense affection and loyalty" (64), Chris directs it primarily toward his father, whose business he will carry on despite his lack of interest in it (and despite his repressed suspicions about his father's crime). Ann comments to Chris, "you're the only one I know who loves his parents"

(83), after a scene in which Chris typically responds *"with admiration"* to his father's recollection of his brazen walk past his neighbors upon his release from jail, "Joe McGuts." Joe replies *"with great force,"* "That's the only way to lick 'em is guts!" (80-81). The remark is typical of a character described as *"a heavy man of stolid mind and build . . . with the imprint of the machine-shop worker and boss still upon him. . . . A man among men"* (58-69, my ellipses). Joe's deep belief in the paternal authority which his build and behavior symbolize is especially apparent in his Act II remark to Chris and Ann after Joe has offered to reinstate Ann's father upon his release from jail. Bewildered by Chris's refusal and Ann's resistance—"I don't understand why she has to crucify the man"—Joe utters *"a commanding outburst:* a father is a father!" (97). The "commanding" outburst blends manner with substance in the play's strongest assertion of the deference due patriarchal authority.

In the final act, we discover guilt over his betrayal of his partner Steve as a hidden motive for Joe's offer, but the deference to fathers he demands is nonetheless sincere, an article of faith for Joe. The reasons for this go beyond the immediate dramatic context. One, as suggested above, is connected to Miller's Judaism. In the first act Joe is troubled by Chris's lack of enthusiasm for taking over the family business, "because what the hell did I work for? [The business is] only for you, Chris, the whole shootin' match is for you!" (69). When his crime is exposed, Joe again presents the transmission of a legacy as the profoundest motive for his crime. "Chris, Chris, I did it for you, it was a chance and I took it for you," Joe cries. "For you, a business for you!" (115). By expecting Chris specifically to take over the *family* business, Joe symbolically expresses a Jewish cultural imperative: to perpetuate a tradition or value by passing it on to one's son. As Linzer notes about the traditional Jewish community,

> Authority is the central concern because only through the force of authority can important values be transmitted to children. . . . The Jewish legal system sought to create a framework for normative family living wherein filial

obedience to parents regardless of their age is unquestioned. . . . thus, *the continuity of the tradition would be ensured by imbuing in children respect for, and obedience to authority.* (96; my emphasis)

In this light, Chris's reluctance to assume his father's business is a threat not just to Joe's authority but to the transgenerational continuity of traditional values. And if, as Linzer concludes, "the major priorities of Jewish families in the course of Jewish history" are "the preservation and transmission of the tradition" (98), Joe's vehemence has a hidden ethnic foundation. Though the Kellers are not presented as a Jewish family, the business legacy Joe defends corresponds to a secularized, economic (albeit corrupted) version of the Jewish traditions that were part of Miller's background. By means of the father-son relationship, Miller may be examining his own mixed feelings as a culturally assimilated Jew toward the spiritual legacy of his forefathers.

But for Miller, an even deeper motive exists, a motive that surfaces in Joe's words when he fears his son will report him to the police. "I'm his father and he's my son. . . . Nothin's bigger than that," Joe cries. "I'm his father and he's my son, and if there's something bigger than that I'll put a bullet in my head!" (120). For the father, the relationship—not the father nor the son individually, but their connection—possesses a transcendent authority which demands the son's forgiveness of the father's crime. As a modern liberal, Miller castigates this narrow, socially irresponsible attitude, and subjects it to tragic irony: the elder son Larry has died as a result of Joe's confused priorities that place family above society. But Joe's remark also articulates Miller's traditionalist view of the father-son relationship as the familial version of the principle of continuity, the connection of past to present. That principle exercises great power over Miller's imagination, as the play's very structure suggests. As is all too apparent, *All My Sons* is an Ibsenesque well-made play in which characters from the past (Ann, her brother George) return to the neighborhood to set in motion a plot which eventually exposes the hidden truth about Joe's past criminal act—a plot that climaxes after the production of a three-year-old letter reveals the most devastating consequence of the crime. As Robert Brustein has pointed out disparagingly, the old-fashioned plot mechanisms resemble those of Newtonian physics (22); but they are inseparable from Miller's intention (emphasized in the 1957 introduction) to make the play "an experience which widens [an audience's] awareness of connection—the filaments to the past and the future which lie concealed in life" (*Theatre Essays*, 128). The primary explicit connection Miller intends to demonstrate may be that between private and public realms, family and society: the dead pilots are indeed all Joe's sons. But the connection between father and son penetrates deeper, since it relates to the very principle of causality—and to the inescapability of the past, of history—which constitutes the play's profoundest (and most universal) level of meaning.

That principle of causality is linked to both father-son relationships. First, the past actions of the father have not only killed 21 pilots but have caused the suicide of his son Larry. Second, the force of Joe's personality and the sacredness of their relationship have had a strong impact on the surviving son Chris, blinding him to his father's crime despite his suspicion of him. As he tells Joe at the end, "I never saw you as a man, I saw you as my father. I can't look at you this way, I can't look at myself!" (125). Chris's outburst reveals not just his reverence for their relationship, but even implies an absorption *into* that relationship (a symbiosis anticipating that of Biff and Willy in Miller's next play). Chris's idealistic condemnations of his father are apparent attempts to escape from that symbiosis—hence, to escape from the past—by ultimately substituting for his reverence toward the father a sense of obligation toward the brother. One connection replaces another. He comments on his fellow soldiers, "they killed themselves for each other," and tells Ann

I got an idea, watching them go down. Everything was being destroyed, see, but it seemed to me that one new thing was made. A kind of . . . responsibility. Man for man. You understand me?—To show that, to bring that on to the earth again like some kind of a monument and everyone would feel it standing there, behind him, and it would make a difference to him. And then I came home and it was incredible. . . . there was no meaning in it here, the whole thing to them was a kind of a—bus accident. (85)

Intriguingly, Miller offers Chris's value of brotherhood as the product of particular historical circumstances, rooted in his experience in World War II. However noble, it is presented as a relative value, as its disregard by the civilians at home helps underscore. For Chris, it nonetheless assumes absolute status, and his final accusation (directed at both parents) is grounded in the proclamation of both actual and metaphorical brotherhood: "Once and for all you can know there's a universe of people outside and you're responsible to it, and unless you know that, you threw away your son [Larry] because that's why he died" (126-27). The gunshot of Joe's suicide melodramatically replies, signalling his recognition of the betrayal of that obligation. Finally for Joe, as well as Chris and Larry, the dead pilots were (in Joe's final words before exiting) "all my sons. And I guess they were, I guess they were" (126). The curtain falls within seconds of these pronouncements, with Kate comforting Chris after Joe's suicide by advising him "Don't take it on yourself. Forget now. Live" (127).

The abruptness of the ending, however, indicates Miller's discomfort with it, stemming from the non-resolution of his own inner conflict. As a liberal moralist, Miller wants to drive home the message that social obligations transcend individual familial ones, and metaphorically substitute the connection of brother to brother for the connection of father to son. (Appropriately, two brothers, both veterans, collude in unintentionally driving the father to suicide.) But the suddenness of the ending implicitly recognizes the problem of setting brotherhood in opposition to fatherhood, rather than seeing them as connected (as Miller the traditionalist wishes them to be). As noted above, the play explicitly presents the value of brotherhood as one developed *in* history.

In contrast, the father-son connection, a metaphor for the inseparability of past from present—the play's central theme, according to the playwright—seems to *be* history, the historical principle of continuity as well as causality, the ground for all which transpires. As a modernist, Miller attempts to substitute a value he has dramatized as relative (brotherhood) for a repudiated absolute (fatherhood) that originates in his traditional religious background: it is one of countless modern variations on Nietzsche's "killing" of God.[7] But as traditionalist, Miller resists the attempt. The asserted connection between brothers remains on the level of rhetoric—especially since Chris's actual brother Larry is already dead—while the connection between father and son remains implicit in the plot structure and deepest level of the play. How, then, can the former be affirmed, the latter "killed"? The quickness of the curtain indicates Miller's confusion in the face of this question, which points to the underlying question that troubles him. How can an ideal of connection between brothers be confidently asserted when the prior, transcendent model of connection (father and son), absorbed from his Judaism, has been repudiated: on what larger basis does the fraternal connection then rest?

That uncertainty is deepened by the inability of the surviving son—the spokesman for brotherhood—to reconstitute the authority he has overthrown. The neighbor Sue Bayliss accuses Chris of "phony idealism," since he holds others (among them Sue's husband Jim) to demanding ideals while resisting his own suspicions about his father's guilt. Chris's words about Joe ironically apply to him: he has a "talent for ignoring things" (68). This flaw would seem to pale in comparison to Joe's more egregious (and murderous) deceptions. But in an illuminating article on the play, Barry Gross perceives instead a decline from father to son. To Gross, Chris lacks the dedication of the father who takes enormous (even criminal) risks to preserve a legacy for his son: a legacy whose tainted nature the son has winked at. Moreover, in contrast to Joe's willingness to kill himself out of his devotion to the father-son relationship ("if there's something bigger than that I'll put a bullet through my head"), Chris is a narcissist who can only love Joe if Joe is innocent, who deceives himself about his father's guilt because his self-image is still so bound up with his image of his father. Idealizing Joe, he idealizes himself, and "cannot look at his father as no better than most because he cannot look at himself as no better than most" (Martine, 13-14). Hence, Gross concludes (alluding to Miller's comment in my opening paragraph), Chris "has achieved neither mastery nor manhood by play's end," and authority has not been "reconstituted" in him (18). I essentially concur—and would add that Chris's final, revealing gesture is to retreat to his mother's arms just before the curtain. His childishness and ultimate passivity are also apparent in his rationalizations of his refusal to perceive his father's guilt, and his subsequent reluctance to turn him in: "I was *made yellow* in this house because I suspected my father and did nothing about it" (123); "I could jail him, if I were human anymore. But I'm like everybody else now. I'm practical now. You *made me practical*" (123); "This is the land of the great big dogs, you don't love a man here, you eat him! . . . *The world's that way*, how can I take it out on him?" (124; my emphases). Seeing himself purely as victim of family and society, Chris is unable to assume responsibility for his actions—in marked contrast to Joe, who ultimately does precisely that.

Chris's inability to take responsibility renders him incapable of restoring authority, leaving a void where the father's power existed before. It also casts doubt on Chris's reliability as a spokesman for brotherhood, and (hence) on the ideal itself.[8] Again, the shattering of father-son continuity makes us question the connection Miller explicitly espouses between brother and brother. Despite his intentions, the traditionalist in him will not permit him to divorce the two. But Miller as modernist betrays the anxiety of their attempted separation. In place of fatherhood and brotherhood, we are left with a discontinuity and fragmentation which implicitly subvert *all* assertions of moral obligation—i.e., all authority—by absorbing them into relativism. Kate Keller's desperate belief, grimly satirized by Miller earlier, needs to be recalled: "God does not let a son be killed by his father," nor (we might add) permit a father to be killed by his son. But these primal crimes are permitted, leaving uncertainty and ambivalence where continuity, connectedness and belief used to be.

Miller's ambivalence regarding authority and brotherhood, as has been suggested, scarcely ends with *All My Sons*. *Death of a Salesman*, though it solves the problem of the abrupt suicidal ending by adding the "requiem" of Willy's funeral, betrays a similar anxiety about killing the patriarch. Biff explicitly repudiates Willy, while Happy affirms his connection with him at the end. And significantly, their father's death frees the brothers to go their separate ways—suggesting much more explicitly that the severance of the father-son bond dissolves the basis for brotherhood as well, though (again) the connection of past to present in the play's structure dramatizes the impossibility of such a severance. *After the Fall* and *The Price* offer a pairing similar to *Sons* and *Salesman*. The former affirms brotherhood—though it is a communion of sinners, now, and women are included—in the face of the void following the collapse of authority; the latter uses an occasion prompted by the father's death years before to imply brotherhood's impossibility. The mixture of Miller's traditional Jewish background with his modernist and liberal beliefs thus creates continual, intriguing tensions within and between individual works throughout his career. And that tension helps account for the continuing power of Miller's drama. The father-son relationship as depicted by Miller dramatizes the longings for authority and connection to the past that, as spiritual beings, we all feel; but its rupture is a symbolic expression of the pervasive sense of betrayal and discontinuity which, as modern western citizens, we all experience.

From *The Journal of American Drama and Theatre* 2, no. 1 (1990): 38-54. Copyright © 1990 by Martin E. Segal Theatre Center, CUNY. Reprinted by permission of *The Journal of American Drama and Theatre*.

Notes

1. *Conversations with Arthur Miller*, 89-90. For Miller's other comments in interviews on fathers and sons, see pp. 50, 54, 91-92, 188-89, 197, 311-12, 327-28.

2. See Malin, *Jews and Americans*, chap. 3.

3. See Freedman, "The Jewishness of Arthur Miller," in *American Drama in Social Context*, 43-58, and Brater, "Ethics and Ethnicity in the Plays of Arthur Miller," in *From Hester Street to Hollywood*, 123-34. Freedman, who emphasizes the "ethnic anonymity" of Miller's drama, claims that only one moment in *All My Sons* (when Kate Keller fawns over George like a Jewish mother) suggests the playwright's Jewish origins. Brater argues that Miller deliberately avoided the ethnic route travelled by Odets, and instead explored universal ethical conflicts "more Judaic than Jewish" in *All My Sons* and subsequent plays. Neither critic discusses the Jewish aspects of the father-son conflict in the play, nor does Richard Loughlin's cursory treatment of the play's Biblical parallels, in "Tradition and Tragedy in *All My Sons*," mention this possibility.

4. Miller reveals his youthful desire to assimilate in *Timebends*: "If ever any Jews should have melted into the proverbial melting pot, it was our family in the twenties; indeed, I would soon be dreaming of entering West Point, and in my most private reveries I was no sallow Talmud reader but Frank Merriwell or Tom Swift, heroic models of athletic verve and military courage" (p. 62). For analysis of the phenomena of assimilation and the forces promoting it, see Oscar Handlin, *The Uprooted*, and Werner Sollors, *Beyond Ethnicity: Consent and Descent in American Culture*.

5. It is interesting to note in this regard Miller's account of the play's composition process in the introduction to the *Collected Plays*. "In (the play's) earlier versions the mother, Kate Keller, was in a dominating position; more precisely, her astrological beliefs were given great prominence. (The play's original title was *The Sign of the Archer.*) And this, because I sought in every sphere to give body and life to connection. But as the play progressed the conflict between Joe and his son Chris pressed astrology to the wall until its mysticism gave way to psychology" (132). I would argue that Miller never fully rid the play of these religious overtones, but instead displaced them onto the father-son relationship—a more comfortable site (given Miller's patriarchal religion) for the mystique attached to connection in the play.

6. As liberal social critic, Miller underscores how widely accepted Joe's inhumane values are by rooting them in the Kellers' neighborhood. "Everyone knows Joe pulled a fast one to get out of jail," Sue Bayliss tells Ann, "but they give him credit for being smart" (94): within two years of his release from jail, everyone has accepted him back into the community.

7. For an intriguing discussion of this in Miller's work from *All My Sons* through *The Price*, see Raymond Reno, "Arthur Miller and the Death of God."

8. Unquestionably, as various critics have observed, the influence of Ibsen's *The Wild Duck* is pronounced here, with Gregers Werle serving as model for a self-righteous (unconsciously), hypocritical young idealist who makes life difficult for others. (For the most stimulating recent discussion of this, see Bigsby, 168-171.) But Ibsen's impact reaches deeper than this. Not only does the abrupt, violent ending recall

Hedda Gabler and *Ghosts*, but the implications of the latter's ending are similar to those of *All My Sons*. *Ghosts* ends with Mrs. Alving screaming as she is faced with the dilemma of whether to kill her own syphilitic son (the victim of her hypocrisy in remaining with her husband). As Francis Fergusson observes, Mrs. Alving thereby fails to attain a final tragic epiphany. Hence, the play's action is "neither completed nor placed in the wider context of meanings" that is found in classical tragedy, partly because Ibsen's romantic imagination did not fit comfortably into the form of the realistic problem play—where his desire to *épater le bourgeois* resulted in a shocking, unresolved conclusion that truncated the development of his protagonist (156-57). Miller's dilemma also consists in striving to place a wider (even absolutist) vision, the product of his Judaism, into the form of the realistic problem play. His desire to attack his society's inhumane business ethic similarly concludes in an abrupt, shocking finale which neither resolves the play's deeper conflicts, nor allows his protagonist, Chris, to develop.

Works Cited

Bigsby, C. W. E. *A Critical Introduction to Twentieth Century American Drama, Vol. II: Miller, Williams, Albee.* London: Cambridge University Press, 1984.

Brustein, Robert. "Drama in The Age of Einstein." *New York Times*, 7 August 1977, II, 1, 22.

Cohen, Sarah B., ed. *From Hester Street to Hollywood: The Jewish-American Stage and Screen.* Bloomington: Indiana University Press, 1983.

Fergusson, Francis. *The Idea of a Theatre.* Princeton: Princeton University Press, 1983.

Freedman, Morris. *American Drama in Social Context.* Carbondale: Southern Illinois University Press, 1971.

Gross, Barry. "*All My Sons* and the Larger Context." *Modern Drama* 18 (March 1975), 15-27; rpt. in Martine, James, ed. *Critical Essays on Arthur Miller.* Boston: G. K. Hall, 1979.

Handlin, Oscar. *The Uprooted.* Second edition. Boston: Little, Brown and Co., 1973.

Linzer, Norman. *The Jewish Family: Authority and Tradition in Modern Perspective.* New York: Human Sciences Press, 1984.

Loughlin, Richard. "Tradition and Tragedy in *All My Sons.*" *English Record*, 14, 3 (1964), 23-27.

Malin, Irving. *Jews and Americans.* Carbondale: Southern Illinois University Press, 1965.

Miller, Arthur. *Collected Plays.* New York: Viking, 1957.

_____. *Conversations with Arthur Miller*, ed. Matthew Roudané. Jackson: University Press of Mississippi, 1987.

_____. *I Don't Need You Any More.* London: Secker and Warburg, 1967.

_____. *Timebends.* New York: Grove Press, 1987.

_____. *The Theatre Essays of Arthur Miller*, ed. Robert A. Martin. New York: Penguin, 1978.

Reno, Raymond. "Arthur Miller and the Death of God." *Texas Studies in Literature and Language*, 11 (1969), 1069-87.

Sollors, Werner. *Beyond Ethnicity: Consent and Descent in American Culture.* New York: Oxford University Press, 1986.

Weales, Gerald, ed. *Death of a Salesman: Texts and Criticism.* New York: Viking, 1967.

"There's No Place Like Home":
Miller's "Poem," Frost's "Play"_____
George Monteiro

In the course of this essay I shall say something about the title of Miller's most famous play, the possibility that the play is related to a classic poem by Robert Frost, and the further possibility that the familiar New Testament Parable of the Prodigal Son contributes to the form and meaning of both Frost's poem and Miller's play.

1. Miller on Frost

By the time Miller was a student at the University of Michigan in the 1930s, Frost's official connections to the university as teacher and poet-in-residence had long since ended although he continued to visit the university frequently. In *Timebends* Miller refers briefly to Frost's behavior at President Kennedy's inauguration and he tells us that among the reading he recommended to Marilyn Monroe was Frost's poems (263, 306, 512). Miller also reports on what may have been the one occasion when he was in Frost's presence. It's something of a shaggy dog story, and it has nothing to do with this paper, but it is mercifully brief. "One evening," writes Miller, "I saw unusual deference paid him [Louis Untermeyer] by the kingly and much older Robert Frost, who sat still for a lengthy lecture from Louis on etymology. That afternoon my young springer spaniel, Red—an unteachable animal I later gave away to my Ford dealer, fleeing his showroom before he could change his mind—had rushed through our Willow Street doorway down the stoop and smashed into the side of a passing car, stunning his brain still further and sending him hysterically running, with me behind him, way up to Borough Hall. In the evening, Frost listened to the story of my chase and then, staring out like one of the heads on Mount Rushmore, drawled, 'Sounds like a comical dog'" (263).

---

2. The Word "Death" in Titles

When Mel Gussow said to Miller in 1986, "It's curious how much a title affects a public understanding of a play," Miller said, simply, "It tells you what to look for." Gussow followed up: "What if *Death of a Salesman* had a different title?" (Gussow 101). Miller did not answer the question, preferring to talk about the recent production of the play in Beijing, but if others had had their way, the play's title would have been different. As Miller tells us, Kermit Bloomgarden, who ultimately produced the play, worried that its title would hurt receipts, and Robert Dowling, the owner of the theater "where the play was to be produced," agreed. He "wanted to keep the title from appearing on the front of the theatre if the word 'death' was to appear in it."

> Bloomgarden suggested that the title be changed to *Free and Clear*, a phrase from Linda's speech in the Requiem. . . . Both Miller and Kazan were adamant about the title, and *Variety* reported finally on 29 December that the "'Death of a Salesman' title for the new Arthur Miller play is being retained at the author's insistence." Noting that the producers disliked the title, "figuring it has a sombre connotation that may tend to repel prospective playgoers, besides being a story tipoff," the article concluded that "Miller has been adamant and under Dramatists Guild rules has final say." (Murphy 12)

Titles with the word "death" in them had some precedent, as Miller notes in *Timebends*: "*Death Comes for the Archbishop*, the *Death and the Maiden* Quartet—always austere and elevated was death in titles," though in his play, he added, it "would be claimed by a joker, a bleeding mass of contradictions, a clown, and there was something funny about that" (*Timebends* 184). Miller does not name them, but there were other uses of the word "death" in titles. There is "Death in the Woods," Sherwood Anderson's story; *Death in the Afternoon*, Ernest Hemingway's book about bull-fighting; and "The Death of the Hired Man," Robert Frost's dramatic narrative in verse.[1]

3. Frost's Poem, "The Death of the Hired Man"

Published in *North of Boston* (1914), this poem has a simple scenario. An old man, who had more than once deserted for higher wages, now has returned, sick and confused, to ask for his old job back from the couple—man and wife—who had formerly employed him. He never appears on "stage"; we learn about him through the conversation between the husband and wife—Warren and Mary—who are out on the porch. Mary is more sympathetic to Silas's plight, having brought him back into the house where he now sleeps back of the stove. Warren argues that Silas, having left him during haying time, does not deserve to be taken back. He should be in the care of the banker brother, who lives just thirteen miles away. Mary reports what Silas has been saying and thinking. He has come back, as Warren correctly surmises, to "ditch the meadow" and to "clear the upper pasture, too"—tasks he seems to have promised to do in the past but not done. He also wants to have another chance to show the "college boy" long since gone on how to stack hay, for instance, saving the boy from becoming "the fool of books." Mary recognizes that Silas has "nothing to look backward to with pride,/ And nothing to look forward to with hope." The dilemma faced by the young couple is whether or not to "take in" the aged, sick Silas, who is obviously no longer useful to them in the economy of the farm. If Mary would take Silas back, if only to give him a "home" in which to die, Warren argues for making Silas endure the consequences of choices he has made in the past.

But at the core of their individual decisions are variant notions of what constitutes one's "home," which are presented as contrary definitions. The wife's definition that home is "Something you somehow haven't to deserve" is put into doubt by the husband, who argues that by leaving the farm for the sake of higher wages elsewhere just when he was needed most—at harvest time—Silas has long since forfeited whatever claim he might have had on this "home." This liberal definition, put forth by Mary, is countered by her husband's perhaps harsher view that "Home is the place where, when you have to go there,/ They have to take you in." These definitions, taken in conjunction, lead implicitly to the idea that, under scrutiny, notions of "home" have already undergone change and redefinition. At the heart of the discussion are two conflicting views of charity and responsibility or what might be called justice. The matter becomes moot—resolution is no longer necessary—when Warren reveals that when he went into the house to talk to Silas, he found him dead.[2]

4. The Play Is a Poem, the Poem Is a Play

In agreement with the director Tyrone Guthrie, Christopher Bigsby writes that *Death of a Salesman* is "a long poem by Willy Loman. For much of the play it is he who hears the voices, shapes the rhythms, creates the rhymes. He turns experience into metaphor, bringing together discrete moments to forge new meanings which then dissolve" (*Critical Study* 121).[3] In an interview in 1977, Miller makes the same point but in other terms: "The play is really one continuous poem. It has no scenes. It has no interstices" (Roudané 276). It is a perfect example of the dramatization of a mind that is at every stage, William James decided in *Principles of Psychology*, "a theatre of simultaneous possibilities" (Baym 732).

Turning to Frost, who described his narrative poem as "a short play, very short" (Cook 359), we see that he keeps Silas off stage. He creates our sense of Silas's life entirely from the outside—from the points of view of the husband and wife; while Miller conceives his entire play as scenes playing themselves out within Willy's mind and around him—even though there are scenes that Willy could not possibly have known about (e.g. Linda's dialogue with her son or the conversations at the restaurant before Willy shows up); these scenes parallel the basic situation in Frost's poem in which Silas, always inside, away from view, is invoked in the conversation that takes place between Warren and Mary out on the porch.

5. The Death of an Old Man

Play and poem both have as their subjective center "old" men who are well beyond their abilities to function at their respective tasks or trades. Reviewing Frost's collected poems in 1949, Charles Poore wrote in the *New York Times*: "'The Death of the Hired Man,' with its poignancies as deep, probably, as the death of any salesman" (25). If poignancy does not make tragedy, this pairing of common men does bring us to Miller's position: "I believe that the common man is as apt a subject for tragedy in its highest sense as kings were" (*Theater Essays* 3). In a different vein, but along the same track, the author of a recent book on obituaries and their writers concludes that "Miller's account of the death of Willy Loman can be read as an elevated obit of a common man" (Johnson 78).

6. The Manny Newman "Story"

In *Timebends* Miller tells of his fascination with Manny Newman, one of his Brooklyn uncles, Manny's wife and children—especially his two sons. So much of *Death of a Salesman* is there: Manny's prevarications, lies (to himself and others), and dreams; Manny's occupation as a salesman driving "all the way through New England in his little car, which in winter was barely kept above freezing by its primitive heater," driving "through every town, stop[ping] at every traffic light" (125); the loyal wife, "alternately flushed and paled as she dreaded and was relieved of the fear that he was making too much of a fool of himself," both of them "still in love"; his two sons "a pair of strong, self-assured young men, musketeers bound to one another's honor and proud of their family," neither of them "patient enough or perhaps capable enough to sit alone and study," "both missed going to college" (127); the son, "filled with the roiling paradoxes of love for me [Miller] and competitive resentment, of contempt for his late failed father and at the same time a pitying love and even amused admiration for the man's outrageousness" (129-30); the revelation that Manny had a dream: "He wanted a business for us. So we could all work together," reveals Miller's cousin. "A business for the boys" (130). "This conventional, mundane wish was a shot of electricity that switched all the random iron filings in my mind in one direction," wrote Miller.

A hopelessly distracted Manny was transformed into a man with purpose: he had been trying to make a gift that would crown all those striving years; all those lies he told, all his imaginings and crazy exaggerations, even the almost military discipline he had laid on his boys, were in this instant given form and point. To be sure, a business expressed his own egotism, but love, too. That homely, ridiculous little man had after all never ceased to struggle for a certain victory, the only kind open to him in this society—selling to achieve his lost self as a man with his name and his sons' names on a business of his own. I suddenly understood him with my very blood. (130)

But Miller admits that he "had imagined all of this and that in reality he was not much more than a bragging and often vulgar little drummer" (131). The one major item missing from this rich store of memories and imaginings as regards the play—*Death of a Salesman*—that would emerge from them Miller would find elsewhere: in the narrative Parable of the Prodigal Son—more specifically, in the surprise ending in which the "lost" son who has squandered all that had been given to him returns not to punishment but to the greatest rewards a loving father can heap upon his head. Except for going off to the war, neither of Manny Newman's sons is reported to have gone much farther away from their family home in Brooklyn than lower Lexington Avenue in Manhattan. Oddly, it may have been the Prodigal Son theme (displaced) in Frost's poem that helped Miller fill-out his play.

"The Death of the Hired Man" offers not a father and a son but an old man and his (presumably) younger employers. The hired man, too, goes away—and does it more than once. His recurrent behavior is that he leaves for more money and then returns. He, too, has dreams, and those dreams involve not a son but a young man who has worked along-side him in the fields but has gone off to college. The hired man wants one more crack at him—to teach him something of value, how to "build a load of hay," hay, so as to keep him from being ruined by what he has learned at college; he wants to "ditch the meadow" and "clear the upper pasture, too"—"he has a plan"; but he "jumble[s] everything."

7. The Parable of the Prodigal Son

A summary of the text of the Parable of the Prodigal Son as it appears in Luke 15:11-32 will do for our purposes: "Having squandered his fortune, starving and destitute in a far country, . . . feeding the forbidden pigs, he [the Prodigal Son] wishes that he could fill his stomach by sharing the food of the pigs he feeds? And how beautifully the father's love is described. Laying aside his dignity, he runs to embrace his son, refuses to hear out his confession, reclothes him in appropriately filial garments, and joyfully celebrates having regained his lost son" (Stein 568).[4] When the son who has stayed at home complains about his father's surprising behavior—his killing of the fatted calf in celebration of the Prodigal's return—his father answers him: "It was meet that we should make merry, and be glad: for this thy brother was dead, and is alive again; and was lost, and is found."

In Frost's poem, the hired man Silas behaves like "family"—even like the Prodigal Son; so, too, does Biff in *Salesman*. Willy's prodigal behavior has long since been revealed to Biff when the son finds the father in a Boston hotel room with a woman. Biff's own prodigal behavior consists of thievery and (out West) jail time. Willy will forgive him these peccadilloes but wants more from Biff than just that. He wants him to be "magnificent." There's no evidence that Biff will forgive Willy his peccadilloes; in fact, he charges him with deceit (at best) when he confronts him with the piece of hose from the cellar. In Frost's poem Silas's prodigal behavior takes the form of desertion—he leaves the "family" at harvest time for employment elsewhere at higher wages. If Mary will forgive him, Warren is reluctant to do so. If Silas is like an animal that has come home to die, so is Willy Loman. It is Willy's fate to kill the "calf" (himself) for Biff's sake (re-ordering the progression of anthropological and religious ritual from human sacrifice to animal sacrifice to symbolic sacrifice).

It would be all too easy to get lost in the literature devoted to the Parable of the Prodigal Son, a good deal of it following closely the story in Luke but much of it displacing the myth in one or many ways. This displacement is especially interesting when it takes place in realistic stories, poems, or plays. I use the terms "realism" and "displacement" as they are defined by Northrop Frye: "Realism, or the art of verisimilitude, evokes the response, 'How like that is to what we know!' When what is written is *like* what is known, we have an art of extended or implied simile. . . . The presence of a mythical structure in realistic fiction [or poetry or drama], however, poses certain technical problems for making it plausible, and the devices used in solving these problems may be given the general name of *displacement*" (*Anatomy* 136). Now I see—no surprise, of course—the presence of the Parable of the Prodigal Son both in Frost's "The Death of the Hired Man" and *Death of a Salesman*, though in neither case is the Parable's structure or its details followed literally or slavishly.[5] It was not possible or desirable to do so. In Miller's case, for starters, as he said in the introduction to his *Collected Plays*, there was the necessity "to cling to the process of Willy's mind as the form the story would take" (*Theater Essays* 144). Though, it must be noted, he does avail himself of the triumvirate present in the Parable of the Prodigal Son: the father and the two sons. As another writer has put it, echoing St. Augustine, though less allegorically, "We are all, like the Prodigal Son, seeking our home, waiting to hear the Father's voice" (Abrams 518).[6] In Frost's poem the Prodigal Son who returns home after his desertion is an old man. Silas's faults are defined by Warren and Mary, who are not his parents but employers—who act in loco parentis, in a way. Silas has in the past deserted them at harvest time, going to work for others at higher wages. He has come home to die, becoming himself the sacrifice (a radical displacement of the "fatted calf," as I have said, of the Parable). As Miller said, famously, "all of tragedy is about the chickens coming home to roost."

In *"Salesman" in Beijing* Miller described his play: *"Death of a Salesman*, really, is a love story between a man and his son" (49). Certainly this is also one way (if an uncommon one) of interpreting Luke's Parable of the Prodigal Son: the father's love of one son over the other is patent, just as Willy's love for Biff over Happy is clear. In *Death of a Salesman* the obvious Prodigal Son is Biff, who has come home after his profligacy out West (he has been in jail) and he is greeted by a father who will do anything for his Prodigal (anything he can to bring into evident reality Biff's "magnificence"), while the "good son," who has not gone West ("Me? Who goes away? Who runs off and—," Happy breaks off in his rebuke of Biff and who—not Biff—actually gives his parents Christmas money that they use to repair the water heater), is excluded from Willy's plans.

In a radical displacement, ultimately it is Willy himself who stands in for the "fatted calf" of Luke's Parable, killing himself to give Biff a $20,000 gift in insurance money. But this isn't the only way the Parable operates deep in Miller's consciousness. For Willy is himself a Prodigal Son, one whose return home has taken place over and over again during his adult life, as he goes out into the territory where his prodigal behavior takes place—the incident of the woman in Boston, for instance, is metonymic. That familiar image of the returning Willy— home from the hapless hunt for sales—seen from the back, weighed down by the suitcases he has lugged all over New England lines him up with all the wanderers, from Odysseus to Cain to Parsifal, as well as the less heroic Prodigal Son.[7] But for Willy there is no "fatted calf," neither at home, nor, as he learns to his stupefaction, at the home office either. Now it is of course possible (perhaps probable) that there is no direct link between Frost's displaced use of the Parable of the Prodigal and Miller's similarly displaced use. But they do share one particular displacement: the younger son has become the old hired man in Frost, while he has been duplicated in Miller, with the son dividing or duplicated into two avatars, one of which is the old, superannuated sales-man. Neither Silas nor Willy is of much, if any, use to the farm, in Silas's case, or the firm, in Willy's. By this point each of them, in terms of occupation or job, has become expendable.

Yet just as there is in the Parable of the Prodigal Son, there is an emphasis on the idea of home in both "The Death of the Hired Man" and *Death of a Salesman*. For the Prodigal Son, home is a place of welcome, forgiveness, and celebration. Things are different in the two modern texts. In Miller's play, Linda warns her two sons: "Someday you'll come here and there'll be strangers here," welcome that erodes quickly into disappointing illusion, and celebration turns rancid and ugly—the dinner the boys plan to have for Willy turns into cruel and vicious rejection (Happy repudiates the father in favor of the girls— "No, that's not my father. He's just a guy."). From that point Willy is totally lost, reversing the text in St. Luke, substituting "father" for "brother": "thy brother was dead, and is alive again; and was lost, and is found." In Frost's "Death of the Hired Man" the husband and wife debate the issue of whether or not to allow Silas, the Prodigal, to come back by offering each other contrary definitions of "home."

Death of a Salesman "grew from simple images," Miller recalled in 1957. "From a little frame house on a street of little frame houses, which had once been loud with the noise of growing boys, and then was empty and silent and finally occupied by strangers. Strangers who could not know with what conquistadorial joy Willy and his boys had once re-shingled the roof. Now it was quiet in the house, and the wrong people in the beds" (*Theater Essays* 141-42). The mother Linda has the foreboding lines, said to the Prodigal Son Biff, that express this loss of "home." "You've got to get it into your head now that one day you'll knock on this door and there'll be strange people here." It has already happened with the home office, as Willy so painfully learns when he goes in to the "home" office to beg for the job that he thinks he was once promised.

8. Summing Up

Frost's poem about the dying hired man anticipates Miller's play about the dying salesman—sometimes by analogue, sometimes by reversal. The old man Silas's returning "home" parallels the young man Biff's returning "home." The wife, Mary, makes a case for Silas; Linda, the wife, makes the case for Willy. Both Willy and Silas want to go back to the past, to correct mistakes, make improvements. Frost writes about Silas from the outside—the points of view are the husband's and wife's—while Miller conceives his play as playing itself out, mostly so, in Willy's head. If all descriptions of Willy are done around him, those of Silas take place in dialogue he does not hear. For Silas, a dying animal returning home to die, the farm is his "home"; for Willy his "home" includes the company (the firm), where the feeling of being "at home" is important, where Willy thinks of himself as part of the family, not as a "hired" hand. If Willy has intimations that he has always been a bit out of sync, he doesn't really understand his situation. He admires the old salesman Dave Singleman, who makes his sales over the phone from his hotel room (a home away from home) and who has the happy fate to die, wearing "his green velvet slippers," in "the smoker of the New York, New Haven and Hartford, going into Boston"—still another home away from home—perhaps the successful salesman's one and only true home.

From *The Arthur Miller Journal* 2, no. 1 (2007): 1-14. Copyright © by St. Francis College. Reprinted with permission of *The Arthur Miller Journal.*

Notes

1. Miller was hardly the first one to highlight the phrase "death of a salesman." On 20 Dec. 1883, the *New York Times* reported the death of a "traveling salesman" from Brooklyn under the headline "Sudden *Death of a Salesman*" (2). Exactly one month later, on 20 Jan. 1884, the *Times* reported the death of another drummer from Brooklyn, once again under the headline "Sudden *Death of a Salesman*" (7). Much closer to the date of Miller's play, however, is the *Times* report "One Dead, One Hurt in Two

Shootings" on 24 Jan. 1946. The result was the *"death of a salesman"* from Jamaica, Queens (27). (Emphasis added throughout.)

2. An awareness of the larger context of "The Death of the Hired Man" generalizes the historical-cultural import of the poem. By the time Frost wrote the poem, as he was well aware, the institution of the "hired man"—usually unmarried and living with his employers—had all but disappeared from the scene.

3. Earlier, in "Arthur Miller: Poet," a piece in the *Michigan Quarterly Review* (1998), Bigsby said something similar: "In an essay on realism, written in 1997, Miller made a remark that I find compellingly interesting. 'Willy Loman,' he said, 'is not a real person. He is if I may say so a figure in a poem.' That poem is not simply the language he or the other characters speak, though this is shaped, charged with a muted eloquence of a kind which he has said was not uncommon in their class half a century or more ago. . . . The poem is the play itself and *hence* the language, the mise en scène, the characters who glimpse the lyricism of a life too easily ensnared in the prosaic, a life which aspires to metaphoric force" (713-14).

4. The Parable of the Prodigal Son is related in Luke (15:11-32): "A certain man had two sons: And the younger of them said to his father, Father, give me the portion of goods that falleth to me. And he divided unto them his living. And not many days after the younger son gathered all together, and took his journey into a far country, and there wasted his substance with riotous living. And when he had spent all, there arose a mighty famine in that land; and he began to be in want. And he went and joined himself to a citizen of that country; and he sent him into his fields to feed swine. And he would fain have filled his belly with the husks that the swine did eat: and no man gave unto him. And when he came to himself, he said, How many hired servants of my father's have bread enough and to spare, and I perish with hunger! I will arise and go to my father, and will say unto him, Father, I have sinned against heaven, and before thee, And am no more worthy to be called thy son: make me as one of thy hired servants. And he arose, and came to his father. But when he was yet a great way off, his father saw him, and had compassion, and ran, and fell on his neck, and kissed him. And the son said unto him, Father, I have sinned against heaven, and in thy sight, and am no more worthy to be called thy son. But the father said to his servants, Bring forth the best robe, and put it on him: and put a ring on his hand, and shoes on his feet: And bring hither the fatted calf, and kill it; and let us eat, and be merry: For this my son was dead, and is alive again; he was lost, and is found. And they began to be merry. Now his elder son was in the field; and as he came and drew nigh to the house, he heard musick and dancing. And he called one of the servants, and asked what these things meant. And he said unto him, Thy brother is come; and thy father hath killed the fatted calf, because he hath received him safe and sound. And he was angry, and would not go in: therefore came his father out, and intreated him. And he answering said to his father, Lo, these many years do I serve thee, neither transgressed I at any time thy commandment: and yet thou never gavest me a kid, that I might make merry with my friends: But as soon as this thy son was come, which hath devoured thy living with harlots, thou hast killed for him the fatted calf. And he said unto him, Son, thou art ever with me, and all that I have is thine. It was meet that we should make merry, and be glad: for this thy brother was dead, and is alive again; and was lost, and is found."

5. While Miller does not refer specifically to the Parable of the Prodigal Son, he does mention the "technique" and "form" of the "three Gospels of Matthew, Mark, and Luke": "you will see the tremendous effort being made to dramatize, to make vivid, an experience which probably none of them really saw—except possibly one" (Roudané 37).

6. Abrams quotes from Bede Griffith's *The Golden String*, an autobiography published in 1954.

7. In the same spirit Bigsby writes: "Willy goes on quests, like some medieval knight, riding forth to justify himself while at the same time his Platonic paradigm for the salesman-warrior is a man in carpet slippers, smoking a cigarette with a telephone in his hand" (*Critical Study* 118).

Works Cited

Abrams, M. H. *Natural Supernaturalism: Tradition and Revolution in Romantic Literature.* New York: Norton, 1971.

Baym, Max I. "William James and Henry Adams." *New England Quarterly*, 10 (Dec. 1937): 717-42.

Bigsby, Christopher. *Arthur Miller: A Critical Study.* Cambridge: Cambridge University Press, 2005.

_____. "Arthur Miller: Poet." *Michigan Quarterly Review*, 37 (Fall 1998): 713-24.

Cook, Reginald L. "Robert Frost's Asides on his Poetry." *American Literature*, 19 (Jan. 1948): 351-59.

Frost, Robert, "The Death of the Hired Man." *North of Boston.* New York: Henry Holt, 1914.

Frye, Northrop. *Anatomy of Criticism: Four Essays.* Princeton: Princeton University Press, 1957.

Gussow, Mel. *Conversations with Miller.* New York: Applause, 2002.

Johnson, Marilyn. *The Dead Beat: Lost Souls, Lucky Stiffs, and the Perverse Pleasures of Obituaries.* New York: HarperCollins, 2006.

Miller, Arthur. *Death of a Salesman.* New York: Viking, 1949.

_____. *"Salesman" in Beijing.* New York: Viking, 1984.

_____. *The Theater Essays of Arthur Miller.* Ed. Robert A. Martin and Steven R. Centola. New York: Da Capo, 1996.

_____. *Timebends: A Life.* New York: Grove, 1987.

Murphy, Brenda. *Miller: Death of a Salesman.* Cambridge: Cambridge University Press, 1995.

Poore, Charles. "Books of the Times." *New York Times* (2 June 1949): 25.

Roudané, Matthew C. (Ed.) *Conversations with Arthur Miller.* Jackson and London: University Press of Mississippi, 1987.

Stein, Robert H. "Parables." In *The Oxford Companion to the Bible.* Ed. Bruce M. Metzger and Michael D. Coogan. New York: Oxford University Press, 1993: 567-70.

Asking "Queer Questions," Revealing Ugly Truths: Giles Corey's Subversive Eccentricity in *The Crucible*

J. Chris Westgate

Theatre and Puritanism may make the strangest of bedfellows. After all, plays were roundly condemned by English Puritans during the Renaissance as inventions of the devil that, with their "wanton gestures" and "bawdy speeches," invited the theatregoer to indulge in a litany of vices, including promiscuity, robbery, and even murder.[1] For American Puritans too, self-fashioning their City on the Hill amid the wilderness of the New World, theatre was associated with any number of sins and was, consequently, forbidden almost altogether. Nevertheless, Arthur Miller yokes together theatre and Puritanism in what has become his most frequently produced play. The question, of course, is why. Why did Miller choose this most curious coupling? In "Journey to *The Crucible*," Miller intimates that his writing of the play was largely an effort to commemorate John Proctor, Rebecca Nurse, and those who had "such belief in themselves and in the rightness of their consciences as to give their lives rather than to say what they thought was false."[2] But Miller was equally appropriating these historical figures to critique the hysteria—driven by fear of Communists instead of witches—of his own day. What Miller may have recognized, as he read the historical documents, is that 1692 Salem was more than just "one of the strangest and most awful chapters in human history."[3] It was the apotheosis of what Victor Turner describes as a "social drama" in which "a public breach has occurred in the normal working of society, ranging from a grave transgression of the code of manners to an act of violence, a beating, even a homicide," and that this transgression—this disruption of society—distills and reveals the essence of that society, just as theatre endeavors to do.[4] The witch-trial itself, in other words, was already a drama, and those sent to the gallows were nineteen characters in search of an author. Adapting history to the stage compelled Miller to take certain well-documented, and understandable, liberties with that history, despite frequent criticism regarding these inaccuracies. After all, "the artist must bring to his work a creative imagination," as historian Edmund S. Morgan observes, "that transcends historical detail in order to recreate living people and situations."[5] What is especially noteworthy in Miller's creative re-imagining of 1692 Salem is how he recasts an apparently minor historical figure through, and for, his aesthetic.

Considering how *The Crucible* foregrounds Proctor's wrestling with his conscience, it is easy to dismiss Giles Corey as little more than an irascible and often feckless old man who, like the other villagers, gets caught up in the hysteria of the witch-hunt. After all, if Miller's Corey, who is based on the historical figure of 1692 Salem, has a literary antecedent, it would have to be Shakespeare's Polonius. When Proctor and Parris have a heated exchange over what "obedience" to the church entails, Corey offers a curious observation: "It suggests to mind what the trouble be among us all these years. Think on it. Wherefore is everybody suing everybody else? Think on it now, it's a deep thing, and dark as a pit. I myself have been six times in court this year" (157). Corey's interjection is a non-sequitur worthy of Shakespeare's officious statesman who, while revealing the "very cause" of Hamlet's lunacy to the king and queen, feels compelled to pontificate on the nature of "majesty." Similarly, when Corey, along with Proctor, confronts Judge Danforth to save their wives, Corey goes from being distraught at the prospect of losing his wife to the gallows—a very real possibility at this point—to describing his litigious prowess by recounting a case that Judge Danforth's father tried years before: "he give me nine pound damages. He were a fair judge, your father. Y'see, I had a white mare at the time, and this fellow come to borrow the mare—" (210-11). Like Polonius, Corey would seem to be too susceptible to free-association to truly appreciate the gravity of the situation and, consequently, to be taken seriously. In fact, it is not entirely clear what Miller thinks of the historical Corey:

He was a crank and a nuisance, but withal a deeply innocent and brave man. In court, once, he was asked if it were true that he had been frightened by the strange behavior of a hog and had then said he knew it to be the Devil in an animal's shape. "What frighted you?" he was asked. He forgot everything but the word "frighted," and instantly replied, "I do not know that I ever spoke that word in my life." (165)

Nevertheless, the fictional Corey, whether Miller intends him to be or not, is much more than the "most comical hero in the history," as Miller describes his historical inspiration (165). In fact, Corey may ultimately have more in common with Lear's Fool than with Polonius.

When Reverend Hale first examines Betty Parris, Corey, amid all the anxiety among the village elders over the girl's mysterious illness, interjects a "queer" question: "Mr. Hale, I have always wanted to ask a learned man—what signifies the readin' of strange books?" (164). Like Corey himself, Corey's "queer" question may be easy to dismiss, as Reverend Hale does, because of its absurdity; but it is because of its absurdity, ironically enough, that it cannot be dismissed. Before discussing how that absurdity works for Corey instead of against him, however, it is worth explicating Corey's question. If taken seriously, the question depends upon, and consequently makes explicit, the assumptions that guide, and to no small degree justify, the investigation of Betty's illness. For the village elders, it cannot be accident or merely pretense that the girl "never waked this morning . . . and hears and sees naught, and cannot eat" (142). Instead, these aberrations in behavior must be signs that "her soul is taken." In fact, the more details that come to light about the girls' activities in the woods the previous night (dancing and, perhaps, conjuring the devil), the more the villagers interpret the illnesses of Betty Parris and Ruth Putnam as unmistakable signs of witchcraft: "Last night, my Ruth were ever so close to their little spirits [of her seven children lost in childbirth]," contends Mrs. Putnam, "For how else is she struck dumb now except some power of darkness would stop her mouth? It is a marvelous sign, Mr. Parris!"

(144). Mrs. Putnam's demand of "how else?" her daughter is "struck dumb," like Corey's question about his wife's reading habits, assumes an unequivocal and readily identifiable relationship between signifier (the girls' illness; or Corey's wife's reading of "strange books") and signified (what these aberrations in behavior portend), to borrow from Saussure's linguistic terminology. This borrowing is more than convenient since Miller's Puritans are obsessed with discovering the signification of anything aberrant. Mrs. Putnam's "how else?' is more than just a distressed question about her daughter's illness; it is equally a plea for expedient explanations of otherwise inexplicable phenomena. Miller's Puritans operate under a worldview that is the ideological equivalent of Newton's Second Law of Motion reversed and reconfigured: every effect *must* have an immediate and identifiable cause. Consequently, when Betty Parris "whines loudly" as the parishioners sing below, her behavior is immediately understood, and justified, as a sign of the Old Boy's influence: "The psalm! The psalm! She cannot bear to hear the Lord's name! . . . Mark it for a sign, mark it!" (152).

But Corey's question does more than just parallel the "seeking of loose spirits" over Betty Parris's sickbed; it equally parodies it (154). After all, the answer to Corey's question would be the default answer that Miller's Puritans ascribe to any aberration: "the Devil's touch"—especially given that the result of Martha Corey's reading was the inhibiting of her husband's prayer. Among the problems with this solution, though, is that Corey prefaces his question by acknowledging Reverend Hale as a "learned man," someone with both the knowledge and the authority to answer the enigma of his wife's disquieting reading habits (164). Indeed, it is because of Hale's extensive "experience in all demonic arts" that he was sent for (142). Ironically, though, Hale's expertise on witchcraft derives from his considerable education that undoubtedly consisted of extensive reading of more than just the Bible. In fact, it is clear that he has read a number of "strange books" himself, as evidenced by the book he describes to Mrs. Putnam upon his arrival: "Here is all the invisible world, caught, defined, and calculated. In these books, the Devil stands stripped of all his brute disguises. Here are your familiar spirits—your incubi and succubi; your witches that go by land, by air, and by sea" (164). Hale's book may be, as Wendy Schissel notes, a copy of the 1486 *Malleus Maleficarum* (*Hammer of Witches*), a medieval guide to identifying and destroying witches.[6] There is, then, something of a paradox at the heart of Corey's question. If Reverend Hale is qualified, not just to answer the question of his wife's reading but also to cleanse Salem of witchcraft, then it is largely due to his reading of "strange books." But, of course, it is the reading of such books that is, in itself, the aberration that is evidence of witchcraft. Does the reading of "strange books" signify "the Devil's touch?" Or does it supply the power to eradicate that "touch"? Within Corey's question, then, the solution is implicated in (and thereby complicated by) the problem. This slippage not only calls into question the authority behind the witch trials that follow but also suggests that the relationship between signifier and signified is, despite Puritan assumptions to the contrary, highly ambiguous . . . if not outright dubious.

Just as significantly, though, this parodying extends to the mechanism for identifying witchery. When Parris and the Putnams insist upon the "sure sign[s] of witchcraft afloat," Hale is adamant that the investigation into these signs will proceed rationally, if not scientifically: "We cannot look to superstition in this. The Devil is precise; the marks of his presence are definite as stone" (163). What Hale demands, in other words, is a careful evaluation of empirical evidence, such as the "bruise[s] of Hell" that he describes as typical evidence of witchcraft. But Hale's methodology, however much he may distance it from the superstition of the village elders, still depends almost exclusively upon interpreting signifiers through Puritan theology; he still depends, in essence, upon the assumption of a stable and identifiable relationship between signifier and signified. It is just this methodology that Corey's question imitates and simultaneously ridicules in his own analysis of the "stoppage of prayer" that resulted from his wife's aberrant behavior. When Martha Corey was reading, as Corey relates the event, he "tried and tried" but could not say his prayers; "then she close her book and walks out of the house" and only then could Corey "pray again" (165). The parallels to Hale's interrogation of Abigail Williams about the girls' activities in the woods are intriguing. When Abigail finally admits that there was a frog in the kettle, even if it only jumped in, Hale interprets the amphibious presence as an unmistakable signifier: "Did you call the Devil last night?" he demands (166). For Hale, the frog becomes "empirical"—and therefore not superstitious—evidence of trafficking with the Old Boy. But Corey's narrative illustrates just how faulty this reasoning is, since to extend the same logic to his wife's reading is to suggest that his inability to pray is "empirical" proof that his wife is a witch, a conclusion that is laughable even to the Puritan elders—at least before the hysteria reaches its fevered pitch. In effect, Corey's question reveals the "critique of empiricism" that poststructuralist thought, influenced by Foucault, has maintained for decades.[7] There is no clear, unbiased relationship between perceiving subject and perceived object. Instead, as Nietzsche observed, "man finds things nothing but what he himself has imported into them."[8] Interpreting signs, in other words, is little more than a Rorschach test that exposes the assumptions of the subject instead of revealing the reality of the object. Corey's observation, if sincere, suggests his own foolishness, not his wife's trafficking with the Devil. Similarly, Hale's declarations about the Devil's presence reveal his predisposition toward finding such evidence, not its authenticity. Hale himself does eventually come to question his own methodology: "I have signed seventy-two death warrants; I am a minister of the Lord, and I dare not take a life without there be a proof so immaculate no slightest qualm of conscience may doubt it" (214). What Corey's question may do, then, is establish that the relationship between signifier and signified, when it comes to identifying witchery, is inherently arbitrary.

If the signifier/signified relationship is arbitrary, though, then that does more than just undermine the methodology for identifying witchery; it threatens Puritan theology itself. Religion is more than just a means of governing and regulating the actions of Miller's Puritans. It is the means of ideologically inscribing the world—both the landscape and those who inhabit that landscape—in which the Puritans live. Miller's Puritans have dearly dichotomized the New World. The forest, where "abominations are done," is juxtaposed with Salem, where the work of God takes place (142). Heathens, who traffic with the Devil, are juxtaposed with Puritans who serve the Lord. This basic binary, which almost certainly recapitulates the biblical juxtapositions of hell and heaven, fallen angels and angels, the Devil and God, is rigid and unambiguous for the Puritans, as Judge Danforth reveals during the trials: "a person is either with this court or he must be counted against it, there be no road between" (209). This moral absolutism, upon which many scholars have extensively commented, extends to and characterizes nearly all aspects of Puritan life. When Rebecca Nurse, weary of indulging the "silly season" of the girls, for example, tells Reverend Parris, "I go to God for you, sir," Parris predictably responds, "I hope you do not mean that we go to Satan here!" (209). There be no road between. This unquestioned and unquestionable binary is comforting for Miller's Puritans because it allows them to readily read, interpret, and apprehend a world that is, without such ideological inscription, a wilderness—both metaphorically and literally. That is why Mrs. Putnam, with "vicious certainty," refuses to see the girls' illness as anything other than unnatural: "I'd not call it sick; the Devil's touch is heavier than sick. It's death, y'know; it's death drivin' into them, forked and hoofed" (164). If there is no road between, it is clear what is behind such aberrations. But Corey's question, with its subversion of the signifier/signified relationship, reveals that this conceptualization of the world is not only constructed but also arbitrarily so. It suggests, in other words, that the Puritans have *mis*read, *mis*interpreted, and *mis*apprehended their world. In so doing, it tugs upon the loose ideological threads that could unravel Puritan theology.

It is clear, then, that Corey is considerably more than just the comic relief within the play. For Miller, he is a surprising but significant voice of social critique. There is some question, though, as to the intentionality of Corey's "queer questions." Does Corey know he's being subversive? Or is he just an eccentric and occasionally feckless old man? In the 1997 film adaptation of Miller's play, Peter Vaughan plays Corey as the latter. Vaughan's Corey is skeptical and suspicious of Putnam but never of the church, nor really of the witch trials for that matter until his own wife is named. His "queer questions" seem to be motivated by sincere concern and curiosity. Nevertheless, there is ample textual evidence to suggest that Corey is a deliberate agitator. In the midst of the village elders discovering "notorious sign[s] of witchcraft afoot," when Betty Parris first takes ill, Corey enters, assesses the situation, and then asks, "Is she going to fly again? I hear she flies" (142). This question could be, and generally has been, read as genuine enthusiasm on Corey's part for the spectacle of the girl's illness. But it would seem more than likely that it is irony cloaked by eccentricity. After all, it is Corey who sees through Putnam's ploy of having his daughter "cry witchery upon George Jacobs" because "if Jacobs hangs for a witch, he forfeit up his property—that's law! And there's none but Putnam with the coin to buy so great a piece" (152). If Corey is capable of recognizing that Putnam is "killing his neighbors for their land," then it seems almost certain that he, like Rebecca Nurse, sees through the girl's pretense and is mocking Parris (a favorite pastime of Corey's) and the Putnams for their gullibility. Moreover, after Corey asks Hale about the "readin' of strange books," he narrates just how his wife's reading "discomfits" him: "last night—mark this—I tried and tried and could not say my prayers. And then she close her book and walks out of the house, and suddenly—mark this—I could pray again!" (211). Corey's "mark this" and "mark this" echo, and parody, Mrs. Putnam's insistence that Reverend Parris "mark" the signs of witchcraft in his daughter's illness. Also, the repetition of "mark this" suggests that Corey is fully aware of his performance here and that he is, quite likely, deliberately embarrassing Parris and the Putnams before Reverend Hale. Corey's ironic intent is further corroborated by his moments of overt sarcasm, as when he interjects "That's deep, Mr. Parris, deep, deep!" when Hale and Parris debate why the Devil would strike the Parris household (165). Interestingly, Walter J. Meserve argues that John Proctor is unintentionally foolish because he fails to appreciate what is happening in Salem (166). Corey, I would argue, deliberately plays the fool because he *does* appreciate what is happening.

The most telling evidence of Corey as a deliberate agitator, though, comes with his death. Unlike John Proctor, Rebecca Nurse, and the others, Corey does not face the noose. Instead, he is, like the historical Corey, pressed to death because, as Elizabeth Proctor explains to her husband, "he would not answer aye or nay to his indictment" (243). If Corey had "denied the charge they'd hang him surely, and auction out his property," but if he had admitted to trafficking with the Devil, then he would compromise his integrity and his standing in the community. It is a daunting dilemma in which Corey finds himself, but it is especially revealing of just how politically and legally astute he is underneath his cloak of eccentricity. Corey chooses to "stand mute" under the most difficult of circumstances, and his silence means that "his son will have his farm." In effect, Corey locates and exploits a loophole within Salem law, by refusing to speak, thereby frustrating the attempt to destroy more than his body. It would seem, then, that Corey appreciates, whether he can articulate it or not, that what he is confronting is more than the weight of the stones piled on top of him; he is equally confronting the weight of social discourse turned against him. If he is condemned as a "wizard," the fundamental "Other" within Puritan theology, it is not just that his family loses everything but also that the village elders, who have endorsed the witch trials, had made him their scapegoat. Corey's silence before his executioners is more than just an act of defiance as Stephen Marino characterizes it; it is an act of subversion. He denies the village elders the justification for the continuance of the trials that they are undoubtedly seeking in his confession since he "died Christian under the law" (243). When Corey finally does speak, moreover, his "More weight" is just as subversive as his silence. In effect, he calls for the very thing destroying him. By seemingly embracing his fate, Corey transforms himself from potential scapegoat into martyr. His death does not justify the witch trials. It actually is the first incident in a series of incidents that ultimately undermines public support for the trials. Corey uses the legal system against itself at his death, just as his "queer questions" used the methodology for identifying witchery against itself during his life. It is not difficult, then, to appreciate Elizabeth Proctor's final words about the old man: "It were a fearsome man, Giles Corey" (244).

Ultimately, the subversiveness of Corey may be a question of performativity, but it is a particularly noteworthy interpretation since it highlights the inherent instability of Puritan theocracy, or at least Miller's depiction of that theocracy, by deconstructing it from the inside out. Miller's play, in other words, does more than just dramatize a "hegemonic world order that demonizes the other" as many critics have thoroughly discussed.[9] It simultaneously illustrates, through Corey's "queer questions," that the potential resistance to, and even subversion of, that hegemony lies in turning hegemonic discourse against itself. What this suggests about the play, then, is that it may be Corey, and not Proctor, who is the central figure in Miller's endeavor to dramatize "the essential nature of one of the strangest and most awful chapters in human history" (133). But, as E. Miller Budick notes,

> the danger which Miller sees for his contemporary American public is not that it will fail to recognize totalitarianism in the Puritans, or even McCarthy. Totalitarianism is too easy an enemy. . . . The danger is that the Americans will not be able to acknowledge the extent to which tyranny is an almost inevitable consequence of moral pride, and that moral pride is part and parcel of an American way of seeing the world.[10]

If Corey's "queer questions" become an indictment of Puritan theocracy, then Miller's play is equally an indictment, however much Miller may conceptualize his art as an "exposition" instead of an "attack," of not just America, as Budick suggests, but instead all societies that willingly or willfully marginalize anything aberrant as Other and then build their ideological identity upon that marginalization.[11] The list of such societies is perhaps as surprising as it is long: Colonial England, Nazi Germany . . . post-September 11th America? Every society, Miller's play would seem to argue, has its witches. The concern of *The Crucible* with what is, perhaps, the fundamental nature of all societies would seem to locate the play, even more than its obvious political inspiration, within Brecht's epic theatre. It is not difficult to imagine a production of the play using titles and screens to project images of other societies upon the stage to remind the audience of the universality of the themes suggested by Miller's Salem.

It is worth noting that Corey's agitation of his society, whether deliberate or not, parallels Miller's conception of the artist, as described during a 1958 interview with Philip Gelb: "The artist is the outcast; he always will be. He is an outcast in the sense that he is to one side of the stream of life and absorbs it and is, in some part of himself, reserved from its implications. . . . He is the enemy usually, I suppose, of the way things are, whatever way they are."[12] Like the artist, then, Corey is both inside and outside of his society, both physically swept up by the witchhunt hysteria yet able to intellectually distance himself far enough from it to comment upon it, both enemy and potential redeemer of his society. But if Miller's conception of the artist reveals much of Corey, then Miller's dramatization of Corey reveals his attitudes toward the artist. Like Corey, the artist seeks to confront, critique, and whenever possible overthrow hegemony, be it religious or secular (for Miller, the obvious example would be the House Committee to Investigate Un-American Activities). But Miller's artist simultaneously endeavors to change attitudes and reconcile Turner's "public breaches." In the same interview with Gelb, Miller admits, "by showing what happens when there are no values, I, at least, assume that the audience will be compelled and propelled toward a more intense quest for values that are missing."[13] This is the objective of all Miller's plays but particularly of *The Crucible*.

Miller's play compels its audience to recognize its own tragic flaws and errors, to see "that moral arrogance, the tendency to render unyielding judgments, is not confined within the American power structure," as Budick notes, but "is at the very heart of the American temperament."[14] *The Crucible*, then, not only documents but also enacts what Turner describes as a "social drama" in that it "suspend[s] normal everyday role playing . . . and force[s] a group to take cognizance of its own behavior in relation to its own values, even to question at times the value of those values. In other words, dramas induce and contain reflexive processes and generate cultural frames in which reflexivity can find a legitimate place."[15] It is the artist who truly asks the "queer questions." But it is the audience who is obligated not only to listen but also to face the ugly truths those questions invariably reveal.

From *The Journal of American Drama and Theatre* 15, no. 1 (2003): 44-53. Copyright © 2003 by Martin E. Segal Theatre Center, CUNY. Reprinted by permission of *The Journal of American Drama and Theatre.*

Notes

1. Phillip Stubbes, *The Anatomie of Abuses*, in *In Shakespeare's Day*, ed. J. V. Cunningham (Greenwich: Fawcett, 1970), 159-160.

2. Arthur Miller, "Journey to *The Crucible*," in *The Theater Essays of Arthur Miller*, ed. Robert A. Martin and Steven R. Centola (New York: Da Capo, 1996), 29.

3. Arthur Miller, *The Crucible*, in *The Portable Arthur Miller*, ed. Christopher Bigsby (New York: Penguin, 1995), 133. Subsequent references will be noted parenthetically in the text.

4. Victor Turner, *From Ritual to Theatre: The Human Seriousness of Play* (New York City: Performing Arts Journal Publications, 1982), 10.

5. Edmund Morgan, "Arthur Miller's *The Crucible* and the Salem Witch Trials: A Historian's View," in *The Golden and Brazen World: Papers in Literature and History*, ed. John M. Wallace (Berkeley: U of California P, 1985), 172.

6. Wendy Schissel, "Re(dis)covering the Witches in Arthur Miller's *The Crucible*: A Feminist Reading," *Modern Drama* 37.3 (1994): 462.

7. Raman Selden, Peter Widdowson, and Peter Brooker. *A Reader's Guide to Contemporary Literary Theory*, 4th ed. (London: Prentice Hall, 1985), 153.

8. Ibid., 185.

9. Thomas P. Adler, "Conscience and Community in *An Enemy of the People* and *The Crucible*," in *The Cambridge Companion to Arthur Miller*, ed. Christopher Bigsby (Cambridge: Cambridge UP, 1997), 95.

10. E. Miller Budick, "History and Other Spectres in Arthur Miller's *The Crucible*," *Modern Drama* 28.4 (1985): 539.

11. Arthur Miller, interview by Phillip Gelb, *The Theater Essays of Arthur Miller*, 195.

12. Ibid., 205.

13. Ibid., 195.

14. Budick, 538.

15. Turner, 92.

Verse, Figurative Language, and Myth in *A View from the Bridge*_____

Stephen A. Marino

No play in Arthur Miller's canon invites a discussion of poetic elements more than *A View from the Bridge*. The play exists in two forms: a one-act version, which was written in an intriguing mixture of verse and prose, opened in New York in 1955; a year later, an expanded two-act version eliminated the verse and premiered in London.[1] Evaluation of the differences between these versions has focussed almost exclusively on how Miller, in response to criticism of the sketchiness of the characters in the one-act play, enlarged the psychological motivations of the principal characters—Eddie Carbone, his wife Beatrice, and their niece Catherine—in order to emphasize the social consequences of the play's central action: Eddie's desire for Catherine. However, criticism has ignored how the poetic elements work in both versions. An examination of the texts reveals how Miller's editing of the poetic elements significantly shifts the focus of Eddie Carbone's action to the psychological and social levels, but deemphasizes the mythic level which is central in the one-act version.

A bare-bones synopsis of the plot of both versions[2] of *A View from the Bridge* shows how the psychological and social elements are integrated in the action of the play. Eddie Carbone, a Brooklyn longshoreman, and his wife, Beatrice, have raised her niece, Catherine, since she was a child. When the play begins, Catherine is seventeen and on the verge of becoming a woman. Eddie's affection as an uncle/step-father has changed into a physical and emotional attraction, which neither Eddie nor Catherine fully perceives, but of which Beatrice is aware. Eddie's emotion is transformed into jealousy when Catherine falls in love and wants to marry Rodolpho, one of two Italian illegal immigrants, the cousins of Beatrice living in the Carbone's Red Hook apartment. Eddie transfers his jealousy into an assault on Rodolpho's masculinity and tells Catherine that Rodolpho is only using her to obtain citizenship.

After Eddie discovers Catherine and Rodolpho coming out of a bedroom, Eddie takes his jealousy outside his family. He informs to immigration authorities—a deed abhorrent to the social codes of the Sicilian-American community—who arrest Rodolpho and his brother, Marco, who publicly accuses Eddie of snitching. Out on bail, Rodolpho intends to marry Catherine, and Marco comes to vindicate his and his brother's honor. Eddie wants Marco to apologize in front of the neighborhood for his accusation because he wants his "name" back. When Marco strikes him, Eddie pulls a knife which Marco turns back on Eddie, killing him.

When the play was published in 1956, Miller wrote an introductory essay, "On Social Plays," which detailed his intention to have the one-act version of *A View from the Bridge* illustrate much more than how Eddie Carbone's individual psychology results in confrontation with his society. Miller explains that when he first heard the tale in his Brooklyn neighborhood, he thought he had heard it before as "some re-enactment of a Greek myth." To Miller, it seemed the two "submarines," the illegal immigrants, set out from Italy as if it were two thousand years ago; he was awed by the destiny of the characters, that "the weaving together of their lives seemed almost the work of fate." Moreover, he wanted to dramatize the story without embellishment, exactly in "its exposed skeleton," because he did not want to interfere with the "myth-like march of the tale" (17-8).

In the writing and production of the one-act version of *A View from the Bridge*, Miller included the mythic quality of Eddie Carbone's story, along with its psychological and social levels, by creating a character, the lawyer Alfieri, who functions as a Greek-like chorus as both a character and commentator. Alfieri's speeches to the audience directly connect Eddie to what Miller sees as the mythic level of the play: Eddie's larger universal fate, his destiny to enact the tragic action. Moreover, the New York production used sparse staging to achieve the "skeletal" quality of the mythic story because as Miller wrote, "nothing existed but the purpose of the tale" ("Introduction," *View* viii).

Miller admits that the meaning of Eddie's fate remained a mystery to him even after writing the play. In revising for the London production, Miller sought to place Eddie more in relation to his Sicilian-American society. Miller realized:

> The mind of Eddie Carbone is not comprehensible apart from its relation to his neighborhood, his fellow workers, his social situation. His self-esteem depends upon their estimate of him, and his value is created largely by his fidelity to the code of his culture. (viii)

In this production, the set was more realistic; more actors played Eddie's neighbors. Miller ultimately judged that "once Eddie had been placed squarely in his social context, among his people, the mythlike feeling of the story emerged of itself, and he could be made more human and less a figure, a force" (ix). Moreover, "The importance of his interior psychological dilemma was magnified to the size it would have in life. What had seemed like a mere aberration had now risen to a fatal violation of ancient law" (ix). Because Miller believed Eddie's action was made more humanely understandable, Miller also included elements of simple human motivation—especially the viewpoints of Beatrice and Catherine. Twenty years later in *Timebends*, Miller commented on how the staging also emphasized Eddie's universal destiny:

> The play began on a Red Hook street against the exterior brick wall of a tenement, which soon split open to show a basement apartment and above it a maze of fire escapes winding back and forth across the face of the building in the background. On those fire escapes the neighbors appeared at the end like a chorus, and Eddie could call up to them, to his society and his conscience for their support of his cause. Somehow, the splitting in half of the whole three story tenement was awesome, and it opened the mind to the size of the mythic story. (431)

Despite his assertion that the two-act version opened up the mythic level of Eddie Carbone's struggle, Arthur Miller's editing of the poetic elements actually deemphasized the mythic level of Eddie Carbone's action that is central to the one-act version. Criticism, too, has debated how the mythic level of the play changes in each version. Some critics argue that the London production more forcefully revealed the mythic importance of Eddie's story and at the same time enlarged the psychological and social connections. For example, Donald P. Costello believes that the London production integrated all the circles—self, family, society, the universe—to which Eddie is responsible. Thus, the play moved "from private to mythic, from Eddie as psychological self to Eddie as participant in universal fate" (447). However, strong critical disagreement also exists about whether the revised version includes a mythic level. Neil Carson judges that "the emphasis seems to shift away from the universal and primitive nature of Eddie's passion to the unique qualities of the man" (101). Similarly, Christopher Bigsby analyzes that the effect of the London production was "to root Carbone more securely in his setting, to move the play away from myth and towards a more substantial reality" (*American Drama* v. 2 203).

An analysis of the poetic elements supports Bigsby and Carson's points. Not enough work has examined how Miller's revisions in language significantly altered the play. The one-act version of *A View from the Bridge* directly elevates Eddie's story to Greek-like mythic status by using both verse form and a series of images, metaphors, and symbols which connect Eddie to a universal destiny which all humans share. The revised two-act play eliminated the verse and altered many significant images. In expanding the psychological motivations of Eddie, Beatrice, and Catherine and placing them more clearly in the social context, Miller reduced the impact of the poetic language on the mythic level.

The one-act version of *A View from the Bridge* uses poetry and prose in an intriguing system where the characters switch from prose to verse in mid dialogue. For example, the lawyer Alfieri's speech, which opens the play, initially uses prose:

Good evening. Welcome to the theatre.

My name is Alfieri. I'll come directly to the point even though I am a lawyer. I am getting on. And I share the weakness of so many of my profession—I believe I have had some amazingly interesting cases.

When one is still young the more improbable vagaries of life only make one impatient. One looks for logic.

But when one is old, facts become precious; in facts I find all the poetry, all the wonder, all the amazement of spring. And spring is especially beautiful after fifty-five. I love what happened, instead of what might or ought to have happened. My wife has warned me, so have my friends: they tell me the people in this neighborhood lack elegance, glamour. After all, who have I dealt with in my life? Longshoremen and their wives and fathers and grandfathers—compensation cases, evictions, family squabbles—the petty troubles of the poor—and yet . . . (86-7)

This initial prose speech places Alfieri in the mid 1950s in Brooklyn in the poor working class culture of the immigrant Sicilian-Americans whose petty legal difficulties he has arbitrated. More importantly, it clearly establishes Alfieri's importance as the narrator who comments on the action, like the chorus in ancient Greek tragedy.

However, in the middle of his speech, suddenly Alfieri switches to poetry, speaking in a free verse dramatic monologue:

> When the tide is right,
> And the wind blows the sea against these houses,
> I sit here in my office,
> Thinking it is all so timeless here.
> I think of Sicily, from where these people came,
> The Roman rocks of Calabria,
> Siracusa on the cliff, where Carthaginian and Greek
> Fought such bloody fights. I think of Hannibal,
> Who slew the fathers of these people; Caesar,
> Whipping them on in Latin. (87)

Alfieri's speech indicates the verse system Miller uses in the one-act version of *A View from the Bridge*. All of Alfieri's commentaries are written in verse and punctuate the beginning and ending of each scene in a fashion similar to the stasimons of ancient Greek tragedy. Moreover, each commentary significantly connects Eddie to the universal fate which Alfieri sees him plunging toward. Using verse for this commentary closely parallels the function of the chorus as the objective voice of society/citizens reacting to the action and, most importantly, judging the tragic hero. Because Miller intended these parallels, we become like the ancient Greek audiences awed by Eddie's action as he moves inexorably toward his destiny.

Other characters in the one-act version also switch from prose to free verse in the middle of dialogue. Eddie, Rodolpho, and Catherine often switch, which effectively elevates the significance of their conversations. Although the shifts to verse are less systematic than Alfieri's commentaries, some notable observations can be made about how these characters use verse and prose—the same way observations are made, for example, about Shakespeare's use of prose and blank verse. Because *A View from the Bridge* attempts to make Eddie a tragic hero, logically he should speak a significant amount of verse. Interestingly, Eddie does not use much verse at all, but his few verse speeches occur at crucial moments of action. For example, he speaks in verse at three highly emotional moments in sc. 1, when he complains about Catherine's inappropriate way of dressing, complaints which illustrate the central conflict of the play: his desire for Catherine. Until the final scene, Eddie speaks in verse only once more, briefly in sc. 7, when he seeks Alfieri's legal advice about Catherine's involvement with Rodolpho and casts doubts about Rodolpho's masculinity. At the climax of the play, Eddie switches to verse in three significant speeches. The first emphasizes his protection of Catherine from turning "into a tramp"; the second demands Marco apologize to him in front of the neighborhood; the third rebuffs the dirtying of his name. Eddie's significant speeches use verse because his tragic action culminates in the last scene. Verse form is appropriate for him to speak since Alfieri's commentaries consistently point to the destiny which Eddie's actions follow. Therefore, the lofty language magnifies his action as a tragic hero.

Outside of Alfieri's commentary, Rodolpho speaks the largest number of verse lines in the direct action of the play. In performance, his Italian accent adds effective lilt to the verse, but Rodolpho's large amount of verse lines has great significance because he is the tragic linchpin of the play. Rodolpho is the unwitting provocateur of the action: he arouses Eddie's perverse jealousy over Catherine; he is the target of Eddie's informing, an action with large social implications in the Sicilian-American community; and he stirs Eddie's confrontation with his masculinity. In addition, Rodolpho and Catherine's conversations switch to verse more than any characters in the play. In fact, Rodolpho and Catherine speak much of their conversations in verse dialogue which is appropriate since their relationship provokes much conflict. In scene 6, in particular, the dialogue between them is almost wholly in verse. This scene is a crucial scene: Rodolpho and Catherine profess their love; they retreat into Catherine's bedroom; and Eddie discovers them. Ironically the form reverts to prose when Eddie enters, the dialogue perhaps imitating his interruption of their romantic interlude.

In addition to verse form, the one-act version of *A View from the Bridge* employs many images, metaphors, and symbols of the sea, shoes, movies, and religion which elevate Eddie's story to its mythic level. Consistent with language use throughout Miller's canon, these poetic devices rely heavily on the tension between their literal and figurative meanings, often including a high level of irony. Many of Alfieri's speeches use these figurative devices at the beginning and end of scenes. For example, Alfieri's two verse speeches, which open and close the one-act play, use the images of the tide and sea to connect Eddie with his mythic fate. In the first stanza quoted earlier in this discussion, Alfieri uses the images of the tide, the sea, and blood to connect the Brooklyn immigrant society of the play to its roots in Sicily—

especially the Sicily of the past. Alfieri compares the actions of modern civilization with ancient civilizations. The ancestors of these immigrant Sicilians were conquered by the Greeks, the Romans, and the northern tribes. They share a bloody history with great mythic heroes, legendary heroes like Hannibal, Caesar, the Carthaginians. Alfieri implies that Eddie, as a descendent, shares in this mythic past.

However, in the next stanza, Alfieri contrasts the mythic heroes of ancient Italian civilizations with the "heroes" of the new civilization in Brooklyn:

> Which is all, of course, ridiculous.
> Al Capone learned his trade on these pavements,
> And Frankie Yale was cut in half
> On the comer of Union Street and President,
> Where so many were so justly shot,
> By unjust men. (87)

The images imply that the "bloody fights"—the euphemism for the savagery of ancient civilizations—has been transformed in the new world. The conquerors like Hannibal and Caesar were transformed into unjust Mafia conquerors like Al Capone and Frankie Yale. Moreover, Alfieri maintains that the savagery apparently has disappeared in the present time of the play:

> It's different now, of course.
> I no longer keep a pistol in my filing cabinet;
> We are quite American, quite civilized—
> Now we settle for half. And I like it better. (87)

The present-day immigrants appear "quite American, quite civilized." Still, Alfieri witnesses how every few years the refinement of the new world is lost when the ancient, bloody savagery rises again. The sea image signifies the connections between the old and new worlds:

And yet, when the tide is right,
And the green smell of the sea
Floats through my window,
I must look up at the circling pigeons of the poor,
And I see falcons there,
The hunting eagles of the olden time,
Fierce above Italian forests. . . .

This is Red Hook, a slum that faces the bay,
Seaward from Brooklyn Bridge. (87-8)

The images set up a series of parallels between the old and new worlds: the green sea of the New York harbor echoes the Adriatic; the circling pigeons of the poor immigrants transform into the falcons and eagles of the ancient world. Moreover, Eddie's savagery parallels the old world savagery.

The sea images of the next stanza raise Eddie's story to the crucial mythic level. Alfieri speaks of a case coming every few years which goes beyond the petty legal squabbles he usually arbitrates:

Once in every few years there is a case,
And as the parties tell me what the trouble is,
I see cobwebs tearing, Adriatic ruins rebuilding themselves;
Calabria;
The eyes of the plaintiff seem suddenly carved,
His voice booming toward me over many fallen stones. (88)

This is Eddie's case. The images of "cobwebs tearing," "Adriatic ruins rebuilding," and "the voice booming over many fallen stones" symbolize how Eddie's fate is rooted to his ancient past. The language implies the mythic "timelessness" of his tale. The final sea image again reinforces Eddie's mythic connection to the old world:

This one's name was Eddie Carbone,

A longshoreman working the docks

From Brooklyn Bridge to the breakwater. . . . (88)

The "bridge" of the play's title gives us the view for Eddie's story. From the Brooklyn Bridge, one can literally see all the docks on which Eddie works as a longshoremen. However, the metaphoric view extends beyond the breakwater, because Eddie's destiny comes from across the sea. The destiny of his ancestors spans a bridge between the old and new world.

* * *

In addition to the figurative language that Alfieri uses in his speeches, other images, symbols, and metaphors are scattered throughout the play. These poetic devices are rooted in the language of the Sicilian-American society in Brooklyn, a language expressing the personal, familial, social, religious, and cultural codes which dictate an individual's behavior and with which Eddie is in conflict. Images, symbols, and metaphors of shoes, movies, religion, riding, and bowling extend throughout the play to indicate Eddie's struggle with these moral codes.

One of the more powerful images of the play—shoes—assumes figurative importance at the beginning of sc. 1. Eddie comes home from work and objects to the high-heeled shoes Catherine is wearing:

EDDIE: What's the shoes for?

CATHERINE: I didn't go outside with them.

EDDIE: Do me a favor, heh?

CATHERINE: Why can't I wear them in the house?

EDDIE: Take them off, will you please? You're beautiful
              enough without the shoes.

CATHERINE: I'm only trying them out. (88-9)

The shoes obviously have caused previous conflict in the home. Eddie has not allowed Catherine to wear these shoes outside the apartment, and now he even does not want her to wear them in the house. His desire to preserve her chaste image is clear from the outset of the play. Although his concern can be explained as normal parental/fatherly protection, Eddie's statement that Catherine is "beautiful enough" without the shoes provides the first hint of his physical attraction to her, a crucial violation of one of the moral codes which operate in the society of the play. In fact, Eddie's next speech shows how the shoes signify a cultural clash for Eddie:

> When I'm home I'm not in the movies,
> I don't wanna see young girls
> Walking around in spike-heel shoes. (89)

In these lines, Eddie associates Catherine's high-heeled shoes with the kind of shoes worn by actresses in the movies and, perhaps, whores in Sicily. Eddie obviously associates movie actresses with a female immorality which he demands Catherine not acquire. The contrast between types of women is consistently reinforced in the play. Eddie illustrates the contrast between Catherine and actresses in his line: "Why don't you wear them nice shoes you got? *He indicates her shoes.* Those are for an actress. Go ahead" (90). Later in the scene, Eddie uses allusions to Greta Garbo and the Madonna, references which vivify his conflicting feelings toward all women, particularly Catherine and Beatrice. Eddie refers to Catherine as Garbo twice in this scene. First he merely teases her: "You do your lessons today, Garbo?" (90). However, when he calls her Garbo a second time, he criticizes Catherine's behavior towards young men:

EDDIE: Listen, by the way, Garbo, what'd I tell you about
            wavin' from the window?
CATHERINE: I was wavin' to Louis.

EDDIE: Listen, I could tell you things about Louis which you
           wouldn't wave to him no more. (92)

The figurative language shows Eddie's clear concern about Catherine's sexuality. In fact, he later uses the image of high heels to symbolize how they attract men:

> Now look, Catherine don't joke with me.
> I'm responsible for you kid.
> I promised your mother on her deathbed.
> So don't joke with me. I mean it.
> I don't like the sound of them high heels on the sidewalk,
> I don't like that clack, clack, clack,
> I don't like the looks they're givin' you. (92)

Thus, the image of shoes reveals Eddie's actual concern with the sexual allure they give, and Eddie's sexual desire for Catherine is at the core of this allure. Eddie does not want Catherine desired by other men like some Garboesque screen-star icon. He does not want her to have any overt sexual attraction, as he says, "Don't walk so wavy like that" (93). Eddie attempts to suppress Catherine's budding sexuality; ironically, he not only notices it, but it also attracts him.

Eddie's suppression of Catherine's sexuality is represented by the other female iconic image of the play—the Madonna. Eddie uses this religious allusion to transmit his awe at how quickly Catherine has grown up:

> Boy, she grew up! Your sister should see her now. I'm tellin' you, it's like a miracle—one day she's a baby; you turn around and she's—*Enter Catherine with knives and forks.* You know? When she sets a table she looks like a Madonna. *Beatrice wipes a strand of hair off Catherine's face. To Catherine*: You're the Madonna type. And anyway, it ain't nice in an office. They don't go for that in an office. (93)

The Madonna allusion works on many complicated levels in the text. The Madonna's purity, chastity, and virginity obviously contrasts with the immoral sexual attractiveness which Eddie associates with the high-heeled shoes and Garbo images. Clearly, Eddie would like to preserve Catherine's chastity, which could be threatened by young men if she flaunts her physical beauty by wearing high heels. Yet, Eddie's desire to keep Catherine's virginity intact is juxtaposed by his physical desire for her, which ironically would destroy her purity. His physical urge clearly is indicated twice later in the play when he passionately kisses her. The Madonna image also has powerful religious connections for Italians which expands Eddie's violation of his cultural codes. For not only does Eddie's violation of Catherine, as her surrogate father, border on incest, his violation of her as a Madonna figure also is grievous sin.

The Madonna image also has powerful psychological connotations. Normally applied to a husband's feelings for his wife, the so-called "Madonna Complex" operates in an intriguing manner in *A View from the Bridge*. Eddie obviously possesses potent feelings for Catherine that resemble the Madonna complex; however, Eddie and Beatrice's marriage bears scrutiny in this vein. There are substantial differences between the one-act and two-act versions of the play regarding the nature of Eddie and Bea's sexual relationship and what the Madonna image implies about it. The one-act version downplays Eddie's impotency which is central in the two-act version. In fact, the only hint of his sexual inadequacy occurs in sc. 3 when Eddie, concerned about Catherine's late night dates with Rodolpho, explains to Beatrice his "responsibility" (108) to her. Beatrice responds, "I just wish once in a while you'd be responsible for me, you know that?" (108). Of course, "responsibility" can be explained many ways, but with Eddie's zealous overprotection of Catherine, especially of her sexuality, we can judge that perhaps he has not been fulfilling his sexual responsibilities as a husband. The two-act version more forcefully portrays Eddie and Bea's sex life. In fact, she asks Eddie, "When am I going to be a wife again, Eddie?" (31); they have not slept together in over three months, which heightens the sexual conflicts. Eddie's inability to sleep with Bea may be explained easily by the Madonna complex, but his sexual feelings are complicated. Although he is unable to perform with Bea, he clearly desires Catherine, but at the same time he does not want her virginity violated. Furthermore, Eddie has possible sexual feelings for Rodolpho, whose masculinity Eddie assaults because he seems both attracted and repulsed by Rodolpho's femininity.

Moreover, the Madonna complex maintains that a husband's sexual inadequacy with his wife occurs as a result of her becoming a mother. The one-act and two-act plays offer quite different versions of this. In the one-act play, Eddie and Beatrice clearly have two children; in the two-act play, references to the children have been cut. This editing has a powerful effect on how we read the images, especially when we also consider how the Madonna image has been cut substantially in the two-act version. The two-act version reduces the impact of the Madonna image by deemphasizing its contrast with the Garbo/actress images. The two-act version does not emphasize the high-heeled shoes and Garbo/actress images at the beginning of the play, but instead emphasizes how "wavy" Catherine walks. Also, this version consistently uses physical terms, like "baby," "little girl," and "big girl" to contrast Catherine with the woman she is becoming. Because Bea and Eddie are childless in the two-act version, they have put all their parental feeling towards Catherine. In a sense, this magnifies Eddie's incestual attraction to her. And because Eddie is so consumed with Rodolpho's masculinity, his own infertility somehow magnifies his inadequacy. The absence of a strong contrast between the Madonna type and the actress type has been reduced in the two-act play, not necessarily to advantage. In fact, the one-act version strongly emphasizes the contrast when Beatrice herself tells Eddie: "Let her be someone else's Madonna now" (109), a line cut from the two-act version.

The shoe and actress images recur when Marco and Rodolpho arrive in sc. 2. In fact, Rodolpho echoes the actress image in an intriguing way. Because the play previously presents Hollywood and movie icons as significant symbols, Rodolpho's Italian name suggests the Hollywood male icon, Rudolph Valentino. Much of Valentino's allure was sexual, and clearly, to Eddie, Rodolpho represents a sexual threat to Catherine as a type of Latin lover. Ironically, Rodolpho does not fit the tall, dark, and handsome stereotype of a Latin lover; rather, "He's practically blond!" (98). Perhaps Rodolpho's blond hair obliquely connects him to the actress image, the blonde bombshells of Hollywood. In fact, Rodolpho's blond hair becomes a point of attack for Eddie, later describing it to Alfieri as platinum, and telling Beatrice "he's like a chorus girl" (108), images which contribute to Eddie's feminization of Rodolpho.

Rodolpho also is a tenor jazz singer, which fits into the Hollywood motif. When he sings "Paper Doll," the lyrics of the song possess significant levels of symbolism, for at this point in the play Eddie already perceives Catherine's attraction to Rodolpho. For example, the line, "It's tough to love a doll that's not your own" (104) refers to both Eddie and Rodolpho, for the emotional and physical possession of Catherine is at the heart of the play. The line, "A doll that other fellows cannot steal" foreshadows Eddie's accusation of Rodolpho's theft of Catherine. After stifling Rodolpho's singing, Eddie again brings the shoe imagery to the forefront: "You got the shoes again" (105) and makes Catherine change the shoes. When she returns, he says, "All actresses they want to be around here" (105). This repetition of the Hollywood motif with its implied loose sexual mores has significance in this scene because Eddie's desire to protect Catherine is about to be challenged by her attraction to Rodolpho. In the two-act play, the Garbo allusion appears for the first time in this scene when Eddie notices the shoes: "What's the high heels for, Garbo?" (28). The one-act version more effectively establishes in the very first scene the stark contrast between types of women: Madonna and actresses. In the two-act version, the Madonna and Garbo images are never directly juxtaposed.

In sc. 2, Rodolpho also employs the image of "riding" which is used literally and figuratively. He romantically and humorously details how he pushes taxis and horse carriages up the hill in his Italian home town, and how he desires to own a motorcycle so he can become a messenger. These literal modes of transportation become figurative in sc. 3 when Eddie and Beatrice are awaiting Rodolpho and Catherine's return from a date. Eddie worries that: "B., he's takin' her for a ride!" a slang tern for taking advantage of her, which includes a significant sexual connotation. Moreover, Bea significantly connects riding with the Madonna image: "All right, that's her ride. It's time already; let her be somebody else's Madonna now" (109). The Madonna image possesses great irony here since Bea clearly understands Eddie's worship of Catherine as a Madonna. Bea wants her husband back as a sexual lover, but Eddie's spiritual love and physical attraction to Catherine interfere with Bea's sex life. Moreover, Eddie's feelings for Catherine are challenged by Rodolpho, and for Catherine to become Rodolpho's Madonna means she must give up her chastity and, ironically, not be a Madonna figure. Later in the scene, Eddie repeats his concern for protecting Catherine's chastity when he warns Rodolpho that he does not want Catherine in Times Square because "it's full of tramps over there" (111). Of course, for Eddie, "Times Square" connotes the same immorality as the actress, Garbo, and shoe images. Moreover, the image of riding continues in the same immoral context. When Eddie tells Catherine his suspicions that Rodolpho is only "bowin' to his passport" (114), Eddie describes him as " a hit-and-run guy, baby; he's got bright lights in his head, Broadway" (114). With the "hit-and-run guy" image, Eddie vividly depicts Rodolpho as a driver intent on running down Catherine's chastity, and leaving the scene. However, when Catherine denies this, Eddie says: "He could be picked up any day. And he's back pushin' taxis up the hill" (114). Eddie ironically applies the original literal meaning to the riding imagery, which exhibits how Arthur Miller consistently creates significant tension between the denotative and connotative meaning of words.

Alfieri's commentary at the beginning of sc. 3 introduces a metaphor of bowling which connects Eddie to his mythic destiny:

A man works, raises his family, goes bowling,
Eats, gets old, and then he dies.
Now, as the weeks passed, there was a future,
There was trouble that would not go away. (106)

Alfieri's reference to bowling at first does not appear important; however, bowling is mentioned two more times in this scene. Eddie is invited bowling by Mike and Louis at the beginning and end of their street conversation about Rodolpho. Bowling becomes intimately connected to Eddie's fate because Alfieri has included it in the activities of a normal man's life. However, Eddie is unlike other men who work, raise families, bowl, eat, and die. Eddie's refusal of Mike and Louis's invitation shows his distinction from other men who have no mythic fate. In Alfieri's commentary at the end of the scene, he also describes Eddie's eyes "like tunnels," its first use in the play. As Eddie moves towards his fate, the light of his eyes indicates the tunnel in which he is trapped. Alfieri describes a passion which "had moved into his body, like a stranger" (115). Of course, this passion has many meanings for Eddie: his desire for Catherine, his jealousy, his hatred—even attraction—for Rodolpho.

Eddie's conversation with Alfieri in his law office in sc. 4 employs many significant images of the play to indicate Eddie's growing crisis. For example, in his attempt to feminize Rodolpho, Eddie describes his hair as "platinum," an echo of the earlier actress imagery. Eddie also says about Rodolpho: "I mean if you close the paper fast—you could blow him over" (117), which recalls Rodolpho's rendition of "Paper Doll." In emasculating Rodolpho, Eddie figuratively attempts to make him into a paper doll. Eddie uses a particularly revealing image when he describes Rodolpho sewing a dress for Catherine: "I mean he looked so sweet there, like an angel—you could kiss him he was so sweet" (118). The angel comparison echoes many of the previous images and allusions. Certainly an angel recalls the Madonna image, for an angel possesses the same whiteness and purity. Moreover, angels often are depicted traditionally as blonde and sexless. Yet the angel imagery also signifies the complicated nature of Eddie's feelings for Rodolpho. Eddie ironically reveals the same attraction to Rodolpho as he does to Catherine. The angel image connotes the same sanctity as the Madonna image, both of which are juxtaposed with physical desire which the kiss indicates. This scene significantly foreshadows Eddie kissing both Catherine and Rodolpho in sc. 6. Although he attempts to emasculate Rodolpho, Eddie ironically perceives him as a sexual threat, as when he says, "When I think of that guy layin' his hands on her I could—" (118). However, Eddie has confused sexuality and masculinity. Eddie's real tragedy is that he does not recognize the tunnel he is walking through. Blind to his own desires, he merely sees Rodolpho as stealing: "He takes and puts his filthy hands on her like a goddam thief" (120). Eddie's blindness is indicated when Alfieri says: "She can't marry you, can she?" Eddie furiously says, "What are you talkin' about, marry me! I don't know what the hell you're talkin' about!" (121).

In Alfieri's commentary in sc. 4, the tunnel imagery again connects Eddie to his destiny:

> There are times when you want to spread an alarm,
> But nothing has happened. I knew, I knew then and there—
> I could have finished the whole story that afternoon,
> It wasn't as though there were a mystery to unravel.
> I could see every step coming, step after step,
> Like a dark figure walking down a hall toward a certain door.
> I knew where he was heading for;
> I knew where he was going to end.
> And I sat here many afternoons,
> Asking myself why, being an intelligent man,
> I was so powerless to stop it.
> I even went to a certain old lady in the neighborhood,
> A very wise old woman, and I told her,

And she only nodded, and said,

"Pray for him."

And so I—*he sits*—waited here. (121)

In this significant commentary, Alfieri gives Eddie over to his fate. The image of the dark figure walking down the hall echoes the previous tunnel imagery of Alfieri's opening commentary in this scene. Moreover, Eddie's consignment to his fate is witnessed by an old lady—an oracle figure who divines Eddie's future. Her statement "Pray for him" implies that only God can help him. Alfieri's waiting indicates his understanding that Eddie is beyond human intervention. His fate awaits him.

Eddie's denigration of Rodolpho's manhood peaks in sc. 5 and sc. 6 where many symbols reinforce the action. For example, in scene 5, Eddie provokes Rodolpho into a boxing match, after he and Catherine begin dancing to a record. The dancing significantly parallels the boxing, by contrasting the physical contact between the lovers, Catherine and Rodolpho, and the antagonists, Eddie and Rodolpho. Catherine and Rodolpho are dancing to "Paper Doll" (although this is less clear in the one-act version than the two-act version, which explicitly states so in the stage directions), an irony given the song's previous connections to Rodolpho's masculinity. In this scene, Eddie's action illustrates his skewed notion of masculinity. He discovers, that in addition to singing and sewing, Rodolpho cooks. Although Eddie is told about the male chefs in European hotels, he does not have a European view of what constitutes masculinity. As an American, Eddie misunderstands his own immigrant Italian culture. For him, masculinity is physical strength, and Eddie, therefore, challenges Rodolpho to a boxing match knowing he can overpower him. After he physically humiliates Rodolpho, Eddie has his own tactic turned on him at the end of the scene when Marco challenges him to lift a chair, and Eddie is unable. This scene signifies Marco's awareness of Eddie's antipathy towards Rodolpho. Moreover, it foreshadows Marco's challenge to Eddie at the end of the play.

In sc. 6, Eddie completes his humiliation of Rodolpho after he discovers him in the bedroom with Catherine. Before the discovery, Rodolpho and Catherine tenderly discuss Eddie's attitude about their relationship. When she suggests they move to Italy, Rodolpho refuses because of the difficulty of making a living there. He uses the same image of stealing, which Eddie used to describe him earlier:

> How can I bring you from a rich country
> To suffer in a poor country?
> What are you talking about?
> I would be a criminal stealing your face. (133)

Although Rodolpho ironically uses the same image as Eddie, it has a vastly different connotation here. He would be a criminal, as Eddie says, but not in the way Eddie thinks. Rodolpho clearly loves Catherine, and his concern for stealing her beauty and well-being is evident.

The dialogue, as Rodolpho and Catherine retreat into the bedroom, differs substantially in both versions of the play. In the one-act version, Catherine initiates their lovemaking when she says, "There's nobody home." Rodolpho answers "Oh, my little girl" (136) and she responds, "Now," signaling her agreement to enter the bedroom. Her womanly initiation of sex vividly contrasts with Rodolpho calling her "my little girl." In the two-act play (the scene is act 2, sc. 1), the language stresses much more the tension between Catherine as a little girl and a grown woman. Before she and Rodolpho retreat to the bedroom, he delivers a line similar to the one-act version: "Oh, Catherine—oh little girl." However, additional dialogue contains images which expand Catherine's psychological motivation:

CATHERINE: I love you, Rodolpho, I love you.
RODOLPHO: Then why are you afraid? That he'll spank you?
CATHERINE: Don't laugh at me! I've been here all my life . . . Every
            day I saw him when he left in the morning and when he

came home at night. You think it's so easy to turn around and say to a man he's nothin' to you no more?

RODOLPHO: I know, but—

CATHERINE: You don't know; nobody knows! I'm not a baby, I know a lot more than people think I know. Beatrice says to be a woman, but—

RODOLPHO: Yes.

CATHERINE: Then why don't she be a woman? If I was a wife I would make a man happy instead of goin' at him all the time. I can tell a block away when he's blue in his mind and just wants to talk to somebody quiet and nice. . . . I can tell when he's hungry or wants a beer before he even says anything. I know when his feet hurt him, I mean I *know* him and now I'm supposed to turn around and make a stranger out of him? I don't know why I have to do that, I mean.

RODOLPHO: Catherine. If I take in my hands a little bird. And she grows and wishes to fly. But I will not let her out of my hands because I love her so much, is that right, is that right for me to do? I don't say you must hate him; but anyway you must go, mustn't you? Catherine?

CATHERINE, *softly:* Hold me.

RODOLPHO, *clasping her to him:* Oh, my little girl.

CATHERINE: Teach me. *She is weeping.* don't know anything, teach me, Rodolpho, hold me.

RODOLPHO: There's nobody here now. Come inside. Come. *He is leading her toward the bedrooms.* And don't cry any more. (60-1)

This scene exhibits Catherine's awareness of becoming a woman. The language certainly echoes Catherine's previous discussion with Bea in sc. 3 about Catherine acting "like a baby" around Eddie. The repetition of the "baby," "little girl," and "spanking" images reinforces this. As a woman, Catherine shows acute sensitivity to Eddie's needs as a man and remarkable perception that Bea does not provide for them. Underlying Catherine's speech are the suggestions that she is aware of how to provide sexually for Eddie. Yet, Catherine cannot provide for Eddie like a wife and, ironically, her own sexual needs are about to be fulfilled by Rodolpho. Intriguingly, her initiation of their lovemaking is somewhat tempered in the two-act version. Although asking Rodolpho to "teach" her clearly can be read as an invitation, her exclamation, "I don't know anything" emphasizes her inexperience and virginity. Rodolpho speaks the line, "There's nobody here now," portraying him much more as the sexual aggressor—which somewhat tempers his femininity. Ultimately, Catherine and Rodolpho's awareness of their sexuality clearly magnifies the shock of Eddie's kiss which occurs moments later.

When Eddie discovers Catherine and Rodolpho in the bedroom, the shoe and baby images occur in both versions of the play. In the one-act play, as he exits the bedroom, Rodolpho says, "Beatrice went to buy shoes for the children" (137). These shoes perhaps contrast Catherine as a woman and as a child. This line is cut from the two-act version since Bea and Eddie are childless, reducing the impact of the shoe imagery here. However, the two-act version includes a line spoken by Catherine immediately before Eddie kisses her: "Eddie, I'm not gonna be a baby any more" (63). The image of her as a baby contrasts with her physical experience as a woman and magnifies Eddie's dramatic kiss— the physical sign of his struggle to love her as a child/baby and desire her as a woman.

In both versions of the play, when Eddie returns to Alfieri's office (sc. 7 in the one-act play; act 2, sc. 2 in the two-act play), several recurring images substantially stress Eddie's march toward his fate. In his commentary, Alfieri again describes Eddie's eyes like tunnels, and Louis again invites Eddie to go bowling. This scene also more forcefully presents the contrast between the social, moral, and legal codes that are operating in the play, codes which have lurked below the surface of the action. Eddie wants to prevent Catherine and Rodolpho's marriage because "the guy ain't right" (139; 65). Alfieri tells him, "morally and legally you have no rights," and Alfieri explains to him how these codes operate in their society:

> I'm not only telling you now, I'm warning you—
> The law is nature.
> The law is only a word for what has a right to happen.
> When the law is wrong it's because it's unnatural,
> But in this case it is natural,
> And a river will drown you
> If you buck it now. (140)[3]

Eddie has little comprehension of Alfieri's explanation of how civil law interprets natural law. Alfieri is operating under a code of modern American society which he describes in his very first commentary in the play as "more civilized." However, in Alfieri's own words, Eddie is not connected to this civilized law; his nature harkens back to his roots in the old world. Eddie's inexplicable action is the "Adriatic ruins rebuilding themselves" (88), the ancient bloody savagery rising again. Eddie lives according to this ancient code, and he will drown when he violates the social and moral codes so powerful in civilized society, especially the ethnic code he breaches by reporting Marco and Rodolpho.

The violation of the ethnic code is enforced in the scene between Alfieri and Marco after his arrest by immigration officials. Marco seeks revenge on Eddie because he has violated the Sicilian ethnic code based on loyalty to one's blood, and the violation exacts terrible consequences: "In my country he would be dead now" (151). Alfieri is reluctant to bail out Marco unless he promises not to exact this revenge: "To promise not to kill is not dishonorable" (153). Ironically, Marco has the same difficulty as Eddie in understanding how the law conflicts with his code:

MARCO:	Then what is to be done with such a man?
ALFIERI:	Nothing. If he obeys the law, he lives. That's all.
MARCO:	The law? All the law is not in a book.
ALFIERI:	Yes. In a book. There is no other law.

MARCO, *his anger rising:* He degraded my brother—my blood. He robbed my children, he mocks my work. I work to come here, mister!

ALFIERI:	I know, Marco—
MARCO:	There is no law for that? Where is the law for that?
ALFIERI:	There is none.

MARCO, *shaking his head:* I don't understand this country. (153)

Marco's frustration at the law not punishing Eddie shows how the law is at odds with Marco's moral code. Here the "civilized" code of American law juxtaposes the ethnic code of Marco's land, which abhors the violation of "blood." For Sicilians this violation must be avenged, because the law does not provide justice.

Ironically, Marco and Eddie both want to avenge their "blood," an image which works on many levels in the play. For Sicilians, blood is the unifying factor of society connecting the individual to his personal family, and to his societal family. Eddie violates all his blood relationships: he violates his paternal relation with Catherine; he violates his conjugal relationship with Beatrice; he violates Rodolpho's masculinity; he violates his immigrant society by informing to authorities. The one-act version of the play uses the blood image only in this one reference by Marco, but the two-act version of the play effectively repeats it twice, assigning it more symbolism. In this version, Rodolpho tries to make peace with Eddie before Marco comes for revenge, but Eddie refuses because his fury is now diverted from Rodolpho to Marco for having sullied his name in front of the neighborhood. When Eddie rebuffs Rodolpho, Beatrice says: "Only blood is good? He kissed your hand!" (83). Of course, Bea refers to the literal shedding of blood, the vendetta which may be avoided only by Eddie, Rodolpho, and Marco's rapprochement. However, in the ensuing dialogue, blood assumes symbolic meaning:

> EDDIE: What he does don't mean nothin' to nobody! *To Rodolpho.* Come on!
>
> BEATRICE, *barring his way to the stairs:* What's gonna mean somethin'? Eddie, listen to me. Who could give you your name? Listen to me, I love you, I'm talkin' to you. I love you; if Marco'll kiss your hand outside, if he goes on his knees, what is he got to give you? That's not what you want.
>
> EDDIE: Don't bother me!
>
> BEATRICE: You want somethin' else, Eddie, and you can never have her!
>
> CATHERINE, *in horror:* B!
>
> EDDIE, *shocked, horrified, his fist clenching:* Beatrice!
>
> *Marco appears outside, walking toward the door from a distant point.*
>
> BEATRICE, *crying out, weeping:* The truth is not as bad as blood, Eddie! I'm tellin you the truth—and tell her good-bye forever!
>
> EDDIE, *crying out in agony:* That's what you think of me—that I would have such a thought? (83-4)

Beatrice clearly refers to blood as "bloodshed." However, because she juxtaposes blood with the truth of Eddie's desire for Catherine, blood assumes figurative meaning as well. For Eddie's desire for Catherine is a violation of the blood that courses through all his relationships with his family and society. Thus, his violation tragically severs the connections with his own blood.

In the two-act play, Eddie's line, "That's what you think of me—that I would have such a thought?" indicates his lack of conscious desire for Catherine, a desire so obvious to everyone, except for himself and

Catherine. This version, which so much more emphasizes the psychology of the characters, deletes from the one-act play the most psychologically revealing action by Eddie in the final scene. Before Marco arrives, Eddie throws Rodolpho out of the apartment and tries to prevent Catherine from following:

> BEATRICE, *rushing to him, her open hands pressed together before*
> *him as though in prayer:* Eddie, it's her husband, it's
> her husband! Let her go, it's her husband!
> *Catherine, moaning, breaks for the door, and she and Rodolpho start*
> *down the stairs; Eddie lunges and catches her; he holds her, and she*
> *weeps up into his face. And he kisses her on the lips.*
> EDDIE, *like a lover, out of his madness:* It's me, ain't it?
> BEATRICE, *hitting his body:* Eddie! God, Eddie!
> EDDIE: Katie, it's me, ain't it? You know it's me, ain't it?
> CATHERINE: Please, please, Eddie, lemme go. Heh? Please? (157-8)

The kiss echoes both the earlier kisses to Catherine and Rodolpho. This crucial action occurs at the climax of the play and reveals the depth of the uncontrollable tragic action to which Eddie has succumbed. In an oblique way, the action recalls Alfieri's tunnel imagery in comparing Eddie to a "dark figure walking down a hall toward a certain door." The very action of this scene occurs in the hallway outside the Carbone apartment and the front door of the house where, prophetically, the confrontation with Marco occurs.

Although the two-act version of *A View from the Bridge* includes an emphasis on blood and name, it substantially deletes some crucial dialogue in the confrontation with Marco that leads to Eddie's death. The strength of the one-act version is how the figurative language supports Eddie's tragedy. In the final scene, many of the significant images of the play recur. Eddie's futile desire to preserve Catherine's chastity is seen when he uses the "tramp" image again. Eddie will not flee his house before Marco arrives, saying, "What did I do that I gotta get outa the house?/ That I wanted a girl not to turn into a tramp?" (156). The imagery of Rodolpho stealing Catherine also appears: "This one and his brother made it bad which they came like thieves to rob, to rob!" (157). The recurrence effectively highlights Eddie's conflict at the moment of its resolution.

The sea images which Alfieri uses in his first speech also echo in his final commentary, which brings significant closure to the one-act play:

> Most of the time now we settle for half,
> And I like it better.
> And yet, when the tide is right
> And the green smell of the sea
> Floats through my window,
> The waves of this bay
> Are the waves against Siracusa,
> And I see a face that suddenly seems carved. (159-60)

Alfieri reinforces Eddie's mythic link to his ancestry from the tides of New York harbor to the seas of the Mediterranean. However, he also integrates the sea images with other significant images he has used in other commentaries in the text. In the two scenes when Eddie seeks legal advice, Alfieri describes Eddie's eyes "like tunnels" to indicate the light and inevitability of the fate through which he was traveling. In his last commentary, Alfieri again uses the tunnel simile:

> The eyes look like tunnels
> Leading back toward some ancestral beach
> Where all of us once lived. (160)

In his most significant commentary in the play, Alfieri combines the tunnel and sea imagery, raising Eddie's story not only to his own mythic level, but to a universal mythic level in which all human beings live. The metaphor of the ancestral beach implies that a savage past lies dormant in us all, that the fateful passion that consumes Eddie could also consume any human. For Alfieri ends his speech suggesting this possibility:

> And I wonder at those times
> How much of all of us
> Really lives there yet,
> And when we will truly have moved on,
> On and away from that dark place,
> That world that has fallen to stones? (160)

However, Arthur Miller deleted this speech from the two-act version, replacing it with a commentary about Eddie in which Alfieri merely "mourns him . . . with a certain . . . alarm" (86). The connection of Eddie to his mythical fate and, most importantly, our connection as reader and audience to Eddie's tragedy are eliminated.

From *A Language Study of Arthur Miller's Plays: The Poetic in the Colloquial* (Lewiston, NY: Edwin Mellen Press, 2002): 81-106. Copyright © 2002 by The Edwin Mellen Press. Reprinted with permission of The Edwin Mellen Press, Lewiston, NY.

Notes

1. A third version exists. Miller rewrote the end for the Paris production because he was advised that a French audience would not accept that Eddie and Catherine could be unaware of the emotions between them. Ostracized by his society, Eddie kills himself. However, the form is the same as the London version (Carson 101).

2. The expansion in the two-act play included primarily dialogue changes for character development in Beatrice and Catherine, not major changes in plot. Some significant deletions and additions of action do exist, which this discussion details.

3. In the two-act version, this speech appears in prose.

Works Cited

Bigsby, C. W. E. *A Critical Introduction to Twentieth-Century American Drama, Volume Two: Tennessee Williams, Arthur Miller, Edward Albee*. Cambridge: Cambridge University Press, 1984.

Carson, Neil. "*A View from the Bridge* and the Expansion of Vision." *Arthur Miller, Modern Critical Views*. Ed. Harold Bloom. New York: Chelsea House, 1987.

Costello, Donald P. "Arthur Miller's Circles of Responsibility: *A View from the Bridge* and Beyond." *Modern Drama* 36 (1993): 443-453.

Miller, Arthur. "Introduction to the *Collected Plays*." *The Theatre Essays of Arthur Miller*. Ed. Robert A. Martin. New York: Viking, 1978.

_____. "On Social Plays." *The Theatre Essays of Arthur Miller*. Ed. Robert A. Martin. New York: Viking, 1978.

_____. *Timebends, A Life*. New York: Grove Press, 1987.

_____. *A View from the Bridge* (with *A Memory of Two Mondays*). New York: Viking Press, 1955.

_____. *A View from the Bridge* (two-act version). New York: Penguin, 1977.

Uneasy Collaboration:
Miller, Kazan, and *After the Fall*_____
Brenda Murphy

Criticism of *After the Fall* has been dogged from the beginning by the play's autobiographical implications. Since the opening night of the premiere production by Lincoln Center in January, 1964, critics have accused Miller of exploiting his marriage to Marilyn Monroe through the character of Maggie. The opening night newspaper and magazine critics all recognized Monroe as the origin of Maggie. Their reactions ranged from the mild disapproval of John McClain in the New York *Journal American*, "I thought the girl might have been permitted to rest in peace" (McClain), to Robert Brustein's condemnation of the play as a "three-and-one-half-hour breach of taste," a "wanton invasion of privacy," and "a shameless piece of tabloid gossip, an act of exhibitionism which makes us all voyeurs" (26-27) in *The New Republic*. The most savage criticism came from the academic critics like Brustein, Richard Gilman, and Susan Sontag, who expressed outrage at Miller's lack of taste. For his part, Miller insisted early on that the play was not about Marilyn Monroe. In an article for *Life* magazine in February, 1964, he wrote:

> The character of Maggie, which in great part seems to underlie the fuss, is not in fact Marilyn Monroe. Maggie is a character in a play about the human animal's unwillingness or inability to discover in himself the seeds of his own destruction. Maggie is in this play because she most perfectly exemplifies the self-destructiveness which finally comes when one views oneself as pure victim. And she most perfectly exemplifies this view because she comes so close to being a pure victim—of parents, of a Puritanical sexual code and of her exploitation as an entertainer. (Miller, "With Respect" 66)

While he denied that Maggie was simply a representation of Monroe, Miller insisted on his right as an artist to make use of the people and

---

events in his own life experience. "An art work's human value lies precisely in its unique ability to share experience which otherwise must remain in darkness," he wrote, and the fact "that elements of my life have been publicized to the point where, in some minds, fiction and design seem to have given way to reportage cannot have prevented me from using my own evidence, any more than if my life were unknown" (Miller, "With Respect" 66). In his autobiography *Timebends*, Miller wrote little about *After the Fall*, but he did insist that the theme of the play was "the dynamics of denial itself, which seemed to me the massive lie of our time," contending that "inevitably, the form of the new play was that of a confession, since the main character's quest for a connection to his own life was the issue, his conquest of denial the path into himself. It seemed neither more nor less autobiographical than anything else I had written for the stage" (520-21).

Miller's treatment of the Marilyn Monroe issue in *Timebends* is typical of his ambiguous, or perhaps ambivalent statements about it over the years. He implies that the character Maggie had been derived from a character called Lorraine in a play he had begun a decade before about a pharmaceuticals magnate, and in the next paragraph tells about the phone call Monroe made asking him to come home after the filming of *The Misfits*, ending the paragraph with the statement, "Now the unstated question posed in [Camus'] *The Fall* was not how to live with a bad conscience—that was merely guilt—but how to find out why one went to another's rescue only to help in his defeat by collaborating in obscuring reality from his eyes. . . . I wanted to write about the participants in such a catastrophe, the humiliated defendants. As all of us are" (521).

In *Timebends*, Miller praised Elia Kazan's direction of *After the Fall*, calling it "a production of great control and truthful feeling, surely one of the best things he had ever done," and writing that "he never tried to simplify his job by thinning out the material, and he faithfully sought to bring out the play's intentions." Nevertheless, he wrote: "My one great regret was my failure to stop [Barbara] Loden from wearing a blonde wig, which seemed to invite identification with Marilyn. Later I had to ask myself if this blindness was my own form of denial, but as usual I was buried in the play's structure, and the characters' resemblance to real models was far from the center of my attention" (537).

It is of course Elia Kazan who is held responsible for that blonde wig. He has written himself that he first thought of Barbara Loden for the part because he had seen her in a blond wig when he was making *Splendor in the Grass* (Kazan 635). Kazan is known as a domineering director who insists on his interpretation, sometimes against the wishes of the playwright, a charge Tennessee Williams made glaringly public with his edition of *Cat on a Hot Tin Roof* in 1955. Kazan admitted in an interview, "I think there should be collaboration, but under my thumb! I think people should collaborate with *me*. I think any art is, finally, the expression of one maniac. That's me" (Ciment 37). Was *After the Fall* a case of Kazan insisting on his own interpretation and imposing it on the play against Miller's wishes? Before we approach this question, it's necessary to consider the circumstances under which this collaboration took place. First, there is of course the background of Miller's relationship with Kazan. They had come together in 1946 to collaborate on *All My Sons*, an important production for both of them, young artists at the beginning of their careers. They immediately found that they were kindred spirits; they had similar backgrounds, values, and ideals; working together was intensely satisfying. By the time they came together to create *Death of a Salesman*, they have both said they were like brothers, and together they achieved their pinnacle of artistic and popular success in the theater. In 1952, however, as they were preparing to do *The Crucible* together, their friendship fell apart, when Kazan not only testified and named names before the Un-American Activities Committee but published an ad in the New York *Times* calling on all good liberals to do the same. Both men felt betrayed, Miller by Kazan's action, and Kazan by Miller's cutting off his friendship afterwards.

In 1962, producer Robert Whitehead, a good friend of both men, was urging them to put their differences behind them in the interest of the new Lincoln Center Repertory Theatre that he and Kazan were to head together. Whitehead could think of no better playwright than Miller to contribute the theater's first play, and perhaps serve as a kind of playwright in residence afterward. Miller wrote that he had "not changed my opinion that [Kazan's] testimony before the Un-American Activities Committee had disserved both himself and the cause of freedom, and I had no doubt that he still thought himself justified," but "what it came down to now was whether his political stance and even moral defection, if one liked, should permanently bar him from working in the theater," the sort of reverse blacklisting by the Left that Miller despised. On the other hand, Miller could not be sure that he "was not merely rationalizing [his] belief that [Kazan] was the best director for this complex play." Either way, to reject Kazan, he felt, "was to reject the hope for a national theater in this time" (Miller, *Timebends* 529-30). Kazan wrote that, although the reconciliation had happened through Whitehead, the "unexpected influence" that made him decide to fully commit to Lincoln Center was "Art Miller. He wanted to be part of this effort and promised us his plays to produce." Although the reasons for their estrangement were never discussed, and Kazan admitted to feeling tense in Miller's company, he wrote that he "admired the effort [Miller] made to come together with me again" (Kazan 586). Despite their determination to work together, the collaboration between these two artists in 1963 was definitely not the joyous and brotherly experience it had been in the forties.

Nevertheless, Kazan began his conferences with Miller on the script in April, and he and Whitehead worked with him throughout the summer and fall. In retrospect, Kazan thought that he was not as helpful to Miller as he should have been: "Invariably we praised and encouraged him, for he had worked hard. I admired his devotion and was grateful for it." But he did not convey what he really thought of the play: "I was so anxious to see him finish that my judgments were not true. Did we have a choice except to encourage him consistently? Our theater was hanging from a rope that we were braiding together" (Kazan 660). Under these circumstances, the rehearsals for *After the Fall* began in October with an unfinished script. According to Richard Meyer, an academic who was spending a sabbatical with the company, "the play Miller brought on this first day was complete but uncut. In spite of the freedom of length granted him, he planned to eliminate a good part of the second of the two acts." Nevertheless, Miller read the whole second act to the company, commenting, "'We don't have to impress each other with a finished product . . . we can share our weaknesses'" (Meyer and Meyer, "Setting" 13).

In hindsight, Kazan wrote that, although he freely offered criticism and suggestions to Miller throughout the writing process, he had "backed away from the truth" when it came to what he called "the overall pseudo confessional concept and particularly that of the first half of the play, which I didn't like then and like less in retrospect." He also disliked the "central figure, based, I had to believe, on Art himself. I found him a bore" (Kazan 630). In the first act, which focuses on Quentin, Kazan thought that "the self-dramatization, the turgid introspection, and a kind of self-favoring in Art's Quentin were heavy going and not interesting. Art's historical viewpoint on Arthur Miller, the hero of the McCarthy crisis, made for dull drama—and that was the first act" (Kazan 630). Kazan was unable to get over the idea that Quentin was a dull, self-important character. In his director's notebook he listed some of the traits he saw in Quentin, just the traits he would later ascribe to Miller:

1. Bewildered . . . puzzling things out.
2. Troubled. Self-doubting.
3. Searching
4. He's all intellectual . . . goes over and over and over his experiences, chewing them like a CUD
5. Extremely inexperienced: Square. Innocent
6. Feels sexually insufficient, uncertain, even inadequate.

7. Feels uncertain intellectually. This uncertainty is a *saving* grace. He also laughs at himself, undercuts his pomposity with humor.

8. Repressed, inhibited, 'like a board.' 'Drives nails into himself because he can't feel enough.'

9. Hard to connect with. He is always half-abstracted. He always seems REMOTE and judging and untouchable. He doesn't smile on cue. He has 'other thoughts.'

10. He once had a great 'charm' (his smile) and he has realized that it was 'they'-ism and has given it up. He had it in College.

11. Hard working . . . (up to when he quit the firm) . . . a Demon Beaver. But he worked as hard as he did mostly to avoid confronting his problems—his relationship with his wife, etc. The fact is that the only thing he got a lot out of is work.

12. Usually avoids direct confrontations . . . writes his anger . . . doesn't directly express it.

13. He is always full of longing.

14. He has given up the old 'answers' He has come to question everything he used to NOT QUESTION. But he is the sort of man who NEEDS 'ANSWERS' . . . must have a firm and strong morality . . . cannot live without a rigid morality (Meyer and Meyer, "After" 49-50).

According to Kazan, Jason Robards "knew immediately" that "the role of Quentin was a dud. Many of the scenes were played around Quentin, not with him; for him to observe and comment on but not take part in. In theatrical parlance, he was frequently 'feeding' other actors lines that they would 'top.' Jason saw this and resented it" (Kazan 667).

Kazan wrote his overall view of the play in his notebook early on. Looking for the dramatic movement or progression through the play, he wrote: "Act I: Quentin blames others. (Psychoanalyst: 'You haven't told me one pertinent thing. You've simply avoided the issue.'). Act II: Quentin really gets down to his complicity in his fall" (Meyer and Meyer, "After" 62). Kazan always saw the real guts of the play in the second act, which he said outright was "about Art's obsessive romance with Marilyn Monroe." Kazan wrote in 1988 that Miller had "denied, foolishly, that the story of that relationship in the play was based on his personal history, denied that his character, Maggie, was based on Marilyn. But he put into the mouth of Maggie precisely what Marilyn had thought of him, and particularly her scorn for him at the end of their marriage. This character is true and has an interesting dramatic development from adoration to contempt. Art is rough on himself, giving us all that Marilyn said in her disappointment and resentment" (Kazan 630).

True to his Method origins, Kazan based his reading of the second act on his own knowledge of Miller and of Marilyn Monroe, with whom he had had his own romantic dalliance in the early fifties. He thought the center of the play was in that relationship, and he urged Miller to rewrite it. Most particularly, Kazan had gone to dinner with Miller in California in 1960, when Monroe was having a rather public affair with Yves Montand. He had seen "the pain on his face and some anger too, manfully controlled." It was that experience that he wanted Miller to get into the second act; "if he'd go all the way and tell the truth of what Marilyn had done and what he'd felt, we might have a strong second act" (Kazan 667). Kazan had also spoken to Monroe after the break-up, and said "she'd revealed her anger at Art and a degree of scorn (which I'd thought unfair). She'd expressed revulsion at his moral superiority toward her and to much of the rest of the world. I knew there were scenes between her and Miller that were a lot more dramatic than those he'd let us see" (Kazan 668). While he didn't speak of this directly, Kazan urged Miller to go back to Connecticut and rewrite the second act while he and the actors were working on the first: "I was playing a hunch that if he went home, troubled by the knowledge that his cast and director thought his second act disappointing, he would dig into his memory and produce something that was intimate and bold, overcoming his play's shortcoming by the strength of its climaxes" (Kazan 668). In Kazan's view, Miller succeeded at this, sparing little of himself in this true representation of his marriage to

Monroe. In Barbara Loden, he cast an actor who not only resembled Monroe but embodied her experience: "I hadn't needed anyone to tell me she fitted the role. I knew her past in detail and knew Marilyn's personal history as well. They'd both been 'floaters' and come out of almost identical childhood experiences, which had left them neurotic, often desperate, and in passion difficult to control"[1] (Kazan 668). William Goyen, a writer in residence on a grant from the Ford Foundation who was present at most of the rehearsals, attested that Miller was quite open with the cast about Maggie's being based on Marilyn Monroe. He wrote that Miller

> showed no self-consciousness when scenes obviously torn from his own life were re-created before him. He spoke with Barbara Loden, who was playing the Monroe figure, frankly and intimately about the woman she was reproducing on the stage, even referred to specific life incidents. He seemed to have nothing to conceal in person as he had nothing to hide in this play. (Goyen 46)

The situation with *After the Fall* seems to have been quite similar to Kazan's experience with Williams on *Cat on a Hot Tin Roof*. Kazan saw what he thought might be a weak script, and he talked the playwright into rewriting it in order to emphasize what he thought was the strongest element in the play. While neither playwright objected at the time, both came to see the rewriting as a mistake, and as something Kazan had demanded without their agency. In order to determine to what extent this was true about *After the Fall*, it's important to consider the collaborative process during the writing and rehearsal of the play. During the summer of 1963, Kazan and Miller conferred regularly about the script, usually at Miller's home in Roxbury, Connecticut. Kazan offered his advice, and Miller rewrote as it seemed appropriate to him. As we have seen, Miller took Kazan's advice on the rewriting of the second act, coming into rehearsals with a considerably revised script at the beginning of December. The versions of the script that are at the Ransom Center in Texas show that this version was again cut a good deal in the next month, during the rehearsal process, preserving the essence of the act as Miller had drafted it, but cutting a good deal of dialogue that developed or elaborated on a point or gesture.[2] Also cut were lines directed at the Listener that make it much clearer that he is Quentin's psychiatrist, a substantial retrospective scene with Louise set in college, which drew her more sympathetically than any of the scenes in the final script, and interestingly, some lines that put Mickey, the character based on Kazan and his testimony to HUAC, in a more sympathetic light and emphasize Quentin's failure to respond to his call for help.[3] These cuts were obviously made with Kazan's approval, and probably at his urging, but they were all made by Miller, as were the additions to the script, many of which are in his handwriting. There is no evidence that Kazan overstepped his role as director in order to suggest specific rewrites, as he sometimes did with Tennessee Williams.

During the rehearsal process, Kazan was far from the domineering director he could often be. Because of the situation with Lincoln Center and his tentative relationship with Miller, he has written that he was "a good boy in the company of the actors we'd selected, and I was one hell of a good boy, compliant and respectful, with Art Miller" (Kazan 660). The accounts of eyewitnesses bear this out. Richard Meyer wrote of Kazan's obvious respect for Miller's script and his words:

> Long before the script was completed, Kazan had spent hours with Miller discussing the theme of the play, the background of the characters, the significance of each line. Even after the play was well into rehearsal, Miller dropped in frequently to watch its progress and was called upon to expand upon the meaning of an action or a bit of dialogue. Kazan himself continued to spend time before and after rehearsals analyzing the written words for more information and searching for new ways to convey this to the audience. (Meyer and Meyer, "Setting" 14)

Goyen described a rehearsal in which Miller and Kazan sat at a table with Jason Robards and Barbara Loden:

> Barbara and Jason would read a few lines of dialogue, then Arthur would interrupt and explain something—with glee and childlike relish. 'Gadg' Kazan waited, watched, relished. He seemed to let Arthur have his full say without interfering, except occasionally to agree heartily with Arthur or even to embellish Arthur's comments. I don't ever remember hearing Gadg take a stand or express a point of view contrary to Arthur's This was a playwright's theater I was in. Miller was in command, it was for him. No theater in America has so given itself over to a playwright as has this one, I thought to myself. (Goyen 45)

Apart from the unusual situation of the production, three things happened during the rehearsal period that help to explain Kazan's uncharacteristic passivity. First Jason Robards, who, as Kazan wrote, was not happy with his part and was having marital difficulties, disappeared from rehearsals for a time, shaking up the entire company. The day he returned, President Kennedy was assassinated, an event that deeply affected many of the people in the company, including Kazan and Miller. Rehearsals were again interrupted. A few days later, Kazan's wife Molly, who had been his major emotional support, his artistic advisor and his conscience, died suddenly of a cerebral hemorrhage. Kazan returned to rehearsals within days of her death, functioning in an efficient and seemingly engaged way, but he later confessed that he was emotionally devastated by his wife's death, just going through the familiar motions of putting on the show in order to keep from collapsing. It is no wonder, as Goyen reported, that "Miller's strength prevailed, and took an even stronger hold" (Goyen 47).

I think there is no doubt that the character Maggie was based on Marilyn Monroe, and that Miller was well aware of it, as his rewriting of the second act and his explanation of the character to the actors shows. Naturally, when critics came out attacking him for what they saw as exploitation of her memory, he backed away from the direct relationship in his *Life* article, saying that Maggie was not Marilyn, although he did say clearly that the play was based on his life, of which she was a part. In *Timebends*, 23 years later, he said that what he regretted was Barbara Loden's blonde wig—in other words, the visual signifier that said Marilyn Monroe to the audience. No doubt this was Kazan's idea. As he said, "although Arthur denied it and still does—why I can't understand—the second act of this play is about one thing: his marriage to Marilyn" (Kazan 667). And, since he found Quentin boring without Maggie, he believed that the second act was what would carry the play. As it did. It seems to me that the obvious conclusion is that Miller was ambivalent about his characterization of Marilyn Monroe and his marriage to her, and that the press reaction truly took him by surprise. As he said, there is no more self-revelation in this play than there is in any of his others. But in this case, he chose as a subject a national icon, recently dead, in whom the public had a stake. It was extraordinary that he thought he could write a play in which he in essence took responsibility for her death and that the average audience would dwell not on that but on the larger, more significant theme of denial, what he called "the massive lie of our time" (Miller, *Timebends* 520) There is great courage and self-revelation in this play in which Miller says over and over again that we are all guilty, we are all responsible for evil, including himself. But in the matter of Marilyn Monroe, perhaps it was Miller himself who was exhibiting denial.

Notes

1. Kazan was deep into a long-term love relationship with Loden at the time he cast her in *After the Fall*, and she was to become his second wife.

2. See *After the Fall*, Mimeo Stage Manager's Copy with A Revisions and Notes, 1963, Harry Ransom Humanities Research Center, University of Texas at Austin. This

script bears a note from Robert Downing, the stage manager, stating that it was the script approximately one month before the final rehearsal script was frozen.

3. In the earlier version, Mickey reminds Quentin that he called three times asking him to come and talk to him, but got no response. He also refers to his knees shaking in fear over the subpoena, and tells Quentin he has been told he will be voted out of the firm if he doesn't testify.

Works Cited

Brustein, Robert. "Arthur Miller's Mea Culpa." *New Republic.* 150 (8 February 1964): 26-28, 30.

Ciment, Michel. *Kazan on Kazan.* New York: Viking, 1974.

Goyen, William. "After the Fall of a Dream: A Behind-the-Curtain Report on What Went Wrong with Lincoln Center Repertory." *Show* (September 1964): 44-47, 86-89.

Kazan, Elia. *Elia Kazan: A Life.* New York: Knopf, 1988.

McClain, John. "Tour de Force by Robards." *New York Journal American* 24 January 1964.

Meyer, Nancy, and Richard Meyer. "'After the Fall': A View from the Director's Notebook." *Theatre, Annual of the Repertory Theatre of Lincoln Center.* Ed. Barry Hyams. New York: Hill and Wang, 1965. 43-73.

Meyer, Richard D., and Nancy Meyer. "Setting the Stage for Lincoln Center." *Theater Arts* 48 (January 1964): 12-16, 69.

Miller, Arthur. "After the Fall." Mimeo Stage Manager's Copy with A Revisions and Notes, 1963, Harry Ransom Humanities Research Center, University of Texas at Austin.

_____. *Timebends: A Life.* New York: Grove, 1987.

_____. "'With Respect for Her Agony—But with Love.'" *Life* 56 (7 February 1964): 66.

All About Talk:
Arthur Miller's *The Price*_____
Gerald Weales

When Arthur Miller's *The Price* opened in New York on February 7, 1968, most of the daily reviewers, whether they praised or damned the play, responded to the talkiness of it. Clive Barnes, condescending to Miller in an essentially favorable review in the New York *Times* (February 8), said, "The action has ended before the play starts, and we the audience have been brought here to listen to the explanations." Richard Watts Jr. complained in the New York *Post* (February 8) that "discussion goes on and on," and an even more disgruntled Martin Gottfried (*Women's Wear Daily*, February 8) insisted that "discussion . . . kills the play." The magazine critics echoed their daily colleagues. Robert Brustein, in one of his typical attacks on Miller (*New Republic*, February 24), reduced the talk to "jabbering and jawing," and my own reluctantly favorable review in *The Reporter* (March 21) noted that "like *Incident at Vichy*, it is little more than a round-table discussion, however emotionally charged." The oddest and in some ways the most interesting reaction to all that talk came from the reviewer on Riverside Radio WRVR—Dr. Walter Sheppard, as his titular billing has it. He likened the play to Bernard Shaw's *Don Juan in Hell*, but having stumbled on that happy comparison, he failed to use it in terms of the set discussion piece, nodded at the four-character similarity and waded into such an addled comment on the play that it is impossible to imagine that he knew what he had with the *Don Juan* reference. For that matter, none of us really knew what we had. Some of us used words like *discussion* as weapons to chastise the play; others (I like to think I am in this group) at least suggested that we were trying to define Miller's method; but none of us really recognized the implications of our responses. Talk, it turns out, is one of the things *The Price* is about. Such a realization need not make either the talk or the play more attractive to the playgoer/reader who is suspicious of Miller's wedding of psychoanalysis with Ibsenite revelation, but at least it gives *The Price* its due. A close look at the play indicates that Miller is using and questioning the dramatic, social, and therapeutic uses of talk and that our understanding of the play, particularly of the ending, hinges on the degree to which the author—and the audience—is willing to admit that there may be efficacy in conversation.

This reading of the play is not intended as a substitute for the standard one. *The Price* is still the story of two brothers who meet again for the first time in sixteen years to dispose of an attic full of discarded furniture—that is, to face the past. Victor is in a kind of spiritual stasis, haunted by the suspicion that his life and his marriage with Esther have no meaning and that there must be someone, something back there to blame for his being a police sergeant instead of a successful scientist, for his having sacrificed career and comfort perhaps unnecessarily to a father, broken by the crash and the depression. Walter, the surgeon brother, who thinks he has accounted for all his losses, is in need of dispensation, forgiveness for the wrong he may or may not have done in letting Victor assume the burden of their father. Miller, as his title indicates, is primarily interested in the recognition that acts, decisions, choices have consequences, often unforeseeable, and that a man, if he is to live,[1] has to accept that he is a product of those consequences, has to pay the price of those acts. If his bills are truly paid—if he has rid himself of guilt for his own past and the need to transfer that guilt to someone else—then the present becomes possible. Although the central thrust of the play is psychological, there is the inevitable social undertone, the suggestion that the choices that both brothers made were dictated by their responses to received attitudes (about success, about the family) just as the situation that called for the decisions was a societal as well as a personal one. This sense of things does not surface, as it does in *After the Fall*, to become an excuse, a rationalization, a family-of-man credit card to absorb the price for the individual.

Although Miller's theme is a major one, both in his work and in twentieth-century literature in general, the fascination of *The Price*, at least for me, lies in the way that theme emerges in a work in which talk is both tool and subject. That is the facet of *The Price* that I want to give my attention to in this essay. The curtain opens on an attic room, cluttered with old furniture, a closed-in playing area, with little space for any but verbal action. A policeman (Victor) enters, in uniform, suggesting to an audience which knows popular plays, but not this one, that a mystery story is about to begin—and, indeed, there is a secret to be unearthed but it has more to do with *Ghosts* than ghost stories. The policeman takes off his jacket, relieving himself of his label, and domesticates the scene as he moves about reintroducing himself to the props. The first sound we hear comes from the harp which he plucks in passing, but the first voices come from a record that he finds on the victrola. It is "Mr. Gallagher and Mr. Shean," the most famous question-and-answer act of the 1920's, and the play gets under way with a conversation routine, a vaudeville ritual.[2] A hint of things to come. There will be questions and answers enough before the play ends—and questions without answers. The point made, Victor takes the record off the phonograph and replaces it with a laughing record, preparation for the end of the play. He is laughing with the performers on the record when Esther enters and the talk begins.

At least, the speeches begin. "What in the world is that?" asks Esther and Victor answers, "Hi!" She asks again and he answers, having kissed her lightly, "Where'd you get a drink?" She replies, "I told you. I went for my checkup." Eventually, after we are well into the scene, Victor does explain what the record is, but by that time the initial exchange has done its job. These two people answer questions with questions, send out words that pass other word clusters en route without even a nod of recognition. In the world of conventional Broadway drama, where indicators are obvious and superficial, that opening could be taken as a standard Failure-of-Communication scene. Miller is not all that simple-minded. There is tension in this marriage, uncertainty on both sides, reflected in Victor's inability to decide about retirement and in Esther's drinking, but there is also closeness, an understanding that hardly knows any longer that it still understands. There are moments in their long first scene together in which one of them purposely deflects an incipient conversation, as when Esther, not wanting to talk about her sense of disconnection now that their child is grown and out of the house, switches abruptly to Victor's failure to reach his brother. There are moments when one of them answers an unasked question, perhaps an imaginary one, as when Victor, nagged by Esther's moody silence, blurts out, "Esther, I said I would bargain!" For much of the time, however, their apparently fragmented talk is the shorthand of two people who know each other well, who can indicate affection or annoyance without having to make a formal presentation. By the time the furniture dealer comes coughing up the stairs to interrupt them,[3] it should be clear that this is a marriage that is under strain, perhaps really in danger of breaking up, but it should also be obvious that there is a solidity here that prepares for the almost unspoken reconciliation at the end of the play.

What grows out of this opening scene is a sense of the way words are used not so much to say something as to suggest it or, just as often, purposely to avoid saying it. There is, however, another sense of talk established, if not practiced, as Victor and Esther fill the time before Solomon's arrival. It is through Esther that this idea of talk emerges. Out of her exasperation comes a need for solutions and, product of her environment that she is, she assumes that solutions lie just beyond the proper gathering of words. If Victor and Walter could talk to one another—*really* talk, to use the soap opera intensive—communicate, to use the jargon—then everything would somehow be solved. This is not a peculiarly American attitude, of course. Nora Helmer, just before she slammed that door to *A Doll House*, confronted Torvald with "We've been married now eight years. Doesn't it occur to you that this is the first time we two, you and I, man and wife, have ever talked seriously together?" Not that Ibsen necessarily assumed that a few more serious conversations would have kept the Helmers together, but I think that dear, dull Nora half suspects that talk might have done the trick. That suspicion is almost an article of faith in the United States and has been for several decades. While I was working on this essay, to catch my breath between paragraphs, I picked up an old copy of *McCall's* (September, 1970) that happened to be lying around the house and read a confessional article by an ex-priest explaining how difficult it is for him to relate to his new wife and her children. The word *talk* runs through the article, an insistent imperative, and it also turns up in a piece by Mary Jo Kopechne's mother in which she explains that Mary Jo was a good girl because she always talked over everything with her parents. Solutions, solutions. This was not an unusual issue of *McCall's*, nor is there anything particularly special about that magazine. All the ladies' magazines, all the newspaper psychologists, all the advice-to-the-love-lorners, licensed and unlicensed, have been telling us for years that holes in marriages, generations gaps, social chasms can be filled with words. The social attitude implicit in this easy adherence to talk operates not only around the dining room table, but in the pages of the presumably serious magazines and in the offices and conference rooms of all our institutions from the federal government down. A symposium in the pages of *Commentary* or *Partisan Review*, a Woman's Lib rap; a group therapy session, "dialogue" kept open on the campus, a national conference on poverty or pollution, a peace conference in Paris—all these are part of a pattern. The assumption is that if enough words are spoken, the magic word will cross someone's lips and the heavens will open. "Baby, Talk to Me," sang the hero in the whiniest song in Charles Strouse's *Bye Bye Birdie*.

This amorphous but very pervasive faith in the spoken word had an inevitable effect on the American theater. Playwrights at their best— from Shakespeare to Chekhov—have always been preoccupied with the strategies of language, the way people use words to confuse, to manipulate, to obscure. Popular drama has never been really comfortable with that degree of ambiguity, but it was only during the late 1940's and the 1950's that the Broadway theater developed the drama of the therapeutic conversation. If *A Doll House* were rewritten in that genre,

Torvald would pick up the clue in Nora's speech and turn confessional; after a rapid exchange of "but-don't-you-sees," they both would, and, joining hands, they would go off to face the dark at the top of the stairs. If that air-clearing conversation could have been taken simply as a theatrical device, a means to a happy curtain, it might have taken its place along with the ritual joining of couples at the end of comedy and the mandatory unmasking of the villain in melodrama, but its creators had greater claims to make for it. The plays were supposed to—and in fact did—deal with real problems and, hence, presumably, real solutions, and an alert couple in the audience might take a message out of the theater with them, might probe their own problems on the train home and thus arrive snarling in Rye and not speak to one another for a week. The more serious playwrights were never comfortable with the device. Tennessee Williams wrote such a scene for *Cat on a Hot Tin Roof*, but when he published the play, he offered both his original and the Broadway versions of the last act, commenting on the latter: ". . . I don't believe that a conversation, however revelatory, ever effects so immediate a change in the heart or even conduct of a person in Brick's state of spiritual disrepair." In *Death of a Salesman*, it is Biff's tears not his words that get through to Willy, who never does understand what the words are saying.

In *The Price*, then, we have a character who believes, with much of her society, in the therapy of talk, and a playwright who has his doubts. Aside from the Esther-Victor opening, Miller provides two conversations—one between Victor and Solomon, the other between Victor and Walter—and both of them have consequences within the play. Both are successful theatrical constructions, taking their form from the characters and the demands of the dramatic action, not from some extra-theatrical idea about the curative power of talk. It is almost as though Miller is using his play not only to question Esther's attitude toward talk, but by implication and example to criticize the audience expectations on that score and the genre that once fed them. Miller's complicated approach to talk as subject and device is apparent in his treatment of Esther. In my discussion I have simply assigned her the prevailing societal faith in words, but although she acts and reacts out of that faith in Act II[4]—she is never simply a vehicle for the idea. Although she harps on "talk," she is as defensive as any of the other characters when the occasion demands, ready to retreat into hurt silence or deflect the conversation to a subject on which she is less vulnerable. Even in her *talk* talk there is no clear line for us to follow. "I mean we ought to start talking the way people talk!" she says at one point, meaning that they should face facts, that Victor should confront Walter and get what the past says Walter owes him. Even if we avoid the obvious ambiguity—that the facts are hers, the past her version of Victor's version—we are faced with her unrecognized doubt about the power of speech. A few lines after the sentence quoted above, she becomes exasperated at Victor's refusal to face the problem of retirement. "It's all I've been talking about since you became eligible—I've been saying the same thing for three years!" she snaps, never hearing how those years of nagging words contradict the point she has just been making. A few seconds later, she is pleading, "Well, why not talk about what you don't understand?" For Victor, although he has certainly tried to call Walter, there is not even Esther's on-again-off-again confidence about talk. When he tries, disbelievingly, to conjure up what went on between him and his father in the attic all those years ago, Esther offers him the reluctant comfort of "Well . . . you loved him." Victor answers, "I know, but it's all words."

It is clear before we are very far into the play that Walter will have to turn up, that he and Victor will have to have some kind of confrontation, but the expectations that hang on that scene are obviously different for Esther, for Victor, and for the audience. Miller, however, has no intention of giving us that scene until we have listened to another conversation, one of a very different character and one that will help shape the Victor-Walter scene when it comes. Solomon arrives to buy the furniture and Esther exits, clearing the stage for him and Victor, leaving a warning hanging in the air, "Well, you give him a good price now, you hear?" The implications of her line—that Victor is a natural sucker, that Solomon is necessarily a crook—is not greatly softened by the old man's "I like her, she's suspicious." The two men are left alone, wearing labels not of their own choosing, and a pattern of approach and retreat begins in which Solomon tries to win Victor over. Solomon is the character that drew the warmest praise from critics, even from those who disliked the play, but a great many reviewers persisted in seeing his scene as a comic interlude, irrelevant to the rest of the play. An old man, pushing ninety, willing to start all over again, to use this roomful of Victor's past as a new beginning, Solomon is obviously a major character in the play's structure of ideas. More important, he has a central dramatic function to perform as well. In New York, he was played in a broadly comic way, achieving his humanity only within the bounds of Yiddish theater stereotypes—a reading that the play allows but does not demand. On the page, he is sadder, tougher, less funny, and, according to Howard Taubman (New York *Times*, October 19, 1968), he was played in Tel Aviv so that his entrance and first line were greeted with a sigh rather than a laugh. In either case, he is a professional dealer, a man who understands the verbal rituals of his own trade. Early in the act, Esther warns Victor that "you're going to have to bargain." Victor insists that he can, that he will, but he has no talent for it. To him, however, bargaining is simply a way for one man to best another, to screw the most profitable deal out of him, and what Solomon is doing, if that is bargaining, is the means by which the second-hand furniture business remains a human endeavor. No one should expect him— particularly at his age—to come crashing into the attic, set a price, pay the money and storm out again. Buying the furniture is not a simple act, it is an event and it demands its mystery. "What're you in such a hurry?" he says. "Talk a little bit, we'll see what happens." So he pokes around the attic, admires the furniture, discusses the state of the world, offers bits of his autobiography, asks Victor questions about himself, philosophizes, jokes, cajoles, badgers, gets politically angry when the deal falters. The effectiveness of the scene depends on an implicit anal-

---

Critical Insights

ogy between it and any swindling scene, for the audience, like Victor, begins to love the old man without being completely convinced that he is anything but a very talented *goniff.* George Oppenheimer was apparently so taken by Solomon's appearance of chicanery that he never got beyond that aspect of the scene, for he wrote in his otherwise enthusiastic review (*Newsday,* February 8, 1968), "We realize that the talk is partially a device to soften Vic . . . for the kill—the offer of a price far below what the furniture is worth."

A device, yes; to soften Victor, yes; but beyond that. . . . All during the first part of his scene with Solomon, Victor fights his interest in, his admiration for, finally his fondness for the old man. He keeps insisting: "I'm not sociable." "I'm not good at conversations." He wants Solomon to "talk money," to be direct, blunt, quick; yet he cannot help, even at the beginning, responding to some of Solomon's statements, feeding the old man straight lines that send him down conversational byways. When, at last, Solomon has played the game as far as it will go, has topped his verbal performance with a last pantomimic postponement, the eating of a hard-boiled egg, he sets to work in apparent earnest, jotting down figures, making his appraisal, "I'm going to go here like an IBM." At this point, it is Victor who interrupts, who reinstates the conversation, "You really got married at seventy-five?" By the time Walter arrives, interrupting them in the middle of the payment, the two men have achieved an unspoken understanding more important than the agreement on a price for the furniture. Talk has turned out to be efficacious after all, but not in the way that Esther imagines, nor even as Solomon intended when he went into his routine. Talk can create something, Miller says, but he does so not by insisting but by putting the creation on stage, by doing the job dramatically. The relationship between Victor and Solomon, whatever it is (at the end of the play, Solomon sits down in the father's chair), is an alliance that is used all during the second act. Banished from the stage by the brothers, Solomon emerges from the bedroom from time to time, interruptions that are intrusive in a more basic way than the original reviewers seemed to think. He tends to come back on the scene, to create a diversion, when Walter has Victor on the defensive, when Esther and Walter have too obviously ganged up on Victor.[5] Even when he is not on stage, he manages to be a presence. Victor's final self-realization does not spring full-blown from his argument with Walter; the seeds are planted in the conversation with Solomon.

Walter and Victor begin their conversation as strangers with a "how's-the-wife" exchange that commits neither to anything. "Relax, we're only talking," says Walter, trying to put Solomon in his place (or the place that Walter thinks ought to be his, for he keeps being surprised that Victor did not know the old man before today). More than a sixteen-year separation lies between the two brothers. There are those unanswered telephone calls, those attempts to reach Walter that Victor so resents, having failed to communicate at third hand, stymied by the machine and the machine-like nurse. Whatever his reason for not answering the phone (he says he was afraid to), Walter is now trying to reach Victor. His scene, at least in the beginning, might be taken as a deadly serious parody of Solomon's, but he is not a professional persuader, his need is too naked, his power to give too limited, finally only material. The reminiscence remains sentimental. His revelations about himself (his divorce, his breakdown, his estrangement from his children) suggest a self-awareness more solid than his picking at Victor implies. He quickly begins to make offers (*cf.*, Solomon's reluctance to reach that point)—that he deny any claim to the furniture, that he take a tax write-off on the furniture and give Victor the money, that he find Victor a job in the hospital. Too much, too soon, and Victor remains unconvinced. All Walter's talk seems to him a way of not talking, of avoiding the questions in their mutual past, and Victor, the man who doesn't believe in talk, decides "I feel I have to say something." At this point, it is Esther, of all people, who tries to stop the incipient conversation. Not surprising, really; from the beginning her call for talk has hinged on the hope of practical results, material consequences. Yet, when Victor indicates that he will not "just take the money and shut up," she falls back to one of her *talk* defenses: "You throw this away, you've got to explain it to me."

Walter is offstage seeing to Solomon when the exchange between Esther and Victor takes place. When he returns, when the possibility of the hospital job is broached, the three streams that will feed the final flood of words begin to bubble. Walter, who wishes "we could talk for weeks," who is "still unused to talking about anything that matters," wants Victor to absolve him for the past, to admit that he chose failure. Victor, not yet ready to give up the cast of characters—helpless father, selfless Victor, villainous Walter—who inhabit his past wants Walter's *mea culpa*. Esther wants a reconciliation between the two brothers and the sentimental and material rewards that would grow out of it; and she wants it so badly that she is almost willing to sacrifice Victor for it. She is the one who stops Walter, when, stung by Victor's ingratitude (noble doctor brother rejected), he starts to storm out: "Vic, listen—maybe you *ought* to talk about it." She insists, over Solomon's protests ("so what's the good you'll tear him to pieces"), that "what's so dreadful about telling the truth," that "We're giving this furniture away because nobody's able to say the simplest things." Walter agrees that "maybe it's just as well to talk now," and in a conventional play this would be the signal for the therapeutic conversation, the truth-telling that would lead to the brotherly embrace. Conversation there is and therapeutic it may be for Victor, but it is not conventional. As revelation follows revelation, as first one brother then the other takes the floor, each tries to score points against the other. Recrimination, accusation, but no understanding. Now one, now another of the participants, Esther included, tries to stop the flow of words when he sees himself endangered, but there is no retaining the flood once it is released. When, finally, Victor emerges from the talk with a new sense of self, it is no thanks to Walter, and it is a self that has no absolution to offer his brother. Earlier in the play, Walter picks up one of their mother's evening gowns, thinking to give it to his dress-designing daughter. Now, in a final wordless fury, he scoops it up and throws it at Victor and then, embarrassed, leaves the stage for good. "After all these years you can't expect to settle everything in one conversation, can you?" Walter had asked earlier. Even now, poor Esther cannot quite let it go, "So many times I thought—the one thing he wanted most was to talk to his brother. . . . It always seems to me that one little step more and some crazy kind of forgiveness will come and lift up everyone." But Esther, as she herself says several times in the play, "can never believe anything I see."

If the mandatory cure-all scene has come and gone and the brothers have not fallen into one another's arms, where does that leave the play? In black despair, some reviewers thought, empty lives displayed in all their emptiness. Brendan Gill, for instance thought the play ended with "three of the four characters . . . even more miserable than they were before" (*New Yorker*, February 17, 1968). Thierry Maulnier, who adapted Miller's play into French, seems to agree. In a note in the program for the French production (*Théâtre Montparnasse*, March 5, 1969), Maulnier, who saw the play's end in its beginning, wrote, "But in the course of that conversation, a man lays himself bare for us and discovers for himself the failure of his life, the absurdity of his failure, and the impossibility for him, even when the occasion arises, to find a reason other than that failure for which to live" (my translation). In a way, Maulnier is right. What emerges from the long talk is the fact that Victor's sacrifice was unnecessary on practical grounds and indefensible in terms of societal values (Walter is persuasive when he denies that their family ever embodied the virtues of loyalty and love). Victor recognizes this and goes beyond it. Maulnier's description is too narrow, the easy label-making of the outsider. Victor does not concede that he is a failure. He acknowledges the consequences of his acts. As Miller said, testifying before the House Un-American Activities Committee in June 1956, "I accept my life." The talk has been effective, but not as a revelatory conversation between the two men. "The confrontation is with each other," Ernest Schier wrote in his review of the Philadelphia try-out (Philadelphia *Bulletin*, January 18, 1968), "but it actually turns out to be . . . a confrontation of each man with himself." Presumably, from Victor's self-confrontation comes a release from the paralysis that has held him, but this is indicated only in small ways, which may explain why some reviewers failed to see it. It would have been impossible for Miller to give Victor a final positive speech—like the one he gave John Proctor in *The Crucible*—for it would have violated the character and, at the same time, have muddied the play's concern with the uses of speech, on and off stage. So we have to catch those small things. The moment when Esther comes over to Victor's side as wife and ally: "Nothing was sacrificed." The acceptance of the present in her willingness that he should wear his uniform when they go out to the movie. His decision to return for the mask and foil of his college fencing days, an acceptance of the past which must be contrasted to Walter's throwing the dress back. Finally, after Esther and Victor leave, Solomon's last non-verbal testimony to life. He puts the laughing record on the victrola. It begins, tinnily, as only an old record can, and then Solomon starts laughing with the record, finally swallowing the mechanical in the human. As at the beginning, laughter has replaced the voices. Being has stilled discussion.

From *The Ohio Review* 13, no. 2 (1972): 74-84. Copyright © 1972 by Ohio University. Reprinted with permission of the author.

Notes

1. There is an interesting "dead" pattern running through the play, a reflection of the paralysis that afflicts Victor and Esther. Very early, recalling a man who once lived in the building, Victor assumes he must be dead, only to realize that at the remembered time the man was "my age now. Huh!" "You're worse than my daughter!" Solomon says, attacking Victor's failure to go beyond his disbelief. "And if you can't do that, my friend—you're a dead man!" Later, when we learn that the daughter committed suicide, the earlier speech comes back, enriched. "Come on, we'll all be dead soon," cajoles Walter, shortly before the recriminative revelations begin, and, as they unfold, Esther says, "We are dying, that's what's true." By contrast, Solomon, who is almost ninety, holds on to the present with "if I'm there tomorrow" or "if I'll live," not with a phrase like "unless I'm dead."

2. The text of the play does not identify the specific Gallagher and Shean record and

I confess that I never thought to make a note of it either time I saw the play. Clive Barnes quotes, "Now Mr. Gallagher, now Mr. Gallagher, will you tell me what that question really means, I just wanted to find out . . ." and Stefan Kanfer (*Life*, March 8, 1968), who found the device "a too obvious billboard for the evening to follow," heard, "Won't you tell me just exactly what you mean?" The Gallagher and Shean exchanges I know, the ones that have been re-pressed in recent years, have no such lines in them, but somewhere in the Gallagher and Shean canon such lyrics may exist. It is possible for a reviewer, wanting to make the implicit explicit, to edit his memory. Barnes and Kanfer may have heard the lines they report, but . . . Absotively, Mr. Gallagher? Possilutely, Mr. Shean?

3. In this play entrances and exits are handled very clumsily if the play is taken as unremittingly realistic. I do not think it should be. The verbal encounters are almost like set pieces and for Solomon to signal his coming with a cough or to pull Walter offstage with "Please, Doctor, if you wouldn't mind . . ." is an admission by Miller of the basic artificiality of his form. Given an attic full of symbolic furniture and a life figure that is also a Yiddish comedy turn, the play is reasonably divorced from the realism that many commentators read into it and found wanting. Much of the incidental, presumably factual material in the play will not hold up under rigid scrutiny. Even the dates and ages are suspect; by my count, Victor would have had to become a policeman around 1940 which would have played havoc with the whole concept of the great Depression sacrifice. So far as I am concerned, these things are unimportant since the play is in the talk, not in what it uncovers, but anyone who dotes on the minor inconsistencies of art might look at Nathan Cohen's acidulous review of the road company production (Toronto *Star*, November 11, 1969) for his is surely the most complete collection of instances of the play's sloppy way with facts.

4. *The Price* opened its Philadelphia try-out in January as a two-act play, but when the production reached New York, it was performed without intermission. Both the first published version (*Saturday Evening Post*, February 10, 1968) and the editions in print (Viking, 1968; Bantam, 1969) are in two acts.

5. The television production made clear what has to be assumed in the theater, that the offstage Solomon is an eavesdropper, willing or not. One shot shows Solomon lying on the bed, eating a candy bar, while the voices of the other three can be heard from outside. That was practically the only thing made clear on television. Produced by the Hallmark Hall of Fame, broadcast over NBC, February 3, 1971, this version of *The Price* was so badly, so stupidly cut that Solomon had no existence as character or symbol and the heart of the play was cut out with him.

Both His Sons:
Arthur Miller's *The Price* and Jewish Assimilation

James A. Robinson

In 1902, writing about the typical son of recent Eastern European Jewish immigrants, Hutchins Hapgood observed,

> He is aware, and rather ashamed, of the limitations of his parents. He feels that the trend and weight of things are against them, that they are in a minority; but yet in a real way the old people remain his conscience, the visible representatives of a moral and religious tradition by which the boy may regulate his inner life. (Howe 254)

Born in 1915, Arthur Miller was himself the son of a Polish Jewish immigrant, Isidore Miller, who emigrated to America at the age of eight around the turn of the century. Though a member of a minority Jewish-American subculture, Isidore did not find "the trend and weight of things" against him. After marrying a second-generation Jew, Augusta Barnett, he lived out the American dream as a young businessman, eventually moving his family out of the Jewish ghetto in lower Manhattan after becoming a wealthy coat manufacturer in the 1920s. His wealth, however, was wiped out by the Stock Market Crash and the Great Depression; and his son Arthur's childhood experience of affluence, followed by loss, not only shaped his politics but served also to produce several plays that focused on the relationship between economics and a son's disillusion with his father. In *All My Sons* (1946) and *Death of a Salesman* (1949), a businessman father morally betrays his sons, thereby forfeiting any claim to the patriarchal authority which might provide the boy with the "conscience" which was the paternal legacy of the immigrants' children, according to Hapgood's quotation above. But in *The Price* (1968), Miller sees the father in a more complicated fashion, a fashion which makes apparent Miller's Judaism and

The Price and Jewish Assimilation **241**

the ethical questions it raised in his mind about his assimilation into modern American capitalistic culture.

In the play, a long-deceased father—like Isidore Miller, a successful businessman who lost nearly everything in the Depression—survives in the minds of his two middle-aged sons, Victor and Walter. Though he was not himself a righteous man, the father's past behavior confronted (and continues to confront) his sons with ethical questions involving a child's obligation to honor his father: the Fifth Commandment of the Mosaic code, at the heart of the Jewish moral tradition. Their differing responses to this obligation engenders their conflict, which is left unresolved. This unresolved conflict reflects Miller's growing recognition of, and ambivalence toward, his internalized Old World Jewish heritage. Thus, the play is only ostensibly about a battle between two brothers. More deeply, it describes a struggle within Arthur Miller to recognize and valorize certain Jewish aspects of his identity which had been obscured from him by his assimilation into mainstream American culture. The play's central conflict, in other words, reflects one within Miller between his Jewish and American heritages. The former is incarnated in Victor, the latter in Walter; and their inability to reconcile reveals the unresolved tension of Miller's own inner struggle.

Irving Malin has observed in *Jews and Americans*, "the archetypal Jew embraces the rule of the father; the archetypal American rebels against the father. Two mythic patterns clash: in this clash [Jewish] writers find tense, symbolic meaning," leading them repeatedly to depict "imperfect father-son relationships in which rebellion supplants acceptance; violence replaces tenderness; and fragmentation defeats wholeness" (33, 35). While Malin does not discuss Miller, his remark describes perfectly the actions of both *All My Sons* and *Death of a Salesman*, where the son's rebellion against the father precipitates an emotional violence that culminates in the father's suicide and the family's fragmentation. It also helps account for the emotional intensity of *The Price*, which depicts the battle between "archetypal Jew" and "archetypal American" in Miller himself. But little attention has been paid by critics to the Jewish elements in Miller's vision, largely because his plays (with the exception of the unpublished apprentice work *They Too Arise*) are so resolutely non-ethnic in language and subject matter.[1]

Unquestionably, the settings, themes and relationships of Miller's plays are most readily identifiable as American, not Jewish. His volume of memoirs, *Timebends* (1987), helps account for this by describing the young Arthur's desire to assimilate into mainstream culture. One childhood episode Miller recalls—involving his father, interestingly—suggests he was at least partially motivated by anxiety over his ethnic background. As a six-year-old at a public library, the boy Arthur was asked his father's name, but "looking up into [the librarian's] blue eyes, I could not bring to voice my father's so Jewish name, Isidore. . . . I had already been programmed to choose something other than pride in my origins, and this despite my father's seemingly confident authority. . . . His minority anxiety had moved into me, I am sure . . ." (24-25, my ellipses). Whatever unconscious discomfort he may have felt, Miller attended public schools, mingled freely with gentiles while growing up in Harlem and Brooklyn, and generally avoided discriminating along religious or ethnic lines—which he also attributes to his father, "whose refusal to attribute naturally superior virtues to all Jews and anti-Semitism to all gentiles may have set up in me, if not a faith in, then an expectation of universal emotions and ideas," he speculates in *Timebends*. "If ever any Jews should have melted into the proverbial pot, it was our family in the twenties; indeed I would soon be dreaming of entering West Point, and in my most private reveries I was no sallow Talmud reader but Frank Merriwell or Tom Swift, heroic models of athletic verve and manly courage" (62).[2]

Miller would later marry a (lapsed) Catholic from the Midwest, Mary Slattery, at a time when his attraction to socialism further submerged any ethnic identification: "Judaism for me and Catholicism for Mary were dead history, cultural mystifications that had been devised mainly to empower their priesthoods by setting people against one another" (*Timebends* 71). Looking back on his first visit to Ohio for the wedding, Miller concludes "I had somehow arrived at the psychological role of mediator between Jews and America, and among Americans themselves as well" (*Timebends* 82). Nor was Miller unique among his generation of educated New York Jews in this respect. As Irving Howe observes in *World of Our Fathers*, the New York Jewish intellectuals who emerged in the 1930s and 1940s (including Philip Rahv, Paul Goodman, and Sidney Hook) represented "the first group of Jewish writers who did not crucially define themselves through a relationship to memories of Jewishness," since "the values controlling Jewish immigrant life by the twenties and thirties were mostly secular, radical and universalist" (599-600).

Despite this apparent assimilation, Miller remains a deeply Jewish writer in several respects, as he implicitly conceded in a 1984 interview. Though claiming "I was never really a religious person in any conventional sense," he conceded that "all of the ideas we are talking about now [i.e, in the interview] are stemming from the Old Testament. The more I live, the more I think that somewhere down the line it poured into my ear, and I don't even know when or how. But I'm reading it again now, and I'm amazed at how embedded it is in me . . ." (*Conversations* 355). As the quotation suggests, Miller's intensely moral vision is rooted in Jewish ethics, an ancient source reinforced by an Eastern European Jewish culture in which, according to Howe, "not beautiful things, but beautiful deeds" were paramount (11). In many Miller plays, deeds both beautiful and ugly occur in a domestic context, reflecting an equally ethnic emphasis on family. Jewish culture from Biblical times has always concentrated on the family as (in Benjamin Kaplan's words) "the nucleus of Hebrew social life," where "the bond existing between members of a family was the strongest cement in their social order" (39); and in Miller's ancestral home of nineteenth century Eastern Europe, Howe remarks, "it was the ferocious loyalty of Jews to the idea of the family as they knew it, the family as locus of experience and as fulfillment of their obligation to perpetuate their line, that enabled them to survive" (20). For the Jew, as David Hartman has commented, the family is the institution which connects the individual to the community and to its history (Linzer 11). And no familial relationships are more important in Jewish tradition than those between parents and children.

The Jewish scholar Gerald Blidstein, in *Honor Thy Father and Mother*, indicates that there is little discussion of the Fifth Commandment in the Bible, the Talmud, or later codes because its "intensity lies elsewhere: in the patriarchal narratives that presuppose the graceful subordination and loyal service of children to parents; in the power and meaningfulness of God's self-description as 'father' of his people Israel; in the strategic location of filial piety in the Ten Commandments, where it is the first of the 'social commands' and indeed the *only* positive demand in the Decalogue made upon man in society" (xi, 4). It is unlikely that life in Miller's highly assimilated American household (at least, as he recalls it) invested the parents with this much transcendent grandeur. But *Timebends* does reveal Miller's childhood sense that "from my father some undefinable authority emanated," a kind of "baronial attitude" that compelled the respect of police, cabdrivers, waiters, even landlords (25). Thus, the particular temperament and demeanor of Isidore Miller during Arthur's early years may have reinforced the deep respect for the father's power—as well as the consequent imperative of filial obedience—that was embedded in thousands of years of Jewish tradition. And the dovetailing of personal and cultural sources led years later to a number of plays (*Sons*, *Salesman*, *The Price*) in which sons feel betrayed by the same paternal figures who had enthralled them as children. Indeed, as the eminent Jewish critic and scholar Harold Bloom has recently asserted, "perhaps all of Miller's works could be titled *The Guilt of the Fathers*, which is a dark matter for a Jewish playwright, brought up to believe in the normative tradition, with its emphasis upon the virtues of the fathers" (3).

Miller's membership by birth in a patriarchal Jewish culture also helps account for the perception of the father-son relationship as transcendent and universal—in a word, archetypal. "It's a very primitive thing in my plays," he claimed in a 1966 interview. "That is, the father was really a figure who incorporated both power and some kind of moral law which he had either broken or had fallen prey to. He figures as an immense shadow. . . . The reason I was able to write about the relationship, I think now, was because it had a mythical quality to me" (Roudané 89-90, my ellipsis). From a sociological perspective, that mythical power results from the interlocking of father, God and history in the Jewish tradition which Miller absorbed as a child. As Norman Linzer has noted in *The Jewish Family: Authority and Tradition in Modern Perspectives*, "as each reinforces the other, the child is exposed to a massive authority system that encompasses the entire Jewish past and is realized in the present" (81). And the male Jewish child is obligated to extend that system into the future, accepting the Law (as embedded in the Torah) from the father and passing it on to his son, so that male continuity becomes crucial to the survival of this patriarchal culture.[3]

The relationship between past and present, father and son, is a central theme throughout Miller's work, which displays both their interpenetration and their conflict. For, as the son of an immigrant, young Arthur Miller experienced to some degree what Geoffrey Gorer describes as the "break of continuity between the immigrants of the first generation and their children of the second generation," a break "of major importance in the development of the modern American character" (26). That break was made easier by the fact that his family had already assimilated to a large extent, a process which encouraged Arthur to largely ignore his ethnic background and thereby resist its patriarchal authority. Thus, the pressure toward absorption into a society that has little regard for history, Jewish or otherwise, became an incentive toward discontinuity, a departure from the ancestral past. And, while Miller never broke fully with his father—his attitude toward him throughout his life was characterized by respect, love and affection— he did experience disappointment with him in his adolescence, during the Depression. By the fall of 1932, Miller notes in *Timebends*, there was an aching absence in the house of any ruling idea or leadership, my father by now having fallen into the habit of endlessly napping in his time at home. . . . I could not avoid awareness of my mother's anger at this waning of his powers; . . . I must have adopted my mother's attitude toward his failure, her impatience at the beginning of the calamity and her alarm as it got worse, and finally a certain sneering contempt for him that filtered through her voice. (109, 111, my ellipses)

The Depression—a time of massive general disillusion with the political system, and with the economic authority of capitalism—also occasioned Miller's personal disillusion regarding the authority of his father. It was during a decade of economic and psychological dislocation and relocation, the 1930s, that Miller largely completed his assimilation into an American culture which was to become the frequent target of his later attacks in his writings. And the same decade furnishes the historical background for the conflict between two brothers over their treatment of their father in *The Price.*

The ethnic basis of the conflict is obscured by—and perhaps from— Miller through an intended critique of American culture. The playwright demands in a "Production Note" appended to the published play that "a fine balance of sympathy" be observed between the brothers' arguments, for "as the world now operates, the qualities of both brothers are necessary to it; surely their respective psychologies and moral values conflict at the heart of the social dilemma" (*Collected Plays,* II, 295). Indeed, the battle between Victor's impulse to sacrifice the self to larger familial obligations, and Walter's drive to realize the self via material success, is scarcely confined to Jewish-Americans. As theatrical classics like *Desire Under the Elms, The Glass Menagerie,* and *The American Dream* make clear, this is inevitably a recurrent theme in the theatre of an affluent, capitalist modern society founded by Christians. And the two brothers in *The Price* could pass for any Eastern urban Americans, since Victor and Walter aren't identifiably Jewish in speech, background, or behavior. But another character is: an elderly furniture dealer named Solomon, who immigrated (like Isidore Miller) from Eastern Europe at the turn of the century. Combined with the Fifth Commandment's crucial thematic role in the action, we will see that the creation of Solomon betrays Miller's growing recognition of the influence of his Jewish background on his morality in general, and his attitude toward patriarchal authority in particular.[4]

The play's plot can be summarized briefly. Two estranged brothers, both in their fifties—one a soon-to-retire policeman, the other a successful surgeon—meet for the first time in 28 years to decide on the disposal of their birth family's furniture, stored in a condemned building in downtown Manhattan. They're unable to agree on the terms of the disposal (Victor, arriving first, agrees to cash from Solomon; Walter subsequently proposes a more lucrative tax write-off), nor can Victor accept Walter's offer to employ him following his retirement. They engage in a prolonged debate, reminiscent of Ibsen, over the source of their estrangement: Walter's virtual abandonment of their father (following the old man's losses during the Depression) to pursue his career, in contrast to Victor's dropping out of college to become a policeman to support his father. The event that cemented their alienation, it is revealed, was Walter's denial of Victor's request for a loan to finish college. Both justify their behavior, and depart unreconciled.

The play can be seen as a series of variations on its title.[5] The obvious action concerns the price obtainable for the furniture. But as the shrewd Solomon points out as he and Victor haggle in the first act, "the price of used furniture is nothing but a viewpoint, and if you wouldn't understand the viewpoint is impossible to understand the price" (321). This declaration of relativity, crucial to the play, pertains specifically to Miller's refusal to side with the "viewpoint" of either brother. The title also refers to the cost of the choices the brothers have made. Walter says about his pursuit of professional success (which has lost him his marriage), "There's too much to learn and far too little time to learn it. And there's a price you have to pay for that. I tried awfully hard to kid myself but there's simply no time for people" (344). Victor likewise pays a price for not pursuing his scientific bent, which disqualifies him (in his mind) for the research position Walter offers: "You can't walk in with one splash and wash out twenty-eight years. There's a price people pay. I've paid it, it's all gone, I haven't got it any more" (361). Moreover, Victor pays a heavy psychological price for his repression of his suspicion about the money his father had, and withheld from him, years before—money which (as Walter knew) could have freed him to complete his education. As Victor's wife Esther, commenting on her husband's inability to decide upon a career following his retirement, notes, "You can't go on blaming everything on [Walter] or the system or God knows what else! You're free and you can't make a move, Victor, and that's what's driving me crazy!" (347). Victor periodically articulates the root cause of his paralysis: his sense of unreality whenever he thinks about his life with his father. "What was he? A busted businessman like thousands of others, and I acted like some land of a mountain crashed. I tell you the truth, every now and then the whole thing is like a story somebody told me" (309).

Victor's confusion recalls that of Quentin in *After the Fall*, but a deeper theme in the play looks back to Miller's earlier work: the inseparability of present from past, as symbolized by the perpetuation of the father in the sons.[6] Indeed, the past's power is visualized before the first line of dialogue is spoken, in a setting which features an overstuffed armchair, a radio from the Twenties, an old wind-up Victrola, and numerous other pieces of furniture that convey the "*weight of time upon the bulging fronts and curving chests*" (297-98). The furniture creates a dramatic situation which allows the brothers to meet again, leads inevitably to a conversation about their father—represented on stage by the chair in which he used to sit—and prompts Walter to offer money, employment, and friendship. In seeking brotherhood, he also seeks freedom from their past estrangement over the father.

But the furniture also occasions a subplot, involving Solomon, which suggests the impossibility of Walter's quest because of the father's lingering power, which casts a shadow over the action. For the

---

The Price and Jewish Assimilation

current business negotiation re-enacts the past event over which the brothers battle. Walter attempts to betray Victor's cash settlement with the old man, not only paralleling Walter's current effort to correct (i.e., betray) Victor's memories of Papa, but also repeating what Victor regards as Walter's economic betrayal of their father by supporting him only minimally ($5/month) during the Depression. Victor, by contrast, refuses to renege on his deal with Solomon, though he would benefit by doing so: as he had years before, he sacrifices himself and honors his commitment to the old man. By this gesture, he gives Solomon (who has come out of retirement to meet Victor) work, which revitalizes him and provides him with hope—as Victor had attempted to provide hope to his stricken father by remaining with him in the past. The two brothers' final gestures toward Solomon summarize their contrasting behavior years before. Seconds before his exit, Walter "*suddenly reaches out and grabs Solomon's face and laughs.* Go ahead, you old mutt—rob them blind, they love it!" (371). Victor's final gesture toward Solomon is to accept the old man's thanks for providing him work, and wish him luck.

If the solidity of the furniture helps embody the victory of past over present, it also points up the related conflict within Miller himself— and perhaps within most Americans, ethnic or otherwise—between the values of the Old and New World. The furniture's "*rich heaviness*" is described as "*almost Germanic*" in the stage directions (298), foreshadowing numerous other references in the dialogue to furniture styles—Louis Seize, Spanish Jacobean, Biedermeier—that draw on European cultures and periods. (Even a minor piece of recurrent business involving Victor's fencing foils, which anticipates the later verbal match between the brothers, alludes to the old European tradition of duelling to defend one's honor.) As noted, in the middle of this Old World style furniture sits the father's old, empty armchair. The setting thus subtly places the role played by Papa in the past action—as mirrored by (the Russian immigrant) Solomon's role in the present—in the larger context of the fatherlands and motherlands left behind by European voyagers to the New World. Those lands in general preached respect for elders, nowhere more so than in European Jewish cultures where veneration of male ancestors corresponded to devotion to a father God. *The Price* thereby evokes the power of Old World patriarchy not just by means of paternal characters, both living and dead, but via the cramped Old World physical environment in which the characters speak and move. The father's chair may be empty, and Europe distant in space and time, but both still exert considerable impact upon the present.

This is only half the story, however, for the furniture is stored in a Manhattan brownstone awaiting demolition: a surrounding context epitomizing a New World culture that rejects permanence, and challenges the patriarchal ideology that maintains tradition. "What is the key word today?" Solomon rhetorically asks Victor. "Disposable. The more you can throw it away the more it's beautiful" (323). Manhattan, the fast-paced heart of urban American culture, constantly disposes of buildings, erecting new ones in their place. And the New York City setting also connotes more broadly the materialistic, individualistic values that are thought of (fairly or not) as American, in contrast to the more communal cultures of Europe. If Victor clings stubbornly to traditional Jewish familial responsibilities, sacrificing opportunities in order to honor his filial obligations, Walter by contrast is stereotypically American, pursuing wealth and self-realization at the expense of family—indeed, "disposing" of his father and brother in the course of his pursuit.

Despite Walter's apparent repudiation of the father, however, he reproduces him in certain vital respects: in the play's moral scheme, both have fully absorbed the materialistic values of modern American culture. Both father and son, for example, embody the destructiveness of success, American-style. Walter achieves fortune and fame at the cost of family (divorced from his wife, he is estranged from his male children) and friends. Significantly, his breakdown occurs after he performs a string of risky, unsuccessful surgeries which other doctors had refused to attempt: true to his ethic of self-concern, he places his need to shine before his patients' right to survival. But this behavior pays tribute to the American model his father provided. For both father and son overidentify with their professional roles, to the point that Papa—a great success before the Crash—is unable to recover from his financial failure, and Walter is driven to a breakdown precipitated by professional setbacks. Papa respects Walter more than Victor because of the former's success, and refuses—in an act imitated by Walter—to share (or even acknowledge the existence of) his money to advance the fortunes of his more loyal son. Finally, in a logical corollary to the capitalist dictum that each should seek his own self-interest, both father and son distrust others. Neither Papa nor Walter expects Victor to remain with his father. "[Papa] was sure you would" walk out "sooner or later," Walter tells his brother. "I don't mean that he wasn't grateful to you, but he really couldn't understand it. . . . I myself never imagined you'd go that far" (364, my ellipsis). Undeniably, Walter is (or at least has been) selfish, but he has unconsciously followed the lead of a narcissistic father.

Victor, by contrast, affirms Miller's value—nurtured by socialism and liberalism, but originating in his Judaism—of connectedness. Maintaining his marriage, Victor also takes great pride in his gifted son: symbolically, he preserves the male continuity which Walter has ruptured, a continuity which Judaism holds sacred. His profession of police work, which upholds the authority of the law, demonstrates the same sense of obligation to protect victims that was apparent in his decision to remain with his father. Indeed, Victor's respect for the father/son bond engenders his respect for other bonds. Without filial devotion, in Victor's view, there exists no sanction for the brotherhood Walter proposes. And Miller seems to manipulate the plot and dialogue to prove this. Thus, Walter's contempt for his father, over his withholding money from Victor, motivates his denial of opportunity to his brother. "I told [Papa] at the time," Walter informs Victor, "if he would send you through [college], I'd contribute properly. But here he's got you running from job to job to feed him—I'm damned if I'd sacrifice when he was holding out on you" (363). And in Victor's mind this scenario of linked betrayals persists, despite the reformed Walter's best efforts to persuade Victor that the real betrayal was that of Victor by the father. Simply, Victor cannot trust a brother who abandons his father: the traditional moralist in him, a sign of the residual Old World Jew in Arthur Miller, finds it impossible.

Ironically, Walter claims a similar respect for the father/son relationship. He feels anguish now for denying money to Victor in the past, describing the action as "despicable" and "frightful" (359); but he also reveals that he reconsidered his brother's request, and called the house to offer Victor the money a few days later, only to speak instead with Papa. When he told his father not to allow Victor to join the police force, the old man replied, "Victor wants to help me. I can't stop him" (359), and dissuaded Walter from his offer. This story is subsequently dismissed by Victor as a rationalization—"if you want to help somebody you do it, if you don't you don't" (360)—and this is partially true. But the episode also suggests the power of the father/son relationship in Walter's (and ultimately Miller's) mind. "You all seemed to need each other more, Vic—more than I needed them [*sic*]. I was never able to feel your kind of . . . faith in him; that . . . confidence" (359). What to Victor constituted a betrayal by his brother is here reconstructed by Walter as an act of respect for a filial bond from which he had been excluded. Hence, "when he said that you wanted to help him, I felt somehow that it'd be wrong for me to try to break it up between you. It seemed like interfering" (359-60).

If we can take Walter at his word, what Miller reveals through both brothers is a deeply Jewish regard for male filiation: a variation on the father/son mystique so prominent in *All My Sons* and *Death of a Salesman*. But, as an *American* Jewish intellectual strongly influenced by Freud, he subjects that mystique to skeptical, secular scrutiny. Perhaps the father, as he claimed, regarded Victor's impulse to serve him as mystifying, but worthy of respect; more likely, the old man deluded himself about this, so he could continue to benefit by his son. More-over, Victor's sacrifice to his father smacks of neurosis and martyr-dom. Finally, the exclusionary nature of the Papa/Victor bond (in Wal-ter's eyes) calls its morality into question, for it is responsible in part for the enmity in Walter toward both father and brother that helps explain his refusal to support them: out of this apparent moral good comes evil.

But that evil is not limited to Walter, nor (as I have been arguing) is Walter limited to evil, even prior to his moral reformation. His past re-fusal to tell Victor about the money's existence may be motivated partly by jealousy, but it is also a product of Walter's belief that Victor "certainly knew [Papa] had *something*" (365)—a "*fact*" which Victor does not deny, though he finds it "*still ungraspable*" (366)—so that Walter recommended Victor take his loan request to his father. Walter's initial refusal, that is, expresses a discretion based not only on resent-ment but on a belief that Victor was his brother in intelligence, and would confront the father (as Walter did) in pursuit of his self-interest. (Victor does, in fact, ask the father for money, only to drop the subject when the father laughs in response.) And Walter's subsequent broth-erly attempt to offer Victor the money, as noted, is defeated by Papa's invocation of the father/son mystique. Furthermore, if Walter's mo-tives were not altogether pure then, they seem more so now. Having confronted his demons as a consequence of his breakdown, he per-ceives that his obsessive pursuit of success had actually originated in "terror": the fear "'of it ever happening to me'—*he glances at the cen-ter chair*—'as it happened to him'" (351). This fear is common to many who lived through the Depression; but Walter is now struggling to free himself from the paranoid model his father provided, and to erect a structure of brotherhood above the ashes of fatherhood. For he sees that same terror of financial failure, epitomized by the father, as the basis of connection with his brother: "we were both running from the same thing," he tells Victor. "I ended in a swamp of success and bankbooks, you on civil service. The difference is you haven't hurt people to defend yourself." After the breakdown, "in the hospital, for the first time since we were boys, I began to feel . . . like a brother. In the sense that we shared something" (352).

If Walter is not simply a villain, Victor is no mere victim. Admittedly, Miller seems to stack the deck in Victor's favor, for—to a modern American audience whose values are Judeo-Christian, and whose tastes still run toward revised versions of sentimental melodrama, as Robert Brustein has recently observed[7]—Victor's defense of his devotion to his father exerts great moral and emotional appeal. "There was no mercy. Anywhere," he explains following his trip, after his father's laughing response to his request, to Bryant Park, where "the grass was covered with men." He continues, "one day you're the head of the house, at the head of the table, and suddenly you're shit. Overnight. And I tried to figure out that laugh—How could he be holding out on me when he loved me? . . . He loved me, Esther! He just didn't want to end up on the grass. It's not that you don't love somebody, it's that you've got to survive. . . . He couldn't believe in anybody anymore, and it was unbearable to me" (367, my ellipses). And Victor is victimized by that devotion: he fails to realize his potential, he and Esther suffer economic deprivation as a result, his life seems unreal to him.

The price paid would be justifiable, however, if the motives were pure and the cause were right; but it is here that Miller centers his attack. For Victor's sense of unreality—in Freudian terms, his neurosis—may not just have resulted from his self-sacrifice, but helped cause it. He realizes his father could have survived without him: when Walter claims "he'd have survived," Victor is *caught by Walter's voicing of his own opinion*" (356). And shortly after Walter reveals the existence of Papa's money, Esther tells Victor, "you haven't believed a word you've said all these years. We've been lying away our existence all these years; down the sewer, day after day after day . . . to protect a miserable cheap manipulator. No wonder it all seemed like a dream to me—it *was*; a goddamned nightmare" (366). There is truth, moreover, in Walter's claim that Victor cannot take responsibility for his feelings toward Walter: "You never had any hatred for me? Never a wish to see me destroyed? To destroy me, to destroy me with this saintly self-sacrifice, this mockery of sacrifice?" (370). Indeed, Victor (like Quentin in *Fall*, who recurrently imagines himself in a crucifixion posture) seeks identity in martyrdom, and uses it as a weapon against his brother. Finally, the father he serves is unworthy of veneration, failing to offer the love which Victor claims is the reason to sacrifice to him. "Was there ever any love here?" Walter asks. "When [Papa] needed [Mama], she vomited. And when you needed him, he laughed. What was unbearable is not that it fell apart, it was that there was never anything here. . . . What you saw behind the library was not that there was no mercy in the world, kid. It's that there was no love in this house. . . . That's what was unbearable. And you proceeded to wipe out what you saw" (368, my ellipses). Walter concludes, "I only saw then what you see now—there was nothing here to betray" (369).

As noted above, Walter's stance corresponds to the secular, modernist, American side of Miller, which perceives a void—an empty chair—where a father God used to be. And it's not just that Papa is no longer there; in a moral sense, he never was. Walter's breakdown has allowed him to experience, then embrace, the emptiness left by the demise of the Father—he is the direct descendent of Quentin in *After the Fall* in this regard—and he seeks to transcend the void via a brotherhood based in humanity, not divinity. "We're brothers," he tells Victor. "It was only two seemingly different roads out of the same trap": the trap laid by their father's legacy of selfishness and fear where love should have been. "'It's almost as though'—*he smiles warmly, uncertain still*—'we're like two halves of the same guy. As though we can't quite move ahead—alone'" (369). But the father must be abandoned before the reunion, and journey, can begin.

This is a powerful counter-argument for anyone in the audience familiar with the popular existentialism of Sartre, Camus, and Erich Fromm. But Victor is unpersuaded, because an unreconstructed and—I would contend—fundamentally Jewish part of Miller resists. That resistance, it is made clear, has no rational basis. "It was idiotic, nobody has to tell me that," Victor concedes. "But you're brought up to believe in one another, you're filled full of that crap—you can't help trying to keep it going, that's all. . . . I can't explain it; I wanted to . . . stop it from falling apart" (368, first ellipsis mine). Though a psychologist might focus on Victor's upbringing as cause here, I believe that his response to his father originates in spaces of the soul that the reason knows not of. For Miller as a Jew, these are the spaces that obligate one to honor one's father—whatever his merits—because abrogation of this absolute, unconditional commandment leaves one open to things "falling apart." Writing on the Fifth Commandment, Gerald Blidstein asserts,

> Hebraic law, as has been pointed out, is fundamentally a system of duties owed, not of rights possessed. The son serves the father not because he 'is in his power,' as the Roman code has it, or because of 'parental authority'; it is the son's responsibility. . . . Service is valued not for its utility alone but as a response to an imperative that a son honor his father. (50)

Moreover, Blidstein argues, "the son is presented with the ethical proposition that his responsibility of filial respect and service remains constant, irrespective of the merits of his parent" (123). To Victor, to the traditional Jew buried deep within Miller, whether Papa morally deserved Victor's devotion is beside the point: he is entitled to it, because he is his father. "However trying the provocation," Blidstein notes, "the honor of the parent remains an absolute in relation to the difficulties of the son" (43).

Miller's internalized Judaic morality also helps account for Victor's desire, above all, to preserve his father's dignity: a dignity that would have been compromised by accepting public welfare, or by being forced to admit the existence of money being withheld from the son. As Blidstein explicates the Talmudic injunction to exhibit reverence (*morah*) toward one's parents,

The Talmud illustrates 'reverence' tersely: *Reverence means that the son must neither stand nor sit in his [father's] place, nor contradict his words, nor tip the scale against him.* The feeling behind this pattern is clear: nothing is to be done that might diminish the dignity, and hence the feeling of worth, of one's parent—either father or mother. (39)

As Victor claims in response to the certainty his father had money, "What does that change? I know I'm talking like a fool, but what does that change? . . . [*Of Walter*] He'd kicked him in the face; and my mother," upon being told by Papa of his bankruptcy, "'vomited.' *Slight pause. His horror and pity twist in his voice.* 'All over his arms. His hands. Just kept on vomiting, like thirty-five years coming up. And he sat there. Stinking like a sewer. And a look came onto his face. I'd never seen a man look like that. He was sitting there, letting it dry on his hands'" (367-68). Victor's shocked response is that of a dutiful son. He engineers the restoration of the dignity his father has already lost, or at least attempts to prevent its further diminishment. As he says—twice—in relation to his vision at Bryant Park, "I just didn't want him to end up on the grass" (367, 370).

Miller's previously cited words from a 1966 interview (only two years before *The Price*'s first production) bear repeating here: the father, he claimed, represented "some kind of moral law. . . . He figures as an immense shadow," and the relationship of father and son "has a mythical quality" as a result. The moral law and mythical quality in *The Price* revolve around the Fifth Commandment, a transcendent obligation which makes Walter's objections about the father's merits irrelevant. And the sacredness of (Jewish) teachings about filial obligations renders Victor unable to trust his brother.

Aiding Victor in his religious resistance is the figure Gregory Solomon, "*a phenomenon; a man nearly ninety but still straight-backed and the air of his massiveness still with him*" (312). He is first of all a realistic, if somewhat fabulous, character: he snacks on hard-boiled eggs, negotiates shrewdly, charms Esther, tires easily, speaks in the

Critical Insights

idiom of a New York Jewish immigrant. Additionally, he functions expressionistically as a projection of the enduring strength of Victor's old-fashioned beliefs. Hence, his repeated interruptions of the conversation between Victor and Walter in Act Two inevitably help prevent Victor from giving in to Walter.[8] He is also, as Ellen Schiff has pointed out, a composite of several stock Jewish stage characters: the usurer, the old-clothes man, the entrepreneur, the wanderer (70). But by naming him Solomon (alluding to the legendary Old Testament king) and equipping him with an air of "massiveness," Miller moves beyond stereotype into archetype. For spiritually, Solomon *is* massive, and ancient as well, since he represents a Judaic tradition that stretches back far into history. And it is this tradition whose laws and injunctions finally control Victor, hence the action, in *The Price*.

Like his Biblical predecessor, Solomon is associated with the creation and enforcement of the law. A former president of the Appraisers' Association, he takes pride in having "made it all ethical," for "before me it was a jungle" (336). Hence, in regard to the furniture, he objects to the deal Walter proposes, pointing out that the transaction between Victor and Solomon has already commenced: "he's got the money in his hand, so the deal is concluded," according to the letter of the law. "He's got the money; I know the law!" (340). By contrast, Walter's proposal, which requires over-valuing the furniture and donating it to the Salvation Army for a $12,000 deduction on his taxes, is slightly shady—or at least it strikes Victor as such. When he asks Walter how he would list his share of the profits, Walter tells him to "call it a gift. Not that it is, but you could list it as such. It's allowed" (345). Victor is *"silent, obviously in conflict"* in response to the proposal. His inner conflict is not so much between the tax code and the Appraisers' code, but between the law (Walter) and the Law (Solomon): the secular and the sacred collide within Victor, and the latter eventually emerges triumphant.

Victor's refusal to abrogate his deal with Solomon, as mentioned earlier, reproduces his decision to stick by Papa years ago, making Solomon patriarchal not only in age and bearing but in function as well. This is reinforced by the advice he dispenses to Victor throughout—like that of King Solomon, it is wise—and a particularly crucial piece of wisdom concerns Victor's unwillingness to trust him as they bargain over the price of the furniture. "Mister, I pity you," he admonishes Victor.

> What is the matter with you people! You're worse than my daughter! Nothing in the world you believe, nothing you respect—how can you live! You think that's such a smart thing? That's so hard, what you're doing? Let me give you a piece of advice—it's not that you can't believe nothing, that's not so hard—it's that you still got to believe it. *That's* hard. And if you can't do that, my friend—you're a dead man! (320)

As in the later exchange between Walter and Victor, "belief" lies at the heart of the debate. Troubled by his suspicions about his father's money, wary of being cheated again, Victor has a hard time trusting this old man; his ultimate insistence on honoring the deal, though, indicates an acceptance of Solomon's fatherly words concerning the necessity of trust. (In contrast, Victor informs Walter, "I couldn't work with you, Walter. I can't. I don't trust you" [370].) To honor the deal is to honor Solomon, is to honor (once again) the father, the Law, in accordance with the Fifth Commandment. For, as Ellen Schiff shrewdly observes about the above speech, "although it is as a merchant that Solomon insists their business can be transacted only in the spirit of mutual confidence, he sounds more like a father lecturing his son on the indispensability of faith" (71).

The Price leaves open whether Victor is to be admired for his morality or criticized for a stubborn inflexibility which maintains faith in a failed father and refuses to embrace a repentant (and more realistic) brother. Perhaps this reflects the ambiguity with which many Americans respond to the faithful, Jew or Gentile, in our contemporary culture. But this is certainly the ambiguity of Miller himself, facing the religious source of his own moral beliefs, here dramatized in the encounters of two sons with two fathers. Despite his genuine attempt to be evenhanded, Miller ultimately sides with Victor, I believe, though it is a split decision: Miller's Jewish moral upbringing ultimately edges out his relativistic, secular, American education as an influence on the play's vision.[9] (Interestingly, his next full-length play, *The Creation of the World and Other Business* [1972], is a modern, half-ironic retelling of the story of Adam and Eve in the Garden of Eden.) While Walter loses his temper and his dignity at the end, Victor retains both, suggesting that Miller (like Victor) sides with Solomon, the father figure—an enormously attractive character who closes the play, overcoming his anxiety about being in business again, "*howling helplessly*" along with an old Laughing Record that Victor had found among the used furniture (373). Miller's respect and affection for this ancient patriarch aligns him with Jewish, not American, culture. As Norman Linzer notes,

In a society where obsolescence is a built-in dynamic in the materialistic lifestyle, and time is an element to be controlled and quantified, parents and certainly grandparents appear as anachronisms . . . [but] Jewish tradition esteems age, history, the spirit. An old person is not out of fashion, but one to be honored. History is not outdated but omnipresent in the consciousness and behavior of the family. (92-93)

Miller remains troubled by the conclusion, I think—a large part of him (the modern American "existential" part) suspects that Victor sacrifices himself unnecessarily, not so much to Solomon as to a principle of past filial devotion that may close the door on his emotional growth in the present. Thus, Miller has described Walter in a recent interview as a "creator," for "without them we"—like Victor?—"are going to stand still" (Bigsby, *Company* 148). Miller dramatizes, in other words, how fatherhood here defeats brotherhood, but he is concerned about the price. Nonetheless, his deepest allegiance still lies with Victor, and with the Jewish morality that is fundamental to Miller's conception of his character.

In the 1984 interview quoted earlier, Miller declared that "all of the ideas we are talking about now are stemming from the Old Testament- . . . . I'm amazed at how embedded it is in me." *The Price* embodies that embeddedness in the values of Victor, the personality of Solomon, and the character of an absent/present father who ironically functions as a symbol of—in my opening words from Hutchins Hapgood about Jewish immigrant fathers—"a moral and religious tradition by which [a second generation immigrant Jewish] boy may regulate his inner life." Interestingly, central to the play's action is the surfacing and recognition of repressed truths. Miller's "Production Note" asserts that by the end, each brother "has merely proved to the other what the other has known but dared not face" (295). For Miller also faces a profound truth about himself—his Jewishness, his allegiance to a patriarchal moral tradition—which his assimilation into American culture had largely concealed from his critics, reviewers, and (perhaps) even his own consciousness.

From *Staging Difference: Cultural Pluralism in American Theatre and Drama* (New York: Peter Lang Publishing, 1995): 121-139. Copyright © 1995 by Peter Lang Publishing Group. Reprinted with permission of Peter Lang Publishing Group.

Notes

1. See Morris Freedman, "The Jewishness of Arthur Miller," in *American Drama in Social Context* 43-58; and Enoch Brater, "Ethics and Ethnicity in the Plays of Arthur Miller," in Sarah B. Cohen, ed., *From Hester Street to Hollywood* 123-34. Freedman, who emphasizes the "ethnic anonymity" of Miller's drama, claims that very few moments in Miller suggest his Jewish background. Brater argues that Miller deliberately avoided the ethnic road previously travelled by Clifford Odets, and instead chose to explore universal ethical conflicts "more Judaic than Jewish" in his drama.

2. Miller's account of this is articulated again in a 1990 interview with Christopher Bigsby, in *Arthur Miller and Company*. Miller considered his birth family "as American a group of people as there was at the time in this country, I suppose. They certainly

were Jews, but they were trying to become, and in some ways did become, indistinguishable from anybody else" (13).

3. In *Timebends*, Miller recollects an experience from his childhood which symbolizes powerfully the centrality in Judaism of the concept of an unbroken male line originating in Jehovah and continuing into the present moment. At an Orthodox service at a synagogue in Harlem, Miller recalls that his great-grandfather "would keep turning my face toward the prayer book and pointing at the letters, which themselves were magical, as I would later learn, and apart from their meaning were lines of an art first inscribed by men who had seen the light of God, letters that led to the center of the earth and outward to the high heavens. Though I knew nothing of all that, it was frightening at times and totally, movingly male. From where I sat, on my great-grandfather's lap, it was all a kind of waking dream; the standing up and then the sitting down and rising and falling of voices passionately flinging an incomprehensible language into the air while with an occasional glance I watched my mother up in the balcony with her eyes on me and [Miller's brother] Kermit, on my great-grandfather and grandfather and father all in a row" (36-37).

4. In *Timebends*, Miller describes encounters with elderly Jewish men, "ur-Hebrews": "on crossing paths with some Ancient of Days, some very old man with a child's spirit, I would sense an unnameable weight upon our relationship, the weight of repetition of an archaic reappearance. Perhaps one of these Gregory Solomon in *The Price*, another, the silent Old Jew in *Incident at Vichy*" (43).

5. See Robert Corrigan, "Introduction: The Achievement of Arthur Miller," in *Arthur Miller: A Collection of Critical Essays*, who declares that the action hinges on the moral debt which Esther (and Walter, implicitly) claims Walter owes to Victor; but Walter cannot satisfy Victor, and the price of this is their relationship (17).

6. Miller stated in a 1983 interview with Steven Centola, "the older one gets, the more of one's parents one recognizes in oneself. You'd think it would be the opposite, but it isn't" (qtd. in Roudané, *Conversations* 355-56).

7. "The Theatre of Guilt," *American Theatre* 21.

8. Corrigan was the first to note this, in "Introduction" 18.

9. Miller describes Victor in the 1990 interview with Bigsby as "an idealist of sorts. He can't help it, he can't kick it. . . . I wouldn't say he's my representative. I'd say that I wish he would win, but I have my doubts" (*Company* 148).

Works Cited

Bigsby, C. W. E., ed. *Arthur Miller and Company: Arthur Miller talks about his work in the company of Actors, Designers, Director, Reviewers and Writers.* London: Methuen, 1990.

Blidstein, Gerald. *Honor Thy Father and Mother: Filial Responsibility in Jewish Law and Ethics.* New York: Ktav Publishing House, 1975.

Bloom, Harold. "Introduction" to *Arthur Miller's All My Sons*, ed. Harold Bloom. New York: Chelsea House, 1988.

Brater, Enoch. "Ethics and Ethnicity in the Plays of Arthur Miller," in Sarah B. Cohen, ed., *From Hester Street to Hollywood: The Jewish-American Stage and Screen*. Bloomington: Indiana UP, 1983.

Brustein, Robert. "The Theatre of Guilt." *American Theatre* 8.12 (March 1992): 18-21, 49.

Corrigan, Robert, ed. *Arthur Miller: A Collection of Critical Essays*. Englewood Cliffs, N.J.: Prentice-Hall, 1968.

Freedman, Morris. *American Drama in Social Context*. Carbondale: Southern Illinois UP, 1962.

Gorer, Geoffrey. *The American People: A Study in National Character*, revised edition. New York: Norton, 1964.

Howe, Irving. *World of Our Fathers*. New York: Harcourt, Brace, Jovanovich, 1976.

Linzer, Norman. *The Jewish Family: Authority and Tradition in Modern Perspective*. Foreword by David Hartman. New York: Sciences Press, 1984.

Malin, Irving. *Jews and Americans*. Carbondale: Southern Illinois UP, 1965.

Miller, Arthur. *Collected Plays*, Vol. II. New York: Viking, 1981.

_____. *Timebends*. New York: Grove, 1987.

Roudané, Matthew, ed. *Conversations with Arthur Miller*. Jackson: UP of Mississippi, 1987.

Schiff, Ellen. *From Stereotype to Metaphor: The Jew in Contemporary Drama*. Albany: SUNY UP, 1982.

The "Line to Measure From":
Arthur Miller's *The American Clock* as a Lesson for the Ages_____

Susan C. W. Abbotson

Arthur Miller's formative years took place during the Great Depression, and this cataclysmic economic, social and cultural event deeply informs all of Miller's work. Several of Miller's plays have been set during the Depression years, but none takes a closer look than his 1980 masterpiece, *The American Clock*: part autobiography,[1] part vaudeville, part tutorial. For Miller, the Depression was the dark night of the American soul, a waking nightmare for those who lived through it, and a dour lesson for times to come. Miller rejects those who paint the period with rose-tinted glasses and nostalgically speak of its welcome camaraderie after a period of intense self-interest. One of Miller's greatest legacies must surely be the timely lesson he encapsulates within *The American Clock*, which is reiterated elsewhere in his work, but receives its most pointed expression in this highly creative, though too often overlooked, play.[2]

The play depicts the forces of optimism and a commitment to life pitted against those of death and despair, invoked through memories of the Depression. In one sense it is as Peter Ferran describes, a "dramatically mythopoetic chapter of America's own biography" (163). But it does more than simply recreate a bygone age, it uses the Depression as an extended metaphor as to how to create a better world for the future. Miller shows characters' attempts to restore a sense of community alongside asserting their necessity for individuality, for it is through community and individuality combined that they will find the strength to deny the chaos they observe surrounding them. This is Miller's central lesson for the ages—and it is one of survival and hope, born, ironically, from his depiction of what he feels was one of the worst periods in American history.

Miller has always sought to explode what he sees as the false myths of American society (materialism, complete happiness and the easy life) and tried to lead people towards an alternative American spirit rooted in a humanistic democracy. This is the main dynamic behind *The American Clock*. "At the play's end . . . we should feel, along with the textures of a massive social and human tragedy, a renewed awareness of the American's improvisational strength, his almost subliminal faith that things can and must be made to work out. In a word, the feel of the energy of a democracy" (*Timebends* 588). It is as Ralph Ellison once told Miller, "Through your art, you affirm the democratic vision" (Bigsby *Company* 1).

In *The American Clock* Miller tells the story of America in the 1930s through the conflated stories of a vast array of characters. We meet businessmen like Jesse Livermore and William Durant who lose everything, and more successful entrepreneurs like Arthur A. Robertson and Theodore K. Quinn. We learn the plight of farmers, like Henry Taylor, young intellectuals, like Joe and Edie, and an assortment of people from all walks of life. At the center, Miller places the Baum family, who are partly autobiographical. Through the Baums he explores, even more deeply, the concerns and demands of such a time. The father, Moe, loses a prosperous business but keeps going, even as his wife, Rose, begins to fall apart under the strain. Their son Lee goes from childhood to adulthood as he travels through the nation, and finally comes to terms with the demands of living in America.

With more than fifty characters, *The American Clock* is, in many ways, one of Miller's most ambitious plays, and strikingly different from those with which America is most familiar.[3] Miller sees it as a mural in which an audience can see individuals at close range, but on standing back, the larger society with its pattern of interconnections becomes visible. In the play, Miller tries to balance epic elements with intimate psychological portraits to give a picture of a society and the individuals who make up that society. "My impulse," he declares, "is usually toward integration of meaning through significant individual action, but the striking new fact of life in the Depression era—unlike the self-sufficient, prosperous seventies—was the swift rise in the common consciousness of the social system" ("Conditions" xiv-xv). In other words, the Depression marks a point in American history when America realized that she would need to recognize both society and the individual to survive. Christopher Bigsby suggests this was "the moment that America entered history" (*Critical* 337). Where many of Miller's earlier plays depict most tellingly the individual's responsibility toward, and place in, their society, *The American Clock* marks a decided change of emphasis as it attempts to show the society's responsibility toward, and place in, the life of the individual.

The Depression was, Miller insists, "only incidentally a matter of money. Rather, it was a moral catastrophe, a violent revelation of the hypocrisies behind the façade of American society" (*Timebends* 115). But it was also a time when the old order had disintegrated, leaving the ground cleared for new structures. The difficulty came in the uncertainty as to what these new structures should be. Miller sees neither socialism nor fascism as offering ideal social systems, as each is too extreme and ultimately flawed. While the former privileges the community, the latter privileges the individual; what is needed is a balance between the two. The people of the 1930s struggled to understand this balance, but the lessons they learned seemed to have been lost over time. Approaching the end of the millennium, Miller saw America as needing to relearn the essential needs of both community and individual in order to combat a mounting spiritual malaise.

By the 1970s, when Miller began writing this play, he saw a growing dismissal of social concerns in the nation and described to Bigsby how he intended to "tell people that there is such a thing as necessity. I wanted to tell them that underneath the surface there is a skeletal structure of human relations which is still there. And you find that when the surface collapses" (*Modern* 116). Austin Pendleton, who directed the 1988 Williamstown Theater Festival version of *The American Clock*, explained his view of the Depression to Leslie Bennetts: "There was a sense of community in this country then and there was a belief in the future, and that created a different atmosphere than exists today. It may be that with the catastrophes that are tumbling down around us now, we're going to have to recover that. This play is an attempt to evoke those two feelings, the belief in the future and the sense of community. The 1980s have been so much about every man for himself, as the 20s were, with the kind of crazy euphoria that comes when people are thinking only about themselves" (C23). Through evoking the sense of community from a bygone age, Miller would offer a jaded 1980s population a restorative vision.

In presenting his mural, Miller allows no scene breaks, and presents us with a fluid montage of constant action. The characters often address the audience directly, as if to include them as part of the throng. The effect he achieves is a collage of the American people, past and present. With so many characters, the work needs a strong collaborative effort, on the part of the cast, to form themselves into a cohesive community. It is a community which is constantly shifting, changing, evolving, and ultimately surviving, before our eyes. Importantly, it is a community we see concretely existing before us. They represent the "whole country" (*The American Clock* 106), that is, the United States of America. To affirm this, Miller begins by presenting on the stage two quintessentially American pastimes—Jazz and Baseball—with the band playing "Million Dollar Baby" to emphasize the American obsession with wealth. Since the play begins in the 1920s, when wealth abounded, everyone willingly joins in the song. Miller creates an additional opening effect, reminiscent of John Dos Passos's great trilogy, *U.S.A.*, in which the speech of the individual people of America blends together to create one voice, the voice of America. Speech flows from one character to another, with Lee continuing the sentence Rose begins, then Moe taking over, then the rest of the cast, and returning to Moe for the conclusion. It suggests a community of one mind, connected by outlook, similar values and beliefs, and desire.

In Miller's view, the 1930s could teach America a lesson for future generations. Gerald Weales has rightly described *The American Clock* as essentially "an account of the collapse of society and of survival despite that collapse . . . [a] diagnosis and prescription and the audience is supposed to see the light" (131). As Miller says, the 1930s showed the people of America "the beginning of a new world in which causalities were revealed and hence responsibilities confirmed, in which a new democracy of suffering suggested a possible democracy of social and moral action" (Bigsby, *Modern* 116). Miller felt such hope needed to be reaffirmed in the decadent 1970s, when he saw America losing her way. He saw her earlier visions and values being replaced by a dehumanizing interest in business and materialism which tended to eradicate both individual and community.[4]

Miller sees the Depression as notable because it was a period when "almost everybody went through the same trauma." As Bigsby describes: "For [Miller] it was above all a brutal decade which offered some brutal lessons" (*Critical* 340). Everyone faced a society-wide insecurity regarding status, property, and jobs, which were all shown to be temporary. "Consequently," Miller continues, "you tend to examine what you believe a little more carefully" (*Mr. Showbiz*). The Depression allowed everyone to reassess, and recognize more clearly, their selves and their relationships to others. As James Flanagan suggests: "For Miller, the Depression and its significance not only indicated the dependency of the family upon outside support but also made him aware of a plane of life where men struggled with issues beyond those of raising a family" (2).

Miller insists that although the Depression was an era of futility and slight hope, which tends to be over-glamorized by Hollywood, he allows *The American Clock* to end on an optimistic note, because he felt optimistic when he wrote it. Miller points out that optimism was not entirely killed in the 1930s, and it is evidenced in the upbeat songs, musicals, and comedies of the period. The vaudevillian form of the play conveys an authentic sense of the Depression era, as vaudeville was an up-and-coming genre of the period which reflected people's comic response to the pressures around them. It was, perhaps, rooted in the sense that things could not possibly get worse so they had to get better. "Underneath it all, you see," Miller suggests, "you were stripped of all your illusions and there's a certain perverse healthiness in that. . . . And I suppose that way in the back of your brain, you knew you were in America and that somehow it was going to work out" (Bigsby, *Company* 204). Miller sincerely believed that the American people have never lost confidence entirely in the idea of America.

America, in Miller's view, improvised her way through the Depression, and survived largely because of the great American spirit. Other societies who have lacked this essential energy have fallen apart under similar pressure, but America pulled through. It is this spirit which Miller tries to depict, in hope that it will strike a chord in his audience so they can rediscover such a spirit in themselves. Dennis Welland points out: "For all the personal elements in it, it is Miller's most deliberate play about America" (152). For Miller, the best part of America is her identity as a nation where hope is possible; this allows her to indulge the people's optimism for the future and encourages them to continually strive for better lives.

There are, importantly, aspects within the play, despite its fluidity and constant shifts of mood, time, and place, which remain fixed throughout. Such aspects allow us to perceive constants which offer a sense of continuity and comforting permanence. The band remains on stage from start to finish, the Baums are a central focus of the play, and a key voice in both this opening chorus and the closing one is Theodore Quinn, a perfect representation of American zeal and spirit. The play is also unified by its joint narrators, Arthur Robertson and Lee Baum. Lee, youthful and initially naive, attempts to make sense of events as they unfold. Robertson, older and wiser, is a man who has an intuitive understanding of events even before they occur. Together they analyze and offer an interpretation of how America survived the calamitous Depression and what lessons we can take from their survival for the future. Both are involved in the action; they are not outside commentators so much as participants, which gives their words a greater credibility. As narrators, Lee and Robertson will, on occasion, offer different interpretations of past events. Miller wants to ensure that we do not uncritically accept either of their views, but recognize that each reads the past, as do we all, through our own individual experiences and perspective. Through these narrators Miller wonders why it was that the Depression did not destroy America for good. The answer he offers is that the American capacity for belief saved the day.

Robertson's opening Biblical image of the country kneeling to a golden calf evokes a prophecy of doom. We all know what happened to those original, misguided idolaters; they paid a harsh price for their faith in little but wealth. These people too, will suffer, as the Wall Street Crash is imminent. The red, white and blue of America's flag, once an emblem of liberty and equality, is denigrated as a wrap for the golden calf, showing how Americans have come to obsess over notions of success and wealth above and beyond notions of democracy. Even the lowly shoeblack Clarence has put all his savings into the almighty stock market, refusing to accept he could possibly lose, despite Robertson's timely advice for him to sell. When the market crashes, Clarence will be left with less than fifty dollars. By showing Clarence as an investor, Miller shows how the Crash had repercussions at every social level.

It is, of course, not just the city people who suffer. Due to weather conditions as punishing as the stock market, we see the more tangible products of the farmers failing as much as the intangible dealings of the city financiers. Miller shows the Taylor's farm being put up for compulsory auction by its bank creditors. In this way, both nature and city finance have a destructive impact on a family. The neighbors, threatened by similar treatment, rally around their fellow-farmer. By a show of physical force, the only power they retain without having any money themselves, they enforce a sale of Taylor's property for one dollar and return it to him. It will be a momentary victory, for he has no money to run a farm whether he owns it or not and he will soon be forced out onto the road to find a living.

Judge Bradley, who initiated the sale, declares that the return of the farm to Taylor for a single dollar is sheer theft and "a crime against every law of God and man" (135), but Miller wants us to recognize the unfairness of this. The judge insists that they all must obey the legal system to ensure order; but Miller asks us to consider where is the order in having your livelihood sold off to the highest bidder, and your family home stripped away? Henry Taylor is a decent family man who has had an unavoidably fallow season. Judge Bradley may have man-made legal laws on his side, but every moral instinct says that Taylor should be allowed to keep his farm. To survive, these people are going to have to rely on the support of their community; not the law, and not God. The initial reaction of many people to the Crash and the events which followed was, unfortunately, to withdraw into their own private little worlds, either through shame, guilt, or despair. Miller has Irene sing "'Tain't Nobody's Bizness" to evoke this isolationist mood, a song which portrays a miserable existence in which the singer insists on complete privacy and detachment. However, such isolation is unproductive.

The real antidote to the calamities of the Depression, and Miller's suggestion of the only possible thing in this world which can be inviolable, is love. It is introduced by the Baums, Rose and Lee, playing and singing "I Can't Give You Anything But Love." The song's sentiments contrast well with the opening scene of acquisitiveness, and it evokes the possibility of people who are not obsessed with things. And yet, this outlook has not yet occurred. The Baums, too, have a lesson to learn in the course of the play. At this point, Lee becomes upset as his sense of his mother is shattered, simply because she has cut her hair short. She is still the same loving mother, as her continued playing indicates, but for the time, he cannot see past the hair. Instead, he rallies himself with the fierce optimism of "On the Sunny Side of the Street," but optimism alone cannot prevent bad things from happening. These people are going to be forced to face the fact that things change, constantly. Such changes are not necessarily for the worse, and they are essentially better than stagnation. One can see a positive side even to the Crash, it was a little like getting one's hair bobbed, because it simplified the lives of many and allowed them to see the world differently.

The Depression allowed America to start anew, to go back to her beginnings where everyone was a stranger and needed to forge new connections. Miller shows how people survive by random acts of kindness, often given by people who do not even know the recipient: Brewster helping Taylor, Callaghan helping Banks, the Baums helping Taylor. Such acts of kindness are positive signs of connections being forged, even though the majority seems to remain out only for themselves. As a recipient of such kindness, Taylor, for his part, is not lazy or expectant. Taylor is prepared to work for his food and does not expect a handout; he is uncomfortable asking the Baums for even that much. His lack of greed is evident when he drinks only half of the glass of water they give him.

Taylor is quite literally starving to death. It is a level of poverty which can still shock the Baums, who survive in comparative comfort. They feed him and Moe gives him a dollar (an ironic echo of the amount for which Taylor's farm was fruitlessly re-bought), but Moe refuses to allow him to sleep in their basement. The dollar will do little lasting good, and is as much a sop for the conscience as a gesture of compassion. The Baums feel sorry for Taylor, but cannot be fully responsible for him; he must accept responsibility for his own condition. Moe explains: "Life is tough, what're you going to do?" (142). Lee, idealistically, does not accept this as a valid response, and is unhappy with what he sees as his father's refusal of responsibility. Grandpa's reaction, however, is worse. He insists that people are not connected and you should only "worry about yourself" (143), as he does. Miller makes it clear that we should not believe Grandpa. Earlier on, we were shown how wrong his views are when he insists that Hitler can only stay in power for six months at most. We have also just witnessed his unrealistic response to Taylor's plight, suggesting the man should simply borrow money to buy his farm back. Grandpa is living in fierce denial of the changing times and what he says is not credible. Moe's philosophy is a lot less selfish and may be a necessary balance; he helps a little, but not to a point where he damages his own prospects.

The issue of responsibility is an important one throughout the play. Ted Quinn introduces a direct argument concerning this issue when he insists that the higher the place a person has in society, the bigger their responsibility should be to others. A popular and carefree figure, shown by Robertson's introduction to him, and by his own song and dance, Quinn seems to have some kind of faith to buoy him up. But what is it in which he believes? Since the GE/Frigidaire price war, he has recognized the farce behind big business conglomerates, in which people become so faceless that they even, occasionally, end up cutting their own throats. He sees such large conglomerates as anti-business because they wipe out the "creative force of competition" (145). Quinn has a conscience and is able to recognize that a company like GE can only get big on the sacrifice of the smaller companies they destroy, and he disapproves. He views monopolies as un-American, because they are un-democratic. He displays a strong belief in America and for what, in his view, she ideally stands: an independent people engaged in healthy competition. In this way, he accounts for both individuals and the larger community.

Robertson suggests to Quinn that his view of America is a dream. Big business is the only possible future as people cannot return to the old ways of small business. In a competitive society, there have to be eventual winners, because the losers cannot keep recuperating indefinitely. He may be right, but Quinn feels it is worth engaging in a fight against such forces, even if victory seems impossible. Quinn even resigns from the presidency of GE to register his disapproval of such monopolies. Quinn has lived the American Dream (having risen to the top from lowly origins), largely by his awareness of the individual elements that go to make up the company as a whole—as in his analysis of the bulbs and knowing the number of bricks in the wall. However, he now sees that the perceived pinnacle of the Dream is an empty goal.

The massive conglomerate that is GE is utterly soulless. He decides to go back to basics in order to assist the "little people" to survive intact in a faceless corporate world. His desire to help others is rooted in his belief in the importance of American individualism. It is these individuals he wants to assist. Despite a lingering uncertainty as to whether it is really so wise to renounce the corporate world, he seems to be ultimately happier once the decision has been made, as evidenced by his song and dance.[5]

As the play progresses, conditions for Americans of the time worsen. There was little one could do to ensure a productive career and future. Despite the fact that even college graduates cannot get jobs, Lee still wants to go to college, but he eventually realizes the unlikelihood of his parents being able to afford it. Lee proves he has spirit by deciding to look for a job instead. Miller sees Lee as the character who asserts the strongest "life force" in the play (Roudané 312). He seems to have more gumption than his cousin Sidney, who sits around playing the piano, dreaming of writing a hit song. But appearances can be deceptive. Sidney may stay at home but he pursues his dreams no less forcefully. It is through Sidney that Miller shows us the redeeming possibilities of love. Sidney's mother suggests that he date their landlady's daughter in the hopes of getting a free apartment. The relationship between Sidney and Doris may begin out of necessity, but actually blossoms into true love, and the couple turn out to be one of the few who survive.

It is Robertson who introduces the clock image of the play's title: "There's never been a society that hasn't had a clock running on it, and you can't help wondering—how long? How long will they stand for this?" (154) This should recall an earlier fragment which had Banks, a man whose family farm had gone under, hitting the road in an unsuccessful search for work. He sings a couple of verses of the song "How Long" to indicate his discontent, which then changes to "The Joint Is Jumpin'" with a group of weary Marathon dancers dancing across the stage. The implication is of a certain indomitableness of spirit, despite wearing odds—these people keep going against all reasonable expectations. Robertson's image sees time as ticking away for everyone, to indicate that nothing lasts forever and all things must change. In this constant change, hope can always be found if sought, for despite the fact that change can be for the worse, it is just as possible that it may be for the better; indeed, change often holds both options simultaneously. For example, although Moe feels humiliated at being reduced to having to borrow a quarter from his son, Lee is able to feel great pride in being able to help his father. Though we see the conditions for the play's characters continue to worsen, as long as they maintain the idea of an American clock which will keep on ticking, they can retain hope regardless.

Robertson views the erection of the Empire State Building during this period as a sign that Americans refused to give in to the Depression and maintained some degree of hope. Robertson reads this as an indication that the majority of Americans stayed sane by keeping faith in the future. Miller describes people in the Depression who were "psychologically traumatized to the point where they would probably never be able to work again. Nor was it only a question of insufficient food; it was hope that had gone out of them, the life illusion and the capacity to believe again" (*Timebends* 114). Without hope, one cannot stave off encroaching death: first of the spirit and then of the whole self. Some failed and ended in suicide, like Joe, or ran out of energy, like Doris, who reaches a point when she cannot even be bothered to get dressed. However, for the most part, like the Baums, the American people continued. Both Moe and Lee realize that survival means never giving in to despair or to whatever bad befalls them. The human spirit has bottomless resilience in its capacity to dream, which can provide the hope towards which they will continue to strive.

Rose and Moe with their son Lee, Rose's sister Fanny with her son Sidney, and Grandpa, make up the Baum family, which is at the heart of *The American Clock*. Miller uses the three main Baums to illustrate the major different reactions he perceived people had to the Depression: Moe responds practically, Lee ideologically, and Rose emotionally. In combination, the three offer a comprehensive picture of the overwhelming impact of the Depression on the American psyche and disposition. Apart, they allow us to explore personalized aspects of the larger social changes which occurred during this period. Wealthy enough, at the start, to have a chauffeur, they, like so many others, over-invest in stocks. We watch as the clock runs out on their prosperity. The whole family is initially distracted by acquisition. Their Grandpa has become a nuisance who has to be shunted back and forth between the sisters rather than embraced as an emblem of the family's connection. They waste their time in petty jealousies and quarrels. Rose is jealous of her mother-in-law; Moe enjoys nastily teasing his sister-in-law. Moe is so busy that he scarcely has time for his own son (unaware of how old he is or when he had his last haircut). They will learn, through the trials of the Depression, how to become a closer, and in certain ways, a more fulfilled family unit.

Moe is an ordinary man who displays extraordinary courage in the way that he deals with his fall in fortune. He recognizes the importance of maintaining a strong sense of self in the face of all that befalls him and his family. He struggles to retain his dignity and honor. Despite bankruptcy, he still tries to pay off his debts. His dismissal of the chauffeur, whom he has been allowing to cheat him for years, is done firmly but without malice. He offers some aid to the suffering community he sees around him—feeding the homeless, handing over small sums of money to people like Henry Taylor and Matthew Bush—without allowing it to grow out of proportion to the family's means.

Miller describes Moe Baum as the opposite of Willy Loman: "He does not have illusions. He is a realistic man and does not surrender to his own defeat." Moe remains a strong figure to the end because he is able to "separate himself from his condition" and avoid self-destructive guilt (Roudané 312-13). What is most important about Moe is his continual refusal to buckle. He strives to provide for his family as practically as possible—moving to a smaller apartment, cutting back on everything but the necessities—and he does not hide behind feelings of guilt or shame when things grow tough. He acknowledges the real state society is in, and remains strong, even as he sees everything around him collapsing and men like Joe killing themselves. "We are going to be alright. . . . It can't go on forever" (198-99), he assures his wife. His final words in the play display this refusal to give in: "I'm trying! God Almighty, I am trying!" (199).

Apart from Moe, the Baums find it hard to face the truth. Rose pretends things will pick up, Grandpa selfishly insists that they get a larger house, and Lee thinks he is going to an Ivy League college. It is clear that the Baums are decent people at heart, but this will not protect them. Lee was lucky enough to withdraw his savings from the bank before it went bust and bought himself a bicycle, but it gets stolen. Lee is a young boy when the Depression hits, and it is in the wake of the eradication of previously thought inviolable beliefs that he must decide the values by which he will live. He displays, throughout, an awareness of his responsibility to others. He knows, instinctively, that the way Taylor gets treated is "all *wrong*" (140). Growing up in a nation which has had the rug pulled from under its feet, and will remain unsure of its footing for some time, Lee searches for an ideology which will satisfy his sense of community. For a long time Lee finds it hard to have faith in anything. He continues to explore the pros and cons of the various ideologies he sees vying for control. He is made to realize, by his university friends, that capitalism will lead to war, as Ralph and Joe point out the relationship between war and the country's economics. Joe also points him in the direction of Karl Marx. Weales suggests that "Lee's social education is important not for its details but as a reflection of individuals cut loose by events and forced to find new ways of coping in a society shed of its old certainties" (131). Miller does not expect us to necessarily embrace the same ideals which Lee does, but simply applaud and emulate his search for ideals.

On leaving college, Lee decides to take a trip to Mississippi to broaden his knowledge. Down South, he becomes dismayed by one effect of the Depression. Instead of helping their fellow man, many turned to violence and anger—just as occurred in Germany. In Germany the anger partly manifested itself in horrific violence against the Jews, using them as scapegoats. The question Miller implicitly asks is who will be the scapegoats in America? The answer appears to be the poor. Lee knows the country has the food to feed its starving, only they cannot afford to buy it as there are no jobs for them to earn a living. This drove many close to madness as they saw their hard-earned skills wasted due to the deflated economy, while a minority continued to get rich by taking irresponsible advantage, such as the tobacco bosses who continued to rake in profits while refusing to pay their workers a living wage. Lee's friend, Joe, struggled to become a dentist but, now qualified, does not have the cash to begin his practice, and is reduced to selling flowers for his meager living. In frustration he turns to Marxism for answers; and this is the same Joe who had, as a boy, written to Herbert Hoover, a staunch Republican president, to wish him success.

Given the evidence Lee witnesses of continued elitist thought, and the human rapacity of the bosses which has been running rampant throughout a capitalistic American society, Lee, like Joe, considers Marxism as offering potential answers. But, unlike Joe, Lee soon sees the flaws in the Communist system, resting largely in its dogmatism and unrealistic expectations of human nature. It is a system which ultimately fails to sustain Joe, who later throws himself under a train in despair. Edie is right when she declares in Communism's defense that "Everything's connected" (186), but she is shown to be, essentially, too idealistic to be entirely credible. She works as a cartoonist, drawing Superman. In the same way her whole world is largely built upon well-meaning fantasy. Marxism describes a capitalistic world in which relationships have come to be ruled by money. When that money is taken away, as in the Depression, the people must find something else to bind them together. Communism's answer unfortunately manifests itself in bloody revolution. Violence and war may be unifying forces, but not ones of which Miller approves.[6] It should be possible to bind people together through love rather than hate. This is the concept Joe espouses, but is unable to pursue in his isolation and despair.

With his mix of characters at the Relief office, Miller allows us to see the idea of America's "melting pot" philosophy, while allowing us to recognize how little "melting" has in fact taken place. Times of trouble tend to set these various groups against each other even more, rather than allow them to bond together. A potential common ideology, such as Communism, allows for some bonding, but it is a solution we know in hindsight will not hold. It is also, as Lee knows from his close scrutiny of the hatred between the strikers at the various car plants, only offering a surface solution which does not reach down very far.

At the Relief office we get a chance to hear from Irene, who espouses Communism and sees it as a sane response to the times, as it encourages a much needed solidarity in an era marked by chaos and loss. Communism will allow, she believes, for the equality promised by the Constitution and Bill of Rights (but denied in practice), to touch everyone, regardless of skin color. She is right that solidarity is the answer, but people need not embrace Communist dogma to find this. We are shown a wonderful image of this solidarity as Irene persuades Grace to give the remains of her baby's bottle to feed the starving Matthew Bush.[7] Apart from Irene, none of these people are Communists. Moe's dime, given to buy the man some more milk, is significantly not given as the ten cents needed for dues to the Workers Alliance, but more as a payment to be a member of a caring human community. It is Irene's knowledge and experience as an African-American woman which will help these people, rather than her belief in Communism. She offers her experience in survival, as someone who has faced hardship all of her life, to all of her fellow Americans, regardless of their color. She informs them that the way to survival is to be part of a community in which everyone willingly helps everyone else. In the resulting unity, each individual will find strength.

Unable to find work as a journalist, Lee applies for a WPA job for which he needs to be on Relief. He can only get on Relief by having his father pretend he hates him and has thrown him out of the house. At

---

first an amusing scene, this charade, nevertheless, brings out in Moe a feeling of disgust towards his son. Moe sees Lee as having compromised both their dignities. Moe is also distraught at his son's evident lack of faith in everything. However, the sacrifice turns out to be worthwhile, as through this work Lee discovers something in which he can believe. Lee's WPA project, to write a detailed American history, is an important one—it will remind Americans of their past, which places them in a time-line, and make it easier for them to hold on for the future. It is through this that Lee begins to get a sense of what he should believe in: America herself. It is a concept he finally understands through his vision of his own mother and the "headful of life" (203) he gains from thinking about all the contradictions for which she stood.

Throughout the various calamities the Baums must face, Rose responds less practically but far more imaginatively, and events take an emotional toll. Rose tries to look on the bright side, pointing out how the Crash has brought families, such as theirs, closer together through sheer necessity. Her efforts to keep happy, however, are motivated by a refusal to admit their real poverty and position; she holds onto dreams of a past gentility in order to survive. For Rose, her piano symbolizes her more glorious past when she was a wealthy woman; it is a past she finds hard to let go. She tries, continuously, to divert herself from acknowledging the harsh realities of their degraded lives. Through her books and songs she avoids truths and pretends that everything is fine and "S'Wonderful," pushing money troubles aside with a carefully chosen lyric. But eventually, the piano must be sold, which, for a time, plunges her into despair. It is a mistake, Miller warns us, to halter one's beliefs to such concrete items, which can so easily be lost. Beliefs linked to intangible hopes and dreams may lack a comforting palpability, but they are likely to be longer-lasting. Miller emphasizes the importance of the scene he has written where Rose is at the piano swearing that she will never let go: "It's the action of a woman trying to resolve her own anxieties. She tries to do so—and fails. The anxieties win over and the piano does not help." At this point Rose is directed to crash down on the keys, for as Miller points out, "that final discord will suggest even to the dullest member of an audience the discords going through the mind of the desperate Rose Baum" (Schonberg 5).

An impending eviction, in which Rose feels she will be totally disconnected from any tangible possessions, threatens to destroy her struggling faith for good. She declares: "The next time I start believing in anybody or anything I hope my tongue is cut out!" (188). Yet, despite her words, we must look to her actions. Rose continues to help other people, such as Stanislaus, who is staying with them and working for his keep. She rests, however, on the brink of madness and despair, not so much because of her own thwarted beliefs and desires, but because of the utter blindness she perceives in others. This is illustrated by the joke about "Gray's Elegy in a Country Churchyard," which Doris and Fanny fail to see (though Lucille finally works it out). Rose is not a fool; she can keep track of a deck of cards just as she can keep track of what is happening to her and her family; it is just that she insists on viewing these events through the lens of her optimism. Rose survives by treading a fine line between hope and despair, and managing to keep her balance by her ability to live in contradictions—as Lee finally recognizes. Though she may lock herself in the bathroom to vent her despair and frustration, in front of others she preserves an attitude of control and keeps on hoping.

Lee's final identification of Rose with America as a whole rests in her ability to accept contradictory beliefs. This is indicative of the binary nature of the American psyche. Rose can simultaneously support concepts of capitalism and freedom, socialism and elitism, humanitarianism and racism—for at the heart of these beliefs lie her essential optimism and belief in life. It is these that allow Rose, and the rest of America, to survive and continue to function. Rose sings out at the close of the play, refusing to give in. Although a little wistful at first, everyone joins in her rendition of "Life's Just a Bowl of Cherries." The country has been saved, not just by the onset of war as Robertson suggests, but also, as Quinn adds, by a reaffirmation of belief in itself, partly engendered by President Roosevelt. Quinn leads the final chorus with his soft-shoe dance, as everybody sings together, including, hopefully, the audience, providing a prime picture of America the brave, prepared to sing and dance with life in the face of every disaster.

Critics have found the upbeat song at the end of the play problematic, insisting that it must be either optimism or sarcasm, when it is both, simultaneously. This is part of the ambiguity Miller wishes to create, to provoke his audience into asking the most important question: "Could it happen again?" Weales insists that there is no need to read the lyrics as true feelings, for these people are not denying their pain; it has been amply portrayed throughout the play. They are aware of the satirical aspects of their song, yet they cannot but be positive about future possibilities. "The play is not simply a chronicle of disaster," Weales insists, "but an account of our coming through" (133). Miller shows a time when deceits were stripped away, and though people suffered in the process, they were able to face the truths which were necessary to face in order for them to get into closer touch with true American values. These people survived, partly due to this, and partly due to their sheer energy, life-force, and their refusal to give in; all of this is evidenced in their singing.

The American Clock uses the horrors of the 1930s to illustrate how America survived in the past, in order to teach her how to survive in the similarly threatening 1980s, and beyond. The Baum family faces difficulties, but survive by recognizing a balance between their own needs and those of others. Moe's dignified strength, Rose's vitality and ability to live with contradiction, and Lee's discovery of the importance of humanity as he sheds off limiting ideologies, all point toward a positive future. The play ends, significantly, with a sense of optimism, even if all the problems the characters face have not been fully resolved. They leave us with a sense of hope, despite the evidence of continued difficulties, because we have been shown that, however bad the world becomes, humanity's capacity for love, faith, and connection cannot ever be fully crushed. As an encomium to the strength of

American democracy in the face of a key American nightmare—utter dispossession—*The American Clock* is one of Miller's most powerful works.

Notes

1. Indeed so many details from Miller's own life have been included in this play that Christopher Bigsby suggests it is "as though Miller has chosen to lay the grid of his personal life over the social history of the time" (*Critical* 346).

2. As Terry Otten states, "*The American Clock* is both experimental and a reiteration of seminal Miller themes" (179). However, outside of the few critics I cite in this article, it has been largely ignored by the scholarly community.

3. The play's uniqueness is partly what makes it stand out so firmly, for there is as Peter Ferran exclaims, "nothing quite like *The American Clock* among Arthur Miller's plays" (153).

4. Miller insists that *The American Clock* is an attempt to grasp "what I felt life in the seventies had all but lost—a unified concept of human beings, the intimate psychological side joined with the social-political. To put it another way, I wanted to set us in our history by revealing a line to measure from" (*Timebends* 587).

5. Terry Otten reads Quinn's final song and dance as a "return to the naive innocence that surely portends another Fall" (184), but such a reading negates Quinn's role in the play as a figure who understands the necessary balance between individuals and community. Robertson may see Quinn's dance as naive, but Miller uses it more as a symbol of the unquenchable American spirit.

6. It is partly World War Two which saves the day, bringing the opportunities everyone seeks. This may show there is a good side even to evil occurrences such as war. But the war is a condition which, beneath the surface, is all too similar to the Depression, only the conflict is more in the open. Miller springs through the years to illustrate the nature of war. Through songs and references to Korean and Vietnamese conflicts, he spins through the 1940s, 1950s and 1960s. War is a constant. War does the same thing every time: kill people. One actor sings "The Times They Are A'Changing," but it is an ironic statement, as they are not changing at all, as all these conflicts blend together. War may return the country to prosperity, but at what price, and could there have been a better way? Miller seeks this alternate path.

7. Strongly reminiscent of Steinbeck's closing scene in his great Depression epic, *The Grapes of Wrath*, where the starving man drinks the mother's milk from Rose of Sharon's breast.

Works Cited

Bennetts, Leslie. "Miller Revives *American Clock* Amid Resonances of 30s." *New York Times* 14 Jul. 1988: C23.

Bigsby, Christopher. *Arthur Miller: A Critical Study*. Cambridge: Cambridge University Press, 2005.

_____, ed. *Arthur Miller and Company*. London: Methuen, 1990.

_____. *Modern American Drama 1945-1990*. Cambridge: Cambridge UP, 1992.

Ferran, Peter W. *"The American Clock*: 'Epic Vaudeville.'" *Arthur Miller's America: Theater and Culture in a Time of Change*. Ed. Enoch Brater. Ann Arbor: University of Michigan Press, 2005: 153-63.

Flanagan, James K. Introduction. In *Arthur Miller*. Eds. June Schlueter and James K. Flanagan. New York: Ungar, 1987: 1-41.

Miller, Arthur. *The American Clock* and *The Archbishop's Ceiling*. New York: Grove, 1989.

_____. "Conditions of Freedom." In *American Clock* and *The Archbishop's Ceiling*. Arthur Miller. New York: Grove, 1989: vii-xix.

_____. Interview. "Mr. Showbiz Celebrity Lounge Interview." *Starwave. Online*. 10 Jan. 1996.

_____. *Timebends: A Life*. New York: Grove, 1987.

Otten, Terry. *The Temptation of Innocence in the Dramas of Arthur Miller*. Columbia: U of Missouri P, 2002.

Roudané, Matthew C., ed. *Conversations with Arthur Miller*. Jackson: UP of Mississippi, 1987.

Schonberg, Harold C. "Joan Copeland Remembers Mama—And So Does Her Brother Arthur." *New York Times* 16 Nov. 1980, sec. 2: 1, 5.

Weales, Gerald. "Watching the Clock." In *The Achievement of Arthur Miller*. Ed. Steven R. Centola. Dallas: Contemporary Research, 1995: 127-34.

Welland, Dennis. *Miller: The Playwright*. 2nd. ed. New York: Methuen, 1983.

Coming to Roost Again:
Tragic Rhythm in Arthur Miller's *Broken Glass*_____

Terry Otten

In his typically caustic tone, Robert Brustein, long one of Arthur Miller's severest critics, called the 1994 Broadway staging of *Broken Glass* "just another spiral in a stumbling career." This "shaky piece of stagecraft," he went on, "is made of fragments from a more shatter-proof phase of Miller's career," when his often "plodding, pedestrian, predictable and a little pompous" works somehow "passed for modern tragedies" (29-30). And David Richards' review in the *New York Times* branded the play "Ibsenism by the book," a rehash of Ibsen's preoccu-pation "with the impact of long-ago deeds on the present" (129). There is some truth in these charges, for Miller does indeed invoke the rhythms of modern tragedy found in Ibsen. In fact, Sylvia Gellburg, the central figure in the drama, is reminiscent of Mrs. Alving in *Ghosts*, who having sinned against herself by remaining in a loveless marriage struggles vainly in the present to evade the ghosts of her past. Miller himself has acknowledged that the first time he realized he could be-come a playwright he was at the University of Michigan when he read "by chance . . . a Greek tragedy and Ibsen at the same time" and discov-ered that "something happens *x* years ago, unbeknownst to the hero, and he's got to grapple with the consequences" (Bigsby, *Arthur Miller and Company* 49). "I've come out of the playwrighting [sic] tradition which is Greek and Ibsen," he continued, "where the past is the burden of man and it's got to be placed on stage so that people can grapple with it. . . . it's the story of how the birds come home to roost" (Bigsby, *Arthur Miller and Company* 201).[1]

But if *Broken Glass* "is a kind of coda to much of Miller's earlier writing," as Sheridan Morley wrote in his review of the performance at the National Theatre in London, it "is in fact a breathtakingly brilliant exploration of the paralysis that overtook America in November 1938 as news of the Nazi persecution of the Jews just after *Kristallnacht*

---

reached their Brooklyn cousins." In an interview published in 1991, Miller acknowledged that his later plays "may seem even more tragic" than earlier texts like *All My Sons* or *Death of a Salesman*, in which "the characters' inability to free themselves gives rise to tragic consequences" (Centola 86-87). And, it might be said, they reveal Miller's sense of the evolving form of tragedy as genre. In *Broken Glass* characters do indeed "face themselves" at the culmination of a circuitous movement through time, reflective of a nearly postmodern vision of shifting reality and truth. The drama's reflection of both the classical pattern of tragedy and Ibsen's adaptation of the genre to the modern age does not constitute a literary offense, after all, nor deny the play's universality or authenticity.

The crisis which triggers the action in the play, the unexplained crippling of Sylvia Gellburg in 1938, parallels the coming of the plague in *Oedipus Rex* or the appearance of ghosts in Ibsen's *Ghosts*. It marks the assertion of the x-factor in Aristotelian terms, which necessitates an unavoidable reckoning with the past. And like *Oedipus Rex*, *Broken Glass*, as some critics have commented, becomes a psychological or spiritual detective story, a quest to resolve the mystery and a return to the "crossroads" where present and past intersect. In the rhythmic structure of the play, every step forward is a step backwards, a confrontation with past failures that erupt in true tragic rhythm in the presentness of the drama. The debilitating paralysis embodies the composite guilt shared by the characters. It represents both public and private, corporate and individual betrayals. Both Phillip, her husband, and Dr. Harry Hyman, her analyst-doctor, suspect that Sylvia's condition is related to her obsession with the news of Nazi atrocities during *Kristallnacht*. Miller of course expressly treats the horrors of the Holocaust in *Incident at Vichy* (1964) and *Playing for Time* (1985). Here he employs the theme more implicitly in the manner of *After the Fall* (1964), in which he links the tyrannies of state terror and individual crimes. Sylvia's "hysterical paralysis" symbolizes a spiritual illness universally shared. As Hyman tells Phillip, "we get sick in twos and threes and fours, not alone as individuals" (504).[2] To live "After the Fall," the characters in *Broken Glass* must somehow be freed from "the temptation of innocence."

As primary investigator, Hyman senses that Sylvia possesses clairvoyant powers. He tells his wife Margaret regarding his taking Sylvia's case, "Something about it fascinates me. . . . there's something about it that I understand" (505). "Sylvia," he scolds his patient, "I know you know more than you're saying" (528). Relating Sylvia's sensitivity to the emerging tragedy in Europe, he later tells Margaret, "I just get the feeling sometimes that she knows something that . . . It's like she's connected to some . . . some wire that goes half-round the world, some truth that other people are blind to" (538).

Sylvia's Cassandra-like vision not only exposes the emerging disaster that exists in the dark moment of history in Europe, but also the secret violations of all the characters. Again like the characters in *Oedipus Rex*, those in *Broken Glass* evade the truth that condemns them and their own criminality. The play is, as John Lahr has written, "an anatomy of denial," a tragic web of "the evasions and hostilities by which the soul contrives to hide its emptiness from itself" (124-25). On the corporate level everyone but Sylvia seems to ignore the Nazi torture of the Jews. Phillip, who cannot tolerate his own Jewishness, tells Hyman, "German Jews can be pretty . . . you know. . . . *Pushes up his nose with his forefinger*" (496). Sylvia's sister Harriet asks her, "What business of yours is that?" and adds that she and her husband Murray agree that Sylvia's preoccupation with *Kristallnacht* "is not normal" (508-09). Margaret, Hyman's gentile wife, asks if "Getting hysterical about something on the other side of the world is sane?" (538). As so often in Miller's plays, characters wash their hands to guard their innocence, ignoring their responsibility as well as their complicity.

But of course tragedy occurs, in the Biblical phrase, in "the fullness of time," the inevitable moment when "the birds come home to roost." In a conversation with Miller, Christopher Bigsby asked, "But surely the most terrible thought is that people don't actually have to pay for their sins?" and Miller responded, "But one does. Somebody has to. . . . You deny it and it keeps coming back in one form or the other" (Bigsby, *Arthur Miller and Company* 202). As in Ibsen's dramas, the past always invades the present and demands retribution. Despite "a desperate wish to refuse responsibility for one's life" (Bigsby, *Arthur Miller and Company* xxxvi), tragedy demands an accountability always present in Miller's tragic texts.

Most guilty, it would seem, is Phillip Gellburg, whose denial of his Jewishness has led to personal violation and the victimization of others. Divided between counter impulses like the traditional tragic hero, he chooses against himself. To conceal his divided nature even from himself, he has for twenty years lived an inauthentic life. Allowing himself to be co-opted by the dominant WASP system that rejects him as Jew, a theme Miller explored in his early novel *Focus*, Phillip has willingly humiliated himself, doing the dirty work for the Brooklyn Guarantee and Trust, where he is the only Jew ever to work for the company. Insisting on his Finnish name, becoming a Republican, coercing his son Jerome to join the army to show that a Jew can become something other than a doctor, lawyer, or businessman, Gellburg is, as Margaret says, "one miserable little pisser" (505). His rejection of his Jewishness is primarily responsible for his alienation from Sylvia, who identifies completely with the Jews in Europe, seeing in the tormented old men cleaning the street with toothbrushes the image of her grandfather. Phillip's self-hatred and self-defensiveness have led him to tyrannize Sylvia, in whose recurring nightmare he assumes the guise of a Nazi who assaults her and starts to cut off her breasts.

But Phillip is not alone in his guilt. Margaret exposes her handsome and jaunty husband's past infidelities. She taunts him about taking on Sylvia's case: "Why not?" she asks—"She's a very beautiful woman" (505). Tempted by Sylvia, Hyman nearly makes love to her and admits to her, "I haven't been this moved by a woman in a very long time" (525). When he reveals his guilt and tries to evade Margaret's accusations, she tells him, "You don't realize how transparent you are. You're a pane of glass, Harry" (537), an obvious evocation of the title and a revelation of his vulnerability. When Hyman says he wonders why he takes Margaret's "suspicions seriously," she quips, "Oh that's easy.— You love the truth, Harry" (538). Even at the end of the play, when Gellburg accuses him of coming around to visit Sylvia "in those boots" (an overt reference to Hyman's riding boots, but perhaps an oblique reference to the boots of German storm-troopers), Hyman reacts all too defensively, "What the hell are you talking about!" Gellburg even suspects that Hyman married "a shiksa" so he "wouldn't look so Jewish." Hyman, too, is driven by guilt in consequence of the tragic pattern initiated by Sylvia's condition.

Nor can Sylvia retreat to a spurious innocence. She also must acknowledge her own culpability. In truth, Sylvia is victim of her own choices and is responsible for them. Both she and Phillip have accommodated themselves to personal failure, accepted their roles as victim and scapegoat, and thereby assured their own defeat. Even as they incriminate each other, they reveal their own offenses. True to the tragic rhythm, whether in Greek drama or in Ibsen's adaptation of the pattern, characters are stripped of their masks; their elusive attempts to preserve innocence ultimately prove futile. David Richards has concluded that "Sylvia Gellburg is unable to walk because her husband is a cripple" (130), but this is too neat and too simplistic. The tragic knowledge she possesses is also about herself, her self-consciousness of personal choices, and her willing acceptance of an inauthentic self. Like all tragic figures she is as much a victim of herself as of others. Faced with "the mores of that time and society, and her amenable personality, and the influence of her mother," Miller has commented, she turns "against herself" (qtd. in Griffin 180).

She appears to be tormented only by others, especially by Phillip. Trying to explain her lost life to Harriet, whose son is determined to turn down a college scholarship, she declares, "If I'd had a chance to go to college, I'd have led a whole different life" (509). She stayed in a failed marriage because, as Harriet tells Hyman, "it would have killed our mother, she worships Phillip, she'd never outlive it" (518). She tolerates her role as long-suffering wife, giving up her fulfilling career in business and remaining with Phillip even though he has twice physically abused her by striking her with a steak and throwing her up a stairs. More poignantly, for twenty years she has lived with Phillip's impotency because she did not want to embarrass him after her failed attempt to gain the Rabbi's help distanced her permanently from her husband. Yet her paralysis empowers her to express her contained hostility to Phillip. She reacts sarcastically to his suggestion that the two of them seek Hyman's help in resolving the impotency. "It's too late for that . . . it doesn't matter anymore," she tells him as she *"draws back her hand"* (514). She openly taunts him when he tries to confess that he once thought about separating from her but has not "felt that way in years now" (515). "I've been here a long time," she retorts: "Well I'm here. . . . Here I am, Phillip! . . . I'm here for my mother's sake, for Jerome's sake, and everybody's sake except mine, but I'm here and here I am and you want to talk about it, now when I'm turning into an old woman?" (515).

Yet despite her bitter condemnation of Phillip and her brutal exposure of his failures, she possesses a tragic *self*-knowledge as well. As John Lahr has commented, "Sylvia can't face her disgust at herself any more than she can face down her husband" (124). "What I did with my life!" she cries out to Phillip. "Out of ignorance. Out of not wanting to shame you in front of other people. A whole life. Gave it away like a couple of pennies—I took better care of my shoes" (553-54). To find some resolve, she must stop blaming others and find the resources in herself. She describes herself as suffering a form of birth trauma, a reflection of the death and rebirth motif tied to the seasons so elemental in traditional tragedy: "It's like I was just born and I . . . didn't want to come out yet" (509). She later tells Hyman, "it's almost like there's something in me. . . . it's like . . . *She presses her chest*—something alive, like a child almost, except it's a very dark thing . . . and it frightens me!" (529).[3] Similarly, Phillip tells Hyman in their last conversation that he is afraid; and

Hyman responds, "If you're alive you're afraid; we're born afraid—a newborn baby is not a picture of confidence" (563).[4] These images suggest the frightening birth of an authentic self, frightening because such a birth can occur only through suffering, at the cost of the public self behind which the characters hide. Frozen by fear and an incapacitating guilt, Sylvia and Phillip have betrayed their true selves—and consequently each other. Only at tremendous price can they achieve a tragic victory in defeat by looking into the mirror.

Phillip reenacts Sylvia's near welcoming of her paralysis after he himself collapses in his boss's office (a scene clearly reminiscent of the one between Willy Loman and Howard in *Death of a Salesman*): "It sounds funny but I felt a happiness . . . that funny? Like I suddenly had something to tell her that would change everything. . . . God, I always thought there'd be a time to get to the bottom of myself!" (560). Like Sylvia's physical collapse, Phillip's marks an end to self-deceit and brings him to a moment of existential awareness. "I don't know where I am" (562), he remarks to Hyman. "My thoughts keep flying around— everything from years ago coming back like it was last week" (562). Faced with what he has been, he confesses, "I feel like there's nothing inside me, I feel empty" (564). It is paradoxically a moment of truth he invites, yet it is only through painful self-confrontation that Phillip can somehow be redeemed from the past. Only by acknowledging his offenses against Sylvia and against himself can he achieve what Miller calls "tragic dimension," when "characters are obsessed with retrieving a lost identity," a true self (Centola 400). He tells Hyman he wants to "talk about being Jews" (562), he struggles to embrace what he betrayed in himself yet always wanted to be, and he wants desperately to heal the breach between him and Sylvia.

Hyman offers the only solution to the tragic dilemma, though of course nothing can rescue the characters from the price tragedy exacts or can alter the past. He advises Phillip to commit the most painful of acts, to look squarely into the mirror, as Miller might say, "After the Fall," and, seeing, "To forgive yourself. . . . And the Jews. And while you're at it you can throw in the goyim" (566). He speaks from experience, as he confesses, knowing his own guilt. And it is this tragic wisdom that Sylvia also expresses at the end when she says to Phillip, "I'm not blaming you, Phillip. The years I wasted I knew I threw away myself. I think I always knew I was doing it" (507). Rejecting a truly crippling innocence, she too admits, "I hate it all now. Everything I did is stupid and ridiculous. I can't find myself in my life." And striking her legs, the symbol of false self, she adds, "I am not this thing" (567). "We wish for a pillow to lay our heads upon," Miller has said of tragedy, "and it's a stone" (Centola 351). Nevertheless, tragedy, Miller insists, ends with a promise of hope. There is some degree of reconciliation, some moral victory through suffering, that melodrama denies.

Only through self-consciousness can responsibility emerge. If a central moment of truth occurs when Hyman tells Phillip, "You can't find anybody who's persecuting anybody else" (566), that all claim innocence, it is transformed into tragic resolve at the end when Phillip begs, "Sylvia, forgive me!" (568), an admission of his Nazi self, his debilitating persona. He gains a moral victory, even though Sylvia insists, "There's nothing to blame!" It is an accounting for Phillip, an act of self-judgment that affirms a moral order. Sylvia comes to a similar point. Before her last scene with Phillip, she informs Harriet, "There is nothing I know now that I didn't know twenty years ago. I just didn't say it. . . . After a while you can't find a true word to put in your mouth" (559). Even as Harriet insists that she cannot blame herself, Sylvia knows that her crime of silence and self-denial has partly precipitated the tragedy. When the apparently dying Phillip falls back in the chair at the very end, she *takes a faltering step*." Pleading with him to "Wait, wait," she gives voice to the pity for him she had early told Hyman she still feels but has been unable to express. The first time she stands after her paralysis comes in a moment of intense anxiety over the events of *Kristallnacht* when she cries out to Hyman, "This is *an emergency*! What if they kill those children! . . . Somebody should do something before they murder us all!" (551). Miller calls this "the first time she is taking her life into her own hands" (qtd. in Griffin 186). This communal gesture of compassion extends to all Jews, and symbolically to all the oppressed. But it is not until the very end, when she stands a second time after her painful journey of self-awareness, that she can fully reach out in compassion for Phillip, forgiving him with whom she is inexorably bound, as a Jewish victim to a Nazi tyrant.

Almost no one, not even Miller, was happy with the ending of the play at its premiere performance in New Haven or shortly later in New York. And despite Miller's alterations it remains a problem for many. Phillip's sudden illness and Sylvia's dramatic if temporary recovery certainly smacks of Hollywood. But Miller describes *Broken Glass* as "tragedy" (qtd. in Griffin 186), and whatever its artistic problems, the conclusion conforms to his concept of tragic action. Although as early as the 1960s Miller recognized that "it is unlikely, to say the least, that since so many other kinds of human consciousness have changed that [tragedy] would remain unchanged," he sees the end of tragedy as consistent, "still basically the same" and traceable back to the Biblical Fall and "the earliest Western literature" (Roudané 200). However dramatically (or over-dramatically), the ending of *Broken Glass* asserts Miller's belief that "the rules of life are powerful and they exist. And that's a tragic view, and therefore hopeful" (Martin and Centola 489). Always for Miller, there are consequences to actions, and the birds eventually *do* return to roost.

Like Ibsen's, Miller's tragic vision is more secular than conventionally religious. Phillip wonders how "can there be Jews if there's no God"; and the scientist-skeptic Hyman recounts, "Oh, they'll find something to worship. The Christians will too—maybe different brands of ketchup" (564). In fact, Miller leaves open the question of divine justice, just as he leaves open-ended the full meaning of Sylvia's "*inward seeing*" and leaves the riddle of existence unanswered. For Miller, the end of tragedy is that "you've got to retrieve what you've spent and you've got to account for it somehow. I don't mean to God, I mean to yourself, or you are totally incomplete always" (Bigsby, *Arthur*

Miller and Company 201). Glimpsing a postmodern age, he has remarked that unlike the classical tragic hero who "is working inside a religious cosmology where there is no mistaking a man for God. . . . We are in a world of scrambled eggs and mucking about in it, and the difference between the points of contact with the man and his god, so to speak, are fused" (Roudané 225). Miller's mission as artist, he has concluded, "my effort, my aesthetic, is to find the chain of moral being in the world, somehow. It's moving in its hidden way through all my work" (Bigsby, *Miller and Company* 178). We know only that the consequences of choices must be faced, that there is always a price to be paid, that suffering is unequivocally part of tragedy; but, nonetheless, such cost bears witness to order in a moral universe that operates with or without God. "You get existential justice," Miller concludes, "but that's about it" (Bigsby, *Arthur Miller and Company* 201). Yet this in itself "makes redemption a possibility at the end," Christopher Bigsby rightly argues, for even after fifty years of writing for the stage, Arthur Miller is not "ready to retract his demand that we acknowledge our responsibility for the world we have made" (*The Portable Arthur Miller* xxxvi)—an insistence, we can conclude, both tragic and redemptive.

From *The South Carolina Review* 31, no. 2 (1999): 17-24. Copyright © 1999 by Clemson University Digital Press. Reprinted with permission of *The South Carolina Review.*

Notes

1. Looking back over his career in the mid 1980s, Miller remarked, "I think probably the greatest single discovery I made was the structure of Greek plays. That really blinded me. It seemed to fit everything that I felt. And then there was Ibsen, who was dealing with the same kind of structural pattern—that is the past meeting the present dilemma" (Roudané 386).

2. I am using the final acting version of the play as reprinted in the revised edition of *The Portable Arthur Miller.* The single volume text published by Penguin in 1994 was subsequently revised in later stage versions. As often noted, Miller has especially rewritten the concluding section since the play's premiere performance at the Long Wharf Theater in New Haven in March of 1994.

3. In *After the Fall*, in 1964, Miller used the image of an "idiot child" that appears in Holga's recurring dream. Suffering from a profound sense of culpability, like Sylvia, she says of the Holocaust that "no one they didn't kill can be innocent again." And she tells Quentin of the idiot child that keeps returning to her lap: "if I could kiss it . . . perhaps I could sleep. And I bent to kiss its broken face, and it was horrible . . . but I kissed it. I think one must finally take one's life to one's arms, Quentin" (22).

4. A short time later Gellburg admits that when he used to make love with Sylvia, "I would almost feel like a small babe on top of her, like she was giving me birth. That's some idea? In bed next to me she was like a . . . marble god" (565).

Works Cited

Bigsby, Christopher, ed. *Arthur Miller and Company*. London: Methuen in association with The Arthur Miller Centre for American Studies, 1990.

_____. *The Portable Arthur Miller*. Revised Edition. New York: Penguin Books, 1995.

Brustein, Robert. "Separated by a Common Playwright." *The New Republic* 30 May 1991: 29-30.

Centola, Steven R. "'Just Looking for a Home.'" *American Drama* 1.1 (1991): 85-94.

Griffin, Alice. *Understanding Arthur Miller*. Columbia: U of South Carolina P, 1996.

Lahr, John. "Dead Souls." *The New Yorker* 9 May 1994. Reprinted in *New York Theater Critics Reviews* 55 (1994): 124-25.

Martin, Robert A., and Steven R. Centola, eds. *The Theater Essays of Arthur Miller*. Revised Edition. New York: Da Capo Press, 1996.

Miller, Arthur. *After the Fall*. New York: Viking, 1964.

_____. *Broken Glass* (Final Acting Version). Bigsby, *The Portable Arthur Miller* 489-568.

Morley, Christopher. "Miller's Crossing." *Spectator* 13 Aug. 1994: 31.

Richards, David. "A Paralysis Points to Spiritual and Social Ills." *New York Times* 25 April 1994. Reprinted in *New York Theater Critics Reviews* 55 (1994): 129-30.

Roudané, Matthew C., ed. *Conversations with Arthur Miller*. Jackson: UP of Mississippi, 1987.

Arthur Miller's Ironic Resurrection_____
Jeffrey D. Mason

> And somehow we are now "post-dread." Something fell down. Nobody's quite sure what it was or is, and whether a structure is re-asserting itself—a new one. But things ain't what they used to be. I think something did fall down, a structure which we look at sometimes comically.... Now what we have is a flow; one thing happening after another without any sensible form or shape.
>
> —Arthur Miller, 20 October 1996[1]

> Power changes everything.
>
> —Arthur Miller, 26 March 2001[2]

Arthur Miller's *Resurrection Blues* (2002) closes with a renunciation of expectations, of any belief that the future could constitute progress beyond the present.[3] After struggling over how to respond to a man who might be the new Messiah, the characters stand together, staring up into the bright light that he radiates as he rises above them, and they cry out, in unison, "Please go away." The light fades, and they say good-bye, "immensely relieved and sorry."[4] If he is the Messiah, they are giving up on salvation, but if we take his messianic status as metaphorical, interpreting him in a secular sense as the one who would lead them to change society and rectify injustice, then they are rejecting activism. From this perspective, the play constitutes Miller's cynical denunciation of a post-millennial age when the values and aspirations he so long defended are, perhaps, no longer viable.[5]

Activism involves working to change and improve the existing order; as such, it requires taking a position that is antagonistic or even subversive in relation to established structures of authority and power. The activist defines a goal, a vision of what society could be, then maps out a strategy for reaching this goal in opposition to the resistance of those who would sustain the status quo. As dramatist and essayist,

---

Miller has taken an activist approach most frequently by identifying a social problem and calling, through either direct or poetic means, for change, and although many characterize him as a social dramatist, both his work and his public life demonstrate a consistently political consciousness.

In *All My Sons* (1947), Miller indicts those who would profit at the expense of others' sacrifice and, more significantly, presents an understanding of community responsibility that goes beyond the conventional boundaries of the family. He attacks betrayal and political repression in *The Crucible* (1953), investigates the guilt for the Holocaust in *Incident at Vichy* (1964), and contemplates the dangers of censorship and surveillance in *The Archbishop's Ceiling* (1984). In these plays and others, Miller comes down firmly on the side of social action, placing his faith in resistance to oppressive authority, the right of the people to live free from tyranny, and the power of the individual to stand against the tide. Offstage, he served as an outspoken and highly visible president of International P.E.N. (1965-69), and he attended two national conventions of the Democratic Party, in 1968 as a delegate for Eugene McCarthy and in 1972 as a journalist sympathetic to George McGovern. In the course of his career, he has denounced Ezra Pound for supporting fascism, protested the burning of Vietnamese villages by American soldiers, censured the Greek government's oppression of writers, advocated for the release of Augusto Boal, and smiled at the prevailing American mistrust of Soviet Russia and the People's Republic of China.[6] He has urged the corrosive question of anti-Semitism in such plays as *Incident at Vichy*, *Playing for Time* (adapted 1980), and *Broken Glass* (1994), as well as the novel *Focus* (1945) and various articles.[7] In his many essays, he has argued that the intimidation of Salman Rushdie was not anomalous; warned that Congressional control of the National Endowment for the Arts would threaten freedom of expression; scolded Newt Gingrich for his position on the relationship of government to the artist; offered a mock-serious proposal that the government arrest and incarcerate each American citizen on her/his eighteenth birthday until a judge accepts evidence of the individual's allegiance; held up to ridicule the honesty not only of Richard Nixon but also of Lyndon Johnson, John F. Kennedy, and Dwight Eisenhower; and attacked a proposal that each American citizen carry an identity card.[8] In all, Miller's work provides a rich record of his response to certain major events and currents of his lifetime: the Great Depression, the Nazi invasion of Europe and the Holocaust, the anti-Communist repression of the 1950s, the anti-war movement of the 1960s, and the fall of the Nixon presidency. David Savran hails the playwright's political commitment: "Miller has consistently dedicated his writing to the exploration of manifestly political issues, including the alienation and commodification of the individual subject in bourgeois society, the mechanics of ostracism, and the ethics of informing on one's own colleagues."[9] Yet as an activist, Miller is more moderate than radical, highly cognizant of the intricacies and ambiguities in society and politics.

Outside the theatre, the most compelling staging of Miller's political persona and activist tendencies took place during his testimony before the House Committee on Un-American Activities on the morning of Thursday, 21 June 1956.[10] Although Miller's reputation as activist and social critic flowered due to his handling of the Committee and various journalists' reports on his testimony, his participation in the scenario did not truly establish him as an unequivocal leftist, activist, or opponent of oppression; rather, the dialogue revealed the subtleties and contradictions in Miller's thought. Early in the hearing, Richard Arens, the staff director for the Committee, asked a series of questions designed to establish that in 1947 alone, the playwright had supported the World Youth Festival in Prague, a *Washington Post* advertisement protesting punitive measures directed against the Communist Party, a statement by the Veterans Against Discrimination advocating the abolition of the Committee, and three actions by the Civil Rights Congress: a rally against the Committee, a statement in support of the Communist Party as a legal American political party, and a press release in support of Gerhart Eisler, whom Arens characterized as "a top-ranking agent of the Kremlin in this country."[11] The Committee regarded all of these organizations and activities as Communist in nature; for example, they listed the Veterans Against Discrimination as a "subversive affiliate" of the Civil Rights Congress, itself "subversive and Communist" and included in a list of Communist organizations compiled from the Attorney General's official reports intended to protect the national security and provide a reference to guide anyone in the government who was reviewing a job applicant's background.[12] Miller asserted that he could not recall whether or not he had given the support that so concerned Arens. He remarked that "in those times I did support a number of things which I would not do now. . . . I would not support now a cause or movement which was dominated by Communists."[13] He agreed that he had exercised poor judgment; not only had he allowed Communists and their supporters to use his name, he committed a "great error" by not using his platform to defend those whom the Communists were persecuting. The Committee regarded his remarks as a confession and acceptance of guilt, but their interpretation aside, he was clearly backing away from embracing these past affiliations.

When the hearing turned to the Smith Act, a law intended to discourage and punish insurgents, Miller took a more aggressive position and offered his well-known defense of advocacy in literature:

> I am opposed to the Smith Act and I am still opposed to anyone being penalized for advocating anything. That doesn't mean that a man is a propagandist. It is in the nature of life and it is in the nature of literature that the passions of an author congeal around issues.
>
> You can go from *War and Peace* through all the great novels of time and they are all advocating something. . . . I am not here defending Communists, I am here defending the right of an author to advocate, to write. . . .
>
> . . . my understanding of [the Act] is that advocacy is penalized or can be under this law. Now, my interest, as I tell you, is possibly too selfish, but without it I can't operate and neither can literature in this country, and I don't think anybody can question this.[14] ("TAM," 4672, 4673)

To write, Miller argued, is to advocate; he traces the process from issues to the writer's "passions" to the consequent work. He evokes a powerful conception of writing as a form of speaking out, of setting out one's ideas for public scrutiny, and of entering into a contentious, engaged discourse. Although he agreed that one should "call out the troops" to subdue a man if he were urging people to blow up the building where the hearing was taking place, he insisted that the Smith Act placed in jeopardy "the freedom of literature without which we will be back in a situation where people as in the Soviet Union and as in Nazi Germany have not got the right to advocate." When Representative Gordon H. Scherer asked whether or not "a poet should have the right to advocate the overthrow of this Government by force and violence in his literature," Miller replied, "a man should have the right to write a poem [concerning] just about anything" ("TAM," 4673, 4674).[15]

Yet Miller equivocated in two respects. First, he cherished a view of the special nature of the artist, and the more Committee members pressed him, the more he limited his defense of advocacy to its literary uses, implying that if literature moves in its own space, then it is harmless, and one can write a poem about anything because the work is "only" a poem. This position rests on a distinction and a boundary between art and politics, one that tends to subordinate and debilitate art, but even the Committee members realized that a poem can serve as a vehicle whose artistic value is of less significance than the ideas it carries. Miller argued that advocacy is essential for literature, and he asked for a special constitutional shield because of literature's artistic nature. In other words, in spite of his defense of advocacy, Miller asks that we appreciate his work for its artistic merits more than for its meaning.

Second, Miller remarked that he had never read the law he disparaged. In fact, the Smith Act specified punishment for anyone convicted not merely of advocacy in general, or even of advocacy of ideas, no matter how aggressive, but specifically of advocating the violent overthrow of the government of the United States.[16] The law did interdict a variety of ordinarily protected activities—to teach, to advise, to print, to publish, to encourage—but only if turned to such a purpose. We are left with the question of whether Miller was acting in ignorance or taking a canny position on a highly sensitive and politicized matter. The Smith Act was undeniably an object of active concern: eleven Communist Party leaders were arrested in 1948 and subsequently convicted under the Act, and the Committee's chair, Francis E. Walter, defended the Act against the argument that the threat of Communist conspiracy was no longer strong enough to warrant the compromise to the right of free speech.[17] We may speculate either that Miller was responding to the Smith Act imperfectly on the basis of hearsay, or that he was turning the Act to his own purposes, finding in it an opportunity to advocate for a certain view of First Amendment rights.

In the course of his testimony, Miller took several carefully selected positions. Although he claimed not to remember offering his support for specific, allegedly subversive causes, he admitted his past affiliation with organizations that the Committee regarded as linked to the Communist Party. However, he had never submitted to the "discipline" of the Party or its cause, and he regarded supporting Communism as a "great error" ("TAM," 4660, 4690). He denounced the Smith Act insofar as it penalized advocacy, but he agreed that the government should restrain someone who incited others to violence. Most significantly, although he insisted that a poet should be able to write about anything and he demanded the right of advocacy in literature, he rested these positions on a meaningful and substantive distinction between literature and political action, apparently implying that literature could have political content even though its writing and publishing were not necessarily political acts. The hearing concluded in a conciliatory mood; the playwright agreed that "it would be a disaster and a calamity if the Communist Party ever took over this country," acknowledged that "we are living in a time when there is great uncertainty," and assured the members, "I believe in democracy [and] I love this country" ("TAM," 4689-90). Miller had found a judicious middle ground: he had not cooperated in the manner of Elia Kazan, Clifford Odets, and Lee J. Cobb, but neither had he resisted as firmly as Lillian Hellman, Pete Seeger, and Zero Mostel.

We should interpret Miller's delicate dance in relation to the political operations and personal risks of the moment. In the very different political climate of the 1960s, Miller took a clearer, more openly activist position. In response to the assassination of Robert Kennedy, he issued a call for social action:

> It must be faced now that we are afraid of the Negro because we have denied him social justice and we do not know how to stop denying him.
>
> We are afraid of the poor because we know that there is enough to go around, that we have not made it our first order of business to literally create the jobs that can and must be created. . . .
>
> We are at war not only with Vietnamese but with Americans. Stop both. We are rich enough to wipe out every slum and to open a world of hope to the poor. What keeps us? Do we want peace in Vietnam? Then make peace. Do we want hope in our cities and towns? Then stop denying any man his birthright. . . .
>
> Between the promise and its denial—there stands the man with the gun. Between the promise and its denial stands a man holding them apart—the American. Either he recognizes what he is doing, or he will take the final, fatal step to suppress the violence he has called up.
>
> Only justice will overcome the nightmare. The American Dream is ours to evoke.[18]

Miller asks his listeners to embrace the moment, to assume responsibility for their society, and to act on the belief that action can lead to results; his is a clarion call to activism. He insists that the United States has the money and the power to effect radical social change, to rectify the wrongs of racism, poverty, and war, and in spite of the remonstrative tone, his message is ultimately optimistic. Here, perhaps, is Miller at his most outspoken, but by the time he wrote *Resurrection Blues*, his confidence in action seemed to have faded.

Resurrection Blues

Resurrection Blues is a political satire that takes aim at such twenty-first-century targets as the power and cultural values of broadcast media, the deceitful rhetoric and compromise of military dictatorship, the wary and unbalanced relationship between the United States and Latin America, and the virtually palpable force of money in a global and corporate economy. Miller brings together these elements in a crisis developing from an impending crucifixion, a plot element that threatens to dislocate the action back to the concerns that led to a hill outside Jerusalem two thousand years ago. The events take place in what Miller describes simply as "a faraway country" but which appears to be a deeply troubled nation located somewhere in the Americas, south of the United States, a Spanish-speaking region whose people still remember the Conquistadors. The country has endured nearly four decades of civil war, and two percent of the people own ninety-six percent of the land. Fathers turn their eight-year-old daughters into prostitutes while small children kill old men for their shoes, and in the most swanky shopping district, pedestrians casually ignore a dead baby lying in the gutter. The air pollution is acrid enough to peel the paint off an eighteenth-century canvas, and a leaking underground aqueduct has so undermined the foundations of homes in one affluent neighborhood that the weight of a grand piano threatens to collapse the house that holds it. Children suffer liver damage from drinking water riddled with blood fluke, and even the powerful must fly to Miami for competent dental care.[19] This "faraway country" has no clearly recognizable model or analogue, although a passing reference to the Andes, late in the play, suggests that Miller might have been thinking of Chile or Argentina, with echoes of Augusto Pinochet or Juan Perón. Yet rather than dismiss it as a generic cartoon of a banana republic, we might do better to regard it as the inverse of the United States, or rather of the self-conceived image of the United States, what the United States, in Miller's satirical commentary, hopes it is not: poor, backward, abused, and abusive.[20]

The story is fairly simple. General Felix Barriaux, the leader of the military junta that rules the country, has captured an alleged rebel usually known as "Ralph" whom he proposes to execute by crucifixion. The largest advertising agency in the United States offers $25 million for the exclusive rights to televise the event, and an account executive, Skip L. Cheeseboro, comes to scout locations with Emily Shapiro, a director of television commercials. They meet Henri Schultz, Felix's cousin, who suffers from chronic guilt over the ruthless operation of his pharmaceutical corporation and who lacks Felix's knack for overlooking the fact that many of the peasants light candles to "Ralph" as the second coming of the Messiah. "Ralph," who never appears on stage, not only generates a dazzling white light, he is apparently able to perform curative miracles. In the end, the characters' various selfish interests drive the debate over whether "Ralph" should stay for his own execution or depart by means of his own transfiguration.

The Operation of Power

The play depicts social and political power as rooted in exploitation and managed through presentation. Miller has explored social power— as distinct from the political processes that frequently express it—most notably in *All My Sons*, *The Crucible*, *The Archbishop's Ceiling*, and even *Death of a Salesman* (1949), which is, in part, an exploration of how exclusion from the currents of power—in the community, in society, in a vocation—relentlessly beats down one man. Yet his concern with power extends well beyond the stage; while serving as president of International P.E.N. in 1966, he offered a perspective informed by what he was learning about oppression outside of the United States. He presents the concentration camp as an expression and consequence of power deployed ruthlessly:

> I have always felt that concentration camps, though they're a phenomenon
> of totalitarian states, are also the logical conclusion of contemporary life. If
> you complain of people being shot down in the streets, of the absence of

communication or social responsibility, of the rise of everyday violence which people have become accustomed to, and the dehumanization of feelings, then the ultimate development on an organized social level is the concentration camp. . . . The concentration camp is the final expression of human separateness and its ultimate consequence.[21]

Just two years earlier, he had finished *After the Fall* (1964), with its dominant scenic image of "the blasted stone tower of a German concentration camp" looming over the entire action and mutely influencing the characters' behavior even while it seems to warn them of the possible consequences of their actions.[22] Here, Miller is suggesting a cluster of associations: concentration camps are productions of totalitarian states, which constitute the most extreme manifestations of institutionalized power, but they also represent the logical extension of an existence rife with violence and fraught with alienation. Power, especially too much power, can crush life. He goes on to explain his fundamental concerns:

> I'm in deadly fear of people with too much power. I don't trust people that much any more. I used to think that if people had the right idea they could make things move accordingly. Now it's a day-to-day fight to stop dreadful things from happening.[23]

Miller made these deeply cynical and pessimistic remarks two years *before* his inspirational response to Robert Kennedy's assassination, so we may conclude that even during the sometimes exhilarating 1960s, he struggled with the problem of how to respond to social calamity, swinging between hope and despair. In *Resurrection Blues*, he explores the option of surrender.

Felix Barriaux constitutes Miller's comic demonstration of the danger of power. He is a composite of every uniformed dictator from Fidel Castro to Saddam Hussein, and the playwright chooses to show not the public persona, the Felix that might appear on CNN, but rather the man behind the scenes who speaks frankly to those who are close to him.²⁴ We hear, therefore, not the political rhetoric itself but the ideas, ambition, and cynicism that drive it, so the character comes across as brutally and comically honest. He is a ruthless pragmatist, completely free from illusions, who advises Henri to "fuck them before they can fuck you" (*RB*, 4). He chooses his concerns and loyalties according to the results he seeks; he knows that dying children are politically insignificant compared with those who will profit if the British erect a warehouse on the waterfront. He so completely scorns the populace that he dismisses the very idea of land reform, assuring Henri that "in ten years the land you gave away will end up back in the hands of two percent of the smartest people! You can't teach gorillas to play Chopin" (*RB*, 16). He states unequivocally that any government must cooperate with the "narco-guerrillas" because they have money and discipline. As for politics in general, "there is only one sacred rule—nobody clearly remembers anything," and since he attaches value to others only insofar as he can use them, he plays everyone he meets (*RB*, 21). Felix is Miller's vision of a despot, of the ostensibly actual substance behind the constructed image, so he constitutes the playwright's attempt to get at the truth of power structures in the worlds of commerce, force, and politics that he explores.

Miller distorts Felix enough that we can choose to laugh at him and not take him too seriously. By contrast, the playwright felt that Danforth, the deputy governor and presiding judge in *The Crucible*, represented so palpable a threat that he should have drawn a darker picture of him. Four years after that play opened, Miller wrote:

> I was wrong in mitigating the evil of this man and the judges he represents. Instead, I would perfect his evil to its utmost and make an open issue, a thematic consideration of it in the play. I believe now, as I did not conceive then, that there are people dedicated to evil in the world; that without their perverse example we should not know the good. Evil is not a mistake but a fact in itself.²⁵

Danforth and Felix both rule, bend others to their wills, and constitute manifestations of what Miller deems wrong with the world. Yet Miller wrote Felix nearly fifty years after he created Danforth; we must take Danforth seriously and deal with his menace, while Felix embodies a situation that has already moved past our control. A Danforth inspires concern and action as we see the possibility to defeat him, but a Felix is too firmly placed and our only option is grim humor.

Through Felix, Miller cultivates his ongoing mistrust of the operation of government and those who govern. At a rally for Eugene McCarthy in 1968, amidst the burgeoning resistance to the Vietnam War, he demanded a departure from the craven leadership he had observed:

> The next President is going to face a revolutionary country and [a] world in revolution, and he will need a lot more than gallantry. He will need the habit of mind to perceive in the institutions he leads [that] what is dead and inhuman must be dismantled. The next President will not be able to lead by consensus, by the expert manipulation of opinion, or by calls for unity, however passionate. . . . The next President will have to weigh every action not for what it will do for our prestige or our institutions but for what it will do to people.[26]

Miller perceives the status quo as a reliance on charisma, good feelings, and expertly-managed spin, so he calls for a higher level of responsibility as well as a greater concern for human welfare.

Throughout his career, Miller has denounced censorship as a pernicious exercise of power and a special form of oppression. He interpreted his 1956 summons by the Committee as no more than his government's attempt to repress his writing.[27] In 1989, possibly looking back to his extensive experience with the repression of writers while serving as president of International P.E.N., he argued that censorship as an abuse of authority was a global problem, used "to steal power from the people and hand it over to the state."[28] *The Archbishop's Ceiling* stages his deep concern over not just censorship but active government surveillance. In the preface to the Grove edition, he wrote:

> Very recently, in the home of a star Soviet writer, I began to convey the best wishes of a mutual friend, an émigré Russian novelist living in Europe, and the star motioned to me not to continue. Once outside, I asked if he wasn't depressed by having to live in a tapped house. . . . Was he really all that unaffected by the presence of the unbidden guest? Perhaps so, but even if he had come to accept or at least abide it fatalistically, the bug's presence had changed him nonetheless. In my view it had perhaps dulled some resistance in him to Power's fingers ransacking his pockets every now and then. One learns to *include the bug* in the baggage of one's mind, in the calculus of one's plans and expectations, and this is not without effect. . . . What, for instance, becomes of the idea of sincerity, the unmitigated expression of one's feelings and views, when one knows that Power's ear is most probably overhead? Is sincerity shaken by the sheer fact that one has so much as *taken the bug into consideration?*[29]

The bug becomes the government, becomes authority, becomes the invasive presence of power that threatens to destroy the individual's mind; Miller sees how the insinuation of official control into private life cannot help but suffocate. Through *The Archbishop's Ceiling*, Miller questioned the integrity not of a specific government but of the very idea of government; the embattled writers in the play regard government as an adversary with no face and virtually limitless authority. One observes, "The government makes it very clear that you must snuggle up to power or you will never be happy."[30]

By 1995, Miller's cynicism over the operation of government had deepened to the point of offering an ironic recommendation that the nation privatize the United States Congress, that businesses and interest groups hire representatives and senators who would openly advocate on their behalf:

The compelling reasons for privatizing Congress are perfectly evident. Everybody hates it, only slightly less than they hate the president. Everybody, that is, who talks on the radio, plus millions of the silent who only listen and hate in private.

Congress has brought on this hatred, mainly by hypocrisy.[31]

He went on to argue that privatization would simply recognize the existence of the corporate state, and he suggested that the transformation extend to the Supreme Court and the Department of Justice so that criminal and civil proceedings could openly consist of striking bargains.

Yet force and tyranny are only the first layers in *Resurrection Blues'* structure of power relations; Miller then turns to the media. He once wrote, "The sin of power is to not only distort reality but to convince people that the false is true, and that what is happening is only an invention of enemies."[32] Felix understands that consolidating power involves managing what people know so that actuality becomes less significant than belief. Skip and Emily can sell virtually anything; they translate experience into the brief, intensely focused moments that they can show on television, and Skip proudly introduces Emily as the director who "has given the world some of its most uplifting commercial images" (*RB*, 29). Felix might, in his public appearances, pay lip service to his duty to his people, but Skip and Emily bear no explicit public responsibility and so can exploit their material more openly; indeed, it is their business to keep their distance from local concerns and especially to make free use of whatever they find. They create propaganda in order to serve the commercial interests that hire them, giving little thought for honesty or accuracy, and insofar as the very nature of a television commercial presupposes that the customer requires persuasion, the relationship between the producer and the customer is inherently antagonistic and the discourse is partisan. Yet their propaganda engages politics at one remove, dealing more directly with the financial influences that support and enable a government like Felix's. Miller is tracing the distance from the 1950s, when the Committee denounced propaganda as the tool of subversives, to the present moment, when propaganda serves the interests of the power elite; surely government fifty years ago used propaganda, but now it does so without shame.

Skip and Emily have become so involved in simulation that they are able to grasp certain realities only through strenuous effort. Emily at first assumes that the execution is part of a feature film that someone else is shooting; only when she sees a team of soldiers digging a hole and bolting together the cross members to construct a genuine crucifix does she realize that they expect her to film an actual crucifixion with actual nails and an actual death. She is incredulous: "Nobody dies in a commercial! Have you all gone crazy?" (RB, 33). Skip, in turn, has difficulty remembering that "Ralph" is not precisely Jesus Christ, and he keeps coming back to questions of how his American customers would react to his treatment of this supposed new Messiah. Crucifixion is actually a standard practice in Felix's country, and when the general cheerfully informs Skip that the typical victim first guzzles a couple of bottles of tequila and might have to be carried to the cross, the advertising man is convinced that many in the United States—specifically born-again Christian viewers "in like dry states . . . Kansas or whatever"—would consider such a debacle to be blasphemous (RB, 44). He is also concerned over the possibility that the condemned man might scream:

> But I should think if he is confident that he is about to . . . like meet his father in heaven, you could put it to him as a test of his faith that he not scream on camera. The camera, you see, tends to magnify everything and screaming on camera could easily seem in questionable taste. . . . I am simply saying that even though he was nailed—the Original, I mean—he is always shown hanging up there in perfect peace. [RB, 48-49]

To Skip, experience is something he arranges, designs, films, and packages; in other words, it is subject to his conscious control with specific goals in mind. Reality is what he devises rather than what happens to him. He and Emily are in the business of managing what people learn and how they interpret it, and the truth of the moment engages them much less than the effect they hope to produce, so they treat actuality as raw material.

As with Felix, Miller stages the media professionals in private rather than in public, showing not the result of the advertising agency's labors but how they operate behind the scenes, and because the potential event is so shattering, even Emily and Skip pause to contemplate their own strategies and how their work affects them. She reminds him that she makes commercials: "My genius is to make everything comfortably fake, Skip. No agency wants real. You want a fake-looking crucifixion?—call me." She shrinks from the prospect before her, assuring him, "I'm totally lost. All I know is that somebody actually dying in my lens would melt my eyeball" (*RB*, 37). When she asks whether or not the project disgusts him, in a moment of candid self-awareness, he replies, "but realistically, who am I to be disgusted?" (*RB*, 36). Skip is seduced by the advantages of the exclusive, so he retreats into cliché Hollywood justifications for the shoot by way of persuading Emily to stick with it:

It's clear, isn't it, that you are not responsible for it happening, right?

[SUDDEN NEW IDEA]

In fact, showing it on the world screen could help put an end to it forever!

[WARMING]

Yes! That's it! If I were moralistic I'd even say you have a *duty* to shoot this! Really, I mean that. . . . In fact, it could end up a worldwide blow against capital punishment, which I know you are against as I passionately am. [*RB*, 36]

When he appears to have convictions, they are completely and conveniently focused on getting the job done; he scorns Emily's suggestion that someone provide a physician to tend to the man they will nail on the cross:

> In all the thousands of paintings and the written accounts of the crucifixion scene I defy anyone to produce a single one that shows a doctor present! I'm sorry but we can't be twisting the historical record!
> [GREAT NEW IDEA]
> ... And furthermore, I will not superimpose American mores on a dignified foreign people. The custom here is to crucify criminals, period! I am not about to condescend to these people with a foreign colonialist mentality! [RB, 43]

Through these comic struggles, Miller engages with the patterns and jeopardies of rationalization and justification. In this presumptive media crisis, the issues have less to do with what people think and do and more to do with what the participants declare and how others read their messages. The politicians have given place to television producers, and the exceptional status of the artist—the standing that supported Miller's 1956 contention for the freedom of the poet—has dissolved in the intersection of art with commerce.

To Felix, Skip, and Emily, appearance is prior to substance; the real is a matter of what they can present through image and rhetoric. They have little interest in truth or genuine experience; they are much more invested in coverage and exposure, in the quality of presentation rather than content, and in the competition over who gets there first and takes the profits. They commodify everything; Felix—who deals not in the reality of his nation but in what he can persuade others to believe about it—speaks of his country in terms of its potential worth, citing coverage in both *Vanity Fair* and *National Geographic* to validate the beauty (and, by implication, the commercial promise) of the views near Santa Felice, while Skip and Emily value the landscape only in terms of what it can help them sell. Emily marvels at the scenery: "Look at that snow. That sun. That light. What a blue. What an orange! What mountains!"

(*RB*, 27). She and Skip remember their travels only in terms of the products their agency was hired to advertise, so Nepal, Kenya, the Caucasus, Colombia, the Himalayas, and Chile are no more than locations where they shot commercials for Ivory Soap, Chevy Malibu, Vidal Shampoo, Jeep, Alka Seltzer, and Efferdent. Skip tells Emily that "what you do is make real things look fake, and that makes them emotionally real," and when she considers "Ralph," she treats him like one more public figure in need of packaging, remarking, "I assume it's important to this man what kind of public impression he makes, right?" (*RB*, 37, 48). Henri, always the intellectual voice of the piece, tries to theorize their strategies, suggesting to Skip that because ancient Egyptian art shows very little about the Jewish captivity in spite of the destruction of the pharaoh's army described in Exodus, the entire episode might have been no more than a work of fiction designed to present a culture's vision of itself. He draws a more recent analogy (and refers to Miller's own activist past) when he points out that the United States justified its military intervention in Vietnam by citing the Gulf of Tonkin incident even though later revelations suggested that the alleged attack on American warships never took place and that President Johnson's government exaggerated and distorted the fragmentary information in order to promote the course of action they desired.

The revolutionaries and the junta have struggled for control of the nation, but Felix and his accomplices are winning not only because they wield greater force but also because they work more closely with foreign business interests, whose financial support is crucial. Miller has traced elsewhere his growing perception that the political and financial sectors are coterminous. After serving as a delegate to the 1968 Democratic National Convention, he wrote that professional politicians regarded the process as a game and the issues as mere tokens for their use.[33] A few years later, he asserted that:

> we've become a corporate state. It has become the function of the state to make it possible for immense corporations to carry on their activities, and

everything else is incidental. There are always conflicts between the corporations and between the Government and the corporations, but fundamentally what we have is a socialism of the individual corporations.[34]

Money and power come together to serve and reinforce each other; money becomes the means of power, and power facilitates profit. It was, perhaps, this vision of the corporate state that led Miller, during the elder Bush's first year in office, to declare the "moral bankruptcy" of politics.[35]

In the end, Felix, Skip, and Emily regard price as the measure of value, no matter whether they are discussing a product, a nation, or a person. When Skip's agency offers $25 million for exclusive rights, everything in Felix's framework changes. The crucifixion now has a certain financial and political worth, and the potential return drives all of the ensuing decisions. The execution of "Ralph" will be about not suffering or commitment, or even punishing a criminal, but rather coverage and profit. The $25 million expands the circle of complicity because the commercial promise of the crucifixion involves even the meanest peasant, who hopes to benefit from tourism. Many of the rural residents hope that their villages will be chosen for the crucifixion, not only for the honor, but also for the effect on property values. One of "Ralph's" followers explains:

> Well, face it, once it's televised they'll be jamming in from the whole entire world to see where it happened. Tour buses bumper to bumper across the Andes to get to see his bloody shorts? Buy a souvenir fingernail or one of his eyeballs in plastic? It's a whole tax base thing, Jeanine, y'know? Like maybe a new school, roads, swimming pool, maybe even a casino and theme park—all that shit. I don't have to tell you, baby, these people have *nothing*. [RB, 121]

This vision goes beyond the trite notion that everything has a price; here, everything carries a price tag, a label that not only fixes its ostensible value but also immures it into a paradigm where nothing has intrinsic value or meaning. The peasants might enjoy the benefit of roads and a new school, but they'll have to hawk phony fingernails and mop floors for Disney. Money takes priority over goods and services, so the point of commerce is the transaction itself, and everything, from "Ralph" to the souvenirs, is cheapened.

The Collapse of Revolution

Standing against Felix's commercial politics is a failed revolution. Miller has set up a situation that meets two criteria he once articulated: that a revolution constitutes a response to intolerable conditions and that a "classic" revolution would involve "a transfer of power between classes."[36] On Miller's terms, this country is ripe for revolution, but we enter the story after the powerful have prevailed. Henri has given up on the struggle and now wrings his hands helplessly, while Jeanine, who took command of the rebels, surrendered to despair and stepped out of an upper-story window in an attempt to end her life. Felix shakes his head over what he regards as her emotionalism, assuring Henri that "she has to know all that is finished, revolution is out" (*RB*, 7). He regards revolution not as a matter of passion, commitment, or historical crisis, but merely as a political strategy, even a social fashion. Even in the aftermath, Henri cannot take it so lightly:

HENRI: A faith in the revolution is what I gave her . . . and then walked away from it myself.

FELIX: I hope I'm not hearing your old Marxism again, Henri.

HENRI: Oh, shit, Felix!—I haven't been a Marxist for twenty-five years!

FELIX: Because that is finished, they're almost all in narcotics now, thanks be to God; but the Americans are here now and they'll clean out the whole lot of them by New Years [*sic*]! Your guerrillas are done!

HENRI: Those are not my guerrillas, my guerrillas were foolish,
          idealistic people, but the hope of the world! These people
          now are cynical and stupid enough to deal narcotics!
          [*RB*, 11]

Savran has traced Miller's evolution from Popular Front Communist to
Cold War liberal, and Henri's weary defensiveness might echo the playwright's look back to earlier days.[37] Jeanine describes the revolution as
"a comedian wearing a black veildon't know whether to laugh or run for
your life," while Henri mourns that "the comical end of everything has
come and gone" (*RB*, 65, 26). Both comments clarify Miller's strategy in
Resurrection Blues; the loss of commitment is so crushing that we must
laugh it off in order to survive. Events have moved beyond serious consideration and submit only to ironic treatment.

"Ralph" is the paradox of the play in that Miller both offers and undermines the correlation with Jesus. If he is divine, then the play veers
towards spirituality, as when Henri tries to explain how seeing the man
made him feel:

> But then, as they were pushing him into the van—it happened quite acci-
> dentally—his gaze rose up to my window and for an instant our eyes
> met.—His composure, Felix—deep inside his pain you could see some-
> thing almost tranquil; his poise was . . . chilling; as though he knew all this
> had to happen. He seemed to transcend everything. [*RB*, 21]

"Ralph" compels the others—the general, the advertising executive,
the television director, the corporate owner, and even the disaffected
revolutionary—to deal with what he implies. There seems to be no
place for faith in the social structure they have all accepted, so each
must find a strategy for coping with him. Felix dismisses him as nothing more than a renegade terrorist, a man whom the government must
execute as an example in order to subjugate the rest of the nation. Yet
because the peasants light candles before his image, Henri argues that a

---

crucifixion will confirm his divinity and bring the simple people down out of the mountains in rebellion. Even Felix can't ignore the prisoner's dazzling luminescence, although he predictably refuses to attach any significance to it:

> All right, I don't understand it! Do you understand a computer chip? Can you tell me what electricity is? And how about a gene? I mean what is a fucking gene? So he lights up; it's one more *thing*, that's all. But look at him, you ever seen such total vacancy in a man's face? . . . That idiot is mental and he's making us all crazy! [*RB*, 23]

Despite his intentions to the contrary, Felix promotes the notion of "Ralph's" divinity by presenting him as ineffable. By positioning "Ralph" as Jeanine's savior, Miller suggests that faith can rescue a decadent and failing revolution; she tells Henri that "Ralph" came to her in the hospital "to quiet my soul," and by the last scene of the play, he has somehow caused the regeneration of her crushed spine, so she is able to limp with the aid of a cane (*RB*, 67). Yet "Ralph" has no answers and can't even guide himself, much less those who look to him for help. He can't make up his mind whether or not he's the son of God and so destined to die on the cross, and even though Felix blames his gunmen for a series of shootings, "Ralph" himself is virtually paralyzed, responding to news of yet another massacre with uncontrollable tears. Jeanine tells Henri that "the wind has more plans than he does," and the bluntly ruthless Felix assesses his status: "He's finished" (*RB*, 67, 14).

Henri realizes that if "Ralph" is actually divine, he represents a profound threat. He argues that while the principal purpose of most human activity is "to deliver us into the realm of the imagination," "Ralph" truly feels everything and so must be hunted down and crucified:

> Imagine, Mr. Cheeseboro, if that kind of reverence for life should spread! Governments would collapse, armies disband, marriages disintegrate! Wherever we turned, our dead unfeeling shallowness would stare us in the face until we shriveled up with shame! [*RB*, 91]

He argues that "Ralph" is calling their various bluffs, that if they truly believe in any of the principles they purport to endorse, they would have to relent. The simplicity and purity of faith, as "Ralph" represents it, seems to argue against actual engagement. Moreover, the status quo of Felix's junta and their offshore business partners relies on treating life with not reverence but contempt; if they respected people, they would no longer be able to operate and a bloodless revolution would take place overnight.

The connection between "Ralph" and Jeanine introduces a contest between faith, in the spiritual sense, and conviction, in the political sense, which leads to a consideration of the material circumstances that Jeanine has sought to change and which the consolation of "Ralph" might mitigate. The advent of "Ralph" clarifies that Jeanine is just as absorbed with the material potential of her country as the others; the difference is that she works toward giving the people the benefit of the nation's resources and of their own labor. "Ralph," however, has more to do with wonder, and if the revolution must turn to such a messiah, then it has, perhaps, lost its way.

Miller has referred to faith as "a belief, one might call it, in man as a creature transcending his appetites," and the erstwhile revolutionaries of *Resurrection Blues* have faltered amidst a crisis of faith, not in "Ralph" so much as in belief itself.[38] In "Ralph," Miller presents faith less as a spiritual matter and more as a metaphor for the kind of commitment that revolutionaries like Jeanine need in order to mount the resistance neces-sary to defeat the junta. They have no money, little materiel, and no al-lies; they are alone with only their determination to support them, but their resolve has proved inadequate. Among "Ralph's" followers is Stanley, an anachronism from the late Sixties with "sneakers, unkempt pony tail, blue denim shirt, backpack" who is also a drug addict, burned-out, and untrustworthy (*RB*, 71). He tells Felix, "I've ruined my life be-lieving in things. I spent two and a half years in India in an ashram; I've been into everything from dope to alcohol to alfalfa therapy to Rolfing to Buddhism to total vegetarianism which I'm into now" (*RB*, 74). Jeanine begs Felix, "Don't ask me to *believe* anything! There are too many young people buried in our earth for anyone to forgive you. It will take five hundred years of snow and rain to wash the memory away" (*RB*, 113). Henri declares simply that "there is no politics any more" and affirms that "the world will never again be changed by heroes" (*RB*, 107). The millennium has turned, and belief has given way to nihilism. Yet the activists have not forgotten what drove them, so they feel the pain of loss. Jeanine asks Henri, "Can't you remember not being afraid of death, Papa? In the mountains? If you died you died for the people, so you would never die. Have you really forgotten how real that was—how pure?" (*RB*, 106). Their skepticism and sense of loss serve to clarify how far Miller has traveled since he wrote characters whose adamant convictions drive such plays as *All My Sons* and *The Crucible*, and since he called upon his fellow Americans to take their future into their own hands and become their own masters. In this regard, *Resurrection Blues* represents the extension of the uncertainty he explores in *After the Fall* and the alienation that characterizes *The Archbishop's Ceiling*.

Because he cannot fully defeat the revolution, Felix seeks to subvert it. Feeling regenerated after a tryst with Emily, he no longer wants to crucify "Ralph" but instead hopes to offer the man a place in his government—rather than destroy his adversary, he will co-opt his influence and connections. To that end, he does his best to suborn Stanley, who denies the ability to know his own mind and reduces "Ralph's" message to "just don't do bad things" (*RB*, 79). Felix hopes, in a sense, that Stanley will name names—will cooperate with the authorities to bring "Ralph" under their control—but to do so presupposes that certain answers are available. Stanley's casual, dazed attitude and haphazard syntax reduce even Felix's determination and "Ralph's" status to a virtually trivial level: "I think he just can't make up his mind, that's all—whether he really wants to—like die. I mean it's understandable, right? . . . with this great kind of weather we're having?" (*RB*, 83). Stanley can't help Felix because he can't perceive the situation in the same terms.

---

320   Critical Insights

Miller has, of course, more than once established his position on the issue of selling out, most notably in *The Crucible*, when a man is called upon to falsely betray others in order to save his life; in *A View from the Bridge* (1956), where a community ostracizes a man who betrays another to the authorities; in *After the Fall*, which explores loyalty, honesty, and the personal cost of turning informer; and in his own refusal to name names before the Committee in 1956. To someone with Miller's personal experience, naming names constituted an act of revelation involving a complex and conflicted mixture of betrayal, penitence, cooperation, and telling the truth while under oath. Miller's response to the Committee's crucial question has become famous:

> I am not protecting the Communists or the Communist Party. . . . I will protect my sense of myself. I could not use the name of another person and bring trouble on him. These were writers, poets, as far as I could see, and the life of a writer, despite what it sometimes seems, is pretty tough. I wouldn't make it any tougher for anybody. I ask you not to ask me that question. . . . I will be perfectly frank with you in anything relating to my activities. I take the responsibility for everything I have ever done, but I cannot take responsibility for another human being. ["TAM," 4686]

In spite of the nuances of Miller's testimony during the two-and-a-half hour interrogation, the salient memory of the hearing is that in declining to name names, he refused to cooperate, to betray others, and to submit to the power of oppressive authority. To refuse to name names remains Miller's signature gesture of resistance.

Like Miller, Jeanine stands in opposition to unjust authority. She has little patience for Emily's naïveté, tersely explaining that the junta has killed over one hundred thousand people to sustain their power, that "they've been crucifying this country for two centuries," and that Emily herself backed their cause simply by paying American taxes, an assertion that urges a complex perception of complicity that Emily finds inconvenient and troubling (*RB*, 63). Emily tries to explain that Henri feels guilty about his failure to live up to the convictions that drive Jeanine:

> EMILY: He's really full of remorse for deserting your people up in the mountains. But he *was* partly right, wasn't he—the revolution had lost the people? And only more pointless killing was left?
>
> JEANINE: Partly right? The secret that eats holes in the heart—is that in the end, whichever side one fought on is partly right no matter how completely wrong it was. Just go down below the Mason-Dixon line and see what I mean.—But all that matters now is that our people are scattered and are still being murdered by some very bad types. [*RB*, 68]

Emily articulates the ambiguity that might have led to Jeanine's sense of inevitable defeat; if both sides are partly right, then there is no possibility of whole-hearted commitment. At bottom, Miller's political concern is with the integrity of one's convictions. In his Committee testimony, he followed the example of his own John Proctor as he tried to protect his sense of himself against the interrogators' attempts to seduce his cooperation and compromise his perception of the truth. Jeanine struggles with both Emily and Henri, insisting on a vision of unmediated history and of principles without negotiation.

The penultimate scene stages Jeanine's resistance to giving up not just "Ralph" but the integrity and humanity that she wishes he could represent. Felix, always looking for an advantage, insists that "Ralph" make the first concession by ordering his followers to disarm, and Jeanine, the last, desperate believer, is distraught when Stanley explains that "Ralph" is weighing the problem of allowing his own crucifixion because he is assessing others' expectations. When Stanley asks, "What's wrong with that?" Jeanine is hurt and outraged: "What's wrong is that it changes him into one more shitty politician! Whatever he does he'll do because it's right, not to get people's approval!" (*RB*,

118). Stanley begs Jeanine to intercede, to persuade "Ralph" to stop his crucifixion, and Henri joins him:

JEANINE: I'm to ask him not to be god.

HENRI: Darling, if he's god he's god, you can't change that; but he doesn't have to die to prove it and bring on a bloodbath.

JEANINE: Which, incidentally, would wreck the value of your company's shares and the farms too . . .

HENRI: All right, yes—I won't deny that. But more blood now is pointless!

JEANINE: We must beg him to live and make things safe for shopping malls!—and justice can go to hell!

HENRI: Very well, yes! Better a shopping mall than a bloodbath! Better hot and cold running water than . . .

JEANINE . . . And the TV idiocy and the car . . .

HENRI: Very well, yes the car too, yes, the car . . . !

JEANINE: And the Jacuzzi . . . !

HENRI: All right, the Jacuzzi too, yes! There is no escape anymore, Jeanine, we must have *things*!

JEANINE: . . . And the emptiness.
[HOWLING]
The e-m-p-t-i-nessssss! [*RB*, 123-24]

Jeanine's agony grows out of her realization that even "Ralph," perhaps, will reconstruct himself in order to serve the commercial and political interests that surround them. To name names seems to involve betraying others, but it really means, as Miller knew in 1956, betraying one's self. Jeanine realizes that Henri wants her to ask "Ralph" to name himself what he is not, to deny himself, to become both Christ and Judas. The others are asking her to give up on activism, but "Ralph" has already done so. The result of his abdication and the others' materialism will be the emptiness that tears at Jeanine, but that emptiness is where the play concludes.

The Ironic Transfiguration

In the final scene, a bright light shines above them, and they realize that "Ralph"—who just the previous night decided to call himself "Charles," producing the inevitable nickname of "Charley"—is transfiguring. Jeanine encourages him to go, and Emily would rather not film him "hanging from two sticks" (*RB*, 130). Skip insists that he respect the contract that the agency has signed with the government, Henri recommends that he depart because his crucifixion "might well bring down a crashing chaos that could kill the economy for endless years to come," and Stanley warns that his return might "light the match that'll explode the whole place again" (*RB*, 131, 132). Felix, who was willing to drop the charges, now realizes that if he loses the television contract, he'll have to return the money: "Listen Charley, get on TV, on that cross and it means ten thousand jobs. I'm talking hotels, I'm talking new construction, I'm talking investment. You care about people? Here's where you belong!" (*RB*, 132). The scene disintegrates as they all shout at each other, quarreling, and then come together in a single upward appeal: "PLEASE GO AWAY, CHARLEE!!" (*RB*, 135). With that, the light fades, and he is gone.

So the play ends not with commitment but with trendy rhetoric, and instead of ideals, Miller gives us commercial interests and emptiness. He has set up the targets quite clearly: the flagrant exploitation of a nation by its military dictator, the capitalist greed that drives the advertising interests, the pointless compassion of the intellectual, the cynical paralysis of the revolutionary, and the general deceit and hypocrisy that suffuse it all. Yet in the end, every tortured soul rejects salvation, and the putative Messiah is, after all, probably some sort of hoax in spite of his impressive special effects. In other words, Miller brings the action to a crisis that seems to demand resolution, but in the last moment, he deflates the situation. The play therefore represents a significant move away from the sacrificial affirmations we find in certain of his earlier works, particularly Joe Keller's decision to take his own life to atone for his selfishness and John Proctor's choice to die for his integrity.

The resolution of *Resurrection Blues* is, in its own way, more shattering than either of those calamities, barely tolerable only because of the wry, comic tone that guides the play.

The through-line in Miller's work is his liberalism, his tendency to perceive action in terms of individual initiative and choice. In 1989, for a new edition of two of his early plays, Miller wrote:

> these plays are somewhat surprising testimony to me that I had not lost the belief in the centrality of the individual and the importance of what he thought and did. . . . I believed it decisive what an individual thinks and does about his life, regardless of overwhelming social forces. . . . Indeed, if these plays are to be credited, there is no force so powerful, politically as well as personally, as a man's self-conceptions.[39]

Indeed, Miller often resolves the action through the will of the individual: thus Chris and Joe Keller, John Proctor, Von Berg in *Incident at Vichy*, and Marcus and Sigmund in *The Archbishop's Ceiling*. Savran has located Miller's work in "the tradition of American liberalism, flattening out class conflicts and prizing individual initiative far more than collective action," and sees in his plays "the liberal humanist subject— that allegedly seamless individual, conceived as author and origin of meaning and action—[who] attempts to construct a linear, unified history."[40] Yet in *Resurrection Blues*, Miller brings the action to the moment when the individual might turn events away from disaster and bring about a moment of thundering closure, but each person retreats. Felix, Skip, Emily, Henri, and Jeanine are, more than their counterparts in Miller's earlier plays, more embodiments of social roles than they are agents of independent action. Miller's liberal humanist subject has failed.

In the end, irony is the essential mode in Miller's work. The theatre of irony is the theatre of denial, staging the refusal to embrace an idea or a position, moving always towards skepticism and detachment, and so leading to stalemate. Miller reaches toward a politics, but in spite of the compassion that suffuses his earlier plays, in *Resurrection Blues*, he hesitates. We can negotiate or contend with those who beset us, as Miller did with the Committee, or we can recognize that we are the problem and that there is no point to action. The *sine qua non* of activism is not just conviction, but faith in one's convictions and in the potential for action to realize them. Miller's detailed vision of his characters' weaknesses leaves him too cynical to find a resolution to the problems they create. The Messiah rises once again, but he rises from life rather than death, departing rather than returning, and all because no one on Earth will listen to him.

Notes

I would like to thank and acknowledge the Office of Research and Faculty Development at the University of Oregon for a Summer Research Award in 2002 that supported and encouraged much of the work that led to the completion of this article.

1. Arthur Miller, interview by Russell Baker, *Broken Glass*, Exxon Mobil Masterpiece Theatre, 20 October 1996.

2. Arthur Miller, *On Politics and the Art of Acting* (New York: Penguin, 2001), 62. First delivered as the 30th Jefferson Lecture in the Humanities for the National Endowment for the Humanities on 26 March 2001.

3. The world premiere of *Resurrection Blues* opened at the Guthrie Theater on Friday, 7 August 2002. Companies planning subsequent productions include The Wilma Theater, Philadelphia (opening 17 September 2003) and The Old Globe, San Diego (opening 20 March 2004).

4. Arthur Miller, *Resurrection Blues* (Minneapolis: Guthrie Theater, 2002), 135. Further quotations are cited in the text and flagged with the abbreviation *RB*.

5. Miller has said that the play is "about the threat of a return of a messiah. Gradually they all get absolutely terrified that it might be Him. . . . It's about American commercialism . . ." ("'Sometimes it takes a hundred years, and then you get it right,'" in Mel Gussow, *Conversations with Miller* [New York: Applause, 2002], 190).

6. Arthur Miller, "Should Ezra Pound Be Shot?" *New Masses* 57 #13 (25 December 1945): 5-6; Miller, "The Age of Abdication," *New York Times*, 23 December 1967; Henry Raymont, "Miller Refuses Greek Book Plan," *New York Times*, 3 July 1969; Robert Anderson, "Repression in Brazil," *New York Times*, 24 April 1971. Miller's thoughts on American relations with Russia and China are most readily available in his *In Rus-*

sia (New York: Viking, 1969) and *Salesman in Beijing* (New York: Viking, 1984).

7. See especially Miller's "The Face in the Mirror: Anti-Semitism Then and Now," *The New York Times Book Review*, 14 October 1984: 3. Later published in his *Echoes Down the Corridor: Collected Essays, 1944-2000*, ed. Steven R. Centola (New York: Penguin, 2000), 205-8.

8. Miller's published essays on these topics include "Arthur Miller on Rushdie and Global Censorship," *Author's Guild Bulletin* (Summer 1989): 5-6; "In the Ayes of the Beholder: With Congress Debating Obscenity in Federally Funded Art, What Will Happen to Free Expression?" *Omni* 13 (February 1991): 10; "To Newt on Art," *The Nation* 261 (31 July-7 August 1995): 118; "A Modest Proposal for the Pacification of the Public Temper," *The Nation* 179 (3 July 1954): 5-8; "The Limited Hang-Out: The Dialogues of Richard Nixon as a Drama of the Antihero," *Harper's* 249 (September 1974): 13-20; "On True Identity," *The New York Times Magazine* (13 April 1975): 111.

9. David Savran, *Communists, Cowboys, and Queers: The Politics of Masculinity in the Work of Arthur Miller and Tennessee Williams* (Minneapolis: University of Minnesota Press, 1992), 21.

10. The ostensible reason for summoning Miller was the Committee's ongoing investigation into violations of passport law. In March 1954, Miller sought to renew his passport in order to travel to Belgium to attend a production of *The Crucible*; the State Department turned him down, citing regulations that restricted anyone believed to support Communist activities and whose travel abroad would therefore not be in the nation's interest. (See "Playwright Arthur Miller Refused Visa to Visit Brussels to See His Play," *New York Times*, 31 March 1954.) For a discussion of the Committee's activities, especially in relation to the arts and the entertainment industry, see the first two chapters of Brenda Murphy's *Congressional Theatre: Dramatizing McCarthyism on Stage, Film, and Television* (Cambridge: Cambridge University Press, 1999).

11. Gerhart Eisler (1897-1968) was an Austrian journalist who worked for the Communist Party in several nations; through his brother, Hanns (1898-1962), a composer, he had ties to the film industry. See Eric Bentley, ed., *Thirty Years of Treason: Excerpts from Hearings before the House Committee on Un-American Activities, 1938-1968* (New York: Viking, 1971), 55-109.

12. House Committee on Un-American Activities, *Guide to Subversive Organizations and Publications*, 82nd Cong., 1st sess., 1951, 109, 33.

13. House Committee on Un-American Activities, "Testimony of Arthur Miller, Accompanied by Counsel, Joseph L. Rauh, Jr.," *Investigation of the Unauthorized Use of United States Passports*, 84th Cong., 2nd sess., 1956, 4663. Further quotations are cited in the text and flagged with the abbreviation "TAM."

14. In the record, *War and Peace* is set in lower-case roman type.

15. Years later, Miller recalled, "When I confirmed that I did think a poet could legally write such a subversive poem, Mr. Scherer actually threw up his hands and turned to the other members as though to say, 'What more do we have to ask?'" (Arthur Miller, *Timebends: A Life* [New York: Grove, 1987], 409). Scherer (1906-88) was a Republican from Ohio, once the assistant prosecuting attorney for Hamilton County, Ohio (1933-41), and the junior member present.

16. More properly known as The Alien Registration Act of 1940, the law specifies

---

penalties for anyone engaged in the following activities with the intent of overthrowing the government: "advocates, abets, advises, or teaches . . . prints, publishes, edits, issues, circulates, sells, distributes, or publicly displays any written or printed matter advocating, advising, or teaching . . . organizes or helps or attempts to organize any society, group, or assembly of persons who teach, advocate, or encourage . . . becomes or is a member of, or affiliates with, any such society, group, or assembly of persons, knowing the purposes thereof" (*U.S. Code*, title 18, sec. 2385; available on the web site of Cornell Law School's Legal Information Institute [http://www4.law.cornell.edu/uscode/18/2385.html]). Congress has amended the law, most recently in 1994, and the language I quote above is from the current version in the United States Code.

17. See Walter's foreword to House Committee on Un-American Activities, *Soviet Total War: "Historic Mission of Violence and Deceit,"* 84th Cong., 1st sess., 1956, v-ix. Walter (1894-1963) was a Democrat from Pennsylvania who served on the Committee from 1949 to his death. He acted as co-sponsor to the 1952 McCarran-Walter Immigration and Nationality Act, which empowered the government to deport any immigrant or naturalized citizen engaging or intending to engage in activities "prejudicial to the public interest" or "subversive to national security."

18. Arthur Miller, "On the Shooting of Robert Kennedy," *New York Times*, 8 June 1968.

19. Blood fluke, or *Schistosoma mansoni*, is a water-borne trematode flatworm that can live parasitically on human blood.

20. The metaphorical potential of the "faraway country" did not escape journalists who reviewed the premiere. Rohan Preston wrote, "it is a play about America. It is about how values can be corrupted by a military-political-electronic-media axis. It is about religious succor and the power of the imagination and art in a time when rampant materialism crushes all things illusory" ("Arthur Miller Lightens Up a Bit in 'Resurrection Blues,'" [Minneapolis-St. Paul] *Star Tribune*, 11 August 2002 [http://www.startribune.com/stories/458/3155518.html]), and Michael Billington described the play as "a funny, pertinent and sharp-toothed satire aimed at the materialist maladies of modern America" ("The Crucifixion Will Be Televised," *The Guardian*, 21 August 2002 [http://www.guardian.co.uk/arts/critic/feature/0,1169,778207,00.html]).

21. Olga Carlisle and Rose Styron, "Arthur Miller: An Interview," in *The Theater Essays of Arthur Miller*, ed. Robert A. Martin and Steven R. Centola (1978; rev. ed. New York: Da Capo, 1996), 289. First published as "The Art of the Theatre II: Arthur Miller, an Interview," *Paris Review* 10 (Summer 1966): 61-98. Miller was referring obliquely to the scenic design of the 1966 Franco Zeffirelli production of *After the Fall*.

22. Arthur Miller, *After the Fall*, in *Arthur Miller's Collected Plays*, volume 2 (New York: Viking, 1981), 127.

23. Carlisle and Styron, 292.

24. Miller has offered some of his thoughts on the public persona of the typical government leader in *On Politics and the Art of Acting*.

25. Arthur Miller, "Introduction," *Arthur Miller's Collected Plays* (New York: Viking, 1957), 43-44.

26. Arthur Miller, "The New Insurgency," *The Nation* 206 (3 June 1968): 717. Speech delivered at Madison Square Garden on 19 May 1968.

27. Arthur Miller, "Writers in Prison," *Encounter* 30 (June 1968): 60.

28. Miller, "Rushdie and Global Censorship," 5.

29. Arthur Miller, "Conditions of Freedom: Two Plays of the Seventies—*The Archbishop's Ceiling* and *The American Clock*," in *Theater Essays*, 474, 475.

30. Arthur Miller, *The Archbishop's Ceiling* (New York: Dramatists Play Service, 1984, 1985), 11.

31. Arthur Miller, "Let's Privatize Congress," in *Echoes Down the Corridor*, 252. First published in *New York Times*, 10 January 1995.

32. Arthur Miller, "The Sin of Power," in *Echoes Down the Corridor*, 172. First published in *Index on Censorship* 7 (May/June 1978): 3-6.

33. Arthur Miller, "The Battle of Chicago: From the Delegates' Side," in *Echoes Down the Corridor*, 76-77. First published in *The New York Times Magazine* (15 September 1968): 29-31, 122-28.

34. Josh Greenfield, "Writing Plays is Absolutely Senseless, Arthur Miller Says, 'But I Love It. I Just Love It,'" in *Conversations with Arthur Miller*, ed. Matthew C. Roudané (Jackson and London: University Press of Mississippi, 1987), 246. First published in *The New York Times Magazine* (13 February 1972): 16-17, 34-39.

35. Janet Balakian, "An Interview with Arthur Miller," *Studies in American Drama, 1945-Present* 6 (1991): 41. Interview took place on 10 July 1989.

36. Steven R. Centola, "'Just Looking for a Home': A Conversation with Arthur Miller," *American Drama* 1 (Fall 1991): 93 (interview took place on 2 August 1990); "Miracles," in *Echoes Down the Corridor*, 127 (first published in *Esquire* 80 [September 1973]: 112-15, 202-4).

37. Savran, 22-26.

38. Arthur Miller, "Arthur Miller on *The Crucible*," in *Theater Essays*, 367. First published in *Audience* (July/August 1972): 46-47.

39. Arthur Miller, "Introduction," *The Golden Years* and *The Man Who Had All The Luck* (London: Methuen, 1989), 8. The first was completed in 1940 and the second was produced in 1944.

40. Savran, 22, 29.

The Fiction of Arthur Miller_____
Laurence Goldstein

Novelists enjoy writing plays; that much we know. They assume that the skills they have mastered in the medium of prose narrative will transfer to the congenial forum of the theater. After all, a plot is a plot, a character is a character, a scene is a scene. . . . But the history of this century suggests that there is something absolutely unique about the experience of crafting a great full-length play, and that the talent required to construct a long fiction might actually militate against the capacity to shape a three-hour performance piece that succeeds on stage. The failures of this century's great novelists are legendary: Henry James's *Guy Domville*, Virginia Woolf's *Freshwater*, James Joyce's *Exiles*, F. Scott Fitzgerald's *The Vegetable*, Ernest Hemingway's *The Fifth Column*, John Steinbeck's *Burning Bright*. But what of playwrights' fiction? Chekhov, Pirandello, and Beckett wrote so much of it, and of such high quality, that one wonders finally in which category of authorship to place them. The chief contemporary examples are Arthur Miller and Tennessee Williams. "His fiction . . . is negligible," writes Martin Seymour-Smith of Williams in *Who's Who in Twentieth Century Literature*, though the positive reviews and decent sales of his *Collected Stories* (1985) suggest otherwise. What of Miller's fiction? Of marginal interest even to admirers—no fiction appears in *The Portable Arthur Miller*, for example—it has been steadily neglected by scholars as well as lay-readers of the playwright's career.

The publication of *Homely Girl, A Life, and Other Stories* in 1995 provides an occasion to look back on Miller's fiction and make some assessments. The bibliography is a short one. Miller established his literary reputation not with plays, though he had written a fair number of journeyman dramas in the 1930s and early 1940s, but with a novel, *Focus*, in 1945. Its theme of American anti-Semitism, coming at a time when the nation was prosecuting a war against Nazism, brought it notoriety, translation into several European languages, and a sale to the

330

Critical Insights

movies; but Laura Z. Hobson's more commercially crafted *Gentle-man's Agreement* (1946) usurped Miller's claim on the controversial subject of prejudice against Jews. The movie was never made, the book went out of print. Short stories published in journals throughout the 1950s and early 1960s were collected in *I Don't Need You Any More* (1967), a volume that received respectful but not enthusiastic notices. Miller chose one of the stories, "The Misfits," as the scenario for a classic film of 1961 and its companion, a book-length prose narrative he described as "neither novel, play, nor screenplay . . . [which] uses the perspectives of the film in order to create a fiction which might have the peculiar immediacy of image and the reflective possibilities of the written word." Busy with theatrical projects in the following decades, Miller published only one piece of fiction, "Bees," in the Spring 1990 issue of *Michigan Quarterly Review*, before the appearance of *Homely Girl, A Life*. And that volume contains only one new story, the title novella, along with two others reprinted from *I Don't Need You Any More*.

The fiction of a famous playwright is guaranteed to attract attention but also a certain measure of condescension. The reviews and literary criticism tend to reproduce the literary world's reservations about Miller's plays, his politics, and his private life, in a minor key. How much easier to critique Miller's use of vernacular, or his moralistic vision, or the Freudian dynamics of his dramaturgy, in speaking of the alternative forum provided by his fiction. Critics who see his play *All My Sons* (1947) as simply an exposé of war profiteering find it easier to dismiss the earlier *Focus* as a "message novel." Was anything ever written about *The Misfits* that did not concentrate on Miller's marriage to and divorce from Marilyn Monroe? There is so little fiction, compared to the output of fiction writers (Faulkner, Cheever, Mailer, Oates, et al.), that the whole corpus became vulnerable to the suspicion that each work was undertaken lightly, as a failed theatrical idea. His stories have very rarely been reprinted in anthologies and are virtually unknown even to general readers who pride themselves on keeping current with the modern masters. Clearly it is time for a new reading, not to make exaggerated claims but to give the fiction a fairer hearing, an "audition" in the old sense of focusing our judgments on the quality of a performance irrespective of public fame.

It may be, however, that fame is the best avenue into the subject of Arthur Miller's fiction. I refer specifically to his short story "Fame," first published in 1966 and one of the two stories he has chosen to reprint in *Homely Girl, A Life*. In this brief, comic narrative a playwright with two hits on Broadway and his face on the cover of *Look* magazine, drops into a bar down the street from one of his productions and responds with "aristocratic graciousness" to the recognition and praise of the patrons. "This is the greatest country in the world," he thinks, where an obscure fellow like himself can be catapulted into the "secret fate" he had nourished as a beginner. A man of his own age approaches and asks, "Are you Meyer Berkowitz?" He turns out to be an old friend from high school, Bernie Gelfand, who has announced himself for the purpose of bragging about his accomplishment since graduation: he is General Manager of the largest shoulder-pad industry east of the Mississippi. When this puffed-up fellow (his upper body enhanced by shoulder-pads) gets around to inquiring about Berkowitz he is abashed to learn that his old schoolmate has beaten him in the fame game. In fact, Gelfand has seen and admired one of the plays without connecting the author to his former classmate. He flees in a kind of panic, collecting his mink-laden wife on the way out.

More of a sketch than a story, "Fame" succeeds in keeping its main character and its reader equally off balance. On one level Berkowitz wins the contest of champions by chasing away his momentary rival. But in the encounter both men's vanity is mortified: both are revealed as smug and narrow-minded in their *amour propre*. The art of the story is a dramatic strategy central to Miller's poetics: bring unlike people from different realms together and let them discover who is the stronger, who has superior bragging rights. Because the turf they contest is Broadway, the playwright wins, but at least for a moment in their competitive struggle Gelfand has triumphed, and may do so again if and when he—or his type of moneybags—exerts some kind of influence over Berkowitz's fate, perhaps by grasping control of the theater itself (or City Hall, or the halls of Congress) at some future time when Berkowitz returns to obscurity. The comic premise, then, is shaded by the reader's sense of the fragility of fame as well as its immense clout in our celebrity culture. Fame, Miller writes in his autobiography, *Timebends*, provokes guilt as a defensive measure. "Guilt is a protective device to conceal one's happiness at surpassing others. . . . It is a kind of payment to them in the form of a pseudo remorse." The dynamics of fame and shame have been much examined in the literature of this century, but rarely in such a highly-condensed and beguiling narrative form.

Two men meet in a significant place to see which is the stronger. Isn't this a familiar scene in Miller's work? *Focus* begins with the protagonist, a personnel manager named Lawrence Newman, meeting with his boss, Mr. Gargan, who upbraids Newman because he has nearsightedly hired a woman, against company policy, who has the facial features of a Jew.

> "Miss Kapp is obviously not our type of person, Newman. I mean she's obvious. Her name must be Kapinsky or something."
>
> "But she can't be, I . . ."
>
> "I can't sit here arguing with you . . ."
>
> "No sir, I'm not arguing. I just can't believe that she . . ."
>
> "You can't see, Newman. Will you tell me why in the world you don't get glasses?"

Gargan is the stronger, Newman the weaker, and the invisible Miss Kapp the weakest of all. The scene with Gargan is reminiscent of the one in *Death of a Salesman* in which Willy Loman pleads with Howard Wagner, the son of his former employer, for his job. Newman, too, loses his job; his new glasses make him look Jewish, though he is in fact gentile, and thus an embarrassment to the giant corporation that employs him. Like Bernie Gelfand and Willy Loman, Newman slinks away from his superior, wondering how in the Darwinian jungle of modern capitalist society he can achieve an identity that restores the sense of rank, of self-worth.

The dynamics of stronger and weaker are learned in the family circle, the primal arena in which each family member aspires to the role that validates his or her desired position. Miller sees clearly that no single role is definitive because the weaker often exerts power over the stronger in the day-to-day activities of a complex family. Who wields the greater power in a parent-child relationship? The parent seems to hold all the highest cards, but in reality—and nobody intuits this more swiftly than the child—the whole point of the family structure is to nurture the child toward self-realization and a happy life in the future. So the child exerts significant control: he or she will be attended to, indulged, often spoiled. He will also be punished with verbal and physical abuse if he falls short of the parents' longing to live vicariously through his success, and his internalization of both nurturing and abuse constitutes the principal crises of his struggle for identity. This is certainly true of the five-year-old in Miller's story "I Don't Need You Any More." The family's youngest, he dominates by means of his tantrums, his aggressive remarks (like the title phrase hurled at his mother), and his visionary moments that set him apart from the more practical parents and brother. He has seen God in the waves along the beach. Much of Judaism haunts and terrifies him, and he strikes at his orthodox family, especially his mother and his older brother, as he seeks reconciliation and love from his patient but often exasperated father. Genesis and Freud inform the story, to be sure, but Miller knows enough to keep them at arm's length, partly by adopting the boy's point of view, and partly by selecting a vocabulary of the most exact realism.

Martin is abusive to his family, the opposite of, say, Maisie in Henry James's novel *What Maisie Knew*, and of the six-year-old protagonist of Henry Roth's novel *Call It Sleep*, to cite two masterpieces told through a child's consciousness. A child eager to learn and master the mysteries of life, and capable of violence if frustrated in his quest, Martin intuits that grown-ups are his antagonists, though he loves them too, in part because they spoil him as the household favorite. "My life consisted of explosions of desires that could not wait to be satisfied," Miller writes in his autobiography. Miller transacted his own struggles for individuality in "a kind of immanent symbolism of menace . . . a beleaguered zone surrounded by strangers with violent hearts." His strategy, like so many of his characters', was to use his intelligence and talent to master his environment. The eyeglasses that Newman acquires in *Focus* are a heavy-handed symbol of the intellectual vision requisite to penetrate to the truth of appearances. Newman's neighborhood seems placid enough, but once his neighbors suspect him of being Jewish, the unwanted result of the glasses, he has to focus on his fellow man with a Jew's perspective. Not money, not marital bliss—for his wife takes the side of the bigoted neighbors against his newly-acquired "Jewishness"—but simple justice becomes the prize for unremitting struggle. In Miller's case, the troubled Jewish son grows up to write plays that trouble the conscience of his extended neighborhood, his society. Those alter-egos who seek salvation in money—the father in *All My Sons*, Willy Loman, Bernie Gelfand—find themselves trumped by the moral authority of their creator.

The love of money is not the sole or even principal evil in Miller's world, even though his characters talk about money all the time. As in the works of his chief early models, Ibsen and Odets in drama and social realists like Sinclair Lewis and James T. Farrell in fiction, the cash nexus is a metonym of the entire network of temptations and desires by which the society sustains itself in the effort to better its condition. Art may (or may not) trump money, but Miller constantly tries to define a way of life that puts both aside in favor of some purer and existential form of self-worth. This is the thematic burden of "Fitter's Night," the other story that Miller has chosen to reprint in *Homely Girl, A Life*.

In this 48-page story of 1966, Miller tries to lay the ghosts of ambition and fame that motivated, and then exhausted, him in the aftermath of his celebrity years as The Heir of Eugene O'Neill and The Husband of MM. The story is set not on Broadway but in the Brooklyn Naval Shipyard during the last years of World War II. (Miller worked there as a steamfitter in the early 1940s and several elements of the story are based on his experience.) The main character is Tony Calabrese, Shipfitter First Class, whose life has been so empty of significance that he chronically derides himself as a failure, "God's original patsy, Joe Jerk." Hoodwinked into an unhappy marriage by the promise of a fortune that never materialized, he thinks enviously of some famous Italian-Americans—Frank Sinatra, Lucky Luciano—who have achieved satisfactions forever denied to him. The story moves between past and present by means of the narrative "timebends" Miller has favored since the composition of *Focus* and *Death of a Salesman*, and finally concentrates upon the ultimate insult to Tony's life, his assignment to do a routine job of repairing the broken depth-charge railing on a destroyer before it joins a convoy the next day. The job seems absurd, unnecessary, "fit for suckers," especially coming on the coldest night of the year.

Everything we know about Tony suggests that he will try to weasel out of doing this job, and justify his laziness by appealing to his low status and his justified resentment with life's humiliations. In fact, he makes an effort to talk the captain into complicity, into postponing the task and doing less than his duty:

> What the hell was the matter with [the captain]? He had a perfect excuse not to have to go to sea and maybe get himself sunk. The German subs were all over the coast of Jersey waiting for these convoys, and here the man had a perfect chance to lay down in a hotel for a couple of days. . . .
> "Captain, listen to me. Please. Lemme give you a piece of advice."
> Expressionless, the captain turned to Tony.
> "I sympathize wichoo. But what's the crime if you call in that you can't move tonight? That's not your fault."

"I have a position in the convoy. I'm due."

"I know that, Captain, but lemme explain to you. Cut outa here right now, make for the Yard; we puts up a staging and slap in a new rail by tomorrow noon, maybe even by ten o-clock. And you're set."

"No, no, that's too late . . ."

Once again, two men from different worlds confront each other. Tony's language distinguishes him as lower-class and he invites the stereotype of a shirker or slacker. The commanding officer speaks the kind of correct English that comes from disciplining speech no less than conduct. The contest of wills seeks to locate the stronger, and in this case it turns out to be the captain. Tony goes to work pounding the rail back to its original position.

What follows is a sustained description of perilous labor, for Tony must hang suspended above the frigid ocean, in a driving wind, in order to get a purchase on the bent rail. This is the crucial scene of the narrative, and it is one that cannot be dramatized in the performing arts. Tony's harrowing work must be articulated moment by moment, with an abundance of descriptive detail that makes the reader vicariously undergo the agony of a strenuous unremitting physical ordeal:

> Tony licked his lips and his tongue seemed to touch iron. His hand on the sledge handle seemed carved forever in a circular grip. The wind in his nose shot numbness into his head and throat. He lifted the sledge and felt a jerky buckling in his right knee and stiffened it quickly. This fuckin' iron, this stubborn, idiot iron lay there bent, refusing his demand. Go back on deck, he thought, and lay down flat for a minute. But with his steel hot now he would only have to heat it up all again. . . . [O]nce having stopped, his muscles would stiffen and make it harder to start again. He swung the hammer, furiously now, throwing his full weight behind it and to hell with his feet—if he fell off the rope would hold him, and they had plenty of guys to fish him out.

Hammering the rail into shape is a means of hammering his flaccid selfhood into shape, a Promethean labor that will, many pages later, command the respect of the captain, who will feel momentarily inferior to this common man capable of so much determined and skillful labor. Tony will not die like John Henry with a hammer in his hand, but go home satisfied with having put in one good night at the end of so many futile ones. His reward is the captain's acknowledgment of Tony's manhood: "that lit face hung alone in endless darkness." He returns to his old unsatisfying life, but in the course of the night he has done something faintly heroic, faintly redeeming.

"Fitter's Night" is a revisionist work about World War II, a conflict that Miller treated with some irony in his journalistic book of 1944, *Situation Normal*. The war, like the Depression it helped bring to an end, figures in Miller's work as an event of immense moral disorder, recapitulated in the private lives of every American citizen. Except in *Incident at Vichy* and his teleplay, *Playing for Time*, Miller does not travel abroad to locate the horror of the war, but instead finds tropes in his own milieu, his own nation, to focus the wider conflict in a determinate site. In *Focus* the predatory world of the early 1940s is crystallized in the figure of the city. That Manhattan and Queens, like Germany, should present a nightmare world of anti-Semitic behavior reinforces Miller's contention in all his work that blame and guilt should not be fixed on individual parties or countries but on social conditions and cultural ideologies that have deformed the whole of humanity.

In *Focus* Lawrence Newman is presented from the first page as someone "yearning for order," someone fixated on neatness, cleanliness, and efficiency. (His name recalls Christopher Newman, the decorous protagonist of Henry James's *The American*.) His life has become complicated by the presence on his block of a newsstand operated by a Jew, Finkelstein, whom the bigoted neighbors have vowed to drive away. Newman, too, tries to persuade Finkelstein to pack up, but the contingency of Newman's own physical resemblance to the Hebrew type makes him a victim as well, leading in the final scenes to solidarity with the Jew as both become targets of street violence. Miller has been criticized for the contrivance of making Newman a gentile rather than a Jew, much as *Gentleman's Agreement* shortly afterward made its gentile journalist masquerade as a Jew, safe from the full effects of prejudice. (The contemporary witticism was that such stories taught readers to be nice to Jews because they might turn out to be Christians after all.) But our own multicultural era might look back on the novel with more respect for the ingenuity of its allegorical construction. Jewish readers will find themselves crossing the ethnic border to identify with Newman because he is persecuted, and gentile readers will have to struggle with the implications and effects of being identified as vicarious Others, not a far-fetched scenario in a culture where prosperous citizens are routinely compelled to assume the guilt of the stronger.

The city is a precise recapitulation in America of the moral universe symbolized by the European conflict:

> The city and the millions upon millions hiving all over it—and they were going mad. He saw it so clearly that it was hardly alarming, for what he understood he no longer feared. They were going mad. People were in asylums for being afraid that the sky would fall, and here were millions walking around as insane as anyone could be who feared the shape of a human face.

Miller has calibrated his descriptions of Newman's tormentors to fit the iconography of Nazi power. The Catholic priest who whips the citizens into a frenzy of anti-Semitism at a huge rally is meant to recall not only Father Coughlin and his ilk but Hitler himself. The thugs who overturn trash cans on the lawns of Jews and beat them on the streets are reminiscent of the Gestapo, the SS, the "willing executioners" of the German public who vented their fear of difference on the most helpless of their citizenry. The most caustic irony at the heart of this urban fable is that Newman's neighbors keep comforting themselves with the thought that when the American troops return from pounding the Nazis they will aid in the persecution of American Jews.

The city as moral wasteland, as a place of intense tribal hatreds and bloody warfare, is a convention in modern American literature, especially during the 1930s when the rise of fascism caused writers like Sinclair Lewis (*It Can't Happen Here*) and Nathanael West (*The Day of the Locust*) to prophesy a mass upheaval on the model of Germany's. But Miller's fiction is remarkable for locating tropes of mass killing, of annihilation on the largest scale, elsewhere than the city, grounded in the dynamics of capitalist commerce that Miller has deplored since the Depression era. His short story "The Misfits" is no less a revisonist work than "Fitter's Night," but the tone is elegiac, not epic, and though the main characters sweat and prevail in their appointed task they emerge by the end of the fiction not as heroes but as the Joe Jerks of the American frontier experience, soldiers in a corrupt and degrading warfare against the ideal of freedom itself.

The main characters, Gay Langland and Perce Howland, 45 and 22 years old, respectively, pride themselves on being "misfits" who stand apart from the constraining domestic and commercial lives of their fellows. In the 1950s there was a widespread anxiety about the transformation of American society into a world of "organization men," of conformist office workers whose individuality was ground down by systems of robotic time-keeping in a corporate world. One result was a mythologizing of the cowboy as exemplar of the free spirit. Miller's story allows its characters to imagine themselves marching to a different drummer. "It's better than wages," is the refrain they use when reassuring each other that their free-ranging life is superior to that of men in gray flannel suits hiving in the city. In fact, the men make a living catching wild mustangs in the mountains of the western states and selling them to industrial producers of dogfood. They are the deluded agents, the shock troops, of commercial forces transforming the living world of nature into a universe of death.

The men are intermittently aware of their sinister role in the degradation of the way of life they embody. They refer to the mustangs as "misfits" just like themselves, and feel genuinely sorrowful at having to capture them. The mustangs have been hunted down for years and now it takes extraordinary efforts to locate and ensnare them. A pilot must fly into the high valleys and stampede the mustangs by shotgun so that the horses run down the mountain into a prehistoric lake bed where Gay and Perce rope and bind them. After their costs are factored they earn perhaps $35 each, hardly enough to sustain them till they move on to the next killing field. As in "Fitter's Night," readers are invited to admire the skill and determination of the laborers, and grant them a certain glamour. The art of the story is in balancing the men's resourcefulness with their murderous task. But the pathos of the horses' captivity, especially a colt's devotion to its doomed mother, alerts the reader to the story's moral argument against a nostalgia for icons of liberty that are so clearly mercenary. Gay and Perce remain cogs in a system of butchery that recalls not just the haphazard violence of warfare but even the Holocaust, as the herds of mustangs face extinction thanks to the irresistible efficiency of their predators.

"Please Don't Kill Anything" is a story with a similar theme. A husband and wife, obviously based on Miller and Marilyn Monroe, are taking a happy walk on the beach when they confront a band of fishermen pulling up nets of fish and dumping them into trucks. The wife feels deeply the pain of this slaughter but is reconciled to it, tentatively, by her husband's explanation that the fish must be sacrificed for the health of humans like themselves. But she is anguished anew when she sees the workers litter the beach with inedible sea robins (flying fish). The ghastly sight of so many creatures left to die revolts her and, it is suggested, endangers her fragile sense of well-being. The husband responds by hurling the sea robins one by one back into the ocean. Like the mustangs, the sea robins are victims of a merchandising process that reduces all living things to consumption items, valued or not for their price in the market. If their mass extinction (for it's clear that teams of fishermen are operating similar nets up and down the coast) recalls wartime atrocities, it also serves as a warning to postwar readers that the conditions of consumer behavior inevitably involve a war against nature in which all of us are implicated.

A final example of this theme is the story "Bees." This is a "story to be spoken," to cite the subtitle, of how a rural householder discovers that the walls of his house are infested with bees and takes steps to exterminate them. Those who have heard Miller read the story in public know that it works perfectly well on the level of stand-up comedy, a "routine" in which the narrator's Sisyphean labors to extinguish the bees draw sympathetic laughter from listeners who have struggled with similar problems in their own domestic spaces. But the story's effectiveness relies, too, on deeper recognitions of the symbolic character of these bees. When the harassed homeowner pumps liquid DDT into the spaces occupied by the bees, and later pries open boards to discover "dead bees eight or ten inches deep," even he concludes, "It was terrible." "Bees" is another fable of the massacre of the innocents belonging to a civilization endowed with technological power (airplanes, winch-operated fishing nets, DDT) sufficient to annihilate large categories of living creatures. In Miller's work, then, the allegorical structure of *Focus*, in which social forces conspire against fellow-citizens marked by difference, yielded to the more effective rhetorical strategy of fabulism. In the stories non-human surrogates for the Jew suffer and die as sacrifices to the machinery of an overwhelming socioeconomic system insistent on its comforts, privileges, and hegemonic power.

Miller's willingness, in his fiction as in his plays, to declare No! in thunder links him with the great tradition of authors in American history who protested the depredations of an exploitive power elite, so often framing their dissenting vision by fables like those described above. James Fenimore Cooper's description of the massacre of passenger pigeons in *The Pioneers* and Melville's depiction of the slaughter of whales in *Moby-Dick* are canonical nineteenth-century texts in this mode, and modern versions are ubiquitous, for example the fable of mass extermination in James Agee's classic story, "A Mother's Tale," and the bear-hunting in Norman Mailer's *Why Are We in Viet-*

nam? (1967, and more likely influenced by *The Misfits* than by the commonly cited novella of Faulkner, "The Bear"). The fatalistic strain of such fictions reminds us that literary distinction in America frequently rests on the perceived oppositional character of an author's writing. The author achieves eminence by articulating subversive truths that audiences both resist and surrender to as workers in systems they acknowledge to be harmful to public well-being. The superior status of the writer, even or especially when he is marginalized, derives from being a reproachful conscience within a culture busy with getting and spending. The culture's dismissive term for such writers is "moralistic" or "didactic," as opposed to "entertaining." Miller has worn this charge as a badge of honor.

* * *

An account of thematic concerns in Miller's fiction would be incomplete without some attention to the positivism imbedded in his stories—a positivism that belongs to the ethical claims he has always mounted for dramatic literature. In *Timebends* he refers to "my conviction that art ought to be of use in changing society," a belief that he rightly links to the Enlightenment assumptions of the 1930s liberal and radical tradition: that reason and socialism, as personal and political principles, respectively, would effect a more humane world, a third force beyond the competing ideologies of capitalism and fascism (including the Stalinist form of fascism). Miller's fiction, beginning with a novel he scrapped in order to rewrite the same story as his first Broadway play, *The Man Who Had All the Luck* (1944), shows an increasing sophistication about the constituents of a moral document capable of persuading mankind to choose good rather than evil. It may be useful to chart his progress in craft by focusing on the role of women in his fiction. Miller acknowledges in *Timebends* that he specialized in "father-son and brother-brother conflicts." In creating an imaginative world so heavily dominated by masculine figures he raises the question of how valid any solution can be in which women are not significant sharers of the revelations and consequences of the mise-en-scène.

Focus offers the most programmatic case in which the main character's evolution of consciousness proceeds by denying the claims of women upon his achievement of superior moral status. In the early portion of the novel Newman fantasizes some perfect woman to share his life in a Romantic dream of ideal union. Yet the woman he chooses to court and marry, Gertrude, is attractive to him in part because she shares his loathing of Jews and his desire to conform to the anti-Semitic neighborhood that plots against the lone Jew at the end of the block, Finkelstein. Constantly Gertrude pleads with Newman to strike out at Finkelstein and make peace with the Jew's tormentors. She serves as a kind of Jungian shadow, a malignant anima who seeks to put Newman on the road to success and riches (significantly, imagined as a Hollywood career). Newman's disabled mother offers him no guidance; in her few appearances she stays glued to the radio. Newman's breakthrough into a redeemed life, as a New-Man of the American era that will succeed the era of fascism, comes when he rejects his wife and takes up arms with Finkelstein against their mutual enemy, battling the local thugs in the street with baseball bats and declaring that they will not be moved from their homes by threats or violence.

The earliest of Miller's short stories, "Monte Sant'Angelo," published in 1951, belongs to the male-bonding tradition of his work of the 1940s. Two friends, one Jewish-American and the other Italian-American, visit an Italian town in search of Vinny's family origins. (*Timebends* provides the autobiographical matrix for this narrative.) Bernstein is delighted that his friend makes contact with some distant relatives but feels bereft of a personal heritage. A visit to Vinny's aged aunt, an inarticulate, lonely, and altogether scary figure, arouses in Bernstein a deeper longing for some connection to his own people, a longing that is satisfied when he recognizes in the ritual gesture of a male citizen of the town some Jewish habits from his own American elders, and concludes that this man, who knows nothing of Judaism, is a revenant from the past, a mediator of the ancient and modern practices of an identity-bearing system of belief he shares with the old man no less than Vinny shares his name and history with ancestors memorialized in the churches of Monte Sant'Angelo.

Looked at from this angle of regard, Miller's imagination of a social world inhabited importantly by women as well as men seems to take shape with "The Misfits" and its later change of form into *The Misfits*, film and novel both. The short story of 1957, as already noted, dramatizes the conventional frontier bonding of male buddies, doomed no less than the wild mustangs hunted to extinction. Gay and Perce think occasionally of Roslyn back in the frontier town, an Eastern schoolteacher with whom Gay lives in a quasi-domestic arrangement. Roslyn disapproves of their occupation and as they rope the horses for slaughter they hear her reproachful voice in their heads. "Roslyn's going to feel sorry for the colt," Gay says to Perce, "so might as well not mention it." Like the compassionate wife of "Please Don't Kill Anything," Roslyn exerts a counter-force in the story against the brute masculine ethic of domination over nature. She is the opposite of Gertrude in *Focus*, who sides with the powerful against the weak. In *Timebends* Miller defines stupidity as "the want of empathic power." Gay and Perce are not stupid, but they are inferior in moral intelligence to the offstage Roslyn.

The novel that Miller made of this short story, like the film of which it is a virtual transcript, features as its most significant change the foregrounding of Roslyn as a major character. The inspiration (or exigency) driving this change is clearly the entrance of Marilyn Monroe into the (re)production process, providing box-office dynamite for what would otherwise be an all-too-straightforward film narrative of futility and defeat. Monroe entered and captured the story because she had first entered Miller's life, so that the film achieved a parabolic status from the first day it was announced. And with Monroe's screen persona comes a radical shift in the nature of Roslyn's character. In the short story we are led to believe that she is one of those "college graduate divorced women" from the East who rebound into Gay's arms after shedding their unsatisfactory mates Nevada style. In the long version Roslyn becomes an "interpretive" dancer who has dwindled to performing in dance halls, and has found even shadier ways of supporting herself. By making her less intellectual and more of a class match for Gay, Miller guarantees that their relationship will not be an uneven struggle in which each partner exerts a formulaic exploitive power over the other (her snob condescension, his sexual allure, the obverse of what the union of Monroe and Miller represented to the general public). What does not change from story to film/novel is the deeper sensitivity that Roslyn displays about the fate of the hunted mustangs, and more generally her refusal to have love on terms degraded by her partner's habit of violence against living things.

The story begins in Reno, "Divorce Capital of the World" (a billboard informs us), no less Babylon than the New York of *Focus*, though here the moral disorder seems more appealing. Displaced people gamble and sin, hucksters ply their trades, and in venues thematically related to Reno, such as the rodeo town, a kind of barbaric "lewdness" erupts constantly into view. An older woman, Isabelle (Thelma Ritter in the film), has befriended the insecure Roslyn, a high school dropout whom Isabelle compares to a little child and chaperones a short distance till Gay assumes the commanding role. Isabelle has a tough-mindedness that recalls Miller's description of his mother in *Timebends*; in a minor mode she anticipates the heroine of "Homely Girl, A Life." Roslyn is all heart and no brain; she drinks "To Life—whatever that is" and Gay remarks to her, "I think that you're the saddest girl I ever met." But she does love life, and Guido, the least sympathetic of the characters, tells her "You have the gift of life." She wants to keep Gay from killing the rabbits desolating his lettuce garden; she loves the birds; she complains about the bucking strap on the rodeo horses. She is, in fact, a rather obvious trope for Nature itself, an Earth Mother who in one scene embraces a tree in a wild dance. "Honey, when you smile it's like the sun coming up," Gay tells her.

As a figure for the life force she contains immense power to change other people by withholding sanction for their ruthless behavior, but she too must undergo change as a human being in a social community far from utopia. She must, for one thing, escape her rote sentiments about the holiness of life and understand Gay's need to capture the wild mustangs in ritual acts of violence. She must acquire a masculine vision of experience if she expects Gay to move a commensurate distance toward her nurturing piety toward nature. The captured colt is the critical figure in the evolving narrative that brings Gay and Roslyn together. The colt represents the child potentially possible between them, their future as a contracted couple. If Gay sacrifices it for the few dollars it would bring in meat (and the colt's mother another thirty dollars or so), he will forfeit the joyful life they might have together beyond the reach of a rapacious commercial system both he and Roslyn despise. The immense pathos of the short story, in which he does, unhappily, accede to financial necessity and his outworn code of honor, yields in the longer version to a happy ending in which he permits Roslyn and Perce to let the mustangs go, except for a stallion which he wrestles into submission and then frees to show that he is still in control. At the end of the novel she mentions the child she believes they can conceive (a line deleted from the film version), and Gay remarks in the last scene, "I bless you, girl."

That the novel is a romance, a fairy tale in the form of a realistic narrative about modern people on the frontier, is more apparent to us when we read it through the retrospective lens of the Miller-Monroe marriage and through Miller's highly unromantic autobiographical play, *After the Fall* (1964). Yet the figure of Roslyn is clearly readable in the vulnerable Maggie of that play; Maggie calls herself "a joke that brings in money" and yet her intellectual husband admires her giving nature. "You're all love, aren't you," he asks, and she answers, "That's all I am." The point is not whether this is an identity satisfying to our current standards—obviously it doesn't satisfy Miller either—but that in rendering such a character's needs and demands in a complex dramatic structure Miller is able to imagine a figure of believable intensity and mythic resonance.

The Misfits is not sentimental about Roslyn; for one thing, she is too sentimental herself to attract the reader's wholehearted sympathy. One gets tired of her fixed angelic nature, what Miller in *Timebends* (speaking of Marilyn) calls "a purely donative femininity," and also of the constant *kvetching* and sniffling and sobbing she carries on throughout the second half of the book. But the reader is snapped back to respect for her powerful feelings of tenderness when she lashes out at Guido, the veteran pilot, constantly evoking the memory of his dead wife as he propositions Roslyn, bargaining with her to save the mustangs if she'll shack up with him:

> "You! Sensitive fella? So full of feelings? So sad about your wife, and crying to me about the bombs you dropped and the people you killed. You have to get something to be human? You were never sad for anybody in your life, Guido! You only know the sad words! You could blow up the whole world, and all you'd ever feel is sorry for *yourself*!"

In speeches like this we hear the proleptic voice of the counterculture in America preparing its critique of the one-dimensional men who prosecuted the Vietnam War later in the 1960s. Roslyn emerges at the end of this narrative as the idealized figure of resistance to the American leaders who justified the slaughter of millions of Asians by turning them into nothing but data. And in summoning the nuclear holocaust, Miller takes aim at the ultimate culmination of the genocidal impulse dramatized in his fabulist fictions. That Roslyn can embody such a range of moral imperatives—not, admittedly, without straining dramatic credibility—speaks well for the relevance of *The Misfits* in a feminist era.

Two later stories develop the theme of female empowerment initiated by *The Misfits*. "The Prophecy," published in 1961, is Miller's earnest effort to enter fully into the consciousness and assess the fate of a female character for the first time. Indeed, it dramatizes the struggle of wills among a group of female characters. The story begins as if it will be an appreciative study of a famous architect, Stowey Rummel, but he is quickly banished from the narrative and the focus turns to his wife, Cleota, and a house party she mounts in her well-appointed country home. Cleota possesses a determined, even rigid demeanor; she looks on most of her invitees with disdain, especially her husband's sister Alice and a fortune teller who later in the story prophesies that Alice will outlive her brother. Cleota also learns that her longtime friend Lucretia has just been abandoned by her husband. The emotional turmoil of these messy lives, in addition to a quantity of alcohol, stirs up Cleota and she makes an impulsive pass at another guest, Joseph, who fends her off. The next day Stowey returns and the couple resumes their married life, more satisfying, perhaps, for Cleota's momentary breakout from the puritanical habits that have brought her a measure of despair.

Plot summaries rarely do justice to complex fiction, and this story, especially, uses a melodramatic structure to generate a considerable number of ideas about love relationships—ideas presented as such in the midst of conversation among intellectuals, or through the consciousness of the characters, the fiction writer Joseph preeminently. Of central importance to our purpose, the story elevates Cleota above the welter of mere ideas (some of them on the futility of thinking when intuitive action is called for), and concludes with her in a state of near ecstasy, "cherishing a rapture, the clear heart of those whose doors are made to hold against the winds of the world." The prophecy proves false, Stowey survives the somewhat mean-spirited Alice, and embraces Cleota in front of the abashed Joseph, as if to make the point that the solidarity of a romantic couple is invulnerable, like a well-designed house. Cleota has not been struck by the lightning of an angry god, but rewarded for making her way through thickets of anxiety (especially about aging), jealousy, and vindictive lust, as well as the arid analytical debates common to her class of sophisticates, to an achieved life; she has conquered the shadow in herself, as Newman did in *Focus* when he matured beyond the infernal temptations offered by his neighbors.

"The Prophecy" is written with an uncertainty and turgidity that critics might point to as a validation of their suspicion about genre-leaping in the verbal arts. It is not quite a "playwright's story," in the sense that it does not resolve its key conflicts through dialogue, but it represents a falling-off in quality from Miller's earlier stories, for all its evocative writing. The same cannot be said for Miller's most recent work, "Homely Girl, A Life," which takes up where first-rate stories like "The Misfits" and "Fitter's Night" left off. In limpid prose and a fluency of dramatic scenes reminiscent of Miller's tableau play *The American Clock* and his autobiography, this chronicle of a woman's life from childhood to old age is unique in Miller's fiction, a full-throated endorsement of the female will to forge a happy life from un-promising circumstances. Janice Sessions is not a cardboard heroine rising miraculously from harsh adversity into one of those successful roles Miller has critiqued throughout his career; she is unusual enough, in appearance and personality, to construct a private life secure against the overwhelming desires of others, even those who mean her well. Like Cleota, she cherishes the rapture of self-creation, of autonomous and gratifying existence, and by so doing she becomes a model for women, and men, suffering from timidity and arrogance alike.

The biographical structure of "Homely Girl" recalls the autobio-graphical structure of *Timebends*, and throughout this novella we sense that Miller is working out once again some of the profound lessons of his own life. Janice's homeliness is something of a metaphor driving the narrative forward. Miller has described himself in *Timebends* as "gangling and unhandsome" to make the point that he was never in danger of succumbing to the fatality of beauty, the easy and treacher-ous path to the future laid out for the picture-perfect faces of an exhi-bitionistic culture. He would achieve by pulling down one form of van-ity in favor of the admiration derived from intellectual and physical labor. In political terms he would work relentlessly to improve the hap-piness and prosperity of mankind by promoting first radical, then liberal causes. It would have been a simple matter to send Janice down the same road. Author and character both begin their adult life in the Depression, and the facts of economic life exert enormous pressure on Janice's leap into maturity:

> This endless waiting-to-become was like the Depression itself—everybody kept waiting for it to lift and forgot how to live in the meantime, but supposing it went on forever? She must start living! And Sam [her husband] had to start thinking of something else than Fascism and organizing unions and the rest of the endlessly repetitive radical agenda. But she mustn't think that way, she guiltily corrected herself.

Janice's guilt comes from wanting to enjoy the present, not sacrifice pleasure for an uncertain future. She is one of those legion of characters in modern fiction trying to awaken from an oppressive history. But Miller does not let such desires reach an easy fulfillment. "A character is defined by the kinds of challenge he cannot walk away from," he writes in *Timebends*. "And by those he has walked away from that cause him remorse."

In this sense, too, Janice is "homely"—she does not think in internationalist terms, her home is not the future but the domestic present where the dominant fact of her consciousness is that she is living a secondhand life in service to husband and Party. During the war she commits an adultery that helps to liberate her from an unsatisfying marriage. She then has an affair with an art history professor, and seems fated to do nothing in life but put her body in service to available males as a way of making a point about her bleak freedom to do so. But Miller would be incapable of an allegory quite that rigid. Janice meets a blind man who works as a recording technician for Decca Records. Their fourteen years of wedded bliss is the only period of genuine happiness in her life. This blindness contrasts interestingly to the near-sightedness of Newman in *Focus*. When Newman obtains the means to see more sharply he achieves the insight to understand how his former anti-Semitism had poisoned his life and that of his culture. Charles's inability to see (and thus impose value on) Janice's homeliness permits both of them the more profound pleasures of personal intimacy apart from the harsh world—the pleasures of sexuality, of music, of compassionate understanding. Though she volunteers some time after his death to the civil rights movement, the core of her life is composed of the union created by this romantic couple.

"The key to the present is always pleasure," Janice thinks at one point, and then rebukes herself as a fraud for such a superficial philosophy. The story is artfully posed between life options that carry highly determinate values: Sam's devotion to the Communist Party, Janice's brother's greedy Capitalism, the hedonism of her lovers, and finally Charles's soulful devotion to the art of music. Janice acquires traits from all these men, inflected toward the future by being "conspiratorially linked" to her father's "arrogant style" in which "guts" not piety forms the self. The absence of strong female characters besides Janice guarantees the story a suspicious reading by feminist critics. If Miller has imbued and ennobled Janice with his own drive, he has withheld from her the saving grace of extraordinary talent, making her dependent on masculine influences to an extent unwarranted by the conditions of postwar society. Nevertheless, her liberation from the controlling forces that threaten to deform her prematurely stands as an affirmation on Miller's part that authentic happiness does come to those who actively quest for it, no matter what the social circumstances. In the last paragraph of the story an aged Janice stands in the city watching a teenage drug dealer drive by in his BMW, rap music blaring, but finds herself immune from the despair threatened by such moral disorder, "filling with wonder at her fortune at having lived into beauty."

* * *

In his introduction to *I Don't Love You Anymore*, Miller writes that he is attracted to the story form because "from time to time there is an urge not to speed up and condense events and character development, which is what one does in a play, but to hold them frozen and to see things isolated in stillness." His choice of terms reveals that he seeks in fiction writing an escape from the highly-wrought intensity that audiences demand in a live-action performance. His stories are quieter, more meditative, more attuned to nuances of consciousness than to the oral rhythms of excited speech; they lack the extremity of feeling that draws his theatrical characters into such fireworks of verbal argument and abuse. Missing in the stories, too, is the intensity of dreaming and longing, and of savage remorse and atavistic hatreds, we associate with the dramaturgy of the stage. Miller's "secret fate" was to be a playwright, no doubt about it. But the fiction does regard the same world, as Miller claims in the Introduction, from a different distance. The chronicle or case study of *Focus* or "Homely Girl, A Life" lays before us the customarily unapprehended textures of an actual life in more detail than a three-act play can comfortably incorporate. The shorter stories, at their best, give us an extended vision into landscapes and lifestyles belonging not only to the familiar universe Miller has half-created these last sixty years but to the modern scene represented by his most talented peers. This neglected corpus of a major writer will not disappoint those readers whose literary taste has been formed and replenished by *Death of a Salesman*, *A View from the Bridge*, and *The Crucible*.

From *Michigan Quarterly Review* 37, no. 4 (1998): 725-745. Copyright © by University of Michigan. Reprinted with permission of the author.

RESOURCES

1915	Arthur Asher Miller is born on October 17 in Harlem, New York City, to Isidore and Augusta Miller; he is the second of their three children.
1929	Miller's family is forced to move to Brooklyn because Isidore Miller's business is struggling.
1933	Miller writes the short story "In Memoriam," which depicts an aging salesman. He graduates from high school and fails to be accepted for admission to Cornell University or the University of Michigan. He re-applies to the University of Michigan and is granted a conditional acceptance.
1934	Miller enters the University of Michigan to study journalism. He becomes a reporter and the night editor on the student newspaper, the *Michigan Daily*, and studies playwriting under Professor Kenneth T. Rowe.
1936	Miller's first play, *No Villain*, is produced and receives the University of Michigan's Avery Hopwood Award.
1937	Miller's play *Honors at Dawn* receives the Avery Hopwood Award, and Miller receives the Theatre Guild's Bureau of New Plays Award for *They Too Arise*, a revision of *No Villain*.
1938	Miller graduates from college with a B.A. in English. He joins the Federal Theatre Project in New York City, where he writes radio plays and scripts.
1939	Miller writes radio plays for the CBS and NBC networks.
1940	Miller travels to North Carolina to collect dialect speech for the folk division of the Library of Congress. He marries Mary Grace Slattery.
1941	Miller works various odd jobs and continues to write radio plays; over the next few years, these include *The Pussycat and the Expert Plumber Who Was a Man* and *William Ireland's Confession*.

1944	Miller's daughter Jane is born. His first Broadway production, *The Man Who Had All the Luck*, closes after four performances but receives the Theatre Guild National Award.
1945	Miller's novel *Focus* is published.
1947	*All My Sons* opens on Broadway on January 29 and goes on to earn Miller a New York Drama Critics' Circle Award. He becomes involved in a variety of antifascist and pro-communist activities. His son, Robert, is born, and the family buys a farmhouse in Roxbury, Connecticut, to use as a vacation home.
1949	*Death of a Salesman* opens on Broadway on February 10 under the direction of Elia Kazan and starring Lee J. Cobb in the title role; it goes on to receive the Pulitzer Prize and the New York Drama Critics' Circle Award. Miller publishes the first of his many theatrical and political essays.
1950	Miller's adaptation of Henrik Ibsen's *An Enemy of the People* premieres but closes after thirty-six performances.
1951	Miller meets Marilyn Monroe for the first time. The first film adaptation of *Death of a Salesman*, starring Fredric March, is released by Columbia Pictures.
1952	Miller visits the Historical Society "witch museum" in Salem, Massachusetts, to conduct research for *The Crucible*.
1953	*The Crucible* opens on Broadway on January 22; it goes on to win the Tony Award and the Donaldson Award for best play.
1954	U.S. State Department denies Miller a passport to attend the opening of *The Crucible* in Brussels because of his alleged support of the communist movement.
1955	One-act version of *A View from the Bridge* premieres on a joint bill with *A Memory of Two Mondays*. The House Un-American Activities Committee (HUAC) pressures New York officials to withdraw permission for Miller to make a film he had been planning about juvenile delinquency in the city.

1956	Miller divorces Mary Slattery and marries Marilyn Monroe. Subpoenaed to appear before HUAC for attending communist meetings, he refuses to name names of others who attended meetings organized by communist sympathizers.
1957	*Collected Plays* is published. Miller is indicted on the charge of contempt of Congress for refusing to name names when testifying before HUAC.
1958	U.S. Court of Appeals overturns Miller's conviction for contempt of Congress. Miller is elected to the National Institute of Arts and Letters. Filming begins on Miller's *The Misfits*, starring Marilyn Monroe.
1959	Miller receives the Gold Medal for Drama from the National Institute of Arts and Letters.
1961	*The Misfits* is released in theaters. Miller and Monroe divorce.
1962	Miller marries Austrian photographer Ingeborg Morath. Marilyn Monroe dies.
1963	Miller's daughter Rebecca is born.
1964	*After the Fall* opens in New York on January 23; *Incident at Vichy* opens in New York on December 3.
1965	Miller is elected president of the worldwide writers' organization International PEN.
1967	Collection of short stories *I Don't Need You Any More* is published.
1968	*The Price* opens on Broadway on February 7.
1969	*In Russia*, a combination photo essay and travel journal on which Miller collaborated with Morath, is published.
1970	One-act plays *Fame* and *The Reason Why* are performed in New York's Theatre Workshop. Miller's works are banned in the Soviet Union as a result of his work to free dissident writers.

1971	First edition of *The Portable Arthur Miller* is published. Television adaptations of *The Price* and *A Memory of Two Mondays* are aired.
1972	*The Creation of the World and Other Business* opens on Broadway but closes after twenty performances.
1974	Television adaptation of *After the Fall* airs.
1975	Revival of *Death of a Salesman* opens in New York.
1977	*In the Country*, a photo essay collaboration between Miller and Morath, is published. *The Archbishop's Ceiling* premieres in Washington, D.C.
1978	First edition of *The Theater Essays of Arthur Miller*, edited by Robert A. Martin, is published. Miller visits China.
1979	*Chinese Encounters*, a photo essay collaboration between Miller and Morath, is published.
1980	*The American Clock* opens in New York but closes after only twelve performances.
1981	*Collected Plays, Volume II* is published.
1982	One-act plays *Elegy for a Lady* and *Some Kind of Love Story* are produced together in Connecticut under the title *2 by A.M.*
1983	Miller directs *Death of a Salesman* at the People's Art Theater in Beijing.
1984	Revival of *Death of a Salesman* starring Dustin Hoffman opens on Broadway. Miller receives Kennedy Center Honors for his lifetime achievement.
1985	Television adaptation of *Death of a Salesman*, starring Dustin Hoffman, airs on CBS and goes on to earn ten nominations for Emmy Awards, receiving three.
1986	Television adaptation of *All My Sons* airs.

1987	*Timebends: A Life* is published. One-act plays *I Can't Remember Anything* and *Clara* open under the title *Danger: Memory!*
1990	Revivals of *The Crucible* open in New York and London.
1991	*The Ride Down Mt. Morgan* premieres in London.
1992	Novella *Homely Girl, a Life* is published.
1994	*Broken Glass* opens at the Booth Theatre on Broadway and goes on to receive the Tony Award for best play.
1995	Miller receives the William Inge Festival Award for distinguished achievement in American theater.
1996	Miller receives the Edward Albee Last Frontier Playwright Award. Critically acclaimed film adaptation of *The Crucible*, starring Winona Ryder and Daniel Day-Lewis, is released.
1998	Major revival of *A View from the Bridge* wins two Tony Awards. Miller is named Distinguished Inaugural Senior Fellow of the American Academy in Berlin.
1999	Revival of *Death of a Salesman* opens on Broadway and goes on to win the Tony Award for best revival of a play.
2000	Revival of *The Ride Down Mt. Morgan* opens on Broadway, as does a revival of *The Price*. Major celebrations of Miller's eighty-fifth birthday are held at the University of Michigan and at the Arthur Miller Center in England. Collection of essays *Echoes Down the Corridor* is published.
2001	Miller receives a fellowship from the National Endowment for the Humanities and the John H. Finley Award for Exemplary Service to New York City.
2002	Inge Morath dies. *Resurrection Blues* premieres in Minneapolis. Miller receives the Premio Príncipe de Asturias de las Letras, an international Spanish award.

2003	Miller is awarded the Jerusalem Prize.
2004	*Finishing the Picture* premieres at Chicago's Goodman Theatre. Miller announces he is planning to marry thirty-four-year-old artist Agnes Barley.
2005	At the age of eighty-nine, Miller dies of congestive heart failure in his Connecticut home on February 10. Memorial services are held in Roxbury, Connecticut, and New York City.

Works by Arthur Miller_____

Plays (date shown is that of first production)
Honors at Dawn, 1936
No Villain, 1936
The Man Who Had All the Luck, 1944
All My Sons, 1947
Death of a Salesman, 1949
An Enemy of the People, 1950 (adaptation of Henrik Ibsen's play)
The Crucible, 1953
A Memory of Two Mondays, 1955
A View from the Bridge, 1955 (one-act version)
A View from the Bridge, 1956 (two-act version)
After the Fall, 1964
Incident at Vichy, 1964
The Price, 1968
The Creation of the World and Other Business, 1972
The Archbishop's Ceiling, 1977
The American Clock, 1980
2 by A.M., 1982 (two one-acts: *Some Kind of Love Story* and *Elegy for a Lady*; later
   published as *Two-Way Mirror*)
Danger: Memory!, 1987 (two one-acts: *I Can't Remember Anything* and *Clara*)
The Golden Years, 1987 (written 1940)
The Ride Down Mt. Morgan, 1991
The Last Yankee, 1993
Broken Glass, 1994
Mr. Peters' Connections, 1998
Resurrection Blues, 2002
Finishing the Picture, 2004

Drama Collections
Collected Plays, 1957
Arthur Miller's Collected Plays, Volume II, 1981
Plays, 1988-1995 (5 volumes)

Long Fiction
Focus, 1945
The Misfits, 1961 (novella)

Short Fiction
I Don't Need You Any More, 1967
Homely Girl, a Life, and Other Stories, 1995
Presence, 2007

Screenplays
The Misfits, 1961
Everybody Wins, 1990
The Crucible, 1996

Teleplay
Playing for Time, 1980

Nonfiction
Situation Normal, 1944
In Russia, 1969 (photo essay; with Inge Morath)
In the Country, 1977 (photo essay; with Morath)
The Theater Essays of Arthur Miller, 1978 (revised and expanded 1996; Robert A. Martin, editor)
Chinese Encounters, 1979 (photo essay; with Morath)
"Salesman" in Beijing, 1984
Conversations with Arthur Miller, 1987 (Matthew C. Roudané, editor)
Spain, 1987
Timebends: A Life, 1987
Arthur Miller and Company, 1990 (Christopher Bigsby, editor)
The Crucible in History, and Other Essays, 2000
Echoes Down the Corridor: Collected Essays, 1944-2000, 2000
On Politics and the Art of Acting, 2001

Bibliography

Bigsby, Christopher. *Arthur Miller: 1915-1962*. Cambridge, MA: Harvard University Press, 2009.

_____. "Arthur Miller: Poet." *Michigan Quarterly Review* 37 (Fall 1998): 713-25.

_____. "Arthur Miller: The Moral Imperative." *Modern American Drama, 1945-1990*. Cambridge: Cambridge University Press, 1992. 72-125.

_____. *A Critical Introduction to Twentieth-Century American Drama*, Volume 2, *Tennessee Williams, Arthur Miller, Edward Albee*. New York: Cambridge University Press, 1984.

_____, ed. *Arthur Miller and Company*. London: Methuen, 1990.

_____, ed. *The Cambridge Companion to Arthur Miller*. New York: Cambridge University Press, 1997.

Bloom, Harold, ed. *Arthur Miller*. Bloom's Major Dramatists. New York: Chelsea House, 1987.

_____, ed. *Arthur Miller's "All My Sons."* Bloom's Modern Critical Interpretations. New York: Chelsea House, 1988.

_____, ed. *Arthur Miller's "Death of a Salesman."* Bloom's Modern Critical Interpretations. New York: Chelsea House, 1988.

Brater, Enoch. *Arthur Miller: A Playwright's Life and Works*. New York: Thames & Hudson, 2005.

_____, ed. *Arthur Miller's America: Theater and Culture in a Time of Change*. Ann Arbor: University of Michigan Press, 2005.

_____, ed. *Arthur Miller's Global Theater*. Ann Arbor: University of Michigan Press, 2007.

Brucher, Richard T. "Willy Loman and *The Soul of a New Machine:* Technology and the Common Man." *Journal of American Studies* 17 (1983): 325-36.

Centola, Steven R., ed. *The Achievement of Arthur Miller: New Essays*. Dallas: Contemporary Research Press, 1995.

Ferres, John H. *Arthur Miller: A Reference Guide*. Boston: G. K. Hall, 1979.

_____. *Twentieth Century Interpretations of "The Crucible."* Englewood Cliffs, NJ: Prentice-Hall, 1972.

Gottfried, Martin. *Arthur Miller: His Life and Work*. Cambridge, MA: Da Capo Press, 2003.

Gussow, Mel. *Conversations with Miller*. New York: Applause, 2002.

Koon, Helene Wickham, ed. *Twentieth Century Interpretations of "Death of a Salesman."* Englewood Cliffs, NJ: Prentice-Hall, 1983.

Koorey, Stefani. *Arthur Miller's Life and Literature*. Metuchen, NJ: Scarecrow Press, 2000.

Langteau, Paula, ed. *Miller and Middle America: Essays on Arthur Miller and the American Experience*. Lanham, MD: University Press of America, 2007.

Marino, Stephen A. *A Language Study of Arthur Miller's Plays: The Poetic in the Colloquial*. Lewiston, NY: Edwin Mellen Press, 2002.

_____, ed. *"The Salesman Has a Birthday": Essays Celebrating the Fiftieth Anniversary of Arthur Miller's "Death of a Salesman."* Lanham, MD: University Press of America, 2000.

Martin, Robert A. "Arthur Miller: Public Issues, Private Tensions." *Studies in the Literary Imagination* 21.2 (1988): 97-106.

_____. "Arthur Miller's *After the Fall*: A Play About a Theme." *American Drama* 16.1 (Fall 1996): 73-88.

_____. "The Nature of Tragedy in Arthur Miller's *Death of a Salesman*." *South Atlantic Review* 61.4 (Fall 1996): 97-106.

Martine, James J. *"The Crucible": Politics, Property, and Pretense*. New York: Twayne, 1993.

_____, ed. *Critical Essays on Arthur Miller*. Boston: G. K. Hall, 1979.

Mason, Jeffrey D. *Stone Tower: The Political Theater of Arthur Miller*. Ann Arbor: University of Michigan Press, 2008.

Miller, Arthur. *Conversations with Arthur Miller*. Ed. Matthew C. Roudané. Jackson: University Press of Mississippi, 1987.

_____. *"Death of a Salesman": Text and Criticism*. Ed. Gerald Weales. New York: Viking Press, 1977.

Miller, Quentin. "The Signifying Poppet: Unseen Voodoo in Arthur Miller's Tituba." *Forum for Modern Language Studies* 43.4 (October 2007): 438-54.

Moss, Leonard. *Arthur Miller*. New Haven, CT: College and University Press, 1967.

_____. "Arthur Miller and the Common Man's Language." *Modern Drama* 7 (1964): 52-59.

Murphy, Brenda. *Congressional Theatre: Dramatizing McCarthyism on Stage, Film, and Television*. New York: Cambridge University Press, 1999.

_____. *Miller: "Death of a Salesman."* New York: Cambridge University Press, 1995.

Murray, Edward. *Arthur Miller, Dramatist*. New York: Frederick Ungar, 1967.

Otten, Terry. *The Temptation of Innocence in the Dramas of Arthur Miller*. Columbia: University of Missouri Press, 2002.

Pagan, Nicholas O. "Arthur Miller and the Rhetoric of Ethnic Self-Expression." *Journal of American Studies* 41.1 (2008): 89-106.

Radavich, David. "Arthur Miller's Sojourn in the Heartland." *American Drama* 16.2 (Summer 2007): 28-45.

Schlueter, June, and James K. Flanagan. *Arthur Miller*. New York: Frederick Ungar, 1987.

Teachout, Terry. "Concurring with Arthur Miller." *Commentary* 127.6 (June 2009): 71-73.

CRITICAL
INSIGHTS

About the Editor_____

Brenda Murphy is Board of Trustees Distinguished Professor of English at the University of Connecticut. Her scholarly work, spanning more than thirty years, reflects her interest in placing American drama, theater, and performance in the broader context of American literature and culture. She has written numerous articles about American playwrights and other writers, but her most significant work is in the ten books she has authored on the American theater. Among Murphy's books are *The Provincetown Players and the Culture of Modernity* (2005), *O'Neill: Long Day's Journey into Night* (2001), *Congressional Theatre: Dramatizing McCarthyism on Stage, Film, and Television* (1999), *Miller: Death of a Salesman* (1995), *Tennessee Williams and Elia Kazan: A Collaboration in the Theatre* (1992), *American Realism and American Drama, 1880-1940* (1987), and, as editor, *Twentieth Century American Drama: Critical Concepts in Literary and Cultural Studies* (2006) and the *Cambridge Companion to American Women Playwrights* (1999). She has been recognized as breaking new ground through her synthesis of the study of the play as literary text and the play as performance in her books on Tennessee Williams, Arthur Miller, and Eugene O'Neill. *Congressional Theatre*, her study of the theater's response to the House Committee on Un-American Activities in the 1950s, was honored by the American Society for Theatre Research in 1999 for outstanding research in theater history and cognate studies.

Professor Murphy has been active in a number of international professional organizations throughout her career. She serves on the editorial boards of several journals and book series and on the boards of several societies that promote the study of American playwrights, and she has served as President of the American Theatre and Drama Society and the Eugene O'Neill Society. Her research has been supported by grants from the National Endowment for the Humanities, the American Council for Learned Societies, the National Humanities Center, and other sources.

About *The Paris Review*_____

The Paris Review is America's preeminent literary quarterly, dedicated to discovering and publishing the best new voices in fiction, nonfiction, and poetry. The magazine was founded in Paris in 1953 by the young American writers Peter Matthiessen and Doc Humes, and edited there and in New York for its first fifty years by George Plimpton. Over the decades, the *Review* has introduced readers to the earliest writings of Jack Kerouac, Philip Roth, T. C. Boyle, V. S. Naipaul, Ha Jin, Ann Patchett, Jay McInerney, Mona Simpson, and Edward P. Jones, and published numerous now classic works, including Roth's *Goodbye, Columbus*, Donald Barthelme's *Alice*, Jim Carroll's

Basketball Diaries, and selections from Samuel Beckett's *Molloy* (his first publication in English). The first chapter of Jeffrey Eugenides's *The Virgin Suicides* appeared in the *Review*'s pages, as well as stories by Rick Moody, David Foster Wallace, Denis Johnson, Jim Crace, Lorrie Moore, and Jeanette Winterson.

The Paris Review's renowned Writers at Work series of interviews, whose early installments include legendary conversations with E. M. Forster, William Faulkner, and Ernest Hemingway, is one of the landmarks of world literature. The interviews received a George Polk Award and were nominated for a Pulitzer Prize. Among the more than three hundred interviewees are Robert Frost, Marianne Moore, W. H. Auden, Elizabeth Bishop, Susan Sontag, and Toni Morrison. Recent issues feature conversations with Salman Rushdie, Joan Didion, Norman Mailer, Kazuo Ishiguro, Marilynne Robinson, Umberto Eco, Annie Proulx, and Gay Talese. In November 2009, Picador published the final volume of a four-volume series of anthologies of *Paris Review* interviews. *The New York Times* called the Writers at Work series "the most remarkable and extensive interviewing project we possess."

The Paris Review is edited by Philip Gourevitch, who was named to the post in 2005, following the death of George Plimpton two years earlier. A new editorial team has published fiction by André Aciman, Colum McCann, Damon Galgut, Mohsin Hamid, Uzodinma Iweala, Gish Jen, Stephen King, James Lasdun, Padgett Powell, Richard Price, and Sam Shepard. Poetry editors Charles Simic, Meghan O'Rourke, and Dan Chiasson have selected works by John Ashbery, Kay Ryan, Billy Collins, Tomaž Šalamun, Mary Jo Bang, Sharon Olds, Charles Wright, and Mary Karr. Writing published in the magazine has been anthologized in *Best American Short Stories* (2006, 2007, and 2008), *Best American Poetry*, *Best Creative Non-Fiction*, the Pushcart Prize anthology, and *O. Henry Prize Stories*.

The magazine presents two annual awards. The Hadada Award for lifelong contribution to literature has recently been given to Joan Didion, Norman Mailer, Peter Matthiessen, and, in 2009, John Ashbery. The Plimpton Prize for Fiction, awarded to a debut or emerging writer brought to national attention in the pages of *The Paris Review*, was presented in 2007 to Benjamin Percy, to Jesse Ball in 2008, and to Alistair Morgan in 2009.

The Paris Review was a finalist for the 2008 and 2009 National Magazine Awards in fiction, and it won the 2007 National Magazine Award in photojournalism. The *Los Angeles Times* recently called *The Paris Review* "an American treasure with true international reach."

Since 1999 *The Paris Review* has been published by The Paris Review Foundation, Inc., a not-for-profit 501(c)(3) organization.

The Paris Review is available in digital form to libraries worldwide in selected academic databases exclusively from EBSCO Publishing. Libraries can contact EBSCO at 1-800-653-2726 for details. For more information on *The Paris Review* or to subscribe, please visit: www.theparisreview.org.

Contributors

Brenda Murphy is Board of Trustees Distinguished Professor of English at the University of Connecticut. Her books on Arthur Miller include *Miller: Death of a Salesman* in the Cambridge University Press series Plays in Performance and, with Susan Abbotson, the casebook *Understanding Death of a Salesman*, as well as a substantial portion of *Congressional Theatre: Dramatizing McCarthyism on Stage, Film, and Television*. She has published many articles on Miller and other American playwrights, as well as books such as *The Provincetown Players and the Culture of Modernity*, *O'Neill: Long Day's Journey into Night*, *Tennessee Williams and Elia Kazan: A Collaboration in the Theatre*, *American Realism and American Drama, 1880-1940*, and, as editor, the *Cambridge Companion to American Women Playwrights*.

Paul Rosefeldt is Professor of English at Delgado Community College in New Orleans, Louisiana.

Richard Beck is a writer living in New York City. He has written articles for *N+1*, *The Boston Phoenix*, *Film Quarterly*, and *The Barnes and Noble Review*.

Pamela Loos has researched or written numerous books of literary criticism. Some of her recent publications include *A Reader's Guide to Amy Tan's "The Joy Luck Club"* (2008) and *A Reader's Guide to Lorraine Hansberry's "A Raisin in the Sun"* (2008).

Stephen A. Marino is the founding editor of *The Arthur Miller Journal*. His work on Arthur Miller has appeared in *Modern Drama*, *The South Atlantic Review*, and *Miller and Middle America: Essays on Miller and the American Experience*. He is the editor of *"The Salesman Has a Birthday": Essays Celebrating the Fiftieth Anniversary of Arthur Miller's "Death of a Salesman"* (2000) and the author of *A Language Study of Arthur Miller's Plays: The Poetic in the Colloquial* (2002). His interview with celebrated actress Joan Copeland, Arthur Miller's sister, appeared in the spring 2008 issue of *The Arthur Miller Journal*. His essay on *The Misfits* was published in the spring 2009 issue of the *Nevada Historical Quarterly*. He is currently writing the critical commentary for the forthcoming Methuen edition of *A View from the Bridge*.

Katherine Egerton is Assistant Professor in the Department of English, Theatre, and Speech Communication at Berea College. Her essays on Arthur Miller have appeared in *The Arthur Miller Journal*, *Text and Presentation 2008*, and *The Journal of American Drama and Theatre*. She serves on the board of the Arthur Miller Society, holding the office of president from 2008 to 2010.

Jane K. Dominik is Professor of English at San Joaquin Delta College in Stockton, California. She earned her Ph.D. from the University of East Anglia, and her dissertation was titled "Image and Word: The Stages of Arthur Miller's Drama." Her work on Miller has appeared in *"The Salesman Has a Birthday": Essays Celebrating the Fiftieth Anniversary of Arthur Miller's "Death of a Salesman"* and *The Arthur Miller Jour-*

nal. She served as the founding editor of *The Arthur Miller Society Newsletter* as well as the society's president and has presented numerous conference papers on Miller and other playwrights.

Steven R. Centola was Professor of English at Millersville University in Pennsylvania and the founding president of the Arthur Miller Society. He designed and taught a variety of American literature courses that often focused on the works of Arthur Miller, F. Scott Fitzgerald, and Ernest Hemingway. He published numerous articles and edited four books, two of which—*Echoes Down the Corridor: Collected Essays, 1944-2000* (2000) and *The Theater Essays of Arthur Miller* (1996)—were created in collaboration with Arthur Miller.

Christopher Bigsby is Professor of American Studies at the University of East Anglia in Norwich, England. He is credited as the author or editor of more than forty books, the most recent being *One Hundred Days: One Hundred Nights* (2008) and *Arthur Miller: 1915-1962* (2008). An esteemed analyst of theater, he is considered the authoritative commentator on Arthur Miller, with whom he shared a thirty-year friendship.

James A. Robinson was Associate Professor of English at the University of Maryland, where he lectured primarily on American and modern drama. He was vice president of the national Eugene O'Neill Society and is considered one of the leading authorities on the playwright.

George Monteiro is Professor Emeritus of English and Adjunct Professor of Portuguese and Brazilian Studies at Brown University. A scholar of American, British, and Portuguese literature, he has published numerous books, collections, translations, and essays, including *Stephen Crane's Blue Badge of Courage* (2000), *The Correspondence of Henry James and Henry Adams* (1992), and *Robert Frost and the New England Renaissance* (1988).

J. Chris Westgate is Assistant Professor of English at California State University, Fullerton. He is the editor of *Brecht, Broadway, and the United States Theatre* (2007), an anthology of essays on playwright Bertolt Brecht. He teaches courses in such subject areas as dramatic literature; Restoration, Elizabethan, and Jacobean drama; and landscape in relation to literature. He is currently working on a revision of his 2005 dissertation for publication.

Gerald Weales is Professor Emeritus of English at the University of Pennsylvania. A drama specialist and theater reviewer, he has contributed to a variety of journals and magazines, including the *Reporter, The Atlantic, Commonweal, The American Scholar,* and *The Georgia Review.* His books include *Canned Goods as Caviar: American Film Comedy of the 1930s* (1985), *Odets the Playwright* (1985), and *Revolution: A Collection of Plays* (1975).

Susan C. W. Abbotson is Performance Editor for *The Arthur Miller Journal* and Professor of English at Rhode Island College, where she lectures on modern and contemporary drama. A previous president of the Arthur Miller Society, she continues to serve on the society's board and manages the society's Web site. Her books include *Thematic Guide to Modern Drama* (2003), *Student Companion to Arthur Miller* (2000), and *Understanding "Death of a Salesman"* (1999).

Terry Otten is Professor Emeritus of English at Wittenberg University. His teaching and research focus mainly on Romantic and modern literature as well as drama. In addition to more than fifty articles, he has published three books: *The Crime of Innocence in the Fiction of Toni Morrison* (1989), *After Innocence* (1982), and *The Deserted Stage* (1972).

Jeffrey D. Mason is Professor of Theatre and Dance and Dean of the College of Arts and Letters at California State University, Sacramento. His publications include plays, articles, edited collections, and books, his most recent being *Stone Tower: The Political Theater of Arthur Miller* (2008). For *Melodrama and the Myth of America* (1993), he received honorable mention for the Barnard Hewitt Award for Outstanding Research in Theatre History.

Laurence Goldstein is an editor, poet, and Professor of English at the University of Michigan, where he served as editor of the *Michigan Quarterly Review* for more than thirty years. His primary research interests include Romantic literature, poetry, film, William Faulkner, and technology in relation to literature. In addition to his four volumes of poetry, he has published several books of literary criticism, the most recent of which is *Writing Ann Arbor: A Literary Anthology* (2005).

Acknowledgments_____

"Arthur Miller" by Paul Rosefeldt. From *Magill's Survey of American Literature*. Rev. ed. Copyright © 2007 by Salem Press, Inc. Reprinted with permission of Salem Press.

"The *Paris Review* Perspective" by Richard Beck. Copyright © 2011 by Richard Beck. Special appreciation goes to Christopher Cox, Nathaniel Rich, and David Wallace-Wells, editors at *The Paris Review*.

"Arthur Miller and the Art of the Possible" by Steven R. Centola. From *American Drama* 14, no. 1 (2005): 63-86. Copyright © 2005 by the American Drama Institute. Reprinted with permission of the American Drama Institute.

"Arthur Miller: Un-American" by Christopher Bigsby. From *The Arthur Miller Journal* 1, no. 1 (2006): 3-17. Copyright © by St. Francis College. Reprinted with permission of *The Arthur Miller Journal*.

"*All My Sons* and Paternal Authority" by James A. Robinson. From *The Journal of American Drama and Theatre* 2, no. 1 (1990): 38-54. Copyright © 1990 by Martin E. Segal Theatre Center, CUNY. Reprinted by permission of *The Journal of American Drama and Theatre*.

"'There's No Place Like Home': Miller's 'Poem,' Frost's 'Play'" by George Monteiro. From *The Arthur Miller Journal* 2, no. 1 (2007): 1-14. Copyright © 2007 by St. Francis College. Reprinted with permission of *The Arthur Miller Journal*.

"Asking 'Queer Questions,' Revealing Ugly Truths: Giles Corey's Subversive Eccentricity in *The Crucible*" by J. Chris Westgate. From *The Journal of American Drama and Theatre* 15, no. 1 (2003): 44-53. Copyright © 2003 by Martin E. Segal Theatre Center, CUNY. Reprinted by permission of *The Journal of American Drama and Theatre*.

"Verse, Figurative Language, and Myth in *A View from the Bridge*" by Stephen A. Marino. From *A Language Study of Arthur Miller's Plays: The Poetic in the Colloquial* (2002), pp. 81-106. Copyright © 2002 by The Edwin Mellen Press. Reprinted with permission of The Edwin Mellen Press.

"Uneasy Collaboration: Miller, Kazan, and *After the Fall*" by Brenda Murphy. From *The Arthur Miller Journal* 1, no. 1 (2006): 49-59. Copyright © 2006 by St. Francis College. Reprinted with permission of *The Arthur Miller Journal*.

"All About Talk: Arthur Miller's *The Price*" by Gerald Weales. From *The Ohio Review* 13, no. 2 (1972): 74-84. Copyright © 1972 by Ohio University. Reprinted with permission of the author.

"Both His Sons: Arthur Miller's *The Price* and Jewish Assimilation" by James A. Robinson. From *Staging Difference: Cultural Pluralism in American Theatre and Drama* (1995), pp. 121-139. Copyright © 1995 by Peter Lang Publishing Group. Reprinted with permission of Peter Lang Publishing Group.

Index

Abbotson, Susan C. W., 48, 265
Abigail Williams. *See* Williams, Abigail
Adamczewski, Zygmunt, 112
Adultery, 15, 21, 47, 114, 289, 351
After the Fall (Miller), 3, 6, 33, 36, 50, 81, 83, 115, 156, 215, 287, 296, 321, 347; critical reception, 134, 215; Elia Kazan's influence, 222
All My Sons (Miller), 3, 9, 15, 24, 30, 35, 48, 61, 75, 106, 138, 142, 146, 152, 157, 217, 298, 331; critical reception, 127
American Clock, The (Miller), 3, 6, 39, 55, 85, 265, 269
American Dream, 20, 40, 59, 67, 71, 101, 109, 128, 274, 303
Anti-Semitism, 54, 58, 115, 123, 136, 298, 330, 338, 352
Archbishop's Ceiling, The (Miller), 3, 7, 65, 85, 298, 309
Ardolino, Frank, 48, 51
Atkinson, Brooks, 75

Barnes, Clive, 84, 227, 240
Barnes, Howard, 77
Barrett, William, 130
Baum family (*The American Clock*), 266, 276
"Bees" (Miller), 342
Bentley, Eric, 3, 129, 132
Bernays, Anne, 47
Betrayal, 59, 108, 116, 150, 217, 241, 250, 253, 292, 321
Biblical allusions, 6, 67, 197, 256, 259, 271, 304, 311
Biff Loman. *See* Loman, Biff
Bigsby, Christopher, 14, 37, 50, 54, 59, 62, 99, 113, 118, 163, 171, 189, 267, 284, 288, 295

Billington, Michael, 328
Blidstein, Gerald, 245, 257
Bloom, Clive, 100
Bloom, Harold, 245
Bordman, Gerald, 133
Boxing metaphors, 43, 204
Brandon, Henry, 107
Brantley, Ben, 34, 79
Brater, Enoch, 89, 157, 262
Broken Glass (Miller), 3, 7, 33, 36, 55, 57, 67, 74, 87, 116, 136, 287; critical reception, 286
Brothers' relationships, 22, 57, 66, 74, 153, 187, 228, 237, 247
Brustein, Robert, 103, 129, 134, 152, 215, 227, 255, 286
Budick, E. Miller, 182
Burke, Kenneth, 51

Carbone, Eddie (*A View from the Bridge*), 35, 186, 191, 194, 202, 208
Carlisle, Olga, 64
Carson, Neil, 189
Chapman, John, 78, 83
Cheating, 25, 29, 43
Chris Keller. *See* Keller, Chris
Christiansen, Richard, 79
Clara (Miller), 6, 86
Clark, Eleanor, 129
Clurman, Harold, 83
Cohen, Nathan, 240
Copeland, Joan (sister), 56, 131
Corey, Giles (*The Crucible*), 174, 179
Corrigan, Robert W., 25, 263
Costello, Donald P., 189
Couchman, Gordon W., 35
Creation of the World and Other Business, The (Miller), 6, 66, 85, 261

Crucible, The (Miller), 3, 5, 9, 15, 35, 46, 50, 68, 80, 113, 131, 173, 298, 307, 321
Crucifixion, 6, 67, 304, 311
Curtis, Penelope, 50

Death of a Salesman (Miller), 3-4, 9, 19, 31, 34, 40, 46, 49, 55, 62, 76, 109, 113, 128, 156, 163, 168, 217, 232, 305; in China, 66; critical reception, 78, 129, 133; success of, 70, 77; title, 161
"Death of the Hired Man, The" (Frost), 162
Depression. *See* Great Depression
Dialogue, 5, 33, 189
Dillingham, William B., 19, 25

Eddie Carbone. *See* Carbone, Eddie
Elegy for a Lady (Miller), 6, 86
Engle, John D., 50
Expressionism, 5, 37, 259

"Fame" (Miller), 332
Family relationships, 15, 19, 29, 37, 59, 85, 106, 140, 170, 209, 244, 251, 277, 334, 344
Father-son relationships, 3, 19, 26, 30, 57, 74, 106, 138, 144, 147, 152, 166, 233, 241, 246, 252, 258, 281
Federal Theatre Project, 9, 38, 60, 73
Feingold, Michael, 104
Fénelon, Fania, 86, 116
Ferran, Peter W., 265, 284
Fiedler, Leslie, 134
Finishing the Picture (Miller), 64, 82
"Fitter's Night" (Miller), 335
Flanagan, James K., 269
Focus (Miller), 58, 74, 115, 124, 289, 330, 338, 344
Freedley, George, 74

Freedman, Morris, 157, 262
Frost, Robert, 160
Frye, Northrop, 167
Fuller, A. Howard, 21

Giles Corey. *See* Corey, Giles
Gill, Brendan, 238
Gilman, Richard, 33, 134, 215
Golden Years, The (Miller), 4, 38, 73
Gorer, Geoffrey, 246
Gottfried, Martin, 83, 89, 134, 227
Goyen, William, 222
Grass Still Grows, The (Miller), 3, 59, 73
Great Depression, 3, 56, 85, 117, 144, 228, 240-241, 246, 254, 265, 299, 340, 351
Gross, Barry, 154
Group Theatre, 4, 63

Hapgood, Hutchins, 241
Happy Loman. *See* Loman, Happy
Hard Times (Terkel), 6, 85
Havel, Václav, 65, 88
Hirschhorn, Clive, 85
Holocaust, 3, 61, 65, 87, 115, 142, 287, 296, 299, 341
"Homely Girl, a Life" (Miller), 350
Homely Girl, a Life, and Other Stories (Miller), 330
Honors at Dawn (Miller), 73
House Un-American Activities Committee, 10, 13, 63, 71, 80, 126, 131, 183, 217, 238, 299, 327
Howe, Irving, 244
HUAC. *See* House Un-American Activities Committee

I Can't Remember Anything (Miller), 6, 86
I Don't Need You Any More (Miller), 331

Ibsen, Henrik, 37, 61, 71, 80, 135, 157, 230

Imagery, 35, 189; birth, 292; blood, 193, 209, 323; crucifixion, 150, 256, 304, 311; names, 51; religious, 35, 48, 157, 197, 271; trees, 41

Incident at Vichy (Miller), 3, 84, 116, 134, 298, 338

Infidelity, 15, 21, 47, 114, 289, 351

Isser, Edward R., 115

Joe Keller. *See* Keller, Joe

John Proctor. *See* Proctor, John

Jones, Chris, 79

Kaplan, Justin, 47

Kate Keller. *See* Keller, Kate

Kauffmann, Stanley, 134

Kazan, Elia, 5, 13, 63, 81, 128, 216

Kazin, Alfred, 124

Keller, Chris (*All My Sons*), 27, 48, 106, 138, 143, 147, 152, 155

Keller, Joe (*All My Sons*), 19, 25, 29, 106, 138, 147, 150; name, 48

Keller, Kate (*All My Sons*), 30, 148, 155

Kerr, Walter, 80, 83, 134

Kong, Belinda, 66

Krutch, Joseph Wood, 33

Lahr, John, 288

Last Yankee, The (Miller), 67, 87

Lawrence, Tony, 84

Linda Loman. *See* Loman, Linda

Linzer, Norman, 140, 150, 246, 261

Loden, Barbara, 82, 217, 222

Loman, Biff (*Death of a Salesman*), 20, 23, 41, 44, 166

Loman, Happy (*Death of a Salesman*), 21, 43, 169; name, 48

Loman, Linda (*Death of a Salesman*), 22, 169

Loman, Willy (*Death of a Salesman*), 4, 19, 31, 40, 45, 109, 112, 163, 168, 171, 277; actors in role, 78-79, 99; name, 47

Loughlin, Richard L., 108, 157

McCarthy, Mary, 129

McCarthyism, 3, 9, 11, 63, 80

McClain, John, 215

Malin, Irving, 142, 242

Man Who Had All the Luck, The (Miller), 4, 9, 61, 74, 147, 343

Marino, Stephen A., 33, 181, 186

Marriage, 15, 30, 87, 198, 208, 229, 252, 286, 290, 336, 351

Martin, Boyd, 77

Martin, Robert A., 59, 101, 109

Mason, Jeffrey D., 54, 297

Maulnier, Thierry, 238

Memory of Two Mondays, A (Miller), 6, 81

Metaphors, 35, 40, 43, 50, 73, 97, 153, 192, 201, 212, 265, 319, 328, 350

Meyer, Richard, 219, 223

Mielziner, Jo, 5, 62, 77

Miller, Arthur; on *After the Fall*, 82, 215; on *All My Sons*, 76, 107, 147, 157; on *The American Clock*, 267, 277, 284; awards and honors, 9, 59, 72, 78; on *Broken Glass*, 294; childhood, 8, 56, 140, 243, 263; on *The Crucible*, 5, 67, 113, 173, 307; on *Death of a Salesman*, 20, 48, 78, 112, 168; education, 57; on father-son relationships, 139; on fiction writing, 353; on Robert Frost, 160; influences, 37, 56, 61, 68, 71, 135, 157, 286, 295; Jewish identity, 58, 74, 123, 138, 144, 149, 157, 242, 248, 257, 262, 335; and Elia Kazan, 63, 81,

217; marriages, 10, 60, 64, 82, 215, 221, 225, 243, 331; on *Mr. Peters' Connections*, 103; politics, 3, 9, 15, 54, 58, 65, 71, 75, 88, 136, 144, 218, 298, 303, 314, 325; on *Resurrection Blues*, 326; on theater language, 33, 36, 97; on *A View from the Bridge*, 187; on Tennessee Williams, 38; writing career, 3, 6, 33, 54, 60, 70, 73, 79

Miller, Augusta (mother), 8, 55, 241

Miller, Isidore (father), 8, 54, 144, 241, 245

Miller, Kermit (brother), 57

Misfits, The (Miller), 64, 331, 340, 345, 348

Monroe, Marilyn, 10, 13, 64, 81, 121, 215, 221, 225, 331, 341, 345

"Monte Sant'Angelo" (Miller), 143, 344

Morath, Ingeborg, 10, 64

Morehouse, Ward, 76

Morley, Sheridan, 83, 286

Moss, Leonard, 34, 50

Mr. Peters' Connections (Miller), 6, 88, 102; critical reception, 103

Murray, Edward, 46

Nadel, Norman, 83

Names and naming, 47-49, 51, 187, 200, 259, 289, 324, 333, 338

Nixon, Richard, 125

No Villain (Miller), 3, 33, 59, 72

Oberg, Arthur K., 34, 50

Odets, Clifford, 4, 37, 51, 59, 262

On Politics and the Art of Acting (Miller), 88, 328

Oppenheimer, George, 235

Otten, Terry, 284, 286

Phelan, Kappo, 77

Playing for Time (Miller), 3, 61, 86, 116, 338

"Please Don't Kill Anything" (Miller), 341

Poetic language, 34, 81, 171, 189

Pound, Ezra, 125

Preston, Rohan, 328

Price, The (Miller), 6, 57, 66, 84, 134, 156, 228, 240-241; critical reception, 227

Proctor, John (*The Crucible*), 114, 181, 239

Prodigal son parable, 74, 160, 165

"Prophecy, The" (Miller), 348

Rahv, Philip, 134

Raine, Nina, 104

Religious imagery, 35, 48, 157, 197

Resurrection Blues (Miller), 3, 6, 67, 88, 297, 304, 310; critical reception, 328

Richards, David, 286, 290

Richards, I. A., 46

Ride Down Mt. Morgan, The (Miller), 7, 36, 48, 67, 86

Robards, Jason, 224

Rosinger, Lawrence, 50

Rowe, Kenneth, 9, 38, 68

Saunders, Frances Stonor, 104

Savran, David, 299, 317, 325

Schier, Ernest, 238

Schiff, Ellen, 259

Schissel, Wendy, 177

Schwartz, Delmore, 134

Simon, John, 33

Simon, Josette, 83

Situation Normal (Miller), 74, 338

Slattery, Mary, 10, 60, 243

Smith, Will, 51

Some Kind of Love Story (Miller), 6, 86

Son-father relationships. *See* Father-son relationships
Sontag, Susan, 134, 215
Sports metaphors, 43
Spurgeon, Caroline F. E., 51
Stein, Mike, 84
Styron, Rose, 64
Suicide, 19, 25, 42, 62, 81, 106, 112, 138, 148, 153, 213, 239, 276

Tammaro, Thomas M., 34, 50
Taubman, Howard, 83, 234
Teachout, Terry, 33
Terkel, Studs, 6, 85
Thacker, David, 66, 88
They Too Arise (Miller), 3, 72, 138, 243
Thomas, Caldwell, 83
Timebends (Miller), 13, 37, 62, 67, 82, 88, 139, 157, 188, 216, 225, 243, 263, 333, 344
Torre, Roma, 79
Turner, Victor, 173, 184

View from the Bridge, A (Miller), 5, 9, 35, 81, 134, 186, 321; comparison of one- and two-act versions, 186; critical reception, 189

Waldorf Conference, 62, 129
War profiteering, 71, 75, 106, 149
Warshow, Robert, 131
Watts, Richard, Jr., 76, 227
Weales, Gerald, 20, 227, 268, 278, 283
Welland, Dennis, 270
Whitehead, Robert, 81, 217
Wilder, Thornton, 38
Williams, Abigail (*The Crucible*), 114, 178
Williams, Raymond, 146
Williams, Tennessee, 34, 38, 217, 232
Willy Loman. *See* Loman, Willy

Yorks, Samuel A., 30

Zeifman, Hersh, 108